Military Courts, Civil-Military Relations, and the Legal Battle for Democracy

The interaction between military and civilian courts, the political power that legal prerogatives can provide to the armed forces, and the difficult process civilian politicians face in reforming military justice remain glaringly under-examined, despite their implications for the quality and survival of democracy. This book breaks new ground by providing a theoretically rich, global examination of the operation and reform of military courts in democratic countries. Drawing on a new dataset of 120 countries over more than two centuries, it presents the first comprehensive picture of the evolution of military justice across states and over time. Combined with qualitative historical case studies of Colombia, Portugal, Indonesia, Fiji, Brazil, Pakistan, and the United States, the book presents a new framework for understanding how civilian actors are able to gain or lose legal control of the armed forces. The book's findings have important lessons for scholars and policymakers working in the fields of democracy, civil-military relations, human rights, and the rule of law.

Brett J. Kyle is Assistant Professor of Political Science, University of Nebraska at Omaha, USA.

Andrew G. Reiter is Associate Professor of Politics and International Relations, Mount Holyoke College, USA.

Military Courts, Civil-Military Relations, and the Legal Battle for Democracy

The Politics of Military Justice

Brett J. Kyle and Andrew G. Reiter

Routledge
Taylor & Francis Group
LONDON AND NEW YORK

First published 2021
by Routledge
2 Park Square, Milton Park, Abingdon, Oxon OX14 4RN

and by Routledge
52 Vanderbilt Avenue, New York, NY 10017

Routledge is an imprint of the Taylor & Francis Group, an informa business

British Library Cataloguing-in-Publication Data
A catalogue record for this book is available from the British Library

Library of Congress Cataloging-in-Publication Data
Names: Kyle, Brett J., author. | Reiter, Andrew G., author.
Title: Military courts, civil-military relations, and the legal battle for democracy: the politics of military justice/Brett J. Kyle, Andrew G. Reiter.
Description: Milton Park, Abingdon, Oxon; New York, NY: Routledge, 2021. | Includes bibliographical references and index.
Identifiers: LCCN 2020033303 (print) | LCCN 2020033304 (ebook) | ISBN 9780367029944 (hardback) | ISBN 9780429019869 (ebook)
Subjects: LCSH: Courts-martial and courts of inquiry. | Military courts. | Military courts–Political aspects. | Military law.
Classification: LCC K4750 .K95 2021 (print) | LCC K4750 (ebook) | DDC 343/.0143–dc23
LC record available at https://lccn.loc.gov/2020033303
LC ebook record available at https://lccn.loc.gov/2020033304

ISBN: 978-0-367-02994-4 (hbk)
ISBN: 978-0-429-01986-9 (ebk)

Typeset in Galliard
by KnowledgeWorks Global Ltd.

Contents

Figures and tables

Figures

Tables

Acknowledgments

This was the most challenging project of our careers. Despite its importance, military justice is understudied and information was often difficult to find. The cross-national nature of the project only magnified the problem. Conducting research on military justice, sometimes covering hundreds of years, in 120 countries was a monumental task and it would not have been possible without the help of our many research assistants, many of whom had invaluable language skills. We would like to thank Mount Holyoke College for providing financial support to hire undergraduates who provided important case study research: Edith Amoafoa-Smart, Sarah Bloomgarden, Lydia Jiang, Juli Kellerbauer, Dhishana Kidambi, Maryanne Magnier, Sarah Painting, Katie Popiela, and Donari Yahzid. Franny Eremeeva helped immensely with the Russian and Israeli cases and Luciany Capra took on an important role in the research on Colombia. We also thank Antonis Gounalakis from the Translation Center at the University of Massachusetts-Amherst for help with the Cyprus case. We extend special thanks to Nora Cyra for covering so many cases and helping with fact-checking and editing. Olivia Yanchik also helped with the preparation of the final manuscript for submission.

We would like to thank the Department of Political Science at the University of Nebraska at Omaha for funding graduate assistants who helped with case research: Media Ajir, Griselda Asamoah-Gyadu, Bryan Brooks, Christopher Schmidt, and Kalynn Stoner. In addition, we would not have been able to complete the research without the resources of the Mount Holyoke College and University of Nebraska at Omaha libraries, in particular the inter-library loan offices which were able to track down sometimes obscure works necessary for the project. Kathleen Pertzborn provided invaluable expertise in helping to develop the figures for the book.

In the early stages of the project we benefited from feedback from our colleagues. The project originated in two graduate seminars at the University of Wisconsin–Madison: Tamir Moustafa's "The Global Expansion of Judicial Power" in autumn 2004 and Helena Alviar's "Latin American Legal Institutions" in autumn 2008. In subsequent years we published two articles, in *Armed Forces & Society* and *Law & Society Review*, that explored the power of military justice systems and attempts to reform them in Latin America. The positive response we received convinced us of the need for a more in-depth, global study of the politics of military justice. As we expanded the project, the discussants and participants at the International Conferences on Law and Society in 2014, 2016, and 2018 provided useful feedback. Camilo Sánchez in particular offered valuable insight on the Colombian case.

When the manuscript was complete, Zoe Everitt, Nancy Rebecca, and many others at the press transformed it into a book. We thank Alison Kirk, the senior editor at Routledge who saw potential in the project early on, convinced us that Routledge was the right home for it, and partnered with us to bring the book to fruition. Finally, we want to thank our families, friends, and colleagues for their support throughout this endeavor. Special thanks to Kathleen for taking on so much during the final months of the project and to Honora for making dad smile each day.

1 Why military justice matters

Introduction

On August 9, 2016, Indian poet and activist Irom Sharmila licked honey from her hand in front of a group of journalists, ending a 16-year hunger strike (BBC News 2016). She began her strike in November 2000 after she witnessed a paramilitary detachment shoot and kill 10 civilians at a bus stop in the city of Malom in the Indian state of Manipur. It was not the massacre itself that pushed Sharmila to take such drastic steps, but rather the fact that the paramilitary forces were within their legal rights to shoot civilians and would not face any legal consequences for their actions.

The 1958 Armed Forces (Special Powers) Act (AFSPA) grants Indian security forces wide ranging powers to search dwellings and arrest individuals without warrants and to use deadly force against civilians when the security forces are of the "opinion that it is necessary so to do for the maintenance of public order."[1] Security personnel have immunity from civilian prosecution for their actions and can only be disciplined in the military court system, effectively creating a condition of martial law (Gautam 2017). The AFSPA originally applied to seven states in the northeast where the government has faced a variety of violent insurgencies (Arunachal Pradesh, Assam, Manipur, Meghalaya, Mizoram, Nagaland, and Tripura), but it was expanded in 1983 to include Punjab and Chandigarh and a nearly identical law was applied to Jammu and Kashmir in 1990.[2] Despite her 16-year struggle, which garnered considerable international attention, Sharmila failed at her ultimate goal—to get the AFSPA repealed. She ended her strike by announcing that she was going to enter electoral politics in an attempt to fight for her cause in a way she hoped would be more effective. In the March 17, 2017 legislative assembly elections in Manipur, Sharmila garnered just 90 votes in a lopsided loss (Sharma 2017). As of this writing, the AFSPA is still active in parts of six states.[3]

Sharmila's resistance is just one event in a long, intense debate over the AFSPA that has embroiled Indian politics. The contestation between the central government, army, and police on one side, and victims and human rights organizations on the other, has been fierce and public. Domestically, opposition to the AFSPA has united a diverse group of human rights, women's, indigenous, student, and legal organizations. In Nagaland, for example, the Naga Students' Federation, Naga Mothers' Association, Naga People's Movement for Human Rights, and Naga Hoho (a Naga tribal body) have held joint anti-AFSPA rallies (Mehrotra 2016). At the local level, victim and survivor networks, such as the Manipuri Women Gun Survivors Network and the Association of Parents of Disappeared Persons, have emerged to help citizens deal with the everyday presence of violence (Bhattacharyya 2018). Internationally, human rights organizations, such as Human Rights Watch [HRW] (2008) and the International Commission of Jurists [ICJ] (2015) have repeatedly documented abuses under the law and called for its repeal. In 2013, a report by the United Nations Special Rapporteur on Extrajudicial, Summary or Arbitrary Executions was critical of the level of repression committed under the AFSPA and recommended its immediate repeal or amendment (United Nations Human Rights Council [UNHRC] 2013a). Those opposed to the AFSPA note the inherent contradiction in a law deemed necessary to end violence that has been in place for more than 60 years.

In the face of this opposition, the government and military are united in their support for the continuation of the AFSPA. They have consistently defended its necessity in combatting rebels and terrorists in those regions, arguing that immunity is required for forces making snap judgments in the face of an armed opposition. The military has taken a hard line and has gone as far as to blame Pakistan's Inter-Services Intelligence for helping citizens file false accusations of human rights violations to discredit India's military and weaken its morale (Singh 2018). In response to criticisms regarding the decades-long application of the law, the military argues that it is not its job to end the insurgency; that task is a political issue that should be left to elected officials. Rather, the military claims that its job is "to keep the insurgency down to a level where the civil administration can carry out its functions" and that those successful peace agreements that have been attained have only been possible because of its actions (Ramachandran 2015).[4] The military has also steadfastly protected its forces and refused to cooperate with civilian authorities. In 2012, for example, the Central Bureau of Investigation (CBI) requested the military turn over eight officers accused of killing five Kashmiri citizens in 2000. Invoking the AFSPA, the military denied the request and said the case would remain under the jurisdiction of military courts (Amnesty International 2012).

The government has been responsive to domestic pressure, often attempting to sympathize with victims, but has not made any substantive changes. In 2004, widespread protests against the AFSPA occurred in Manipur, culminating with a group of Manipuri mothers undressing in front of the Assam Rifles headquarters, which forced the government to establish a committee, led by retired Justice B. P. Jeevan Reddy, to review the law. The final report called the law "a symbol of hate, oppression and instrument of high handedness" and recommended its repeal (Reddy 2005). The government, however, refused to release the report for over a year, only after human rights organizations leaked it to the press, and thereafter the government ignored the recommendations (Varadarajan 2006).

Similarly, in December 2012, following a gang rape of a 23-year-old woman that incited mass protests, the government created the Justice Verma Committee to review the country's laws on sexual violence. Its final report criticized the AFSPA for creating a culture of impunity and recommended that the immunity provided for members of the armed forces be revoked for sexual offenses (Verma 2013). While the government revised the criminal code and enacted new legislation on sexual crimes, it ignored the recommendation to amend the AFSPA.

In the battle over the AFSPA the civilian judiciary has found itself in the middle, with the power to tip the scales in favor of one side or the other. In 1997, the Supreme Court heard the first challenge to the AFSPA when it combined several writ petitions filed by human rights organizations in the 1980s into one case. In its judgment, the Court upheld the law, declaring that the powers it provided to the military were neither unreasonable nor unconstitutional. It did, however, attempt to regulate these powers, creating a list of instructions (referred to as the "Do's and Don'ts") for the military to follow, including providing written justifications for the refusal to prosecute any personnel.[5] Compliance by the military has been weak, and the ruling merely changed how, not whether, the military could invoke immunity for its forces.

The fight came to a head in 2016 when the Extra Judicial Execution Victim Families Association demanded a probe into what it alleged were 1,528 "fake encounter" deaths in Manipur over the last decade, where extrajudicial killings by security forces were masked as self-defense. On July 8 of that year, the Supreme Court ruled in its favor, declaring that:

> It does not matter whether the victim was a common person or a militant or a terrorist, nor does it matter whether the aggressor was a common person or the state. The law is the same for both and is equally applicable to both .... This is the requirement of a democracy and the requirement of preservation of the rule of law and the preservation of individual liberties.[6]

In the landmark ruling, the Court gave the petitioners one year to gather more evidence on the cases prior to authorizing an investigation.

The ruling was a serious blow to the government and military, who for the first time faced judicial pressure that threatened the survival of the AFSPA. In April 2017, the government challenged the ruling, filing a curative petition that argued that the judgment would hinder the military's ability to confront insurgent and terrorist threats. Moreover, it contended, opening up past behavior for judicial review would harm morale (Pervez 2017). Just two weeks later, the Supreme Court rejected the petition and upheld its previous ruling (Shivshankar 2017). On July 14, with new evidence in hand, the Court directed the CBI to set up a five-member team to examine at least 87 of the 1,528 killings (HRW 2017a).

In the aftermath, state security forces have intimidated and threatened activists, lawyers, and the plaintiffs involved in the case (HRW 2018). Hundreds of military personnel have also filed collective petitions to the Supreme Court protesting against the dilution of the AFSPA (Indian Express 2018b). In a sign that the military was unprepared for the Court's resoluteness, this move has created divisions within its ranks. The upper echelon sees this as an unnecessary move that could trigger a broader court ruling on the constitutionality of the law. Army Chief General Bipin Rawat has spoken out publicly against the lower ranking officers who have filed the petitions, saying: "The Army was fighting these cases, the government is aware of these cases, and AFSPA is a very strong law which provides protection to the soldiers. Now, if these guys (the petitioners) lose the case, what will happen?" (Indian Express 2018a). The fight over the fate of the AFSPA continues to rage in India.

The Indian case is not unique. Many governments grant security forces extra-judicial powers when combatting armed threats. Indeed, the AFSPA is not as far reaching as many laws. While in India the military justice system provides immunity for its personnel, any civilians arrested by military or paramilitary forces must be immediately turned over to the regular police and are processed through the normal civilian judicial system. In neighboring Pakistan, in contrast, a January 2015 constitutional amendment authorized the use of secret military tribunals for civilians suspected of terrorism-related offenses. In this system, the accused were defended by an assigned military lawyer; trials were held in secret without media access; cases were ruled on by military judges, many without law degrees, who did not have to justify their verdicts; and there was no right to appeal (ICJ 2019). In Lebanon, military courts have jurisdiction over a wide range of crimes. There are many reports of torture being used to extract confessions, the courts tried over 300 children in 2016 alone, and the government is increasingly using the system to try human rights lawyers and activists (HRW 2017b).

The threat of Islamic terrorism in particular has sparked a resurgence in the use of military courts. In response to incursions by Boko Haram from neighboring Nigeria, Cameroon passed a controversial anti-terrorism law in 2014 that allows military tribunals to try civilians. The law is written broadly to include a range of behavior beyond terrorism, and the government has used it to repress dissent in the Anglophone northwest (Cameroon Concord News 2017). On May 23, 2017, Philippine president Rodrigo Duterte declared martial law in the southern region of Mindanao as the government battled the Islamic armed group Maute in the city of Marawi.[7] The declaration allowed military courts to try civilians and suspends habeas corpus for those charged with rebellion (HRW 2017c). On July 4, the Supreme Court upheld the declaration; though Duterte had said that he would have ignored the court anyway if it had ruled against him (Villamor 2017). In each instance, the decision to extend additional judicial powers to the military was not without debate or controversy, with government and military leaders, domestic and international human rights organizations, the civilian judiciary, and external states all pursuing their own agendas.

To be clear, the existence of military courts is not inherently problematic. Militaries have unique characteristics that require the maintenance of their own judicial systems. A military is recognized to be its own society, separate from the broader civilian population, with its own judicial needs born out of the codes of conduct and the exceptional demands of the institution. Military effectiveness relies on discipline, hierarchical leadership, and adherence to commands. Many of the offenses defined in military legal codes exist to compel obedience to orders and otherwise ensure the ability of the institution to operate under its unique circumstances. Many military crimes have no equivalent in the civilian world, such as disobedience, insubordination, dereliction of duty, or being absent without official leave. Moreover, military service places personnel in a position of responsibility for military property, ranging from machinery and weapons to food and clothing. The improper use, damage, or sale of such property can be a crime that falls under military legal jurisdiction. A military may also maintain legal authority to punish those individuals who attempt either to join or to leave the armed forces through fraudulent means (Morris 2010, 64–70, 79–81). In addition, penalties imposed by military courts can be quite different than in the civilian system, including confinement to quarters, the performance of menial tasks, assignment of extra duties, or exercise to the point of exhaustion (Rowe 2006, 64). More substantial sanctions such as forfeiture of pay, loss of rank, and even administrative separation from the armed forces (Morris 2010, 158–62) are military punishments not generally present in civilian legal systems. The unique needs of a military provide a justifiable rationale for the institution to maintain its own legal system.

The expansion of military court jurisdiction over non-military crimes and the civilian population, however, is an alarming development. Where military courts have too much power they represent a direct challenge to civilian control of the armed forces and undermine civilian judicial systems and the rule of law, essential components of a well-functioning democracy. The overall outcome is an increase in human rights violations as militaries are left unchecked to carry out internal security as they see fit and to use expanded judicial power to counter any opposition to themselves or the governments that empower them.

Military legal power and democratic rule

The extent of the legal power of militaries has an oversized impact on the quality of democracy due to its intersection with multiple components necessary for democratic rule. Government officials, elected in free and fair elections, must be able to govern without interference from external forces. The judiciary must have the ability to check the government's behavior to prevent abuse of power, and citizens require an expectation of fair trials. The government also has a duty to protect its citizens from human right abuses, including unlawful killings, forced disappearances, torture, and arbitrary arrest and detention. Military courts that have too much power threaten all of these components of democracy.

One of the first goals of the civilian leadership in a new democratic setting is to establish firm civilian control over the armed forces (Diamond and Plattner 1996) so that the military answers to civilian leaders who are accountable to the people through free, fair, and frequent elections (Dahl 2000; Schmitter and

Karl 1991). As an armed actor, the military always maintains the latent power to intervene in politics through force or threats of force (Finer 1962). The central paradox of civil-military relations is how a society simultaneously can be protected by and from its military (Feaver 1996). A military strong enough to protect the state is capable of threatening it. Short of abolishing the military altogether, civilian governments are forced to find ways to subordinate it to their authority.

The demands of modern war fighting shifted military affairs from the realm of aristocrats, militias, or temporary citizen-soldiers to standing armies with professional officer corps (Kohn 1997). Samuel Huntington (1957) posited that objective civilian control could be best achieved through a clear separation of civilian and military responsibilities—the civilian leadership sets national strategy, defines the missions, issues the orders, and leaves the military to execute the orders, thereby turning the military into a politically neutral "tool of the state." Morris Janowitz (1960), to the contrary, saw the "narrowing skill differential" between civilian and military elites to mean more overlap and similarity between the two than the rigid separation Huntington imagined.[8] In long-standing democracies, where civilian supremacy is established, civil-military relations has come to be seen as a matter of "shared responsibility" between civilian and military leadership, with debate, healthy disagreement, and interactive decision-making (Bland 1999). Rather than the dichotomy of civilian versus military supremacy, civil-military relations is an ongoing management process, in which the health of the system depends on successful demonstration of civilian understanding of military culture and mutual respect between the groups (Herspring 2013; Schiff 2009).

In democratizing countries, new civilian leaders are faced with an acute need to roll back previously institutionalized military political powers. These leaders undertake wide-ranging reforms and put in place new institutional controls in an effort to curtail military prerogatives and secure the new democracy against undue military influence in government (Croissant and Kuehn 2017). These controls include the elimination of military-appointed members of government (Hunter 1997; Pion-Berlin 2005); (re-)organization of defense ministries, including the establishment of a civilian minister of defense (Pion-Berlin 2009); reduction of military involvement in non-military government administration (Serra 2010); institution of legislative oversight, especially control over budgets (Giraldo 2006); formalization of chains of command and civilian-military communication channels (Droz-Vincent 2013); and reform of military missions, including limiting the use of the military in internal policing duties (Goodman 1996; Pion-Berlin 2018). In the post-communist context, new democratic governments also sought to reform the preceding civil-military systems by severing communist party ties to the military (Bebler 1997).

Addressing the judicial prerogatives of the military is an important aspect of this process of asserting civilian control. After transitions from authoritarian rule, civilian-military bargaining often takes place over who has jurisdiction over members of the military accused of human rights violations during the previous regime (Pion-Berlin 2010). Militaries also desire the ability to police themselves in future deployments by the new democratic government. Legal prerogatives are particularly sticky, and reform efforts that do not engage with the military directly typically fail to effect change or achieve long-term compliance even when written law is successfully modified (Kyle and Reiter 2013). Military judicial systems with expansive jurisdiction thus represent a direct challenge to the positive civil-military relations required for a functioning democracy.

Another crucial task for democratic actors is to strengthen courts, to ensure that all actors adhere to the rule of law, and to engender renewed societal faith in the justice system (e.g. Magalhães 1999).[9] In the transitional context, establishing the rule of law is an essential characteristic of democratic consolidation (Linz and Stepan 1996). Deepening the quality of democracy relies on the continued commitment to ensuring individuals' rights and to treating all persons equally before the law (O'Donnell 2004). While there are notable exceptions (e.g. Fiss 1993), a strong line of scholarly work finds a positive impact of the rule of law on democracy (e.g. Gloppen, Gargarella, and Skaar 2004; Morlino and Palombella 2010) and holds that furthering democratic values through the judicial branch is vital to the stability of democratic regimes (Hammergen 1998).

To do so, courts must be sufficiently independent to make decisions free from pressure from other branches of government (Shetreet and Forsyth 2012), and a level of internal independence must exist where courts can make rulings without interference from higher courts (Ríos-Figueroa 2016). Furthermore, the range of cases upon which civilian courts can rule (Finkel 2003; Larkins 1998) and the extent to which other actors comply with courts' decisions (Gloppen, Gargarella, and Skaar 2004) are vital to establishing the rule of law. Courts are political actors whose interests should, within constitutionally provided boundaries, serve to check executive and legislative power (Iaryczower, Spiller, and Tommasi 2006; O'Donnell 1998). Democracies new and old have established constitutional courts, some explicitly empowered with judicial review, enabling them to rule on the constitutionality of actions taken by the elected branches (Bhanu Mehta 2007; Ginsburg 2003; Rose-Ackerman 2005).

Where military courts have too much power, they can influence civilian judges and prevent civilian court rulings from being followed. Contradictory court rulings over similar issues challenge the internal independence of the judiciary. Where military courts retain jurisdiction over a large number of crimes and refuse to transfer cases, in defiance of civilian court rulings, the rule of law is weakened substantially. This can lead a democratic society to lose faith in the entire judicial branch, resulting in increased corruption and vigilantism, as citizens doubt the court system's ability to function as a neutral arbiter in disputes.

Finally, human rights violations are intrinsically tied to the quality of democracy. A regime's ability to engage past human rights violations effectively may secure democratic transitions and accelerate democratic consolidation. The literature on transitional justice is divided on the proper approach to address human rights violations committed by previous regimes, but more recent and more comprehensive analyses find a clear causal link between prosecutions of past abuses and improvements in democracy and physical integrity rights (Dancy et al. 2019; Olsen, Payne, and Reiter 2010).[10] Where military courts retain jurisdiction over past human rights violations, thereby preventing members of the military from being prosecuted, democratic consolidation is stunted.

Preventing future human rights violations is then a component of the quality of democracy. Where military courts control the prosecution of members of domestic security forces when they are accused of human rights violations, a culture of impunity develops. Security forces are more likely to abuse their power in the line of duty knowing there will be few repercussions. The use of excessive force in policing and anti-terrorism operations is likely to increase, with adverse effects on innocent civilians. In addition, the ability of militaries to try civilians for particular crimes is a human rights violation itself, given that the key components of a fair trial with due process are often not observed and punishments are typically more severe.

The maintenance of a proper relationship between military courts and human rights is also reflected in international law. This is well-trodden ground (e.g. UNHRC 2013b) and we will not re-summarize the arguments here, but the use of military courts to protect perpetrators of human rights violations from prosecution contravenes the standards and requirements found in a plethora of international and regional human rights treaties. While often not made explicit in the treaty text, courts and international organizations have interpreted the trial of civilians by military courts to be in violation of international human rights standards (e.g. the Inter-American system, see Cerna 2016; United Nations Commission on Human Rights 2006). Court rulings invoking international treaties have played an important role as a catalyst for military court reform in a number of countries.

In sum, when military courts overstep their boundaries, victims do not receive justice for past human rights violations, future human rights violations are not deterred, civil-military relations suffer, the rule of law is weakened, and, as a result, democratic consolidation is hindered. Understanding where militaries retain legal power and how this changes over time is vital for each of these concerns.

Despite the significance of military courts, they are understudied and their political impact is poorly understood. Most of the existing scholarship devoted to military courts is legal in nature (e.g. Rowe 2006), with an aim of understanding how military justice systems operate, almost exclusively in well-established democracies (e.g. Duxbury and Groves 2016; Morris 2010), including the United States where issues surrounding Guantanamo Bay and the War on Terror have attracted attention (e.g. Ní Aoláin and Gross 2013). Scholarship on civil-military relations, while extensive and valuable to understanding interactions between the military and other elements of society, typically does not take into consideration the legal power of militaries (e.g. Barany 2012). An innovative literature has begun to address questions around judicial politics within authoritarian regimes, where military courts typically play a prominent role (e.g. Ginsburg and Moustafa 2008; Pereira 2005), but there is little examination of those systems after democratization. Those works that do study judicial systems across transitions typically only focus on civilian courts (e.g. Helmke 2004; Popova 2012).[11]

Our work goes beyond existing studies by devoting significant attention to the larger political role of military courts in democracies. We treat military courts as an instrument through which militaries (and often the state) exert their power and as independent political actors with their own agendas. Even where the main purpose of military courts is to aid the state in maintaining security, they also at times challenge the state and (re)define law according to their own views (e.g. Israel, see Hajjar 2005). As political players, military courts are embedded in a larger political-institutional environment comprised of a variety of actors with interests in using military justice to their advantage or in opposing it to accomplish their own goals. As we discuss above, governments frequently turn to military courts to address internal security threats and buttress shaky regimes, and militaries rely on them to protect their own forces from prosecution. Yet opposition political parties, domestic and international human rights activists, and civilian judges often oppose expanded roles for military justice. Politicians working to rein in overly powerful militaries can enact legal reforms through legislation or new constitutions and amendments (Serra 2010).[12] Independent decisions from civilian judges can determine the trajectory of judicial reform (Hilbink 2007) and shape the landscape of civil-military relations (Ríos-Figueroa 2016). Domestic and international pressure is often a driving force behind the actions of politicians and judges.

Military legal subordination

To examine the political role of military courts, we develop and employ a framework of "legal subordination," defined as the degree to which military courts are subordinated to democratic, civilian control. The concept centers around who can be prosecuted in military courts (personal jurisdiction, or *in personam*) and for what crimes (subject matter jurisdiction, or *rationae materiae*). In this framework, we characterize military legal subordination as a range from *full subordination* to *jurisdictional contestation* to *military overreach*. In systems of full subordination, military courts either have been abolished completely or operate only for a narrow set of offenses necessary to maintain good order and discipline. There are no serious disputes between civilian and military courts regarding the jurisdiction of cases. Military overreach is characterized by a military justice system that is largely unchecked by civilian actors. In such systems, military courts try civilians for specific crimes against the state and typically retain jurisdiction over members of the armed forces for most crimes. Finally, in cases of jurisdictional contestation, military courts have jurisdiction over some civilian crimes committed by members of the military, including human rights violations, and there are often public disputes over who has the right to hear cases. Military courts, however, do not try civilians. We go into more detail on the process by which we define each type in Chapter 2.

Implicit in this scale is our view that full subordination is the goal to which democratic states should strive. Only under those systems is there a reasonable expectation that the military will remain subordinated to civilian leaders and that sufficient rule of law and respect for human rights will exist. Legal subordination of the military is an essential component of well-functioning, democratic societies. States can move along this continuum over time in two ways—rapidly and gradually—and in two directions—toward or away from full subordination.

States may establish their first system in any of the three categories and maintain that system indefinitely. Movement from one category to another, however, is common. There are two distinct pathways by which states transition to full subordination, which is the ultimate goal of those advocating reform. In the first scenario, full subordination is realized immediately at a critical juncture in national politics. During democratic transitions, major turnovers in government, or the end of internal or external wars, governments enact new laws and constitutions that reconfigure the armed forces and the judiciary, leading to rapid change from jurisdictional contestation and, at times, even from military overreach to full subordination. In the second scenario, those actors advocating reform are able to bring about positive change in the face of resistance incrementally over time. The process usually plays out in fits and starts, with important reforms separated by periods of stability until interrupted by new reforms, often due to significant court rulings or resurgent pressure from civil society following high-profile human rights violations.

States may either reform up or backslide down into the jurisdictional contestation category. In many states, reform efforts have been successful but remain incomplete. The combined efforts of the civilian judiciary, government actors, and reform movements within civil society have reduced the legal power of the military over time. Yet the military has successfully resisted and maintains enclaves of legal power, and full subordination has not been achieved. Partial subordination is also often baked into democratic transitions. Efforts to rein in the military occur during the democratization process but full subordination is not realized. Contestation becomes the status quo. In other cases, states in the full subordination category see militaries gain more legal power over time, eroding the degree of civilian control. Cases of backsliding are typically associated with the development of new internal or external security threats, which push civilian actors to devolve more power to security forces.

Finally, as with full subordination, states can shift to the category of military overreach immediately or incrementally. States may see civilian control erode and backslide into this category. Alternatively, there may be a complete breakdown of civilian control due to the emergence of an internal security threat or a major regime change, leading a state to collapse at once into military overreach.

Using the military legal subordination framework and the typology of change outlined above, we answer three distinct but interrelated research questions. First, what is the status of legal subordination of militaries worldwide? Or to what degree, if any, has each state experienced reform? As of yet, there is no clear picture of how much legal power militaries have, whether this has increased or decreased in the past decades, and how much variation there is within countries over time.

Second, what explains the varying degrees of legal subordination around the world? Where there has been partial or full reform, research is needed to show which actors led those efforts and what tactics proved effective. Where reform efforts have failed, we need to understand why and who resisted attempts to change the system. Finally, what causes some countries to backslide, with the military gaining more legal powers? For all of those scenarios above, it is important to understand the role of the larger political context in shaping behavior. Political transitions, government turnover, civil wars, organized crime, and terrorism all play a role in determining the direction of change in military legal subordination.

Third, what is the relationship between legal subordination and human rights, civil-military relations, and democracy? While empirical examples suggest that a lack of subordination is detrimental to all three outcomes of interest, there is a lack of systematic studies that examine these relationships across cases and time. A full picture is necessary to understand the degree to which legal subordination of the military matters, particularly for policymakers working on these issues in nascent democracies.

Case selection and methodology

To answer the crucial questions outlined above, we have constructed a global dataset of military justice over time in 120 countries—all countries that have been nominally democratic at some point since the beginning of the Third Wave of democratization in 1974 through 2017 (Huntington 1991).[13] We focus on democratic regimes, because they must protect themselves from threats in order to survive but face the inherent dilemma of needing to do so in a manner that stays within a constitutional framework and does not subvert democracy itself (Loveman 1993, 19). It is also only in a democratic context where we can assume an attempt to maintain human rights standards and a desire to reserve political power to elected officials rather than members of the military. We trace the trajectory of military court jurisdiction across authoritarian and democratic periods in all of those countries.[14]

To develop our dataset, we analyzed national constitutions and legislation, military codes, domestic and international court rulings, as well as other primary and secondary sources to detail the jurisdictional authority of military courts across cases and over time.[15] The endnotes for each chapter provide extensive links to original documents, and we have made all of them available on a dedicated website.[16] Countries maintain an array of institutional configurations with military courts, military tribunals, courts martial, and special tribunals.[17] We use the term "military courts" to refer collectively to any judicial body operated by the military.[18]

We are most interested, however, in what actually happens in practice. Therefore, in addition to the legal status of military courts, we use a wide range of reports by governments, international organizations, and non-governmental organizations, coupled with news sources and academic publications, to document the legal power of militaries in practice in each country. Using our typology of legal subordination, we then present a global map of the legal power of militaries across more than four decades.

In examining military legal power, we do not assume that all civilian judiciaries in democratic regimes are inherently independent and impartial. Many civilian judiciaries are under-resourced, actively subverted by the government, or corrupt. Nor do we assume that military courts cannot be independent and impartial. Indeed, under certain circumstances, military court jurisdiction over civilians may even be compliant with international law, provided there are sufficient safeguards (Livoja 2016; Rowe 2006, 99–102).[19] Military courts, however, struggle to maintain independence because their judges are often prosecuting cases of opponents of those in the military or executive branch who appoint them to their positions. Impartiality is also difficult to maintain because those being prosecuted by military courts have typically been captured and held by the military (Weissbrodt and Hansen 2013, 310–12). Moreover, it is not only the *actual* level of independence and impartiality of a court that matters. Rather, "perceived bias" (Weissbrodt and Hansen 2013, 311) or the "*appearance* of a lack of independence or impartiality" is "sufficient to show that the court lacks independence or impartiality or both" (Rowe 2006, 83).[20] Military courts are viewed as inherently biased in most contexts. Delivering equality in legal outcomes and avoiding the appearance of bias are essential to the health of a democracy.

Finally, we restrict our analysis to situations where courts have jurisdiction over their own citizens. We thus exclude foreign occupations where military courts may have temporary jurisdiction over conquered peoples or where military courts were used to govern colonies, which was a common practice. France, for example, relied on military courts in its colonies in Africa and Southeast Asia, and during the colonial wars of the 1950s–60s, it used them extensively "both as a means of punishing those fighting for independence and in order to ensure that the excesses committed by the colonial troops … would go unpunished" (Andreu-Guzmán 2004, 269). Overt military occupations of foreign territory are also largely historical (Hathaway and Shapiro 2017). Russia's annexation of Crimea from Ukraine in 2014 is the notable divergence from this trend, but it was quickly incorporated into Russia's state and legal system (Petrov 2016). In addition, we exclude discussions of how military personnel attached to international peacekeeping operations are held legally accountable.

The approach of creating and analyzing a large dataset has the advantage of categorizing the world, uncovering broad trends, and identifying potential causal factors that explain outcomes. We present a clear picture of military justice in more cases and across a greater timespan than any previous study. Moreover, while other work has tracked legal changes over time, our study is the first to examine the politics of military justice at such a scale. This approach, however, has limitations. It is unable to isolate and assess the relative importance of variables or identify the causal mechanisms of change. We thus combine this method with qualitative case studies that are fine-grained and deeply historical.

We selected seven case studies to illustrate our outcomes of interest and the different causal factors and pathways states take to arrive at them. Portugal (Chapter 4) was one of the earliest states to develop a modern military justice system in Europe and demonstrates how the historical legacies of original systems persist over time, in this case centuries. Portugal also illustrates the shifts in military legal subordination that accompany the military seizing power and major democratic transitions. We then show that its strong domestic judiciary and an absence of security threats explain the stable system of full subordination since the 1974 democratic transition.

In contrast, the case of Colombia (Chapter 4) shows how and why states break from past practices upon independence. It is then a prominent example of a security threat driving decisions over military justice. As the state fought a bloody civil war for over 50 years, the government, supported by much of the population, empowered the military to use whatever means necessary to end the conflict. Colombia then illustrates how a combination of factors for reform coalesced and overcame the influence of this security threat. Despite the conflict worsening, Colombia shifted into jurisdictional contestation and then eventually the full subordination category with the help of pressure from domestic and international human rights organizations, international court rulings, a shift in public opinion following major human rights violations attributed to the military, and a strong domestic judiciary stemming from a critical juncture in Colombian politics that led to a new constitution.

Indonesia (Chapter 5) represents a case where a military with well-entrenched political power, stemming from its birth as a revolutionary army that freed the country from colonial rule, is able to resist full subordination of its military justice system despite the presence of many other factors that would normally predict reform—a major democratic transition, a strong civil society movement, and the creation of a new constitutional court. The constitutional court lost its influence early on, new security threats emerged, and the military worked hard to improve its image within the population at large, leading to a stalemate and stalled reform. Fiji (Chapter 5) is an example of a former British colony that established a system of full subordination immediately after independence, as most other states in that situation did. A gradual growth in military power over time led to it becoming political and ruling directly. The case shows how fear of accountability for human rights violations can lead to a perpetual cycle whereby the military intervenes repeatedly to ensure its legal protections remain intact. The absence of strong factors for reform has meant that the country remains mired in the jurisdictional contestation category.

Like Indonesia, Brazil (Chapter 6) experienced a major democratic transition, in this case after a long period of institutionalized military rule. The military has come under heavy criticism from domestic and international actors for human rights violations committed during its rule. International courts have ruled against the government's practices. These factors in favor of reform, however, are negated by the persistent internal security threat of organized crime and drug-trafficking. The population, and in turn politicians seeking to win office, have increasingly turned to the military to confront those issues. The military's strong image within the population is aided by the fact that the former military regime was relatively peaceful for those who did not directly oppose it. While Brazil is an example of a persistent security threat resulting in static military overreach, Pakistan (Chapter 6) shows how the ebb and flow of security threats and the corresponding direct interventions by the military in politics explain the repeated shifts between jurisdictional contestation and military overreach. The country remains locked in this vicious cycle, with almost none of the factors necessary for reform present.

Finally, the United States (Chapter 7) demonstrates how military legal subordination can transform over time absent any significant political transition. The United States has been a democracy since its independence and like other British colonies established a system of full subordination immediately thereafter. Civil society has been strong and politicians respond to their constituents as they compete in free and fair elections. With those factors constant, changes in military justice are explained by a delicate balance between the strength of courts and the severity of internal security threats. In the face of extreme security threats, such as the US Civil War, military legal power has expanded significantly, with civilian courts and the military typically avoiding a direct confrontation with each other. When the threats subside, civilian courts have attempted to condemn past practices so as not to set a precedent for the abuse of military courts going forward.

Our case studies are situated in the approach of comparative historical analysis, in that we analyze historical sequences with the objective of identifying "causal configurations that produce major outcomes of interest" (Mahoney and Rueschemeyer 2003, 11). We engage in "structured, focused comparison," whereby we ask a common set of questions related to specific aspects of each historical case (George and Bennett 2005). Moreover, we conduct within-case analysis for each country, allowing us to examine the causal factors underlying dozens of shifts in military legal subordination. This tactic enables us to demonstrate the degree to which our cross-national findings are observed within countries ("pattern matching," see Campbell 1975).

Most importantly, we employ the methods of process tracing (Bennett 2010) and causal narrative (Sewell 1996) in our case studies. Such an approach is especially important in our study where the explanatory and outcome variables may be separated by significant time (e.g. R. Collier and D. Collier 1991). Our goal is to provide a fine-grained picture of each case by unpacking variables and disaggregating sequences of events, working to highlight the complex interactions between causal factors that lead to our outcomes of interest. Overall, we find strong support for our cross-national findings in our case study analysis.

Plan of the book

In Chapter 2, we begin by examining the history and role of military justice and defining each of our three systems of military legal subordination in depth. We then describe our new dataset and the process of its construction. We conclude the chapter by using it to present an overview of the degree of military legal subordination around the world over time and to examine the relationship between military justice and democracy and human rights. Overall, we show that military legal subordination has increased over time, particularly since the end of the Cold War. At the same time, we find that many civilian governments still do not have firm control over their military's legal prerogatives.

In Chapter 3, we further draw on our dataset to examine the ways in which states create and change their military justice systems. We identify key patterns in the establishment of military justice around the world. We then present our model of change to explain reform and backsliding through interactions among three principal actors—the government, the military, and high courts—whose positions are influenced by a variety of domestic and international factors. Chapters 4, 5, 6, and 7 then apply that model to our case studies, as we discuss above. We conclude the book, in Chapter 8, by discussing the implications of our work for successful activism and outlining several avenues of future research.

Notes

1 *Armed Forces (Special Powers) Act (AFSPA), 1958* (Act No. 28 of 1958) [11th September, 1958], http://legislative.gov.in/sites/default/files/A1958-28.pdf. The AFSPA has its origins in the 1942 Lord Linlithgow ordinance used by the British to suppress the 1942 Quit India movement.

2 *Armed Forces (Punjab and Chandigarh) Special Powers Act, 1983* (Act No. 34 of 1983) [8th December, 1983], http://legislative.gov.in/sites/default/files/A1983-34.pdf; *Armed Forces (Jammu and Kashmir) Special Powers Act, 1990* (Act No. 21 of 1990) [10th September, 1990], http://legislative.gov.in/sites/default/files/A1990-21.pdf.

3 The government repealed the 1983 Armed Forces (Punjab and Chandigarh) Special Powers Act in 1997. It removed the AFSPA from Tripura in 2015 and removed it from Meghalaya and reduced it to limited areas of Arunachal Pradesh in 2018.

4 The quote is from Lieutenant General (retired) Raj Kadyan, a former Vice-Chief of Army Staff.

5 *Naga People's Movement of Human Rights, etc.* v. *Union of India*, AIR 1998 SC 431, https://main.sci.gov.in/jonew/judis/13628.pdf.

6 Judgment, Writ Petition (CRL) No. 129 of 2012, Supreme Court of India, https://main.sci.gov.in/supremecourt/2012/29000/29000_2012_Judgement_14-Jul-2017.pdf.

7 Maute is also referred to as the Islamic State of Lanao.

8 Conversely, other scholars (e.g. Finer 1962; Fitch 1998) have found that in the context of developing countries, military modernization can actually threaten civilian supremacy if it leads the military to see itself as the institution that should dictate national development.

9 For a discussion on the concept of the rule of law, see Maravall and Przeworski 2003.

10 For a contrasting view that prosecutions should be eschewed in favor of amnesties that appease potential spoilers and safeguard democratic transitions, see Snyder and Vinjamuri 2003.

11 A notable exception is a recent work by Julio Ríos-Figueroa (2016), which examines the role of constitutional courts as mediators between the military and civilian actors in three Latin American democracies.

12 Political reformers are not necessarily democratic reformers. Turkey has become more authoritarian under President Tayyip Erdogan and one of the steps he took was to rein in the legal prerogatives of the military through a constitutional amendment, an effort that may help "coup-proof" the government following the 2016 coup attempt by a faction of the armed forces (Aybet 2017).

13 We use the Polity5 dataset to determine our cases (Marshall and Gurr 2008). We present more details on our case selection in Chapter 2.

14 This includes examining the role of military courts in predecessor states for those that have recently become independent.

15 We are particularly indebted to the International Commission of Jurists' two-volume work on military jurisdiction and international law (Andreu-Guzmán 2018; Andreu-Guzmán 2004) and the database of national constitutions maintained by the Comparative Constitutions Project (Elkins, Ginsburg, and Melton 2018). In addition, the Global Military Justice Reform Blog (http://globalmjreform.blogspot.com/) was an invaluable source for current events related to military justice.

16 Because URLs inevitably change, all documents in the public domain are also available for download at http://andyreiter.com/military-justice/.

17 While some countries do not maintain a uniform code of military justice and each branch (e.g. army, navy) operates its own judicial system instead, there are typically no significant divergences in their jurisdictional reach or relationships with civilian courts.

18 Governments frequently create special courts to deal with national security issues and to prosecute their opponents for political reasons. We only consider them military courts if they are predominantly run by the military. In many cases, special courts have military aspects, including some military judges, but they are otherwise civilian courts operated by civilian authorities.

19 The Third Geneva Convention, for example, states that courts martial are appropriate for prisoners of war, see Geneva Convention relative to the Treatment of Prisoners of War, August 12, 1949, 75 U.N.T.S. 972, https://treaties.un.org/doc/Publication/UNTS/Volume%2075/volume-75-I-972-English.pdf. Most human rights treaty monitoring bodies, however, have come out strongly against civilians being tried in military courts (Conte 2013).

20 The emphasis is in the original.

References

Amnesty International. 2012. "India: Pathribal Ruling a Setback for Justice in Jammu and Kashmir," May 12. https://www.amnesty.org/en/press-releases/2012/05/india-pathribal-ruling-setback-justice-jammu-and-kashmir/.

Andreu-Guzmán, Federico. 2004. *Military Courts and Gross Human Rights Violations. Vol. 1. of Military Jurisdiction and International Law.* Geneva: International Commission of Jurists. https://www.icj.org/military-jurisdiction-and-international-law-military-courts-and-gross-human-rights-violations-vol-1/.

Andreu-Guzmán, Federico. 2018. *Fuero militar y Derecho internacional: Los civiles ante los tribunales militares. Vol 2. of Military Jurisdiction and International Law.* Geneva: International Commission of Jurists. https://www.icj.org/wp-content/uploads/2018/05/Universal-Tribunales-Militares-Vol-II-Publications-Reports-Thematic-reports-2018-SPA.pdf.

Aybet, Gulnur. 2017. "Turkey's Good-Governance Referendum." *New York Times*, April 14, https://www.nytimes.com/2017/04/14/opinion/turkeys-good-governance-referendum.html?mcubz=2&_r=0.

Barany, Zoltan. 2012. *The Soldier and the Changing State: Building Democratic Armies in Africa, Asia, Europe, and the Americas.* Princeton: Princeton University Press. DOI: 10.1515/9781400845491.

BBC News. 2016. "Irom Sharmila: World's Longest Hunger Strike Ends," August 9. http://www.bbc.com/news/world-asia-india-37007494.

Bebler, Anton A. 1997. "The Regionwide Perspective on Post-Communist Civil-Military Relations." In *Civil-Military Relations in Post-Communist States: Central and Eastern Europe in Transition*, ed. Anton A. Bebler. London: Praeger, 65–76.

Bennett, George. 2010. "Process Tracing and Causal Inference." In *Rethinking Social Inquiry: Diverse Tools, Shared Standards*, eds. Henry E. Brady and David Collier. 2nd ed. Lanham, MD: Rowman & Littlefield, 203–20.

Bhanu Mehta, Pratap. 2007. "India's Unlikely Democracy: The Rise of Judicial Sovereignty." *Journal of Democracy* 18 (2): 70–83. DOI: 10.1353/jod.2007.0030.

Bhattacharyya, Rituparna. 2018. "Living with Armed Forces Special Powers Act (AFSPA) as Everyday Life." *GeoJournal* 83 (1): 31–48. DOI: 10.1007/s10708-016-9752-9.

Bland, Douglas. 1999. "A Unified Theory of Civil-Military Relations." *Armed Forces & Society* 26 (1): 7–26. DOI: 10.1177/0095327X9902600102.

Cameroon Concord News. 2017. "Do Anti-Terrorism Laws in Cameroon Shackle the Hands of Justice?" April 7. http://www.cameroonconcordnews.com/do-anti-terrorism-laws-in-cameroon-shackle-the-hands-of-justice/.

Campbell, Donald T. 1975. "'Degrees of Freedom' and the Case Study." *Comparative Political Studies* 8 (2): 175–93. DOI: 10.1177/001041407500800204.

Cerna, Christina A. 2016. "The Inter-American System and Military Justice." In *Military Justice in the Modern Age*, eds. Alison Duxbury and Matthews Groves. Cambridge: Cambridge University Press, 325–46. DOI: 10.1017/CBO9781107326330.017.

Collier, Ruth Berins, and David Collier. 1991. *Shaping the Political Arena: Critical Junctures, the Labor Movement, and Regime Dynamics in Latin America.* Princeton: Princeton University Press.

Conte, Alex. 2013. "Approaches and Responses of the UN Human Rights Mechanisms to Exceptional Courts and Military Commissions." In *Guantánamo and Beyond: Exceptional Courts and Military Commissions in Comparative Perspective*, eds. Fionnuala Ní Aoláin and Oren Gross. New York: Cambridge University Press, 321–40. DOI: 10.1017/CBO9780511920721.019.

Croissant, Aurel, and David Kuehn. 2017. *Reforming Civil-Military Relations in New Democracies: Democratic Control and Military Effectiveness in Comparative Perspectives.* New York: Springer. DOI: 10.1007/978-3-319-53189-2.

Dahl, Robert A. 2000. *On Democracy.* New Haven: Yale University Press.

Dancy, Geoff, Bridget Marchesi, Tricia D. Olsen, Leigh A. Payne, Andrew G. Reiter, and Kathryn Sikkink. 2019. "Behind Bars and Bargains: New Findings on Transitional Justice in Emerging Democracies." *International Studies Quarterly* 63 (1): 99–110. DOI: 10.1093/isq/sqy053.

Diamond, Larry, and Marc F. Plattner, eds. 1996. *Civil-Military Relations and Democracy.* Baltimore: Johns Hopkins University Press.

Droz-Vincent, Philippe. 2013. "Prospects for 'Democratic Control of the Armed Forces'? Comparative Insights and Lessons for the Arab World in Transition." *Armed Forces & Society* 40 (4): 696–723. DOI: 10.1177/0095327X12468881.

Duxbury, Alison, and Mathew Groves, eds. 2016. *Military Justice in the Modern Age.* Cambridge: Cambridge University Press. DOI: 10.1017/CBo9781107326330.

Elkins, Zachary, Tom Ginsberg, and James Melton. 2018. Characteristics of National Constitutions [v.2.0]. www.comparativeconstitutionsproject.org.

Feaver, Peter D. 1996. "The Civil-Military Problematique: Huntington, Janowitz, and the Question of Civilian Control." *Armed Forces & Society* 23 (2): 149–78. DOI: 10.1177/0095327X9602300203.

Finer, Samuel E. 1962. *The Man on Horseback: The Role of the Military in Politics.* London: Pall Mall.

Finkel, Jodi. 2003. "Supreme Court Decisions on Electoral Rules after Mexico's 1994 Judicial Reform: An Empowered Court." *Journal of Latin American Studies* 35 (4): 777–99. DOI: 10.1017/S0022216X03006989.

Fiss, Owen M. 1993. "The Right Degree of Independence." In *Transition to Democracy in Latin America: The Role of the Judiciary*, ed. Irwin P. Stotzky. Boulder: Westview, 55–72. DOI: 10.4324/9780429269578-5.

Fitch, Samuel J. 1998. *The Armed Forces and Democracy in Latin America.* Baltimore: Johns Hopkins University Press.

Gautam, Khagesh. 2017. "Martial Law in India: The Deployment of Military under the Armed Forces Special Powers Act, 1958." *Southwestern Journal of International Law* 24 (1): 117–45.

George, Alexander L., and Andrew Bennett. 2005. *Case Studies and Theory Development in the Social Sciences.* Cambridge: MIT Press.

Ginsburg, Tom. 2003. *Judicial Review in New Democracies: Constitutional Courts in Asian Cases.* Cambridge: Cambridge University Press. DOI: 10.1017/CBO9780511511189.

Ginsburg, Tom, and Tamir Moustafa, eds. 2008. *Rule by Law: The Politics of Courts in Authoritarian Regimes.* Cambridge: Cambridge University Press. DOI: 10.1017/CBO9780511814822.

Giraldo, Jeanne Kinney. 2006. "Defense Budgets, Democratic Civilian Control, and Effective Governance." In *Who Guards the Guardians and How: Democratic Civil-Military Relations*, eds. Thomas C. Bruneau and Scott D. Tollefson. Austin: University of Texas Press, 178–207.

Gloppen, Siri, Roberto Gargarella, and Elin Skaar, eds. 2004. *Democratization and the Judiciary: The Accountability Function of Courts in New Democracies.* London: Cass. DOI: 10.4324/9780203485408.

Goodman, Louis W. 1996. "Military Roles Past and Present." In *Civil-Military Relations and Democracy*, eds. Larry Diamond and Marc F. Plattner. Baltimore: Johns Hopkins University Press, 30–43.

Hajjar, Lisa. 2005. *Courting Conflict: The Israeli Military Court System in the West Bank and Gaza.* Berkeley: University of California Press.

Hammergen, Linn. 1998. *The Politics of Justice and Justice Reform in Latin America: The Peruvian Case in Comparative Perspective.* Boulder: Westview.

Hathaway, Oona A., and Scott J. Shapiro. 2017. *The Internationalists: How a Radical Plan to Outlaw War Remade the World.* New York: Simon & Schuster.

Helmke, Gretchen. 2004. *Courts under Constraints: Judges, Generals and Presidents in Argentina.* Cambridge: Cambridge University Press.

Herspring, Dale R. 2013. *Civil-Military Relations and Shared Responsibility: A Four-Nation Study.* Baltimore: Johns Hopkins University Press.

Hilbink, Lisa. 2007. *Judges Beyond Politics in Democracy and Dictatorship: Lessons from Chile.* Cambridge: Cambridge University Press. DOI: 10.1017/CBO9780511511509.

Human Rights Watch. 2008. "'These Fellows Must Be Eliminated': Relentless Violence and Impunity in Manipur," September 29. https://www.hrw.org/report/2008/09/29/these-fellows-must-be-eliminated/relentless-violence-and-impunity-manipur.

Human Rights Watch. 2017a. "India: Top Court Orders Manipur Killings Inquiry," July 15. https://www.hrw.org/news/2017/07/15/india-top-court-orders-manipur-killings-inquiry.

Human Rights Watch. 2017b. "'It's Not the Right Place for Us': The Trial of Civilians by Military Courts in Lebanon," January 26. https://www.hrw.org/report/2017/01/26/its-not-right-place-us/trial-civilians-military-courts-lebanon.

Human Rights Watch. 2017c. "Philippines: Martial Law Threatens Escalation of Abuses," March 25. https://www.hrw.org/news/2017/05/25/philippines-martial-law-threatens-escalation-abuses.

Human Rights Watch. 2018. "India: Manipur Victim Families, Activists Harassed," April 12. https://www.hrw.org/news/2018/04/12/india-manipur-victim-families-activists-harassed.

Hunter, Wendy. 1997. *Eroding Military Influence in Brazil: Politicians Against Soldiers.* Chapel Hill: University of North Carolina Press.

Huntington, Samuel. 1957. *The Soldier and the State: The Theory and Politics of Civil-Military Relations.* Cambridge: Belknap. DOI: 10.2307/j.ctvjf9wx3.

Huntington, Samuel. 1991. *The Third Wave: Democratization in the Late Twentieth Century.* Norman: University of Oklahoma Press.

Iaryczower, Matías, Pablto T. Spiller, and Mariano Tommasi. 2006. "Judicial Lobbying: The Politics of Labor Law Constitutional Interpretation." *American Political Science Review* 100 (1): 85–97. DOI: 1017/S0003055406062022.

Indian Express. 2018a. "AFSPA: Army Chief Bipin Rawat Asks Why Officers, Soldiers Filed Plea in SC," September 4. https://indianexpress.com/article/india/afspa-army-chief-bipin-rawat-asks-why-officers-soldiers-filed-plea-in-sc-5338214/.

Indian Express. 2018b. "Over 380 Army Personnel Move Supreme Court on AFSPA," September 1. https://indianexpress.com/article/india/over-380-army-personnel-move-supreme-court-on-afspa-5334622/.

International Commission of Jurists. 2015. "India: Repeal Armed Forces Special Powers Act Immediately," November 5. https://www.icj.org/india-repeal-armed-forces-special-powers-act-immediately/.

International Commission of Jurists. 2019. "Military Injustice in Pakistan," January. https://www.icj.org/wp-content/uploads/2019/01/Pakistan-military-courts-Advocacy-Analysis-brief-2018-ENG.pdf.

Janowitz, Morris. 1960. *The Professional Soldier: A Social and Political Portrait.* New York: Free Press.

Kohn, Richard H. 1997. "How Democracies Control the Military." *Journal of Democracy* 8 (4): 140–53. DOI: 10.1353/jod.1997.0060.

Kyle, Brett J., and Andrew G. Reiter. 2013. "Militarized Justice in New Democracies: Explaining the Process of Military Court Reform in Latin America." *Law & Society Review* 47 (2): 375–407. DOI: 10.1111/lasr.12019.

Larkins, Christopher M. 1998. "The Judiciary and Delegative Democracy in Argentina." *Comparative Politics* 30 (4): 423–43. DOI: 10.2307/422332.

Linz, Juan, and Alfred Stepan. 1996. "Toward Consolidated Democracies." *Journal of Democracy* 7 (2): 14–33. DOI: 10.1353/jod.1996.0031.

Livoja, Rain. 2016. "Trying Civilian Contractors in Military Courts: A Necessary Evil?" In *Military Justice in the Modern Age*, eds. Alison Duxbury and Matthews Groves. Cambridge: Cambridge University Press, 81–105. DOI: 10.1017/CBO9781107326330.006.

Loveman, Brian. 1993. *The Constitution of Tyranny: Regimes of Exception in Spanish America.* Pittsburgh: University of Pittsburgh Press.

Magalhães, Pedro C. 1999. "The Politics of Judicial Reform in Eastern Europe." *Comparative Politics* 32 (1): 43–62. DOI: 10.2307/422432.

Mahoney, James, and Dietrich Rueschemeyer. 2003. "Comparative Historical Analysis: Achievements and Agendas." In *Comparative Historical Analysis in the Social Sciences*, eds. James Mahoney and Dietrich Rueschemeyer. New York: Cambridge University Press, 3–38.

Maravall, José María, and Adam Przeworski, eds. 2003. *Democracy and the Rule of Law.* New York: Cambridge University Press. DOI: 10.1017/CBO9780511610066.

Marshall, Monty G., and Ted Robert Gurr. 2018. "Polity5 Project: Political Regime Characteristics and Transitions, 1800–2018." http://www.systemicpeace.org/polityproject.html.

Mehrotra, Deepti Priya. 2016. "Manipur's Common Cause: Anti-AFSPA Struggle Unites Diverse Groups and Multiple Strategies in the Fight for Peace." *Indian Express*, September 15. https://indianexpress.com/article/opinion/columns/irom-sharmila-fast-manipur-afspa-protest-supreme-court-indian-army-3031474/.

Morlino, Leonardo, and Gianluigi Palombella, eds. 2010. *Rule of Law and Democracy: Inquiries into Internal and External Issues.* Leiden, the Netherlands: Brill.

Morris, Lawrence. 2010. *Military Justice: A Guide to the Issues.* Santa Barbara: Praeger.

Ní Aoláin, Fionnuala, and Oren Gross, eds. 2013. *Guantanamo and Beyond: Exceptional Courts and Military Commissions in Comparative Perspective.* Cambridge: Cambridge University Press. DOI: 10.1017/CBO9780511920721.

O'Donnell, Guillermo. 1998. "Horizontal Accountability in New Democracies." *Journal of Democracy* 9 (3): 112–23. DOI: 10.1353/jod.1998.0051.

O'Donnell, Guillermo. 2004. "The Quality of Democracy: Why the Rule of Law Matters." *Journal of Democracy* 15 (4): 32–46. DOI: 10.1353/jod/2004.0076.

Olsen, Tricia D., Leigh A. Payne, and Andrew G. Reiter. 2010. "The Justice Balance: When Transitional Justice Improves Human Rights and Democracy." *Human Rights Quarterly* 32 (4): 980–1007. DOI: 10.1353/hrq.2010.0021.

Pereira, Anthony W. 2005. *Political (In)Justice: Authoritarianism and the Rule of Law in Brazil, Chile, and Argentina.* Pittsburgh: University of Pittsburgh Press.

Pervez, Ayesha. 2017. "Shielding the Armed Forces for Actions Under AFSPA, But at What Cost?" *The Wire*, April 17. https://thewire.in/law/bjp-modi-afspa-manipur-kashmir.

Petrov, Nikolai. 2016. "Crimea: Transforming the Ukrainian Peninsula into a Russian Island." *Russian Politics and Law* 54 (1): 74–95. DOI: 10.1080/10611940.2015.1160715.

Pion-Berlin, David S. 2005. "Political Management of the Military in Latin America." *Military Review* 85 (1): 19–31.

Pion-Berlin, David S. 2009. "Defense Organization and Civil-Military Relations in Latin America." *Armed Forces & Society* 35 (3): 562–86. DOI: 10.1177/0095327X08322565.

Pion-Berlin, David S. 2010. "Informal Civil-Military Relations in Latin America: Why Politicians and Soldiers Choose Unofficial Venues." *Armed Forces & Society* 36 (3): 526–44. DOI: 10.1177/0095327X09352961.

Pion-Berlin, David S. 2018. *Military Missions in Democratic Latin America.* New York: Palgrave Macmillan. DOI: 10.1057/978-1-137-59270-5.

Popova, Maria. 2012. *Politicized Justice in Emerging Democracies: A Study of Courts in Russia and Ukraine.* Cambridge: Cambridge University Press. DOI: 10.1017/CBO9781139055345.

Ramachandran, Sudha. 2015. "India's Controversial Armed Forces (Special Powers) Act." *The Diplomat*, July 2. https://thediplomat.com/2015/07/indias-controversial-armed-forces-special-powers-act/.

Reddy, B. P. Jeevan. 2005. "Report of the Committee to Review the Armed Forces (Special Powers) Act, 1958." Government of India, Ministry of Home Affairs.

Ríos-Figueroa, Julio. 2016. *Constitutional Courts as Mediators: Armed Conflict, Civil-Military Relations, and the Rule of Law in Latin America*. Cambridge: Cambridge University Press. DOI: 10.1017/CBO9781139942157.

Rose-Ackerman, Susan. 2005. *From Elections to Democracy: Building Accountable Government in Hungary and Poland*. Cambridge: Cambridge University Press.

Rowe, Peter. 2006. *The Impact of Human Rights Law on Armed Forces*. Cambridge: Cambridge University Press. DOI: 10.1017/CBO9780511616198.

Schiff, Rebecca. 2009. *The Military and Domestic Politics: A Concordance Theory of Civil-Military Relations*. London: Routledge. DOI: 10.4324/9780203892305.

Schmitter, Philippe C., and Terry L. Karl. 1991. "What Democracy Is...and Is Not." *Journal of Democracy* 2 (3): 75–88. DOI: 10.1353/jod.1991.0033.

Serra, Narcís. 2010. *The Military Transition: Democratic Reform of the Armed Forces*. Cambridge: Cambridge University Press. DOI: 10.1017/S1537592710002938.

Sewell, William H., Jr. 1996. "Three Temporalities: Toward an Eventful Sociology." In *The Historic Turn in the Human Sciences*, ed. Terrence J. McDonald. Ann Arbor: University of Michigan Press, 245–80.

Sharma, K. Sarojkumar. 2017. "Irom Sharmila Suffers Defeat, Gets Only 90 Votes." *Times of India*, March 12. http://timesofindia.indiatimes.com/elections/assembly-elections/manipur/news/irom-sharmila-suffers-defeat-gets-only-90-votes/articleshow/57601062.cms.

Shetreet, Shimon, and Christopher Forsyth. 2012. *The Culture of Judicial Independence: Conceptual Foundations and Practical Challenges*. Leiden, the Netherlands: Brill.

Shivshankar, V. 2017. "Supreme Court Upholds Order Against Use of Excessive Force by Army in Manipur." *The Wire*, April 27. https://thewire.in/law/supreme-court-upholds-order-use-excessive-force-army-manipur.

Singh, Bikram. 2018. "A Great Nation Must Stand with its Soldiers." *Hindustan Times*, September 20. https://www.hindustantimes.com/analysis/a-great-nation-must-stand-with-its-soldiers/story-nBtryyOMzjffNXnNHJ7agI.html.

Snyder, Jack, and Leslie Vinjamuri. 2003. "Trials and Errors: Principle and Pragmatism in Strategies of International Justice." *International Security* 28 (3): 5–44. DOI: 10.1162/016228803773100066.

United Nations Commission on Human Rights. 2006. "Draft Principles Governing the Administration of Justice Through Military Tribunals." E/CN.4/2006/58 at 4. https://undocs.org/pdf?symbol=en/E/CN.4/2006/58.

United Nations Human Rights Council. 2013a. "Report of the Special Rapporteur on Extrajudicial, Summary or Arbitrary Executions, Christof Heyns: Mission to India." A/HRC/23/47/Add.31. https://www.ohchr.org/documents/hrbodies/hrcouncil/regularsession/session23/a.hrc.23.47.add.1_en.pdf.

United Nations Human Rights Council. 2013b. "Report of the Special Rapporteur on the Independence of Judges and Lawyers, Gabriela Knaul." A/68/285. https://undocs.org/pdf?symbol=en/A/68/285.

Varadarajan, Siddharth. 2006. "Repeal Armed Forces Act: Official Panel." *The Hindu*, October 8. https://www.thehindu.com/todays-paper/repeal-armed-forces-act-official-panel/article18485943.ece.

Verma, J. S. 2013. "Report of the Committee on Amendments to Criminal Law," January 23. http://www.prsindia.org/uploads/media/Justice%20verma%20committee/js%20verma%20committe%20report.pdf.

Villamor, Felipe. 2017. "Philippine Supreme Court Upholds Duterte's Martial Law Edict." *New York Times*, July 4. https://www.nytimes.com/2017/07/04/world/asia/philippines-supreme-court-martial-law-rodrigo-duterte.html?mcubz=2&_r=0.

Weissbrodt, Davis S., and Joseph C. Hansen. 2013. "The Rights to a Fair Trial in an Extraordinary Court." In *Guantánamo and Beyond: Exceptional Courts and Military Commissions in Comparative Perspective*, eds. Fionnuala Ní Aoláin and Oren Gross. New York: Cambridge University Press, 305–20. DOI: 10.1017/CBO9780511920721.018.

2 The role of military justice in the modern world

Introduction

As long as there have been militaries there have been systems, of some form, of military justice to accompany them. For a variety of reasons, militaries require the ability to maintain internal discipline and adjudicate violations of rules that are specific to the military. In this chapter, we begin by tracing the history of military justice as it has evolved into modern court systems and then describe the necessary role that they play in a properly functioning military. Next, to understand the variation in relationships between military courts and civilian authorities, we turn to our framework of legal subordination, which delineates the degree to which military courts are subordinated to democratic, civilian control. We define and illustrate three distinct systems—full subordination, jurisdictional contestation, and military overreach—and discuss the political ramifications of each. Finally, we conclude the chapter with a global overview of military courts over the past half-century. Using our new dataset, we present trends over time and examine the relationship between military legal subordination and democracy and human rights. Overall, military legal subordination has increased over time. More countries have reined in the use of military courts as a shield of impunity, and the use of military courts to try civilians has declined significantly since the end of the Cold War. Nevertheless, even today over a third of the countries in our dataset have military justice systems with expansive jurisdiction or troubled practices, where civilian governments do not have firm control over the military's legal prerogatives.

The evolution of military courts

The military is a unique institution. Its members are trained specifically in the use of lethal force to achieve objectives on behalf of the state. Moreover, its success—in protecting the state and keeping its members alive—depends on operating efficiently and cohesively. Commanders need to ensure that their orders are obeyed without provocation or hesitation. Military justice serves a vital function in maintaining the good order and discipline necessary to ensure obedience to superiors. Violations of military codes need to be punished swiftly, and at times harshly, in order to deter future violations and to inculcate a clear understanding that order must be maintained. Such violations also have to be adjudicated fairly to prevent the erosion of morale or the stoking of dissent within the ranks. These demands necessitate a formalized system with written rules and associated punishments.

When professionalized and organized standing armies developed, they also took on a number of characteristics that reinforced their distinct identities and evolved into what some have called a "separate society" (Hirschhorn 1984).[1] They wear special uniforms, use their own language, and practice traditions that help to engender unit cohesion. In most cases, they live together, in effect making them 24-hour employees of the state. Military personnel share an unmistakable corporate identity based on appearance, codes of conduct, routine practices, and training that set them apart from the civilian population. Instilling values and skills necessary for military life are essential components of modern military training. Professionalization of the officer corps, in particular, includes specialized instruction in command (Abrahamsson 1972; Huntington 1957). Military personnel uniquely must be prepared to risk their lives in battle and to sacrifice themselves if ordered to do so. The need for unwavering discipline and adherence to the chain of command is of utmost importance.[2] Commitment to these values sets them apart from the rest of society. This division between military and civilian cultures can be at the root of civil-military tensions. Not only do militaries view themselves as distinct entities within society, but they may also develop a sense of holding a position that is above society, where the duty of the institution is to serve as "guardians" of the state, even from internal threats and the government itself (Nordlinger 1977).

Given those unique characteristics, all militaries have maintained some system to ensure internal order and discipline. Early armed groups typically handled this informally at the unit level with commanders meting out often cruel punishment on subordinates who disobeyed their orders or engaged in behavior harmful to the mission. As militaries modernized and professionalized, they more clearly defined their rules of behavior and enforced their associated penalties through more formalized systems.

In the Roman Empire, laws related to maintaining *disciplina militaris*—including punishments for desertion, theft, and insubordination—were written down, and these military codes were then adjudicated in a hierarchical system (Hebblewhite 2017, 128–39). *Centurians* were empowered to summarily punish minor violations, with more serious crimes being referred to *tribunos* who would conduct an investigation before ruling (Postma 1968, 68). All capital crimes were referred to the commanding general, who was the only one with the authority to impose the death sentence. Bestowed with the military *imperium*, or supreme power, he would often rule from a *tribunal*, which frequently was a raised mound or a wooden structure in the center of the camp (Brand 1968, 55, 68–70). While punishments sometimes took the form of humiliating violators, most sentences were extremely harsh and involved some form of corporal punishment (Phang 2008, 111–51). In severe cases, the general could order the punishment of ***decimation***, whereby every tenth soldier in the unit was sentenced to death (Phang 2008, 123–29; Postma 1968, 68). At the same time, military law benefitted the military's members. Soldiers were given special legal privileges not available to civilians (Hebblewhite 2017, 120–28) and were even granted the right to "object to being tried by a civilian judge when he is charged with the commission of a common-law offence" (Postma 1968, 69).

Throughout the Middle Ages, European militaries gradually expanded and codified military law and established the antecedents of modern military justice systems. In 1190, England's King Richard I (Richard the Lionheart) laid out clear laws for crusaders sailing to the Middle East during the Third Crusade. Killing someone on board a ship was punishable by death, with the perpetrator, alive, tied to the victim's dead body and thrown overboard. The laws also addressed numerous small infractions: using foul language, for example, was penalized with a fine of one ounce of silver. King Richard II of England published the comprehensive Ordinances of War in 1385, which covered many offenses related to military discipline, but also included rules against the destruction of church property and guidelines for the treatment of prisoners. Violations of some of the more serious rules were punishable by death or various forms of corporal punishment, but many others resulted in the forfeiture of the knight's horse and armor. It became customary for each English king to issue his own Rules and Ordinances of War before each military campaign. Swedish King Gustavus Adolphus's 1621 Articles of War went further than previous efforts and established a detailed system of military courts to adjudicate an exhaustive list of military laws, which were required to be read aloud publicly to each regiment once a month.[3]

The modern British military justice system has its origins in the late 1600s (Samuel 1816). King James II of England laid out a detailed system of courts martial in 1686 and the first Mutiny Act of 1689 established the right of the king to enact articles of war (Winthrop 1920, 919–30). From the beginning, there was a clear distinction between military legal powers within England's borders and those in its overseas dominions. Military courts had no jurisdiction over civilians in England during peacetime, and by the early 1700s, courts martial could not try British soldiers for ordinary felonies committed on British soil either (Wiener 1967, 14–15). In the British Empire, particularly in North America, courts martial continued their jurisdiction over civilians, but the government restricted them over time, beginning during the Seven Years War (1756–63). Exceptions still existed, however, including provisions allowing for military justice in territories where no civil authority had been established (Wiener 1967, 64–77).[4] As they were revised throughout the 1700s, British military law and practice served as a model for many countries in the world. The first articles of war in the United States, for example, were nearly identical to the British articles in force at the time of the revolution (Davis 1915, 339–564; Winthrop 1920, 931–46, 953–60).

Other colonial powers during this time also developed distinct legal systems to govern their military forces. Most notably, reaffirming the idea of a separate society, Spain granted its military its own *fuero*, or set of privileges, adjudicated by its own courts.[5] The *fuero militar* has its origins in the mid-1500s and took full form in the late-1700s when, as part of the Bourbon Reforms, King Charles III created new privileges for the reorganized and expanded standing army controlling its empire (McAlister 1957). Reflecting its role in maintaining internal order in Spain and its colonies, the military's tribunals could exercise legal authority over civilians, especially in instances of public disturbances or crimes against the state, such as treason and sedition (Loveman 2001, 251–52). In most circumstances, military courts tried members of the military for nearly all types of civil and criminal offenses. Members were also allowed to use military courts for other legal matters, such as the preparation of wills and settlement of estates (McAlister 1957, 7). Some of the privileges extended to the family members and even domestic servants of members of the military, and many were retained after a soldier retired. The military valued the *fuero militar*, and attempts to revoke it became a contentious issue that plagued civil-military relations in most former Spanish colonies long after their independence.

Parallel legal systems for the armed forces are commonplace today. Nearly every state that has a military has some type of separate military justice system to govern it. These systems, however, vary considerably in whom they can prosecute for what crimes. In the next section, we describe a system of full subordination, where military courts restrict their operations to trying members of the military for a narrowly defined set of military crimes. Such a system, we argue, is compatible with democracy and is the ideal type toward which states should strive.

Full subordination

Civilian control of the armed forces is fundamental to modern democracy. For popular sovereignty to be exercised, the military must answer to elected officials who ultimately answer to the voting public. Having a military that is unaccountable to civilian authorities, including in the legal realm, weakens democracy. Democratic states must manage the contradiction of a need for a separate justice system that maintains the military's internal discipline while preventing that separate system from delivering unequal justice by shielding the military from accountability or acting as a tool of repression against the civilian population. In countries characterized as full subordination, military judicial powers are limited to judging only military personnel for offenses necessary to maintain good order and discipline, with minimal exceptions. In the event of jurisdictional conflicts, the military defers to civilian authorities and transfers cases, and civilian authorities have sufficient oversight over military courts to prevent abuses.

Military-specific crimes

Military-specific crimes over which military courts have jurisdiction are those offenses necessary to maintain good order and discipline, stemming from the imperative of command effectiveness. Military justice may need to be carried out in unique circumstances such as on the battlefield or aboard ship where conventional civilian police and judges are unavailable. Additionally, proceedings must be conducted quickly to restore order, deter further insubordination, and prevent dissention in the ranks that may arise from a failure to address wrongdoing.

If a military is to be effective in executing the policies of the civilian democratic government, military personnel must adhere to the chain of command that stretches from the elected commander-in-chief to the individual soldier. Maintaining this disciplined structure requires defining offenses that do not exist in a civilian legal code and the means to punish violations of them. Among civilians, missing work might mean getting fired from one's job, but that is likely the extent of the punishment. In a military context, missing work is a criminal offense. For example, as defined in the United States Uniform Code of Military Justice (UCMJ), failing to show up for deployment, known as "missing movement" (Article 87), can result in discharge from the forces and imprisonment for up to two years.[6] Any number of unauthorized absences, including making oneself unavailable for duty through feigned illness or intentionally inflicted injury (Article 83), abandoning one's post (Article 86), or desertion (Article 85), are military-specific crimes punished accordingly (Articles 77–134). These actions are significant offenses in a military context because they represent a threat to the unit's ability to carry out operations. As Lawrence Morris (2010) writes: "fundamental to good order and discipline is the requirement that soldiers serve where they are told when they are told" (66).

Similarly, maintaining the military chain of command requires defining disobedience and disrespect against superiors as violations of military law. The US UCMJ articulates separate acts of disrespect toward a superior commissioned officer, including assaulting that person (Article 89), disobeying a superior commissioned officer (Article 90), insubordination toward a non-commissioned officer (Article 91), and the failure to obey a general order or regulation (Article 92). Meanwhile, there are further catch-all provisions, such as Article 133, which permits charges against "Conduct unbecoming an officer and a gentleman," and Article 134, the "General article" against any action "to the prejudice of good order and discipline in the armed forces." The US system is emblematic of established democracies. Almost all have similar codes of military justice that define these unique military crimes and empower military courts to adjudicate violations of them.

In sum, there are a host of military-specific crimes that, by necessity, are judged in military courts. The distinct nature of the job and the serious implications of breaking military rules require a specialized justice system. Where they are limited to adjudicating military-specific crimes, as we discuss above, they are compatible with a democratic regime.

Overlap with civilian criminal codes

Full legal subordination of the armed forces requires military justice to be limited to clearly internal affairs, but scholars and practitioners have debated the service-related distinction because military law often includes common crimes, such as theft, that would also be recognized in the civilian realm. Common crimes can be seen as "no less a breach of discipline than a purely military offence" (Rowe 2006, 80) given the unique conditions of military life, including soldiers living in close quarters and needing to be able to trust each other in order to maintain effectiveness. Thus, theft among soldiers or sailors is not solely about the act of theft but also the acrimony and erosion of trust that accompanies it (Gibson 2008, 37), thereby meriting potentially harsher punishment than would exist for the equivalent civilian crime. Established democracies have dealt with these inevitable overlaps differently in practice. The United Kingdom considers service members subject to civilian criminal law when they are serving in the United Kingdom and subject to military law when abroad. The Canadian National Defence Act includes various offenses that overlap with civilian law but stipulates that specific crimes, including murder and manslaughter, never fall under military jurisdiction.[7] In the 1960s, the US Supreme Court ruled that a "service connection" was necessary for military justice to apply, rather than allowing military law to serve as a blanket for all judicial proceedings involving military personnel, but this interpretation lasted only until a 1987 ruling, which did away with this distinction (Morris 2010, 37). Furthermore, some countries, such as the United States and Canada, consider military courts and civilian courts to be "separate sovereigns," making it possible for a soldier to be tried in both venues (Morris 2010, 40).

To conclude, while military courts should never try serious crimes committed against civilians, such as murder, there is justification for military courts to retain jurisdiction of some common crimes committed by their personnel, and to adjudicate them differently than would civilian judicial systems. As a matter of civilian control of the armed forces, however, legal subordination requires any potential conflict between civilian and military jurisdiction over those crimes to be settled in favor of the civilian authority, just as a civilian congressional decision on the military budget or a civilian president relieving a general of their command would be respected by the armed forces. In practice, for full subordination to be in effect, military jurisdiction must be limited and the military must routinely cooperate with civilian authorities when there is a potential conflict between the two.

Civilian authority over military justice

Finally, while modern military justice systems are designed to deal with crimes separate from civilian codes, they are nevertheless rooted in the authority provided by the country's constitution and require thorough civilian oversight for there to be control over the armed forces in a democracy. Even in well-established democracies with highly professionalized armed forces, military justice systems often concentrate decision-making power in the hands of soldiers' immediate superiors when it comes to what offenses to charge and how severely they are to be punished, which raises fears of unevenness in the application of military law (West 1970; 1977). For accused military personnel and civilian victims in instances of human rights abuses, it is crucial for codes of military justice to contain provisions against unlawful command influence and to include articulated procedures for interacting with civilian legal authorities, including, for example, the means to turn military personnel over to them to stand trial when appropriate.[8]

The limits placed on the power of military courts are as important to protecting soldiers' rights as they are to safeguarding the state and society (Generous 1973). Internally, a military is not a democracy, yet it is called on to serve a democratic state and draws its members from a democratic society that values debate, dissent, and a plurality of views and opinions. Meanwhile, the military cannot indulge such behaviors deemed essential to meaningful political life in the society at large; a soldier does not engage in debate and compromise with superiors in response to an order. When serving in the armed forces of a democratic state, individuals accept limits on many of their liberties, but they do not entirely surrender their rights or cease to be citizens of that state. While some restrictions are nearly universal—prohibitions on organizing labor unions for armed forces personnel, for example—military codes of justice in democratic states seek to curtail fundamental rights such as freedom of speech only to the extent necessary to maintain discipline and effectiveness.

For example, while the US UCMJ specifies "Contempt toward officials" (Article 88) as an offense that can be tried by court martial, it defines the crime narrowly and with the intent to reflect the importance of military subordination to civilian control. The article applies only to commissioned officers, only prohibits "contemptuous words" against current political officials, and includes an exemption for "purely private conversation."[9] Indeed, there is an irony of democratic civil-military relations that rights to speech, protest, or organizing—seen as necessary for a country to be called democratic and which the democratic country's military exists in part to defend—are limited for those who serve in the armed forces (J. Finn 1971). Military judicial systems thus attempt to balance the need for discipline with the expectation of fair conduct in proceedings, including a soldier's right to appeal a ruling, potentially even putting the case in the hands of a civilian high court after military venues have been exhausted. Moreover, while military judicial systems enforce good order and discipline, they must avoid arbitrary deprivation of rights or maltreatment of personnel. The earliest modern military justice systems, such as that of nineteenth-century Prussia, eliminated corporal punishment and protected recruits from physical abuse by superiors in order "to make military service tolerable to the masses," expecting them "to come forward freely and train rigorously, without undue coercion" (Dolman 2004, 132). Safeguards against internal abuse are especially important in the all-volunteer forces now common in established democracies.

In sum, the category we describe as full subordination requires that military judicial powers are limited to judging military personnel for military offenses. Military codes of justice are understood to be necessary to maintain discipline and command effectiveness by defining and punishing crimes specific to the military profession. Where military law overlaps with civilian criminal law, any significant dispute must be resolved in favor of civilian authorities as a matter of routine. Full subordination does not preclude the possibility of conflicting military and civilian jurisdictions, but states in this category are those whose militaries consistently cooperate with investigations and turn cases over to civilian authorities without delay when requested. Finally, while the mechanisms of military justice exist within the military, they ultimately are derived from the constitutional authority of the democratic state and must remain subordinate to and under the oversight of civilian courts and elected officials.

Jurisdictional contestation

We define jurisdictional contestation as those countries in which military courts have jurisdiction over non-military crimes, including human rights violations, committed by military personnel and the military is regularly uncooperative with civilian authorities when jurisdictions conflict.[10] In this category, however, military courts do not try civilians.[11] In jurisdictional contestation, militaries retain an enclave of legal power, either in statutes on the books or through routine behavior, which significantly limits civilian authority. In these circumstances, a system of military justice intended to support good order and discipline within the armed forces extends military power in a way that harms civil-military relations and undermines the rule of law and democracy by shielding the military from accountability.

States face an inherent challenge in maintaining the appropriate domain for military courts. The government needs to ensure that the armed forces remain a tool of the state rather than a threat to its survival. At the same time, it must be careful not to undermine the military autonomy that is necessary for the institution to function effectively and apolitically. Samuel Huntington's subjective and objective models of civilian control of the armed forces are instructive here: in the subjective model, competing groups of civilian elites invoke the idea of civilian control of the armed forces as an "instrumental value" aiming for "a distribution of power favorable to its own interests" (Huntington 1957, 83), effectively replicating within the military the divisions that exist in civilian politics. By contrast, objective civilian control seeks to professionalize the military, keeping it occupied with its specialized training and away from factional civilian politics, which enables the military to be "ready to carry out the wishes of any civilian group which secures legitimate authority within the state" (Huntington 1957, 84). Only objective civilian control accords with sustained democracy and military effectiveness because it focuses the military on its primary task of war fighting rather than politicking. It also reduces the ability of competing civilian elites to cultivate factional relationships with military allies to intervene against civilian rivals. Civilian control of the military in a democracy therefore contains a paradox that is especially problematic for legal subordination of the armed forces—the military must answer to elected civilian authorities, but civilians must also respect a degree of military autonomy in order to avoid undue political influence over internal military affairs that could compromise the apolitical outlook of the institution and its members.

The ultimate expressions of disobedience—mutiny, sedition, or rebellion—illustrate the need for civilian care in addressing military legal prerogatives. Military codes of justice are necessary to prosecute instances of outright subversion of the chain of command within the military, but the nature and extent of the insurrection can raise questions regarding whether it is internal to the military and therefore appropriately prosecuted by military courts, or a threat to the democracy itself, and therefore in the civilian domain. In many African cases, for example, where junior soldiers have used mutiny routinely to voice demands against senior leadership, they have been punished internally and therefore less harshly than those involved in coup attempts against the constitutional order who have been tried in civilian courts (Dwyer 2017). Conversely, in Argentina, the 1951 Code of Military Justice made mutiny a more severe crime than a coup, which channeled military agitation into attempts to overthrow civilian governments instead of rebellions against the military high command.[12] Consequently, after the transition to democracy in 1983, a series of reforms asserted civilian jurisdiction over challenges to the constitutional order, whether they came from the armed forces or from civilian rebel groups (Norden 1996, 164–67).

The more that civilian leaders attempt to control the military justice system, however, the more likely it is for civil-military relations to become antagonistic. The "civilianization" of military law is deeply contentious (Sherman 1970). The military regards increased judicial scrutiny as a direct attack on its ability to operate effectively (Dunlap 2015), even going as far as to characterize it in terms of "legal ambush" or "legal encirclement" (Waters 2016, 43). This has been particularly acute in relation to the application of international humanitarian law to modern warfare (Hansen 2013). Militaries argue that this "lawfare," as coined by Charles Dunlap (2001; 2008), risks undercutting their ability to operate effectively. While much of the debate has focused on international operations, the deployment of the military within the state's own borders is no less legally fraught. Military courts carry an innate capacity to judge criminal accusations against their personnel, potentially allowing them to act as a shield against accountability for human rights violations committed in the conduct of military operations.

The risk has intensified as states increasingly use militaries domestically in unconventional missions such as urban and rural policing, anti-gang and anti-drug operations, guarding capital assets such as oil pipelines, and patrolling national borders (e.g. Latin America, see Kyle and Reiter 2019). This practice brings military personnel more frequently into contact with civilian populations, raising the likelihood of military offenses against civilians and disputes over who can hold the military accountable. In many instances, democratically elected governments find themselves under pressure from voters fed up with failures of police and the courts and thus turn to the armed forces in a desire to be seen as responsive. Empowering militaries in this way simultaneously intensifies the potential for human rights abuses against civilian populations and heightens the military's incentives to maintain control over judicial processes to deal with them.

Countries characterized as jurisdictional contestation face this dilemma in practice whereby military courts retain jurisdiction over members of the military for a wide range of crimes, including human rights violations. Where civilian and military jurisdictions conflict, militaries routinely fail to comply with civilian legal authorities. As a matter of civilian control of the armed forces, legal prerogatives challenge the traditional binary characterization of military intervention or non-intervention in politics. Even where the military poses a minimal overt threat to civilian control of the state, the quality of democracy and health of civil-military relations are at stake when military authorities contradict civilian jurisdiction over investigating, charging, and prosecuting crimes by military personnel.

Military overreach

In systems that we describe as military overreach, not only do military courts have jurisdiction over members of the military for non-military crimes, including human rights violations, but they also routinely try civilians. In some states, provisions for some crimes committed by civilians to be tried in military courts are a permanent part of the legal system. These typically include terrorism and other crimes against the state of a military nature, justifying, in the eyes of the government, a military legal response in kind. In most democratic states, however, the trial of civilians in military courts, which are designed primarily for internal military discipline, is by definition exceptional. The nature of the exception varies in reach, time, and geographical scope. During regimes of exception (e.g. states of emergency, siege, or war) specific crimes committed by civilians can be temporarily shifted to military court jurisdiction.[13] In such scenarios, the government determines that existing national (or regional) conditions necessitate the expansion of military court jurisdiction as part of a larger effort to manage the crisis and restore order. In extreme cases, governments declare martial law and give military courts jurisdiction over all civilians for all crimes in the country or in a geographically defined zone. The civilian judicial system is suspended and replaced by military justice (Rossiter 1948, 9).[14]

Virtually all constitutions acknowledge the "inevitability of crises and the need for expansive powers to cope with them" (J. E. Finn 1991, 14), and where they do not exist, states operate under the principle of constitutional necessity (Gross and Ní Aoláin 2006, 40–54).[15] There is a large debate, however, over whether it is justifiable to suspend civil liberties and other democratic principles when democracy itself is under threat (Friedrich 1957).[16]

Many early thinkers were firmly in support of governments using undemocratic means when necessary to safeguard democracy. Thomas Hobbes, for example, believed that it was the government's right to determine threats to the state, at home and abroad, and for a leader to do "whatsoever he shall think necessary to be done" to preserve peace and security (Hobbes [1668] 1994, 113). John Locke concurred, arguing that the executive must have the power to act "according to discretion, for the public good, without the prescription of law, and sometimes even against it" (Locke [1690] 1988, 375). In other words, national survival matters above all (e.g. Schlesinger 1973). Modern day scholars of the "accommodation approach" agree that a democracy must be flexible and constitutional protections can be relaxed during times of emergency (Gross and Ní Aoláin 2006, 17–109; R. Posner 2003, 292–308).[17]

Those holding this position view the Roman republic, after the fall of the monarchy in 509 BC, as the ideal model (Rossiter 1948, 15–28). When faced with an emergency, the government would appoint a "dictator" to take control of the state. Those who determined the existence of an emergency could not serve as the dictator themselves and the position was limited to a maximum, non-renewable term of six months. The dictator's powers were also well defined, and he was limited to managing the defense of the republic from foreign threats. Most emblematically, Lucius Quinctius Cincinnatus was named dictator in 458 BC and stepped down just 15 days later once he had defeated the enemy.

There are significant risks, however, to granting government leaders increased power. Niccolò Machiavelli agreed that there has to be a way for democracies to react quickly during crises, and he advocated for states of exception in the Roman model. Yet he acknowledged that where people are willing to grant unlimited power for an unspecified duration, there is a great risk of falling into dictatorship (Machiavelli [1531] 1996, 74–77). Jean-Jacques Rousseau likewise argued that it is inevitable that at some point members of the government will exceed their authority and usurp the sovereign, sending the state into tyranny (Rousseau [1762] 1997, 106–8). Scholars point most prominently to Weimar Germany as a cautionary tale (Rossiter 1948, 29–73). Article 48 of the constitution helped enable Adolf Hitler and the Nazi Party to seize power: "If the public safety and order in the German Reich are seriously disturbed or endangered, the President of the Reich may take the measures necessary to the restoration of public safety and order, and may if necessary intervene with the armed forces."[18]

There are several inherent problems in the expansion of power at the expense of democratic values. First, during crises, fear and panic often reign, and "what seems unreasonable in reasonable times may look reasonable in unreasonable times" (Lasswell 1950, 141). Governments often overreact and opt for measures—one of which is to empower military courts—that are more authoritarian than necessary to combat threats (Gross 2003, 1038–42). Second, policies enacted during times of crisis often have staying power long after they are over (J. E. Finn 1991, 54). What are viewed as temporary policies "have a peculiar tendency to become entrenched over time and thus normalized and made routine" (Gross 2003, 1090). Finally, a "ratchet" effect may occur where recurring crises are interpreted as a failure to successfully manage previous ones, justifying the use of even more extreme responses.[19]

These inherent flaws represent a recipe for democratic breakdown. Government leaders exploit and manipulate public fears to crack down on opponents and accumulate more power for themselves. The six-month term limit on the Roman dictator has little practicality today and those in power often get to decide when the threat is over. In many cases, states of exception are continuously renewed and a “normalization of the extraordinary” develops (Gross 2003, 1089–90). Furthermore, there is little practical difference between a democratic regime that has suspended democracy for an undefined temporary period and an authoritarian regime (Linz 2000, 62–63). Indeed, scholars note that even Rome fell victim:

> Eventually, of course, certain Roman dictators violated these limitations. Sulla used the dictatorship to introduce a new constitution and remained well beyond the customary six months (ca. 84 B.C.). Caesar made the dictatorship a more permanent form of political rule (ca. 49–44 B.C.), and his grandnephew, Octavian, presided over the transition from republic to empire (after 31 B.C.) (Loveman 1993, 19).

While some established democracies have shown restraint during crises and returned to pre-crisis practices, in many instances, authoritarian regimes have come to power under conditions of real or perceived crisis. Unresolvable political cleavages, internal security threats, or severe economic disruptions have provided the opportunity for the sudden end to democracy through military overthrow or party usurpation, in which political leaders seize unlimited power often after having been elected to office (Brooker 2013; Linz 1978). The case, noted above, of the end to the Weimar Republic in Germany through the passage of the Enabling Act in 1933 is among the best known (Ermakoff 2008; Lepsius 1978).[20]

We do not take a stance on the overall debate about whether some aspects of democracy can be sacrificed to confront threats to the democratic system, but we firmly believe that any responses should be limited (see Ackerman 2004) and argue that the extension of military courts to civilians should not be included. When civilians are placed under military jurisdiction, basic tenets of the rule of law are imperiled and thus the practice should be avoided (Joinet 2002; United Nations Commission on Human Rights 2006). In judicial proceedings in a functioning democracy, defendants have expectations of equal treatment before the law, knowing the evidence being brought against them, and the right to a public trial in which an impartial judge or jury rules without having prejudged the case. These basic practices are unlikely to be guaranteed to civilian defendants in military court proceedings because of their tendency to take place out of public view and for evidence to be concealed on the basis of national security concerns. Military jurisdiction over civilians is also logically inconsistent with the widely accepted justification for the existence of military courts—maintaining good order and discipline within the institution. Civilians are not part of the institution and therefore cannot be considered to be subject to the disciplinary demands enforced by military justice. Finally, as we discuss in Chapter 1, even where military courts have adequate safeguards, it is the perceived bias that these courts do not have sufficient independence and impartiality that matters most, making them an instrument that should not be applied to civilians (Rowe 2006, 83; Weissbrodt and Hansen 2013, 311).

Table 2.1 A typology of military legal subordination

Type of system	*Defendants, venue, and crimes*
Full subordination	Military courts try members of the military for offenses necessary to maintain good order and discipline. Military courts do not try civilians.
Jurisdictional contestation	Military courts try members of the military for offenses necessary to maintain good order and discipline and some civilian crimes, including human rights violations. Military courts do not try civilians.
Military overreach	Military courts try members of the military for offenses necessary to maintain good order and discipline and some civilian crimes, including human rights violations. Military courts try civilians for some crimes.

We summarize these definitions as a conceptual typology of military legal subordination in Table 2.1. As an ordinal scale, this framework arranges the three categories—full subordination, jurisdictional contestation, and military overreach—by how desirable each system is for a democratic society (Collier, LaPorte, and Seawright 2012, 219). Full subordination of military legal prerogatives to civilian control is most conducive to stable civil-military relations, respect for human rights, and adherence to the rule of law. Then, in descending order, jurisdictional contestation represents significant challenges to elements of democratic practice, where the military competes with civilian authorities. At the bottom of the scale is military overreach, in which the military additionally has legal power over civilians. The conceptual typology structure permits a clear articulation of mutually exclusive categories, demonstrates the ordered relationship among the categories, and "map[s] out variation in the outcomes being explained" (Collier, LaPorte, and Seawright 2012, 226). In the next section, we describe our new dataset and present cross-national trends over time. Our aim is to provide a clear picture of how military legal power has evolved over the past four decades as well as its relationship to democracy and human rights. This sets up Chapter 3 where we present our theoretical framework for understanding change—positive and negative—between systems in individual states.

A global overview of military justice

Understanding the relationship between military justice and democracy, human rights, the rule of law, and civil-military relations requires a comprehensive analysis across cases and over time. We address this need by creating an original global dataset on military legal subordination. We include all countries that the Polity5 dataset codes as being at least a partial democracy in at least one year from 1974 to 2017, corresponding to the time since the beginning of the Third Wave of democratization (Huntington 1991).[21] Polity5 is a widely used dataset that provides detailed information on political regime characteristics for every country in the world over 500,000 in population from 1800 to 2018 (Marshall and Gurr 2018). Including partial democracies means incorporating some states generally considered to be authoritarian or that have only minimal characteristics of democratic institutions. It is important to include such cases because many sources view the use of military courts for non-military crimes and non-military personnel as human rights violations and in turn do not consider states where such behavior occurs democratic. Excluding these cases would prevent us from examining the relationship between military court jurisdiction and the quality of democracy, a key question of this study. We thus cast a broad net, only excluding countries that have been firmly authoritarian where so many other characteristics of the regime are undemocratic that military court jurisdiction would have no effect on our outcomes of interest.[22] Our dataset contains 120 countries (see appendix).

While we select our cases based on their regime type since 1974, for each we analyze military justice as far back historically as we are able to reliably document state practice in the context of codified laws. The oldest country in our dataset is the United Kingdom, which we begin in 1689 with the first English military justice system. We are able to trace the operation of military justice in the major colonial powers of France, Spain, and Portugal, as well as the United States, to the 1700s. For many Western European countries, we include data starting from their independence or unification in the 1800s. For Latin America, we document military justice for almost all countries from the time of their independence from Spain, Gran Colombia, and the Federal Republic of Central America in the first half of the 1800s. Most countries in Asia and Central Europe are in our dataset since the end of World War II, when their borders and political systems were reconstituted. We examine military justice in Africa since decolonization. Finally, there is a subset of countries that gained their independence following the dissolution of the Soviet Union and Yugoslavia in the early 1990s.[23]

To code the legal subordination of the military in each case, we focus first on documenting the existence and configuration of military courts. Some countries have no military or there are no separate military courts.[24] If civilian courts have full legal control of all security forces, we code those countries as full subordination. Where military courts exist, we examine the personnel and crimes under their jurisdiction, and any legal contexts, such as states of exception, that change that jurisdiction. To do so, we analyze each country's constitution, relevant national laws, and military codes of justice.[25]

We are most interested in what happens in practice. The level of compliance with written laws varies considerably across countries: militaries can refuse to transfer cases; there may be open battles over jurisdiction; civilian judges can decide not to apply the law in this area; expanded powers under states of emergency may be possible but are never used. In categorizing country cases, we identify routine practices and widespread activity of militaries, their courts, and contention with civilian actors. To determine state practice, we draw on numerous primary and secondary sources, including government documents, domestic and international court rulings, reports by human rights organizations and think tanks, news coverage, and academic books and articles. With this information, we construct a times-series dataset with a corresponding system—full subordination, jurisdictional contestation, or military overreach—coded for each country in each year.[26] The dataset contains 10,431 country years, of which 2,402 are coded as military overreach, 3,875 as jurisdictional contestation, and 4,154 as full subordination.[27] We present the findings from this dataset below and provide the full details for each country in the appendix. We also use those sources above to chronicle the factors accounting for changes in systems within each country over time, which we present in Chapter 3.

Figure 2.1 provides an overview of the legal power of militaries since 1800. Because the number of states in the world varies over time, we use the percentage of states in our dataset in a given year as our reference point. The data paint a clear picture of increased military legal subordination over time. Beginning with the conclusion of World War I, militaries in many parts of the world went through a professionalization and de-politicization process, becoming fully subordinated to civilian, democratic governments. This trend accelerated dramatically following the end of the Cold War. The figure also shows the temporary expansion of military courts to try civilians during both of the world wars. High levels of military overreach persisted throughout much of the Cold War. While the use of military courts to try civilians has decreased markedly over the past four decades, in many countries militaries have resisted attempts to curtail their legal prerogatives. The percentage of countries in the jurisdictional contestation category has been relatively stable, fluctuating between 30% and 40% from 1979 to 2012, and remains at 25% today.

Figures 2.2 to 2.6 display regional trends, using the United Nations Regional Groups.[28] Given the strength of democracy in the region, it is not surprising that Western Europe has had the most success in curtailing the military's legal

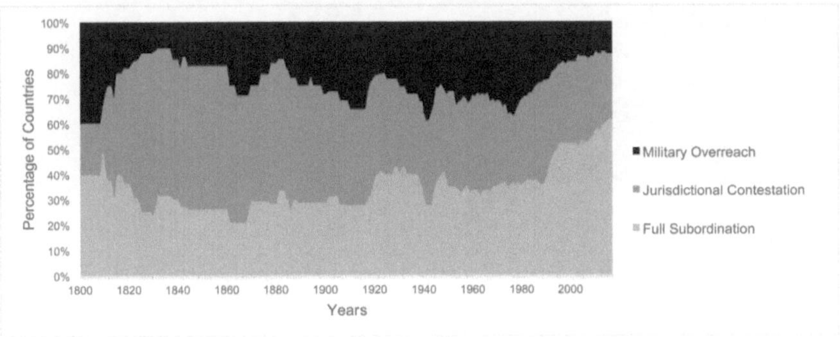

Figure 2.1 Military legal subordination in the world (1800–2017)

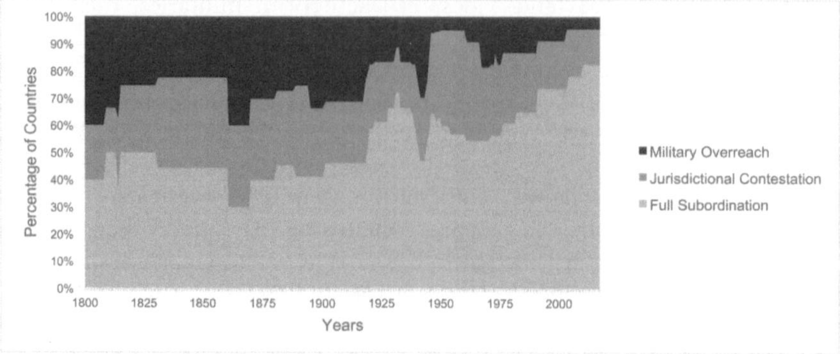

Figure 2.2 Military legal subordination in Western Europe and others (1800–2017)

power. Since the mid-1800s, civilian governments in Western European countries have steadily asserted control over military justice systems. The practice of using military courts to try civilians has nearly been abolished and in only a few cases do military courts have excessive power vis-à-vis civilian courts. In contrast, in Africa and the Asia and Pacific region, military legal power has remained relatively steady. For over half of those countries, military courts continue to try civilians and/or protect their own forces from accountability in civilian courts. Eastern Europe is unique in the high percentage of states in the full subordination category over time. This is due to communist parties having firm control over the armed forces in many one-party states during the Cold War and then a swift process of bringing military justice systems in line with Western European countries in the 1990s. Finally, the most dramatic changes have occurred in Latin America. Militaries largely kept the legal privileges enjoyed in the Spanish military upon independence, but the use of military courts to try civilians was uncommon. Shortly thereafter, military courts began to try civilians with increasing regularity, peaking in the middle of the Cold War—in 1974, 62%

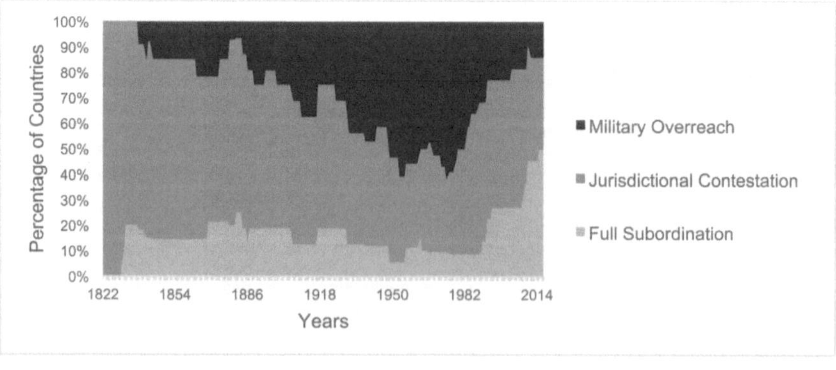

Figure 2.3 Military legal subordination in Latin America and the Caribbean (1822–2017)

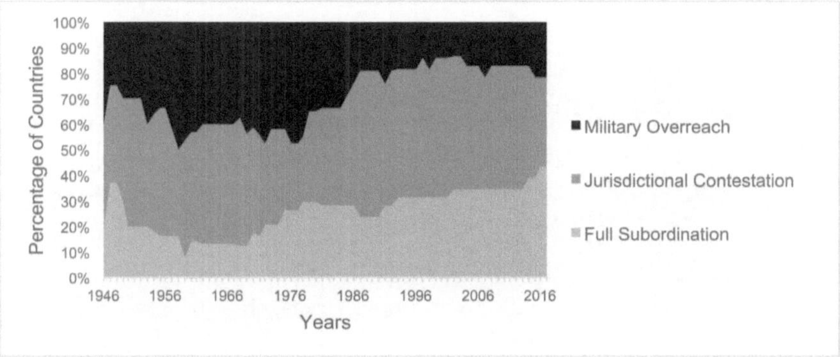

Figure 2.4 Military legal subordination in Asia and the Pacific (1946–2017)

of countries in the region routinely did so. Since then, there has been a long, gradual process of rolling back this practice. Militaries in the region, however, continue to resist civilian oversight, with only half of the countries in the full subordination category.

Table 2.2 illustrates the relationship between military legal subordination and democracy and human rights. The first indicator is the average POLITY score for countries in years in which they are classified in each system, which ranges from –10 (fully autocratic) to 10 (fully democratic).[29] To measure human rights, we include two indicators. The first comes from the Political Terror Scale, which measures "violations of basic human rights to the physical integrity of the person by agents of the state" in each country (Gibney et al. 2019).[30] Scores range from 1, indicating that citizens are relatively safe and protected from wrongful imprisonment and torture, to 5, where terror has expanded to the entire population. The dataset contains three distinct scores for each country-year based on sources and we use the average of all three. We also include the average of the civil liberties and political rights scores from

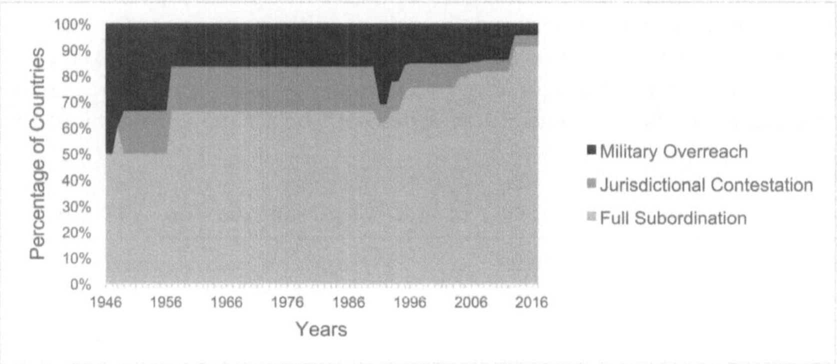

Figure 2.5 Military legal subordination in Eastern Europe (1946–2017)

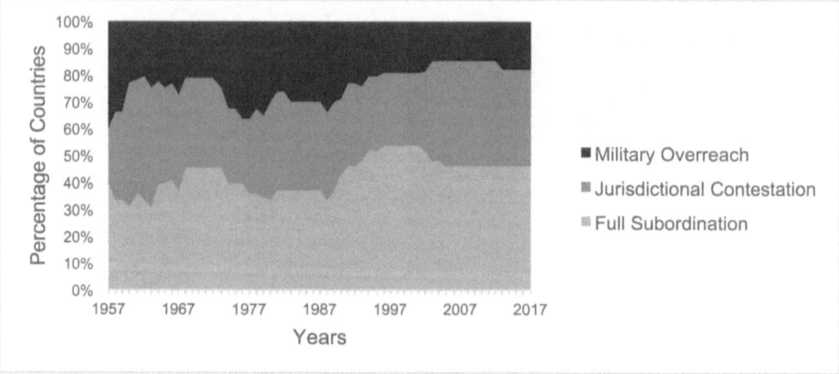

Figure 2.6 Military legal subordination in Africa (1957–2017)

Freedom House's Freedom in the World dataset, which range from 1 to 7, with 1 representing the greatest degree of freedom and 7 the smallest degree of freedom (Freedom House 2018).[31] To make comparison to the POLITY score easier, we have inverted the human rights measures so that higher numbers indicate better human rights conditions.

In general, the more democratic a country is, the more its military's legal powers are subordinated to civilian control. The POLITY averages, however, indicate that many countries scoring in the positive range of democratic practice (3.85) on the elements considered by POLITY—ability of the public to express preferences for leaders, constraints on executive leadership, and respect for civil liberties—do not have full control over their military's legal powers. Additionally, as the average POLITY score for countries experiencing military overreach (−0.44) demonstrates, a military's ability to put civilians on trial is a major flaw that can exist in democratic systems or those that are only marginally in the autocratic range. Military overreach can endure beyond an era of authoritarianism into a new democracy, or even be enabled by a sitting democratic government. The potential for such a broad use of military power reinforces how important it is to understand the role of military courts as a contentious prerogative with ramifications for democratic civil-military relations, the quality of democracy, and the rule of law. The human rights indicators presented in Table 2.2 show that, in general, countries with better human rights practices

Table 2.2 Democracy, human rights, and military legal subordination, 1974–2017

Type of system	*Polity*	*Political Terror Scale*	*Freedom House*
Full subordination	6.64	4.13	5.56
Jurisdictional contestation	3.85	3.37	4.56
Military overreach	−0.44	2.80	3.42

have higher degrees of subordination of military legal power. Simultaneously, the fact that countries with jurisdictional contestation systems have demonstrably worse human rights records underscores the troubling recognition that not only do more violations happen in these cases than in those of full subordination, but also there is a greater level of impunity for those abuses. Finally, the lowest scores on human rights practices are among countries with systems of military overreach, confirming that the use of military courts against civilians coincides with the use of other forms of state repression. Overall, these findings are consistent with our argument that countries should strive to establish and maintain a system of full subordination.

Conclusion

Overall, we are cautiously optimistic about the evolution of military legal subordination. The operation of military courts today is remarkably different from the way it was 50 years ago when such courts tried civilians at will in large parts of the world. This improvement, however, was not a foregone conclusion. Successful reform only occurred because of bold actions by politicians, judges, and activists who took advantage of important political openings to push for change. At the same time, militaries have resisted attempts at reform or have taken advantage of the emergence of security threats to gain more legal power, and in many countries in the world, civilian governments still do not have full control over their military's legal powers. In the following chapter, we draw on our dataset to identify patterns in how countries established military justice systems, from late modern to nineteenth-century Europe to the post-colonial and post-Cold War periods. We then present a dynamic model of change to explain shifts in military justice systems after their initial establishment, centered on interactions among three principal actors—the government, the military, and high courts. The model serves as the framework for the case studies to follow in Chapters 4–7.

Notes

1 The notion of the military as a separate society was famously articulated by the US Supreme Court in *Orloff* v. *Willoughby*, 345 U.S. 83 (1953), https://cdn.loc.gov/service/ll/usrep/usrep345/usrep345083/usrep345083.pdf.

2 It is not guaranteed that all personnel will accept these ideas, however, and military organization is so dependent on the successful implementation of these values that courts martial are used to deter challenges to them or to punish those who seek to express dissent while in uniform (J. Finn 1971).

3 The full texts of the *Ordinance of Richard I*, *Articles of War of Richard II*, and *Articles of War of Gustavus Adolphus* can be found in Winthrop (1920, 903; 904–6; 907–18).

4 The circumstances of the American War for Independence led to the expansive use of British courts martial against civilians. The British Army occupied the major cities of the American colonies—Boston, Newport, New York, Philadelphia, Charleston, and Savannah—subjecting residents to military justice "not only for war offenses

[such as] corresponding with or aiding the enemy … but in a far greater number of instances, on charges of committing ordinary common law felonies" (Wiener 1967, 92–93). Military law for civilians in these instances often carried extremely harsh penalties, including the death sentence for burglary (Wiener 1967, 277–300).

5 There were 34 *fueros* in total, the most prominent being the *fuero eclesiástico*, which governed the clergy (McAlister 1957, 6).

6 *Uniform Code of Military Justice, U.S. Code* 10 (2019) §§ 801 et seq., https://uscode.house.gov/browse/prelim@title10/subtitleA/part2/chapter47&edition=prelim.

7 National Defence Act, RSC 1985, c N-5, Article 70, https://www.canlii.org/en/ca/laws/stat/rsc-1985-c-n-5/latest/rsc-1985-c-n-5.html.

8 *Manual for Courts-Martial United States (2019 Edition)*, Rule 106, https://jsc.defense.gov/Portals/99/Documents/2019%20MCM%20(Final)%20(20190108).pdf?ver=2019-01-11-115724-610.

9 *Manual for Courts-Martial United States (2019 Edition)*, Article 88, https://jsc.defense.gov/Portals/99/Documents/2019%20MCM%20(Final)%20(20190108).pdf?ver=2019-01-11-115724-610.

10 While *human rights violations* is an expansive term, we are referring to violations of the subset of civil and political rights known as physical integrity rights, which includes such abuses as extrajudicial murder, disappearance, torture, and political imprisonment, see Cingranelli and Richards 1999.

11 Many codes of military justice allow for some types of civilians to be tried in military courts, such as those employed directly by the military. In addition, in situations in which civilians and members of the military are involved in a large conspiracy together, some codes allow for the case to be consolidated in military courts. In most countries, military courts rarely, if ever, try civilians under those criteria. If a country abuses the law and applies military justice to civilians more broadly, we classify it as military overreach.

12 Sanción Ley 14.029, "Código de Justicia Militar," 4 de julio de 1951, http://servicios.infoleg.gob.ar/infolegInternet/anexos/105000-109999/105438/texact.htm.

13 Terminology varies considerably across countries (Gross and Ní Aoláin 2006, 40–46). When discussing a specific case, we use the term used in that country.

14 For the most comprehensive overview of the concept of martial law and the origins of its practice, see Birkhimer 1914.

15 For an overview of emergency powers, see Ferejohn and Pasquino 2004.

16 This is often referred to as the debate over "reasons of state."

17 The extra-legality model agrees that democracies need flexibility to meet crises but argues that provisions for the suspension of rights should not be built into the constitution. Rather, elected leaders should "break the law" when faced with threats, with the public ratifying or rejecting the decisions *ex post* (Gross 2003; Gross and Ní Aoláin 2006, 110–70).

18 Constitution of the German Empire of August 11, 1919 (Weimar Constitution), http://ghdi.ghi-dc.org/sub_document.cfm?document_id=3937. Karl Lowenstein (1937) argued that Germany and other European democracies should have used these provisions themselves first to crack down on anti-democratic groups to prevent them from rising to power.

19 For a detailed critique of the ratchet and fear/panic arguments, see E. Posner and Vermeule 2003.

20 *Law to Remove the Distress of the People and the Reich (The Enabling Act)*, March 24, 1933, http://ghdi.ghi-dc.org/sub_document.cfm?document_id=1496.

21 The dataset's POLITY variable is a weighted score derived from coding the competitiveness of political participation, the regulation of participation, the openness and competitiveness of executive recruitment, and constraints on the executive. The scale ranges from –10 to 10, where a partial democracy is defined as a score of

1–6 and a full democracy 7–10. We use the POLITY2 variable, which provides a treatment to the POLITY variable to account for years with missing data, enabling it to be used more easily for time-series analysis.

22 We exclude several countries that experienced extended periods of civil war, state failure, or foreign intervention, during which government institutions largely ceased to function in all or most of the territory: Central African Republic, Côte d'Ivoire, Democratic Republic of Congo, Iraq, Serbia and Montenegro (1992–2002), and Yemen. Similarly, Liberia was embroiled in civil war from 1989 to 2003, after which it created a new military with foreign assistance, but it did not enact a new code of military justice until 2017 (Carter 2017). We also do not include the Republic of Congo in which party militias played the predominant role in internal security for much of its history (Bazenguissa-Ganga 1999). Similarly, beginning in 1964, there was complete fusion of civilian and military institutions in Haiti, and the *Tonton Macoute* paramilitary organization served most of the functions of the military (Laguerre 1993, 120–22). In addition, for some small countries international human rights monitoring is insufficient to accurately code state practice: Bhutan, Cabo Verde, Comoros, Djibouti, Gabon, Lesotho, and Mauritania. Finally, we do not include Kosovo given that the United Nations and the North Atlantic Treaty Organization served many of the government's functions, including providing security, until very recently.

23 For some countries, there is a lag between independence and when they enter our dataset due to the time needed to fully design and construct state institutions, including the military.

24 Those countries in our dataset without a formal military are the Solomon Islands since independence in 1978, Mauritius since independence in 1968, Botswana from independence in 1966 to 1976, Gambia from independence in 1964 to 1984, and Costa Rica since 1948. In addition, Japan and West Germany did not operate their own militaries after World War II until 1954.

25 The Characteristics of National Constitutions Dataset contains every constitution in the world from the late 1700s to present (Elkins, Ginsberg, and Melton 2018).

26 We code each year based on the system that exists when the year concludes. There are three exceptions: Panama (1987), Pakistan (1953), and Thailand (1991). In each case, governments granted military courts the power to try civilians, yet rescinded those powers within weeks or months, thereby shifting each state into the military overreach category and back to the jurisdictional contestation category within the same calendar year. In those cases, we code the full year as military overreach, starting jurisdictional contestation in the subsequent calendar year.

27 In several cases, the time series is interrupted. We do not include data for Austria during its annexation by Germany (1938–44), Cambodia during the Khmer Rouge regime (1975–80), and for periods of state collapse due to civil war in Burundi (1993–2004), Ethiopia (1991–95), and Sierra Leone (1991–2000).

28 We use the United Nations Regional Groups: Africa, Asia-Pacific, Eastern Europe, Latin American and Caribbean, and Western Europe and Others, see https://www.un.org/dgacm/content/regional-groups. We include the United States, Israel, and Turkey in the Western Europe and Others region and Taiwan in the Asia-Pacific region.

29 For this analysis we use Polity5's POLITY2 variable, which converts periods of transition, interregnum, and interruption into standard POLITY scores.

30 The Political Terror Scale begins in 1976.

31 Another widely used measure is the CIRI Human Rights Dataset, but it is limited to the years 1981–2011 for most countries (Cingranelli, Richards, and Clay 2014).

References

Abrahamsson, Bengt. 1972. *Military Professionalization and Political Power*. London: Sage.

Ackerman, Bruce. 2004. "The Emergency Constitution." *Yale Law Journal* 113 (5): 1029–91. DOI: 10.2307/4135710.

Bazenguissa-Ganga, Rémy. 1999. "The Spread of Political Violence in Congo-Brazzaville." *African Affairs* 98 (390): 37–54.

Birkhimer, William E. 1914. *Military Government and Martial Law*. 3rd ed. Rev. Kansas City: Franklin Hudson.

Brand, C. E. 1968. *Roman Military Law*. Austin: University of Texas Press.

Brooker, Paul. 2013. *Non-Democratic Regimes: Theory, Government and Politics*. New York: Palgrave Macmillan.

Carter, J. Burgess. 2017. "Sherman Submits Draft Law on Legislative Continuity." *Daily Observer*, August 31. https://www.liberianobserver.com/news/draft-law-on-legislative-continuity-submitted-to-senate/.

Cingranelli, David L., and David L. Richards. 1999. "Measuring the Level, Pattern, and Sequence of Government Respect for Physical Integrity Rights." *International Studies Quarterly* 43 (2): 407–18.

Cingranelli, David L., David L. Richards, and K. Chad Clay. 2014. "The CIRI Human Rights Dataset." Version 2014.04.14. http://www.humanrightsdata.com.

Collier, David, Jody LaPorte, and Jason Seawright. 2012. "Putting Typologies to Work: Concept Formation, Measurement, and Analytic Rigor." *Political Research Quarterly* 65 (1): 217–32.

Davis, George B. 1915. *A Treatise on the Military Law of the United States Together with the Practice and Procedure of Courts-Martial and Other Military Tribunals*. 3rd ed. New York: John Wiley & Sons.

Dolman, Everett Carl. 2004. *The Warrior State: How Military Organization Structures Politics*. New York: Palgrave Macmillan. DOI: 10.1057/9781403978264.

Dunlap, Charles J., Jr. 2001. "Law and Military Interventions: Preserving Humanitarian Values in 21st Century Conflicts." Carr Center for Human Rights, John F. Kennedy School of Government, Harvard University, Working Paper. https://people.duke.edu/~pfeaver/dunlap.pdf.

Dunlap, Charles J., Jr. 2008. "Commentary, Lawfare Today: A Perspective." *Yale Journal of International Affairs* 3 (1): 146–54.

Dunlap, Charles J., Jr. 2015. "Civilianizing Military Justice? Sorry, it Can't—and Shouldn't—Work." *War on the Rocks*, October 8. https://warontherocks.com/2015/10/civilianizing-military-justice-sorry-it-cant-and-shouldnt-work/.

Dwyer, Maggie. 2017. *Soldiers in Revolt: Army Mutinies in Africa*. Oxford: Oxford University Press. DOI: 10.1093/oso/9780190876074.001.0001.

Elkins, Zachary, Tom Ginsberg, and James Melton. 2018. Characteristics of National Constitutions [v.2.0]. www.comparativeconstitutionsproject.org.

Ermakoff, Ivan. 2008. *Ruling Oneself Out: A Theory of Collective Abdications*. Durham: Duke University Press. DOI: 10.1215/9780822388722.

Ferejohn, John, and Pasquale Pasquino. 2004. "The Law of the Exception: A Typology of Emergency Powers." *International Journal of Constitutional Law* 2 (2): 210–39. DOI: 10.1093/icon/2.2.210.

Finn, James, ed. 1971. *Conscience and Command: Justice and Discipline in the Military*. New York: Random House.

Finn, John E. 1991. *Constitutions in Crisis: Political Violence and the Rule of Law*. New York: Oxford University Press.

Freedom House. 2018. "Freedom in the World 2018." https://freedomhouse.org/report/freedom-world/freedom-world-2018.

Friedrich, Carl J. 1957. *Constitutional Reason of State: The Survival of the Constitutional Order*. Providence: Brown University Press.

Generous, William T., Jr. 1973. *Swords and Scales: The Development of the Uniform Code of Military Justice*. London: Kennikat.

Gibney, Mark, Linda Cornett, Reed Wood, Peter Haschke, Daniel Arnon, Attilio Pisanò, and Garry Barrett. 2019. "The Political Terror Scale 1976–2018." www.politicalterrorscale.org/.

Gibson, Michael R. 2008. "International Human Rights Law and the Administration of Justice through Military Tribunals: Preserving Utility while Precluding Impunity." *Journal of International Law and International Relations* 4 (1): 1–48.

Gross, Oren. 2003. "Chaos and Rules: Should Responses to Violent Crises Always Be Constitutional?" *Yale Law Journal* 112 (5): 1011–134. DOI: 10.2139/ssrn.370800.

Gross, Oren, and Fionnuala Ní Aoláin. 2006. *Law in Times of Crisis: Emergency Powers in Theory and Practice*. New York: Cambridge University Press. DOI: 10.1017/CBO9780511493997.

Hansen, Victor. 2013. "The Impact of Military Justice Reforms On the Law of Armed Conflict: How to Avoid Unintended Consequences." *Michigan State International Law Review* 21 (2): 229–72. DOI: 10.1017/cbo9781107326330.007.

Hebblewhite, Mark. 2017. *The Emperor and the Army in the Later Roman Empire, AD 235–395*. New York: Routledge. DOI: 10.4324/9781315616018.

Hirschhorn, James M. 1984. "The Separate Community: Military Uniqueness and Servicemen's Constitutional Rights." *North Carolina Law Review* 62 (2): 177–254.

Hobbes, Thomas. [1668] 1994. *Leviathan*. Ed. Edwin Curley. Indianapolis: Hackett.

Huntington, Samuel. 1957. *The Soldier and the State: The Theory and Politics of Civil-Military Relations*. Cambridge: Belknap. DOI: 10.2307/j.ctvjf9wx3.

Huntington, Samuel. 1991. *The Third Wave: Democratization in the Late Twentieth Century*. Norman: University of Oklahoma Press.

Joinet, Louis. 2002 "Issue of the Administration of Justice through Military Tribunals." UN Sub-Commission on the Promotion and Protection of Human Rights. E/CN.4/Sub.2/2002/4. https://undocs.org/pdf?symbol=en/E/CN.4/Sub.2/2002/4.

Kyle, Brett J., and Andrew G. Reiter. 2019. "A New Dawn for Latin American Militaries." *NACLA Report on the Americas* 51 (1): 18–28. DOI: 10.1080/10714839.2019.1593684.

Laguerre, Michael S. 1993. *The Military and Society in Haiti*. Knoxville: The University of Tennessee Press.

Lasswell, Harold D. 1950. *National Security and Individual Freedoms*. New York: McGraw Hill.

Lepsius, M. Rainer. 1978. "From Fragmented Party Democracy to Government by Emergency Decree and National Socialist Takeover: Germany." In *The Breakdown of Democratic Regimes: Europe*, eds. Juan J. Linz and Alfred Stepan. Baltimore: Johns Hopkins University Press, 34–79.

Linz, Juan J. 1978. *The Breakdown of Democratic Regimes: Crisis, Breakdown, and Reequilibration*. Baltimore: Johns Hopkins University Press.

Linz, Juan J. 2000. *Totalitarian and Authoritarian Regimes*. Boulder: Lynne Rienner.

Locke, John. [1690] 1988. *Two Treatises of Government*. Ed. Peter Laslett. Cambridge: Cambridge University Press. DOI: 10.1017/CBO9780511810268.011.

Loveman, Brian. 1993. *The Constitution of Tyranny: Regimes of Exception in Spanish America*. Pittsburgh: University of Pittsburgh Press.

Loveman, Brian. 2001. "Historical Foundations of Civil-Military Relations in Spanish America." In *Civil-Military Relations in Latin America: New Analytical Perspectives*, ed. David Pion-Berlin. Chapel Hill: University of North Carolina Press, 246–74.

Lowenstein, Karl. 1937. "Militant Democracy and Fundamental Rights." *American Political Science Review* 31 (3): 417–32. DOI: 10.2307/1948164.

Machiavelli, Niccolò. [1531] 1996. *Discourses on Livy*. Trans. Harvey Mansfield and Nathan Tarcov. Chicago: University of Chicago Press. DOI: 10.7208/Chicago/9780226500331.001.0001.

Marshall, Monty G., and Ted Robert Gurr. 2018. "Polity5 Project: Political Regime Characteristics and Transitions, 1800–2018." http://www.systemicpeace.org/polityproject.html.

McAlister, Lyle N. 1957. *The "Fuero Militar" in New Spain: 1764–1800*. Gainesville: University of Florida Press.

Morris, Lawrence J. 2010. *Military Justice: A Guide to the Issues*. Denver: Praeger.

Norden, Deborah. 1996. *Military Rebellion in Argentina: Between Coups and Consolidation*. Lincoln: University of Nebraska Press.

Nordlinger, Eric A. 1977. *Soldiers in Politics: Military Coups and Governments*. Englewood Cliffs, NJ: Prentice-Hall.

Phang, Sara Elise. 2008. *Roman Military Service: Ideologies of Discipline in the Late Republic and Early Principate*. New York: Cambridge University Press. DOI: 10.1017/CBO9780511497872.

Posner, Eric A., and Adrian Vermeule. 2003. "Accommodating Emergencies." *Stanford Law Review* 56 (3): 605–44. DOI: 10.2139/ssrn.441343.

Posner, Richard A. 2003. *Law, Pragmatism, and Democracy*. Cambridge: Harvard University Press.

Postma, L. V. 1968. "Roman Military Law." *South African Law Journal* 85 (1): 65–70.

Rossiter, Clinton L. 1948. *Constitutional Dictatorship: Crisis Government in Modern Democracies*. Princeton: Princeton University Press.

Rousseau, Jean-Jacques. [1762] 1997. *Rousseau: "The Social Contract" and Other Late Political Writings*. Trans. Victor Gourevitch. Cambridge: Cambridge University Press. DOI: 10.1017/9781316584606.

Rowe, Peter. 2006. *The Impact of Human Rights Law on Armed Forces*. Cambridge: Cambridge University Press. DOI: 10.1017/CBO9780511616198.

Samuel, E. 1816. *An Historical Account of the British Army, and of the Law Military*. London: William Clowes.

Schlesinger, Arthur, Jr. 1973. *The Imperial Presidency*. Boston: Houghton Mifflin.

Sherman, Edward F. 1970. "The Civilianization of Military Law." *Maine Law Review* 22 (1): 3–103.

United Nations Commission on Human Rights. 2006. "Draft Principles Governing the Administration of Justice through Military Tribunals." E/CN.4/2006/58 at 4. https://undocs.org/pdf?symbol=en/E/CN.4/2006/58.

Waters, Christopher. 2016. "Democratic Oversight through Courts and Tribunals." In *Military Justice in the Modern Age*, eds. Alison Duxbury and Matthews Groves. Cambridge: Cambridge University Press, 36–56. DOI: 10.1017/CBO9781107326330.004.

Weissbrodt, Davis S., and Joseph C. Hansen. 2013. "The Rights to a Fair Trial in an Extraordinary Court." In *Guantánamo and Beyond: Exceptional Courts and Military Commissions in Comparative Perspective*, eds. Fionnuala Ní Aoláin and Oren Gross. New York: Cambridge University Press, 305–20. DOI: 10.1017/CBO9780511920721.018.

West, Luther C. 1970. "A History of Command Influence on the Military Judicial System." *UCLA Law Review* 18 (1): 1–156.

West, Luther C. 1977. *They Call It Justice: Command Influence and the Court-Martial System*. New York: Viking Press.

Wiener, Frederick Bernays. 1967. *Civilians under Military Justice: The British Practice since 1689 Especially in North America*. Chicago: University of Chicago Press.

Winthrop, William. 1920. *Military Law and Precedents*. 3rd ed. Washington, DC: Government Printing Office. https://www.loc.gov/rr/frd/Military_Law/pdf/ML_precedents.pdf.

3 Judges, generals, and politicians: The fight over military justice

Introduction

Military justice systems have a profound effect on the quality of democracy, human rights, and the rule of law. In this chapter, we analyze the establishment and change in military justice systems, developing a dynamic model of key actors and interests to explain reform, stagnation, and backsliding in civilian control of military legal power. We begin by briefly outlining patterns of change between system categories. We then describe the establishment of military justice in late modern to nineteenth-century Europe, detailing the systems that would eventually spread to much of the rest of the world. In the following section, we identify patterns of adoption of military justice systems in the course of state (re-)formation in the wake of independence from colonial rule, after the dissolution of the Soviet Union and Yugoslavia at the end of the Cold War, and through external installation after defeat in interstate war. Finally, we present our dynamic model of change to explain shifts in military justice systems after their initial establishment. The model is centered on three principal actors—the government, the military, and high courts—whose interaction in a decision-making nexus determine the system of military justice. The behavior of these principal actors is influenced by several domestic (public sentiment and civil society) and international factors (human rights courts, non-governmental organizations (NGOs), inter-governmental organizations (IOs), and external states). Overall, we argue that the strength of domestic courts and the prevalence and severity of security threats—which change the preferences and level of influence of the government and military—play major roles in shaping military justice policy. Shifts in these factors help to explain reform and backsliding. In addition, transformations in government represent critical junctures in politics that often allows for the reshaping of military justice practices. While not decisive, other domestic and international factors can help to tip the balance in debates over the military's legal subordination.

Establishment and change of military justice systems

As outlined in Chapter 2, in this study we develop a conceptual typology of military justice systems based on the jurisdiction and practice of military courts and how these institutions interact with the civilian government and population. This "organized system of types" (Collier, LaPorte, and Seawright 2008, 152) produces three distinct categories describing the extent to which a military is subordinated to civilian control in the legal domain—full subordination, jurisdictional contestation, and military overreach—an ordered scale from positive to negative regarding observing the rule of law, respecting human rights, and maintaining good civil-military relations in a democracy. In systems of full subordination, military courts exercise legal power over their own personnel for the offenses necessary to maintain good order and discipline within the forces. In the event of disagreement between civilian and military authorities over a case, military authorities routinely cooperate by transferring cases and personnel to civilian jurisdiction. Under systems of jurisdictional contestation, military courts have expanded jurisdiction over their personnel for nearly all crimes, including human rights abuses. In these systems, the supremacy of civilian courts is not guaranteed, militaries are routinely uncooperative with civilian authorities, and military courts serve as a shield of impunity. Finally, under systems of military overreach, military courts have legal control over their own forces and extend their jurisdiction over civilians, putting them on trial for a broad array of offenses such as crimes against the state or violations of martial law regulations.

Countries may establish their first system in any of the three categories and maintain that system indefinitely. Movement from one category to another, however, is common, and we visualize the types of change that countries experience in Figure 3.1. The top two horizontal lines in the figure depict positive change (reform). A state may move immediately from military overreach to full subordination, simultaneously wresting control of cases against civilians and excessive military power over its own personnel in one episode of reform. A state may also

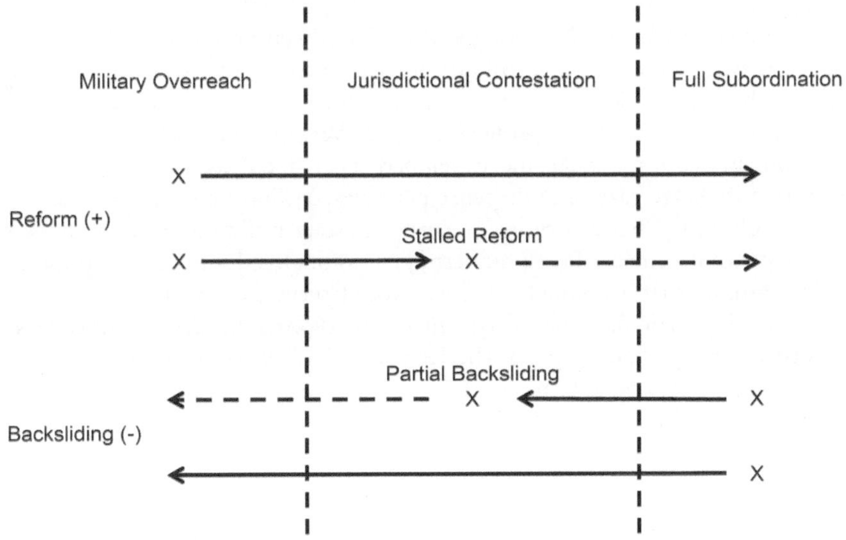

Figure 3.1 Reform and backsliding in military justice systems

experience incremental change, either by beginning in the jurisdictional contestation category and successfully moving to full subordination or by beginning in the military overreach category and reforming into jurisdictional contestation. In the latter scenario, the state may experience further reform in a subsequent episode of change that brings it into the full subordination category or it may fail to achieve additional gains, remaining in the middle category (stalled reform).

The bottom two horizontal lines in the figure depict negative change (backsliding). First, mirroring the incremental positive change described above, a state may experience negative movement into the jurisdictional contestation category from full subordination and make no further changes (partial backsliding), or subsequent erosion of civilian control may move the country into military overreach. Second, as the final horizontal line in the figure depicts, a state may move immediately from full subordination to military overreach in one episode of backsliding. In our dataset, we document 146 episodes of change between systems within countries. Of those, 83 episodes (57%) are positive—reform from military overreach to full subordination (20, 14%), jurisdictional contestation to full subordination (22, 15%), or from military overreach to jurisdictional contestation (41, 28%). The remaining 63 episodes (43%) of change are cases of backsliding—from full subordination to jurisdictional contestation (7, 5%), full subordination to military overreach (14, 10%), and jurisdictional contestation to military overreach (42, 29%). More than half of the episodes of change (83, 57%) are shifts between the lower two categories on our scale. In the rest of the chapter, we apply the framework of establishment and change in military justice systems to the world from the development of modern systems in Europe to the present.

The birth of modern military justice in Europe

As we discuss in Chapter 2, as long as there have been organized fighting forces there has been some form of military justice. Initially this was informal, typically with commanders meting out harsh punishments to subordinates who violated orders. As militaries professionalized over time, military justice did too. Governments codified rules and developed specialized institutions and procedures to adjudicate cases and dispense penalties. Military justice, as we know it in the world today, has its origins in European state-building in the seventeenth to nineteenth centuries. These modern, professionalized militaries and military justice systems that accompanied them would serve as models for the rest of the world. In particular, the major European colonial powers spread their systems throughout their empires, the legacies of which continue to shape how post-colonial states operate today. Table 3.1 provides an overview of the establishment of the first modern military justice systems in Europe.

Longstanding democracies

A number of European countries long maintained a position of neutrality in international politics, had few colonial ambitions, and largely avoided

Table 3.1 The establishment of military justice in Europe

Country	*Year*	*Military justice system*
England	1689	Full subordination
Spain	1701	Jurisdictional contestation
Portugal	1763	Jurisdictional contestation
France	1791	Military overreach
Sweden	1809	Full subordination
Netherlands	1814	Jurisdictional contestation
Norway	1814	Full subordination
Belgium	1831	Jurisdictional contestation
Italy	1861	Military overreach
Luxembourg	1881	Full subordination
Switzerland	1889	Jurisdictional contestation

becoming embroiled in major wars. These countries have had good civil-military relations and military justice systems have held little power. In Sweden, military justice originated with the courts martial system of King Gustavus Adolphus, established in 1621 and formally codified in 1795 (Lindeblad 1963, 122). The 1809 Instrument of Government, which was in effect until the government enacted a new constitution in 1974, required that all crimes committed by members of the military be tried in civilian courts during peacetime.[1] Eventually, Sweden would abolish the military penal code entirely (1949) and prohibit the creation of military courts even in wartime (1962) (Sherman 1973, 1413–16).[2]

Norway's first constitution in 1814 did not allow military courts in times of peace (Gammelgaard and Holmøyvik 2014, 245).[3] Luxembourg has also always maintained a clear distinction between civilian and military crimes, beginning with the Act on the Organization of the Armed Forces in 1881, with military courts only having jurisdiction over a narrow range of the latter.[4] Belgium would remain in the jurisdictional contestation category from its independence in 1831 until the late twentieth century. In practice, however, civil-military relations have been strong and there have been few conflicts between military and civilian courts, likely because the "armed forces have never played any role in the political history of the country" (d'Argent 2003, 185).

Military justice in Switzerland dates to the fourteenth century; the current system has its origins in the 1889 Law on Judicial Organization and the Code of Military Criminal Procedure for the Federal Army.[5] Military courts can only try civilians in exceptional circumstances related to war or war crimes, but the courts have broad jurisdiction over members of the military for almost all crimes. Like Belgium, there have been no serious issues related to military justice given the fact that they do not have a history of operating domestically. The military's autonomy in many areas, including military justice, is due to national pride in the military and a long-held belief that a large force with mandatory service for all male citizens has deterred adversaries and kept it out of European wars (Haltiner 2003).

Major colonial powers

The great powers of Europe had large militaries that played a significant role in interstate wars and colonization. In turn, these militaries retained significant legal autonomy. With the exception of Great Britain, military courts had near complete jurisdiction over members of the military and, in some cases, also tried civilians.

The naval powers—the Netherlands, Portugal, and Spain—granted military courts broad jurisdiction over members of the military for most crimes. While not used to try civilians, military courts in the Netherlands long maintained jurisdiction over members of the military for civil and criminal offenses, stemming from the Dutch Code of Military Procedure of 1814 (Gilissen 1963, 87). Despite a number of reform attempts, this system lasted until 1991. Some form of military justice existed in Spain from at least the fourteenth century and took on a formal structure in 1701 with the first Flanders Ordinance (Depósito de la Guerra 1873, 41). Military courts heard nearly all cases, civil and criminal, committed by members of the military (Andreu-Guzmán 2004, 320–22).[6] The *fuero militar* became a valued privilege of military service (Andújar Castillo 1996). Portuguese military justice followed a similar pattern. Military law, separate from civilian justice, developed in the seventeenth century and was updated and formalized in 1763 by royal decree.[7] The Lisbon Council of War (*Conselho de Guerra*) was a privileged forum of justice for military personnel (Souza 2015), placing Portugal in the jurisdictional contestation category at the outset of its modern system.[8] We discuss the Portuguese case at length in Chapter 4.

It is not surprising that Italy and France, who dealt with more conflict at home, began with military justice systems in the military overreach category. After its unification, Italy maintained the 1869 Sardinian Military Code, which allowed the government to use military courts to try civilians to deal with the many political and economic protest movements embroiling the Italian peninsula at the time (Andreu-Guzmán 2004, 286–87). Italy remained in the military overreach category through World War II.

Some aspect of military justice has existed in France since 1347. In the ensuing centuries, the system maintained a distinction between military and ordinary crimes, with civilian courts adjudicating the latter. There were no clear codes of military justice, however, and so in practice military courts had broad jurisdiction over members of the military. Moreover, military courts had jurisdiction over civilians during the state of siege (*état de siege*), the first of which was declared in 1791.[9] The government used the state of siege regularly to deal with unrest throughout the next century, placing France in the military overreach category in practice until the end of World War I (Radin 1942, 636–38).

The British exception

Unlike the other great powers, Britain developed a system of full subordination early on and maintained it even as it established the world's largest empire. Beginning in the late 1600s, English kings issued their own Articles of War for troops fighting abroad. In 1689, the Mutiny Act established, for the first time, a military justice system in times of peace and introduced the process of courts martial (Samuel 1816). From the beginning, military courts did not have jurisdiction over civilians in Britain during peacetime, stemming from rights first laid out in the 1628 Petition of Right.[10] They could only exercise control over civilians during periods of martial law but the last declaration was in 1780 and the expansion of the government's powers during the period was limited (Rossiter 1948, 139). Military courts were also limited in their jurisdiction over members of the military. By the early 1700s, courts martial could not try British soldiers for ordinary felonies committed in Britain (Wiener 1967, 14–15). This strong military legal subordination would influence many of the United Kingdom's colonies as they became independent in the twentieth century.

Military justice and state (re-)formation

While the states we discuss above most commonly arrived at their first systems of military justice through a long evolutionary process, we identify three particular sets of cases that experienced a political cleavage followed by a critical juncture that served as a founding moment—post-colonial states, states (re-)formed at the end of the Cold War, and states that experienced foreign installation of a new system after defeat in war and subsequent occupation. In each of these experiences, the institutions and practices of the ruling power or predecessor state formed the antecedent conditions influencing political actors. A critical juncture is a moment of contingency in which rules are in flux and new systems may be established that have the potential to endure for long periods, shaping politics and government for generations to come (Capoccia and Kelemen 2007, 353–54; R. Collier and D. Collier 1991, 30). We discuss cases from each of these categories of state formation below.

Post-colonial states

Through colonialism and empire building, the European states we discuss above spread their systems of military justice to colonies across the globe. Thus, when post-colonial states gained their independence, they were not starting with a blank slate. The former colonies of the United Kingdom and Spain, in particular, experienced high degrees of institutional continuity, whereby newly independent states maintained the systems of their colonial powers or adopted new systems that closely resembled the ones they replaced. Legacies of British institutions were more positive than those of other European colonizers (Lipset, Seong, and Torres 1993). The British tendency toward democracy and liberal constitutionalism translated to legal restraint on power in many post-colonial societies (Daniels, Trebilcock, and Carson 2011). This positive pattern was true for the initial adoption of military justice systems as well—new states most commonly adopted the British system of full subordination at independence, as shown in Table 3.2.

Table 3.2 Post-colonial military justice systems

Country	*Year*	*Military justice system*
United Kingdom: Full subordination		
Australia	1901	Full subordination
Botswana	1966	Full subordination
Cyprus	1960	Full subordination
Fiji	1970	Full subordination
Gambia	1965	Full subordination
Ghana	1957	Full subordination
Guyana	1966	Jurisdictional contestation
India	1947	Full subordination
Ireland	1922	Full subordination
Jamaica	1962	Full subordination
Kenya	1968	Full subordination
Malaysia	1972	Full subordination
Mauritius	1968	Full subordination
Myanmar	1947	Full subordination
New Zealand	1971	Full subordination
Nigeria	1960	Jurisdictional contestation
Pakistan	1947	Jurisdictional contestation
Sierra Leone	1961	Full subordination
Solomon Islands	1978	Full subordination
Sri Lanka	1949	Jurisdictional contestation
Sudan	1957	Military overreach
Tanzania	1964	Full subordination
Trinidad and Tobago	1962	Jurisdictional contestation
Uganda	1962	Jurisdictional contestation
United States	1789	Full subordination
Zambia	1964	Full subordination
Zimbabwe	1980	Jurisdictional contestation
Spain: Jurisdictional contestation		
Argentina	1810	Jurisdictional contestation
Bolivia	1825	Jurisdictional contestation
Chile	1818	Jurisdictional contestation
Mexico	1824	Jurisdictional contestation
Paraguay	1811	Jurisdictional contestation
Peru	1821	Jurisdictional contestation
Uruguay	1825	Jurisdictional contestation
France: Jurisdictional contestation		
Algeria	1963	Military overreach
Benin	1960	Jurisdictional contestation
Burkina Faso	1960	Jurisdictional contestation
Cambodia	1954	Military overreach
Guinea	1958	Jurisdictional contestation
Madagascar	1960	Military overreach
Mali	1960	Jurisdictional contestation
Niger	1960	Full subordination
Senegal	1960	Full subordination
Tunisia	1957	Military overreach
Portugal: Jurisdictional contestation		
Brazil	1822	Jurisdictional contestation
Guinea-Bissau	1974	Military overreach

Table 3.2 Post-colonial military justice systems (Continued)

Country	*Year*	*Military justice system*
The Netherlands: Jurisdictional contestation		
Indonesia	1946	Military overreach
Suriname	1975	Jurisdictional contestation

The United States is emblematic of colonial continuity in former British territories. As the United States was fighting for independence, it adopted a military justice system nearly identical to that of the British, and many of the provisions set forth in that code remained part of US military justice for over a century (Wiener 1967, 21–23). Similarly, Australia continued to use the Naval Discipline Act 1866 and Army Act 1881 to govern its military justice system well after independence.[11] The Defence Force Discipline Act 1982 finally created a unified system for trying members of the armed forces for service-related crimes (Denton 2016).[12] The military discipline system exists under parliament's defense power, granted to it by Article 51(vi) of the constitution.[13] Any non-disciplinary crimes are tried in the country's regular judicial system.

Widespread decolonization of British territories in the 1960s and 1970s most commonly produced continuity. Cyprus' first military criminal code, following its independence in 1960, restricted the jurisdiction of military courts to military crimes committed by members of the military.[14] Zambia, independent in 1964, also adopted a system of full subordination and has maintained stable civil-military relations (Phiri 2001). The 1964 Defence Act limits the jurisdiction of military courts to military offenses.[15] In New Zealand, the Armed Forces Discipline Act 1971 governs military justice.[16] It does not allow civilians to be prosecuted by military courts and only provides for jurisdiction over members of the military for military-related crimes. There are few political disruptions or security problems to create civil-military clashes in these countries.

Other states do face such challenges yet maintain their systems of full subordination adopted at independence. Notably, in Malaysia, following the withdrawal of the British military presence in 1971, the government began to build and professionalize its military and enacted the Armed Forces Act 1972, which provides for courts martial for members of the military for military crimes only.[17] The law remains in place today and there have been very few tensions between the military and the civilian government, owing in part to the dominance of the ethnic Malay in both. In combatting militants and other political opposition, the government has used the Internal Security Act 1960 and later the Security Offences (Special Measures) Act 2012 (Lee 2002).[18] Neither law, however, allows for the use of military courts against civilians. Similarly, Jamaica has maintained a system of full subordination despite a long history of violence, dating back to its independence in 1962 (Sives 2010). Criminal and gang violence have increased over time as the country has become a major transit point for cocaine and a supplier of marijuana to the United States. Frequently, the government has declared states of public emergency, during which it can deploy the military domestically, but it has resisted expanding the power of military courts.

Some former British colonies had no military at all at the point of independence—Botswana, Gambia, and Mauritius—and we consider those states full subordination. In Gambia and Botswana, however, the subsequent establishment of standing armies and military justice systems led to serious civil-military challenges, including military rule in Gambia from 1994 to 1996 and overly broad military court jurisdiction in Botswana that protects personnel from prosecution for almost all common civil and criminal offenses (Wiseman 1996).[19] Fiji, which had a very small military at independence in 1970, followed a similar course. The military became increasingly influential over time and a coup in 1987 ruptured the initial post-colonial system of full subordination. We discuss the Fijian case at length in Chapter 5.

Not every former British colony followed the pattern of colonial continuity. Those cases are largely explained by pervasive security threats. Trinidad and Tobago adopted a jurisdictional contestation system when it became independent. The 1962 Defence Act allows members of the military to be tried in military courts for most crimes.[20] The military has a long history of involvement in domestic security (Phillips 1997), and the government has invoked a state of emergency on several occasions. An increased threat of Islamic terrorism in recent years has reinforced these practices. Trinidad and Tobago faced an attempted coup in 1990 by the fundamentalist group Jamaat-al-Muslimeen, and more recently the Islamic State established a presence in the country (Badri-Maharaj 2017).[21] Military courts typically handle abuses committed by the military in the line of duty.[22]

Colonial continuity in the former Spanish colonies of Latin America meant maintaining jurisdictional contestation after independence. Spanish colonial institutions were rigidly hierarchical with control centralized in the hands of the monarchy (Hanson 1974). Colonial judicial institutions, especially the *fuero militar*, kept the military outside of civilian law, and militaries in newly independent countries of Latin America sought to maintain these privileges (Kahle 1951; McAlister 1957). Spanish military forces played a significant role in managing the colonies, especially in the nineteenth century following the Bourbon Reforms (Lynch 1992). This praetorian role set the stage for post-colonial militaries to see themselves as separate from and above civilian government. The wars of independence separated the colonies from Spanish control but did not revolutionize the stratified societies established during centuries of colonialism. American-born creole elites filled the former role of the Spanish elites and continued many of the practices of the colonial era (Andrews 1985).

New states in Latin America commonly continued enforcing Spanish royal ordinances related to military justice for long periods after independence. Argentina passed legislation in 1815–17 specifically maintaining Spanish military criminal law (Andreu-Guzmán 2004, 169). In 1895, the government established a new code of military justice that gave military courts jurisdiction over all crimes committed by military personnel.[23] Peru followed the same path, explicitly retaining Spanish military codes in the first post-independence constitution in 1823 (Andreu-Guzmán 2004, 300). In Bolivia, the Spanish royal ordinances remained in effect until 1904 when the government established a new military code (Castro and Lara 2008, 14).[24] The *fuero* was abolished in 1910, but military jurisdiction remained contentious.[25] The frequent use of regimes of exception in this period reinforced military power (Loveman 1993, 237–61). In Chile, the government maintained the Spanish ordinances until 1839 when it adopted a new system still in the jurisdictional contestation category (Castro and Lara 2008, 16). Similarly, upon independence in Mexico, the country continued the *fuero* and codified the separate privileged system into Mexican law in 1843.[26] Paraguay enforced Spanish military ordinances after its independence in 1811 until its first code in 1887 reined in military legal prerogatives, moving the country to full subordination (Andreu-Guzmán 2004, 296).[27] Spanish military law continued to operate in Uruguay after independence in 1825 until the government abolished the *fuero* in 1831 (Castro and Lara 2008, 19; Salgado 1905, 218–21).[28] The Portuguese colony of Brazil followed the same pattern as its Spanish neighbors. Upon independence in 1822, Brazil retained the colonial system of Councils of War (*Conselhos de Guerra*), keeping it in the jurisdictional contestation category in the early post-colonial period (Souza 2015). We discuss the Brazilian case at length in Chapter 6.

Former French colonies exhibit considerable variation in their initial codes and practices after independence. There are fewer indications of deliberate efforts to maintain continuity in these cases than in the former British and Spanish colonies. Nineteenth-century French colonialism in Africa and Southeast Asia left a problematic legal and military legacy for the independent states that would emerge in the 1950s and 1960s. French colonialism was less institutionalized and less intentional than British colonialism of the same era (Betts 2004; Firmin-Sellers 2000). French colonies often had been acquired or expanded by ambitious military commanders acting opportunistically without the approval of authorities in Paris (Gershovich 2000, 4–7), and they were similarly managed with little direct civilian oversight from the center. The military commands in the colonies were responsible for administration, blurring civil-military lines, especially on the eve of independence (Menard 1967, 67). The legal systems inherited from France were also ineffective in establishing and maintaining the rule of law (Joireman 2001). Moreover, continued French military involvement in West Africa in particular, enhanced the role of domestic militaries and undermined civilian authority in that region (Luckham 1982).

Militaries in many former French colonies seized control of government almost immediately upon independence or shortly thereafter. Civilians did not have control over militaries, including in the legal sphere, placing several countries in the jurisdictional contestation category at their founding. The military has dominated politics in Burkina Faso since independence in 1960 (Harsch 2017). There have been seven successful coups, two failed coup attempts, and at least six recorded coup plots (Dwyer 2017, 150). Benin similarly experienced numerous military coups after independence and has not been able to assert civilian legal authority over the military (Houngnikpo 2000). In Mali, General

Moussa Traoré seized power in a coup in 1968 and ruled until 1991 when he was overthrown in another military coup (Bennett 1975; Clark 1995). Guinea uniquely separated from French control by a successful "no" vote in the 1958 referendum on the proposed creation of a new French Community for territories in West Africa (Schmidt 2009, 4–6). The new state was in the hands of civilian leaders, yet they relied heavily on the military to bolster their rule with little accountability for military actions. Military courts had jurisdiction over all crimes committed by military personnel until 1988 (Sidibe 2018).[29]

Some former French colonies adopted systems of military overreach upon independence, largely due to violent wars of independence that ruptured French colonial systems. The Algerian military has exercised considerable formal and informal influence in politics, including decisions on who serves as president (Cook 2007, 33). From the 1971 military code, Algerian military courts have jurisdiction over civilians accused of crimes against state security and political offenses (International Commission of Jurists [ICJ] 2005).[30] The war for independence in French Indochina produced a similar legacy of disruption in colonial control followed by a high level of military influence in politics for Cambodia. After independence in 1953, the government subjected civilians to trial in the military courts established in 1954 and the Special Military Court established in 1959, which had jurisdiction over crimes against the state and did not allow for appeals (Amnesty International 1999).

Post-Soviet and post-Yugoslavia states

The second major pattern of adoption and reform of military justice systems upon new state formation came in the wake of the breakup of the Soviet Union and Yugoslavia in the 1990s. Both had been multinational and communist political entities. Nationalist mobilization helped bring about their dissolution and a major moment of nation-state (re-)formation (Beissinger 2002; Roeder 2004). While the militarized societies and ideologically oriented armed forces of communist countries were far from ideal for building democratic civil-military relations (Barany 2012, 213–15), the communist legacy of civilian control of the military helped to diminish the potential for militaries to be politically powerful in the transitions or immediately after (Cottey, Edmunds, and Forster 2006; Herspring 1992). In contrast to many of the post-colonial states we discuss above, the democracies that emerged from the Soviet Union and Yugoslavia most commonly did not exhibit continuity with the military justice systems of those predecessor states.[31] Instead, they reformed immediately from military overreach to full subordination, as depicted in Table 3.3.

In the Soviet Union, the 1958 Statute on Military Tribunals governed military justice (Grzybowski 1960). The 1977 Soviet constitution and the 1980 Military Courts Act further refined aspects of the system. Military courts had jurisdiction over members of the military for all crimes and over civilians for some crimes against the state, most notably espionage, though there were few trials of civilians in practice (Berman and Spindler 1972, 97; Golovko 2008).

Table 3.3 Post-Cold War military justice establishment and reform

Country	*Year*	*Military justice system*
Former Soviet Union		
Armenia	1991	Military overreach
Azerbaijan	1991	Military overreach
Belarus	1991	Military overreach
Estonia	1991	Full subordination
Kyrgyzstan	1993	Jurisdictional contestation
Latvia	1991	Full subordination
Lithuania	1992	Full subordination
Moldova	1992	Full subordination
Ukraine	1993	Full subordination
Former Yugoslavia		
Croatia	1996	Full subordination
North Macedonia	1991	Full subordination
Slovenia	1991	Full subordination

Military justice in the Soviet Union had a federal structure, centralizing authority in Moscow, unlike the civilian legal systems that functioned independently in each Soviet republic (Schmitt and Moody 1991, 21). Thus, the total collapse of the overarching Soviet structure facilitated newly independent states making a significant break from the previous system.

After independence, some states—Armenia, Estonia, Latvia, and Lithuania—did not establish military courts at all. Article 92 of Armenia's 1995 constitution allowed for military courts, but the government never passed implementing legislation to create them (Manukyan 2001). In Latvia, after independence in 1991, the government reinstated the 1922 constitution, which permitted the creation of military courts only in the event of a war or a state of emergency.[32] The 1993 Law on Judicial Power and the 2005 Law on Military Courts reinforced these restrictions.[33] Such courts can try civilians for specified crimes, but the government has never created them.

Ukraine, Moldova, and Georgia established new military courts but with limited powers, characterizing them as full subordination. In Ukraine, the military justice system established in 1993 was a specialized part of the regular civilian judiciary (Vashakmadze 2018, 1). Military courts were limited to prosecuting members of the military. The 1992 Law on the Military Court System in Moldova approved the creation of military tribunals, but they were similarly restricted to handling military cases.[34] In Georgia, the years immediately following independence were chaotic, with rival militias vying for power while engaged in conflict with Russia and separatists in Abkhazia and South Ossetia. It was not until 1995 that the government "weakened the militias, and established a modicum of central-state control" (Levitsky and Way 2010, 223). The 1995 constitution only allows for military courts to operate during periods of martial law and within the regular judicial system.[35] The 1997 Organic Law of Georgia on Common Courts reaffirmed this system.[36]

Three post-Soviet cases took different paths following independence, quickly becoming dominated by personal dictators who implemented military overreach or jurisdictional contestation systems. All three, however, would eventually fully reform—a stark reminder that subordination of military legal prerogatives is not synonymous with liberal democracy. Under President Ilham Aliyev (2003–present), who took over power from his father, Heydar Aliyev (1993–2003), Azerbaijan collaborated with the World Bank's Judicial Monitoring Project to gradually reform the judicial system, bringing the country to the full subordination category in 2013.[37] Belarus moved into the full subordination category in 2013 after Alexander Lukashenko, who has ruled since independence, reformed the entire judicial system, including abolishing military courts.[38] Finally, Kyrgyzstan abolished military courts completely in 2016, largely based on budgetary grounds, and shifted all cases to civilian courts (Sputnik 2016).

Russia remained in the military overreach category after the breakup of the Soviet Union. It undertook a series of reforms to the military justice system, over time closely integrating it into the civilian justice system. This effort culminated in a 1999 law that removed most civilian crimes from the jurisdiction of military courts.[39] The crime of terrorism, however, is still included and in recent years the government has prosecuted suspected terrorists in military courts (Human Rights Watch [HRW] 2020). Moreover, military courts still cover all crimes committed by members of the military, and the military has used its courts to protect its personnel from prosecution for crimes committed during the First and Second Chechen Wars (Kovalev 2008).

Like the Soviet Union, Yugoslavia maintained a system of military overreach. Modern military justice in Yugoslavia originated in World War II when partisans fighting to liberate the country from Axis occupation established military courts and local councils to try those accused of undermining the war effort (Central Intelligence Agency 1948). After the war, military courts retained this expansive authority to try anyone, including civilians, for national security offenses. Broadly written criminal codes permitted severe punishment for crimes that threatened the economic or military strength of the country (Curtis 1992, 279). Also like the Soviet Union, Yugoslavia's successor states transitioned to full subordination upon or shortly after independence.

Slovenia, the first republic to secede, did not establish military courts after independence. The 1991 constitution explicitly prohibits the creation of military courts in peacetime, making the country a case of full subordination.[40] Similarly, North Macedonia, after gaining its independence in 1991 established no military court system. Civilian courts judge all cases involving military personnel beyond disciplinary procedures.[41] These two states were able to secede relatively peacefully, which facilitated the movement away from military overreach. Croatia, however, experienced a long and violent struggle for its independence. During the conflict, Croatia established new military courts and used them to try civilians for security-related crimes (HRW 1995). After the war ended, Croatia reformed its military justice system to reach full subordination. In 1996, by presidential decree, the government abolished military courts (Kutnjak Ivkovich 2001, 59).

Foreign installation after defeat in war

The final type of critical juncture in which a new military justice system is created is foreign installation after defeat in war. In this scenario, a state loses a war and experiences occupation or otherwise has its sovereignty compromised to the extent that it cannot resist the creation of new institutions. This path to adoption or reform of a new military justice system is akin to the "Externally Monitored Installation" path of redemocratization identified by Alfred Stepan (1986), in which a foreign power is able "to dismantle the military and political institutions and other features of the authoritarian state apparatus ... [which] removes an important obstacle to redemocratization" (71). As with the story of general change in regime type, West Germany and Japan in the aftermath of World War II exhibit this pathway of change, as does Panama after the US invasion in 1989.

In Germany, the Nazi regime (1933–45) used military courts extensively, sentencing over 30,000 people to death (Müller 1991, 183–91). After Germany's defeat in World War II, new national institutions were established by the occupying Allied forces. When West Germany (Federal Republic of Germany) was formed in 1949, its new constitution prohibited military courts in peacetime, only allowing for them to be created in times of national defense or if members of the military were serving abroad.[42] West Germany did not even have a military again until 1954, making the country a clear case of full subordination. Upon reunification in 1990, East Germany adopted the constitution of West Germany, and present-day Germany maintains a "strict distinction between the prosecution of criminal offences and the punishment of disciplinary offences."[43] Japan's experience after World War II was similar. The victorious Allies established a new constitution in 1947 that prohibited Japan from maintaining a standing army (Article 9) and forbid the creation of any extraordinary tribunals (Article 76).[44] As with Germany, the occupied country had no armed forces until 1954, when the United States assisted and supervised the creation of the Japan Ground Self-Defense Force (GSDF) (Hunter-Chester 2016).[45] Prime Minister Shinzō Abe (2012–20), sought to relax the restrictions on Japan's forces, raising concerns that a system of courts martial could return.

Finally, Panama is a case of foreign installation of a new military justice system after war. After the United States invaded in 1989 to remove General Manuel Noriega from power, it oversaw an end to the National Guard and its courts (Fishel 2000). A constitutional amendment in 1994 made the move permanent.[46] Today, all Panamanian police and border guards are under the civilian Ministry of Public Security and accountable to the regular judicial system.[47]

A model of change

As noted above, countries' first military justice systems may be established in any of our three categories—full subordination, jurisdictional contestation, or military overreach. Reform or backsliding may then occur over time. We argue that the degree of military legal subordination in each country is determined by interactions among three principal actors—the government, the military, and high courts—in a decision-making nexus. These interactions are also influenced by an array of domestic (public sentiment and civil society) and international factors (human rights courts, NGOs, IOs, and external states). We explain each of the actors and influences below and illustrate the model in Figure 3.2.

Principal actor: The government

The government—in the form of an executive and legislature—is a principal actor in creating, maintaining, or reforming a military justice system. This is the actor with the authority to legislate, issue decrees, and institute and reform constitutions, all of which spell out the rules governing the armed forces of the state. The government is also responsible for deciding on the budget, deployment, and doctrines of the military and establishing institutional controls and performing oversight (Matei 2013, 29–33). In a democratic state, these rules and behaviors are crucial to ensuring that the military ultimately answers to the people, through its elected officials.

Regime type is an important determinant of the interaction between the principal actors in the struggle over military justice. First, civilian control of the armed forces is an essential condition of democracy (Dahl 1998, 147), and the liberalizing moment of democratization is an opportunity for governments to

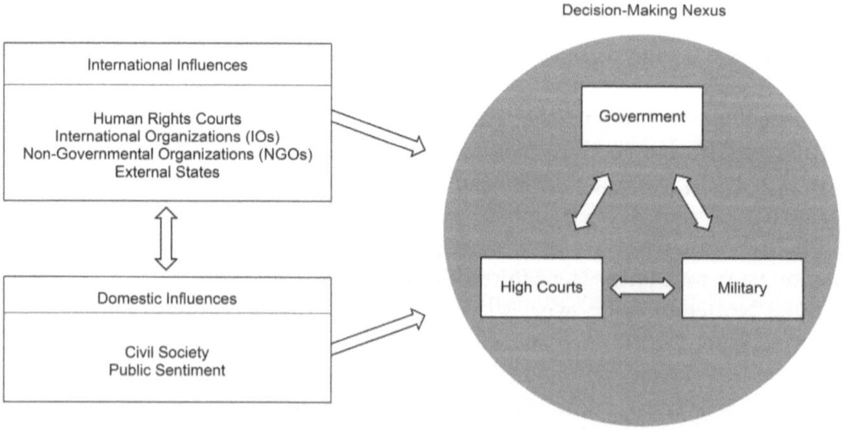

Figure 3.2 Military justice: A model of change

"roll back" military prerogatives that may have gone unchecked in the previous non-democratic period (Barany 2012, 33). To assess the effect of democratization on military justice reform, we use the Polity5 dataset's REGTRANS variable to examine military justice in the context of all major democratic transitions from 1974 to 2017 for those countries in our dataset (Marshall and Gurr 2018).[48] There were 104 cases in which the country was in the military overreach or jurisdictional contestation category prior to the transition. Of those, nearly a third (31, 32%) reformed on our scale during the transition itself or immediately after, demonstrating that democratic transitions represent critical junctures that dramatically influence the trajectory of military justice. In Nigeria, for example, democratization in 1999 brought with it a new constitution that banned the trial of civilians in military courts.[49] In Argentina, reforms following the end of military rule in 1983 ended military jurisdiction over civilians.[50] In Taiwan, the government lifted martial law in 1987 as part of a broad liberalization process (Ginsburg 2003, 114).

Second, we find that populist leaders, while consistently a threat to democracy in their own way, can be reformers of military justice. Populists come to power with an ambiguous nationalist agenda and a mobilized segment of "the people" as their source of support (Brubaker 2020). Their appeals often invoke military imagery and praise for martial values, but in practice they frequently clash with the armed forces (Kuehn and Trinkunas 2017). The populist drive to dismantle national institutions and consolidate power in the hands of the individual leader plays out in the battle over military justice through reducing military legal prerogatives. Under the leadership of Recep Tayyip Erdoğan, Turkey's military justice system has gone from jurisdictional contestation to full subordination. A series of constitutional reforms in 2010 restricted military courts to military crimes by members of the military, and in 2017, further amendments to the constitution abolished military courts completely.[51] In Ecuador, where the military has consistently been a powerful political actor responsible for overthrowing numerous leaders, Rafael Correa, riding a high level of popular support when he was elected in 2006, purged the higher echelons of the military and enacted a new constitution in 2008 that created a unified justice system, eliminating military courts (Romero 2008).[52]

Finally, with the collapse of democracy or other illiberal transitions, we observe backsliding in military legal subordination. Particularly when the military seizes control of government, the interests of the two actors become largely inseparable. Expansion of the military legal prerogative is often tied to the motivation to take power—justifying military rule by the need to restore public order or combat a security threat—and implementing martial law to do so. In Thailand, for example, the military has carried out 19 coups or coup attempts since 1932, often citing some combination of defense of the monarchy and separatist insurgency in the southern part of the country as justification for intervention in government, followed by extending military jurisdiction over civilians (Albritton 2005; Farrelly 2013). Thailand has moved back and forth between jurisdictional contestation and military overreach numerous times between the 1950s and the present day, reflecting a status quo of a military that is legally unaccountable to civilian leadership and punctuated by moments of power over civilians. We elaborate this pattern in detail with the case of Pakistan in Chapter 6.

Principal actor: The military

The military is a principal decision-maker in the fight over military legal subordination. The modern military is a unique institution, imbued with its own norms, values, and corporate interests that influence its behavior when dealing with the other two principal actors—government and domestic high courts. Military professionals are "specialists on violence" (Lasswell 1941) who "share a sense of organic unity and consciousness of themselves as a group apart from laymen" (Huntington 1957, 10). The group cohesion and social solidarity of the armed forces go beyond those of the average profession, because service in the military is "a complete style of life" (Janowitz 1960, 177). Given the gravity of the profession and the exceptional unity required to carry out their duties, militaries have their own codes of conduct and law that they use to uphold professional standards (Huntington 1957, 10). This internal self-perception and presence of unique rules raise the fundamental question of whether a military is competent to police and judge itself. In the courtroom, the sense of corporate unity and the duty to protect each other as a community can become obstacles to justice because they run afoul of a fundamental principal of the rule of law that no one can be their own judge.

As a corporate entity, the military has specific prerogatives they seek to enhance or defend, including the fundamentals of mission, size, and budget (Young 2006). Militaries seek to protect institutional powers such as a military officer serving as Minister of Defense (Red de Seguridad y Defensa de América Latina 2016, 33–34) and control over other offices, especially intelligence services (Weeks 2008). Civilian politicians and high-ranking military officials in democratic states engage in a cooperative, if at times tense, relationship of consultation and oversight (Schiff 2009), and military leaders naturally try to influence policymakers to act in accordance with military preferences (Barany 2012, 27). Military budgets, and the process by which they are decided (e.g. Ball and le Roux 2006), are exceptionally important, because the civilian leadership's "authority to prepare, enact into law, disburse, and scrutinize the military's management of the budget is its most powerful tool for controlling the armed forces" (Barany 2012, 32). From the military perspective, the budget is about both money and prestige. The immediate material interest of having up-to-date weapons and sufficient supplies for training and mission preparedness is joined by the longer-term issue of potential for career advancement in an institution where personnel are adequately paid, they have a "self-image" of honor, and enjoy the respect of the nation (Barany 2012, 33; Janowitz 1960, 225–26). Poor service conditions erode morale and undermine effectiveness (Barany 2007, 61–69).

As an institutional prerogative, military courts occupy the material and the intangible space. Seeking to retain control over military courts is simultaneously about avoiding the risk of prison sentences for human rights violations as well as preserving the reputation of the institution. The potential for accountability threatens the military's claim that its actions are right and the natural expression of its duty to fight enemies of the state. This is especially important in post-authoritarian contexts, which we illustrate with Indonesia in Chapter 5 and Brazil in Chapter 6, where militaries saw maintaining control over any potential prosecution as a core interest to defend.

The security environment significantly influences the battle over military judicial prerogatives. In general, a high external security threat level tends to produce positive civil-military relations as civilian leadership and the military work together to fight the external foe, while a high internal security threat level produces discord and frequent military intervention against civilian governments (Desch 1999). We find that the locus of the security threat is less of a determining factor regarding the power of military justice systems, but military legal subordination is a greater challenge where security issues dominate the national political debate because the military is naturally a central actor under such conditions. The threat of terrorism, in particular, brings the military into politics because civilian politicians "pull" the military into government decision-making as they try to address the danger, or the military will leverage its unique war-fighting role to "push" its way in (Bove, Rivera, and Ruffa 2020). The extreme version of the latter is the military seizing control of government completely, implementing martial law, and extending jurisdiction of military courts over the civilian population.

Finally, military clashes with domestic courts are characterized by consistent refusal to cooperate with investigations and turn accused personnel over to civilian authorities, or otherwise obstruct civilian justice. The Zimbabwean military has taken control of the National Prosecuting Authority, which was established by the 2013 constitution to provide independent judicial oversight of state actors—over three-quarters of the Prosecutor's General Staff is comprised of military officers (Zimbabwe Independent 2016). In Cambodia, conflicting statutes lead to defiance of the courts. After the collapse of the Khmer Rouge regime, Cambodia reformed its military courts, limiting their jurisdiction to members of the military for military crimes. This was reaffirmed in the new criminal code of 1992 (Amnesty International 1999). At the same time, however, Article 51 of the 1994 Statute on Civil Servants declares that civil servants may not be prosecuted for any crimes without the consent of their supervising ministry.[53] This measure did not apply to the military, but it invoked it anyway as a shield against prosecution (Adhoc, Licadho, and HRW 1999).[54] Where civilian courts attempt to try members of the military, it has pressured civilian judges to release defendants (United States Department of State [USDS] 2011).

In the case of Bangladesh, the military has historically been a powerful actor since the country's independence from Pakistan in 1971 and has at times ruled through martial law. Today, Bangladesh is in a state of jurisdictional contestation due to continued inability of civilian legal authorities to exercise oversight. In addition to the military continuing to hold considerable influence over civilian government by occupying important offices (Smith 2018), the military constrains civilian court actions. For example, in 2014, when members of the paramilitary Rapid Action Battalion were accused of the murder of seven people, civilian legal efforts against the three army and navy officers were only possible after the military leadership gave its permission to act (bdnews24.com 2014).

Principal actor: High courts

Domestic high courts are major actors in the contest over military legal subordination.[55] They engage the issue in a variety of ways. In their position, they hear challenges brought by civilians against the use of military courts. They rule on jurisdictional disputes between military and civilian courts. High courts also rule on whether legislation, including codes of military justice and national security laws, are compatible with the constitution and international treaty obligations. In many cases, we find high courts to be a deciding factor in military court reform and in preventing backsliding.

The power of domestic courts is usually conceptualized around judicial independence, which includes judicial autonomy and judicial influence. Judges need to be able to make their decisions without undue influence from other political actors and have their decisions in turn constrain the behavior of those actors (Ríos-Figueroa and Staton 2014). Scholars have long noted the importance of judicial independence for democratic consolidation (e.g. Linz and Stepan 1996; O'Donnell 1998). Empirical evidence indicates that judicial independence can help ensure the survival of democracy (Gibler and Randazzo 2011; Reenock, Staton, and Radean 2013) and reduce state repression and human rights violations (Keith 2002).

When it comes to issues related to security and the military, however, the relationship is less clear. It is perhaps in these situations where political jurisprudence (Shapiro 1963) is at its strongest and court behavior is driven more by political considerations than impartial judgments. The crisis jurisprudence approach contends that "judicial deference to democratic executives is amplified during war" (Epperly and Sievert 2019, 701), and some argue emphatically that courts should give the government wide latitude to use any legal means at their disposal to combat security threats (Posner and Vermeule 2007). New empirical evidence also suggests that security threats, like terrorism, reduce the confidence citizens have in the judiciary as their preferences shift to granting the executive branch more power (Miller 2017), creating a disincentive for courts to contest the expansion of military legal power. In many cases, we find domestic courts unwilling to challenge the government on these issues. In Greece, for example, until the end of the military regime in 1974, the civilian judiciary viewed its position as subservient to the state and its role as one of protecting state interests (Pollis 1987, 599–611). It consistently upheld emergency laws and the expanded use of military courts to try civilians to combat the threat of communism.

Other scholars, however, argue that this relationship is not unidirectional. Civil conflict acts as a critical juncture in which judicial independence can increase or decrease (Epperly and Sievert 2019). High courts serve as a mediator between civilian governments and the military, especially during periods of armed conflict (Ríos-Figueroa 2016). In post-authoritarian settings, domestic courts have directly challenged the government and the military, successfully overturning amnesty laws and bringing members of the military complicit in past human rights violations to trial (e.g. Skaar 2011). In sum, even in the most difficult circumstances, high courts are sometimes able to shape policy regarding the military's power.

Domestic high courts have been crucial in declaring military laws unconstitutional throughout Latin America, as we demonstrate in our discussions of the Dominican Republic (2001), Mexico (2012), and Peru (2003)—often aided by rulings from the Inter-American Court of Human Rights (IACtHR), as we discuss below. In Spain, a high court ruling was necessary to finally settle the issue of military justice where ambiguity reigned for years. During the rule of General Francisco Franco (1936–75), military courts could try members of the military for any crime and civilians for crimes against the public order (Osuna 2014, 145). As part of the transition to democracy, the leaders of all of the major political parties and the labor unions signed the Moncloa Pacts in 1977, agreeing on a broad set of political, legal, and economic reforms. Chapter 7 was specifically dedicated to reforming the military justice system (Serra 2010, 126). The new constitution signed in 1978 specifies that military courts only have jurisdiction for crimes within a military framework, but leaves the definition of that term to legislation.[56] The military courts continued to adjudicate a wide range of cases, including those involving civilians (Ballbé 1983). The government enacted four organic laws between 1985 and 1989, including a new military code of justice (Osuna 2014, 179). It was not until 1991, however, when Constitutional and Supreme Court rulings established a clear interpretation on a limited role for military courts that cases were finally adjudicated appropriately (Andreu-Guzmán 2004, 329–30).

At the same time, court decisions are not self-enforcing. They depend on governments revising legislation and changing their behavior in response. In addition, as we discuss above, militaries often refuse to cooperate with court rulings and obstruct investigations, meaning that de jure changes made by the courts are not realized in practice. In Nepal, for example, the Supreme Court has consistently supported human rights, including invalidating the military justice provisions of the Army Act 2006 and ordering the government to convene a task force to review the statute (ICJ 2013, 86). The government, however, has consistently failed to implement the court's judgments. In extreme cases, overly assertive courts can lead to backlash. In Colombia and Indonesia, as discussed in Chapters 4 and 5, governments reacted to adverse rulings by attempting to pack the courts and curtail their power.

Domestic influences: Public sentiment

Public sentiment plays an important role in setting the domestic environment in which the core actors make decisions about the military justice system. Where the military is unpopular, discredited by human rights abuses past or present, or a high-profile event provokes public outrage, government leaders find it easier or politically beneficial to challenge military privileges or roll back draconian practices. Conversely, where the public views the armed forces favorably, there is less incentive and it is more difficult for government to pursue reform. In addition, public sentiment may condition a country for backsliding when faced with large-scale problems such as terrorism and widespread violent crime that stoke fear and lead to calls to empower the military to address them. For public pressure to play a significant role in military justice reform or backsliding, it must be sufficiently widespread and intense to shift the cost-benefit calculations of those in power. We find two distinct scenarios in which popular pressure can lead to reform.

First, authoritarian regimes are sensitive to popular opinion as they seek to remain in power. Lacking genuine elections as a source of legitimacy, authoritarians attempt to bolster their right to rule through foundational myths, personal loyalties, and delivering results for key constituencies (von Soest and Grauvogel 2017). They control information and produce propaganda to craft the public view of conditions in the country (Geddes and Zaller 1989). One-party states in particular also rely on constant mobilization around a unifying ideology to co-opt the population into the political project of the regime (Corner 2009; Linz 2000). Authoritarian regimes frequently use military courts as a tool of repression, prosecuting civilian opponents and protecting security forces from accountability for human rights violations committed in the context of suppressing dissent. High levels of repression, however, particularly as it becomes more indiscriminate, can fuel popular resistance (Mason and Krane 1989), in turn threatening the regime's survival. In such scenarios, some authoritarian leaders choose to grant concessions to reduce discontent with their rule. In some cases, the opposition directly targets military courts, leading the regime to sacrifice that power to placate the opposition while holding on to other prerogatives. A prominent example is in Thailand, where student protests against martial law in 1968 forced the government to lift it in the capital of Bangkok (Prizzia 1985, 49–50).

Second, in democratic regimes, public pressure on military justice issues can lead politicians to reform the system. The expectation of responsive government is a defining feature of democratic systems. Built on inclusive participation and competition, the public is sufficiently connected to decision-making to reflect the will of the people in selecting leaders and shaping government policy (Dahl 1971). The expectation of regular elections and the public's ability to express preferences in between elections creates a system in which "political leaders will be somewhat responsive to the preferences of some ordinary citizens" (Dahl 1956, 131). At times, military justice can be an important issue for voters.

In Taiwan in 2013, for example, public outrage and mass protests following the death of Hung Chung-chiu, a 24-year-old corporal, brought swift change. As punishment for a minor infraction, he was "subjected to arduous punishment exercises in the hot sun," which induced heatstroke and organ failure. Anti-military sentiment left over from the era of martial law (1949–87) and Taiwan's system of compulsory military service made the scandal a matter of national concern (BBC News 2013).[57] Under public pressure, the government revised its military code, making soldiers subject to the Code of Criminal Procedure and abolishing the military court system (Amnesty International 2014).[58]

In Mexico, public outcry over widespread human rights abuses—and the consistent impunity for military personnel—led to reform on paper. The administration of President Felipe Calderón (2006–12) ratcheted up state violence in prosecuting the drug war when he came into office. Human rights violations committed by military personnel increased dramatically, and military courts routinely shielded soldiers from accountability. Public pressure to move cases to civilian jurisdiction resulted in a successful change in the law in 2014.[59]

There are limits, however, to the effectiveness of public pressure on reform. Despite the new law, the Mexican military resists cooperating with civilian authorities. Similarly, although the 1968 protests in Thailand achieved immediate gains, the military continues to be heavily involved in politics and resists any reform efforts that would curtail its power. As we discuss in Chapter 1, large protests over time have not been able to change the 1958 Armed Forces (Special Powers) Act in India.[60]

Moreover, public pressure can be a source of stagnation or backsliding as well. For example, Uruguay struggled for more than two decades to pursue accountability for the human rights abuses of the military dictatorship (1973–85) (Skaar 2015). The post-dictatorship administration enacted an amnesty, the Expiry Law, which prevented prosecution for past crimes.[61] Despite efforts by civil society actors to overturn it, the public voted twice in national referendums (1989 and 2009) to retain the law.

In addition, when the public demands action on current threats such as terrorism or overwhelming criminal activity, democratic governments find themselves pressured to deliver results quickly or risk their electoral standing. Combined with the fact that publics frequently hold their national armed forces in high esteem, politicians frequently turn to the military to show they are "protecting the homeland" from terrorism or being "tough on crime." For example, in the aftermath of the September 11, 2001 terrorist attacks on the United States, public opinion came to support sacrificing the protection of civil liberties for a feeling of security (Davis and Silver 2003; Huddy, Feldman, and Weber 2007). As we discuss in Chapter 7, this influenced the government's choices in how it handled captured terrorists. Terrorism also dominates the political debate in Pakistan and in turn its use of military courts, which we discuss in Chapter 6.

Fear of crime presents the same dynamic. National surveys in the Latinobarómetro, the Afrobarometer, and the World Values Survey routinely find respondents showing high levels of confidence in the military while having lower levels of confidence in the regular police and the judiciary. Such attitudes condition political leaders to valorize the military and task it with duties well beyond its conventional war-fighting role, especially policing (Pérez 2015). In Latin America, in particular, leaders across the political spectrum empower the military in this manner, suggesting sustained popular pressure, rather than the expression of one party or leader's preference, drives the use of military as police (Kyle and Reiter 2019).

Domestic influences: Civil society

In some cases, domestic civil society organizations (CSOs) are able to influence major actors' decision-making on military justice reform. As we discuss below with international NGOs, domestic NGOs, think tanks, and human rights organizations, work together to document abuses, highlight systemic problems, and advocate for change. Domestic civil society provides important indirect information to the general public and mobilizing infrastructure for large-scale reform campaigns as well as placing direct pressure on governments to act.

Politicians and governments must deal with a wide range of national challenges and day-to-day crises while time and attention is limited. CSOs have a key role in putting military reform on the agenda and working to ensure that it is not lost amidst the chaos of politics or ignored and rejected by uncooperative governments unwilling to listen. The ability of CSOs to influence politics is heavily contingent, however, on the resources at their disposal (Jenkins 1983) and the political opportunity structure in which they operate (McAdam, McCarthy, and Zald 1996).

CSOs are more likely to be effective when they have material resources such as money and office space and social resources such as organizing capacity and useful technical skills of their members, including knowledge of the bureaucracy and legal system. Moreover, as we discuss in the section on international influences on reform, domestic CSOs are most effective when they have connections to their counterparts in other countries. This gives them the ability to build and use an epistemic community to raise awareness of a domestic issue cross-nationally. These international connections enable domestic groups to find new avenues to pressure for reform when their direct ability to pressure government is closed (Keck and Sikkink 1998). Domestic-international interaction also facilitates civil society success by grounding universalistic human rights in the local context. Strong domestic civil society can carry international human rights norms and advocate change while pushing back against claims of human rights as unwelcome foreign influence (Hafner-Burton 2013, 151–59). Finally, domestic CSOs utilize the international commitments of their own governments, especially ratification of human rights treaties, to press those governments for reform and to monitor compliance (Hafner-Burton and Tsutsui 2005; Simmons 2012).

Even well-resourced and internationally-connected CSOs, however, are limited by the political opportunity structure around them. They are likely to be more effective in established democratic systems where there are multiple points of access to the political system. Nevertheless, the nature of military justice reform in particular, and security sector reform in general, makes CSO efforts often at their most essential in unfavorable political environments, including post-authoritarian states where the military or other security forces remain politically powerful (Neild 2012). For example, human rights organizations in Burkina Faso have consistently protested the military's behavior in its fight against Islamic militants, including documenting its execution of as many as 60 people in front of their families in 2019 (Reuters 2019). Military courts retain jurisdiction over military operations and there is little expectation of accountability. It is thus not surprising that we find civil society, while active in most cases where abuses are occurring, is only instrumental in bringing about change to military justice in exceptional cases where the right conditions exist.

For example, in the Dominican Republic, where the military and police retained their legal powers long after democratization in 1978, human rights violations committed in internal security operations mounted with little accountability. In 2000, a coalition of six civil society groups submitted an "Act of Unconstitutionality" to the Supreme Court on the legality of using separate security courts for human rights violations (USDS 2001). The Supreme Court ruled that in peacetime civilian courts should be used. In 2002, the legislature passed a new criminal code that explicitly removed cases of human rights violations from military and police courts to civilian courts.[62] Though it was not until a 2010 constitutional reform that full compliance occurred, the efforts of CSOs were crucial in launching the process of change.[63]

Similarly, in South Korea, civil society played a role in pushing for further reforms after democratization. From 1972 to early 1981, the country was in a state of martial law, during which military courts tried civilians. With the beginning of the Fifth Republic (1981–87) under Chun Doo-hwan, the government lifted martial law and spearheaded major reforms that eventually transitioned South Korea to democracy in 1988. Since the end of martial law, military courts have not tried civilians, but they retain broad jurisdiction over military personnel. In response to human rights violations committed by members of the military that go unpunished, CSOs have pressured the government to reform, successfully initiating a process to integrate the military justice system with the regular civilian judiciary (Korea Herald 2018).

In addition to pressing for reform, domestic civil society can be an important source of resistance against the military or its allies in government attempting to gain more legal power. In Peru, for example, vigilant civil society actors helped to keep civilian legal options against the military viable in the aftermath of the Alberto Fujimori regime (1990–2000). In the context of rulings by the Constitutional Tribunal, a very public battle between the government and the Inter-American Court of Human Rights, and lack of military cooperation with civilian legal authorities, the government issued Decree 1097, which set a statute of limitations for crimes committed by the military during the civil war.[64] This would have facilitated the military continuing to obstruct and delay cases until they would be closed, thereby preventing convictions. Strong opposition from international and domestic human rights organizations, however, forced the legislature to repeal the measure (Freedom House 2010; Washington Office on Latin America 2010).

In sum, domestic civil society influences the decision-making of the core actors. Domestic CSOs are a valuable expression of human rights pressure for reform as well as a restraint against backsliding. Civil society is most effective in advocating for military justice reform when it is able to connect with international actors.

International influences: Human rights courts

International human rights courts (IHRCs) represent one type of external influence on military legal subordination. The IACtHR and, to a lesser extent, the European Court of Human Rights (ECtHR) have been active in many debates around military justice reform. By ruling on cases related to military court behavior, these courts exert pressure on states to reform.

The ability of IHRCs to effect change, however, is heavily dependent on domestic political and legal conditions (Hillebrecht 2014). While all international courts are "implementer-dependent" institutions (Hall 2011) that require domestic actors to carry out their judgments, compliance with IHRCs is particularly difficult. An IHRC ruling is a case of second-order compliance (Fisher 1981) after the state has already failed to comply with its human rights treaty obligations (Simmons 1998, 78) and where those actors required to implement reform may be the ones responsible for the human rights violations identified in the case. The right conditions must exist for IHRC rulings to create meaningful reform on issues like military legal subordination.

In particular, the independence, strength, and position of domestic courts are crucial. IHRCs have more success in bringing about change when the executive can adopt policies that address the issue, but that is highly dependent on whether the executive expects the domestic judiciary to implement court orders (Haglund 2020). Domestic judges are even more likely than presidents and legislatures to shirk the court's rulings (Huneeus 2011). IHRCs thus need domestic courts to serve as "compliance partners" in implementing their rulings, but in recent years they have increasingly come to view themselves as "gatekeepers" instead, limiting the power of IHRCs (Kunz 2020). On the issue of military justice, domestic courts have a mixed record of partnering with IHRCs, and other political factors have further limited their ability to effect reform.

The greatest influence of IHRCs on military justice has been in Latin America through the IACtHR. Established by the Organization of American States in 1979, the court has a strong history, aided early on by partnering with domestic courts in the region to overturn amnesty laws put in place to protect those involved in human rights violations in prior authoritarian regimes. It has engaged the issue of military court jurisdiction throughout its history and has been a significant factor in reform attempts in several countries. At the same time, other countries have ignored or overtly contested judgments in this area, and even successful reforms on paper have often not materialized in practice. This is part of a growing feeling in the region that the court has become too intrusive in domestic politics. Governments have withdrawn or threatened to do so, and domestic judicial pushback has grown (Contesse 2019).

In addition to Colombia, which we discuss in detail in Chapter 4, the most successful efforts came in Argentina, where the prospect of a case was sufficient to spur reform. In 2004, the Inter-American Commission of Human Rights ruled that a petition challenging the use of military courts in Argentina was admissible and that it planned to refer the case to the IACtHR. Rather than leading to a trial, this led to a friendly settlement whereby Argentina promised to reform its military justice system.[65] The Ministry of Defense created a commission to study the issue and in 2008 congress enacted a new code of military justice, which replaced the 1951 version and removed all non-disciplinary crimes from the military justice system.[66] It came into force on February 27, 2009, shifting the country from jurisdictional contestation to full subordination. This success, however, was contingent on larger political developments in the country. Néstor Kirchner assumed the presidency in 2003 and actively pushed for military reform, but he engaged in a bargain with the military that expanded its budget and upgraded its equipment to ensure its loyalty (Kyle and Reiter 2013, 398). This facilitated the military's acquiescence to eroding its legal prerogatives.

In Chile and Peru, the IACtHR was able to help domestic actors remove civilians from the jurisdiction of military courts, but full subordination remained unreachable. In 2005, the court, in *Palamara Iribarne* v. *Chile*, ordered the government to revise its legislation to restrict the jurisdiction of military courts to active members of the military for military crimes.[67] Eventually, in December 2010, the Chilean government passed legislation to amend the military justice system to eliminate their jurisdiction over civilians and over all cases involving minors.[68] The military, however, has continued to resist additional reform and the country remains in the jurisdictional contestation category (HRW 2017a).

The IACtHR ruled against Peru's use of military courts in several high-profile cases in the early 2000s.[69] This occurred during a period in which domestic courts were actively rolling back the military's legal prerogatives following the end of Alberto Fujimori's authoritarian regime (1990–2000). From 2002 to 2009, the Peruvian Constitutional Tribunal struck down much of Fujimori's anti-terrorism legislation and reduced the power of military courts significantly, including removing their ability to try civilians (González-Ocantos 2016, 159; Ríos-Figueroa 2016, 105–15).[70] Reform stalled, however, and the military resisted efforts to reduce the jurisdiction of military courts over its members, openly contesting or failing to comply with rulings, and ultimately deciding to wage a "silent but steady legal battle" (Ríos-Figueroa 2016, 110).

In *Radilla-Pacheco* v. *Mexico* (2009), the IACtHR examined a 1974 case of a disappearance committed by the military.[71] In its judgment, the court ordered Mexico to reform its military code of justice to ensure the transfer of such cases to civilian courts. The court reiterated this obligation in subsequent cases over the next year. The Mexican Supreme Court ordered a review of the *Radilla-Pacheco* case and in 2011 voted to support the ruling and ordered all judges to comply.[72] In a 2012 *amparo* review, the Supreme Court declared parts of Article 57 of the Military Code of Justice unconstitutional.[73] Congress subsequently reformed the code in 2014, shifting all cases involving human rights violations committed against civilians to civilian courts.[74] The military, however, continues to obstruct investigations by tampering with crime scenes, limiting access to its members for interviews, and providing false testimony (Suárez-Enríquez 2017). Impunity remains high.

Finally, demonstrating the importance of domestic allies, the IACtHR has failed to have any meaningful effect in cases where local reform efforts are not present. In 1996, the court found Venezuela's Code of Military Justice incompatible with the Inter-American Convention on Human Rights.[75] The court ruled against Venezuela on this issue again in 2006 and 2009.[76] Military courts continued to shield their own forces from accountability and to prosecute civilians, and they are taking on an even more prominent role in President Nicolás Maduro's (2013–present) crackdown on opposition to his rule (Casey 2017; Rueda and Viana 2017). Brazil has also rejected the court's rulings on its human rights issues (Rosenn 2014, 331).[77]

While the primary impact of international courts has been in Latin America, the ECtHR has also played a role in bringing about military justice reform, albeit a minimal one due to the fact that most of the parties to the European Convention on Human Rights have long maintained full subordination systems. Most of the court's jurisprudence on military justice has been related to reforming the structure and procedures of military courts within that category. The United Kingdom, for example, has reformed its military justice system numerous times following a succession of ECtHR rulings against it beginning in the late 1990s (Kosař 2017, 116–17).[78]

In two instances, however, the court had a direct impact on reform across categories. Belgium's military justice system, which was firmly in the jurisdictional contestation category since its establishment in 1831, was found to be incompatible with the European Convention on Human Rights (Lambert Abdelgawad 2007, 128), and a new law subsequently abolished military courts in times of peace in 2004.[79] In Turkey, military courts were first formally recognized in the 1961 constitution and established by the 1963 Military Criminal Procedure Law.[80] They had broad jurisdiction over members of the military and civilians. A series of ECtHR rulings against Turkey beginning in the late 1990s forced the country to eliminate its State Security Courts.[81] In 2003, spurred by a case before the court, the government ended military court jurisdiction over civilians (Greer 2013, 347–49).[82] A series of constitutional reforms in 2010 restricted military courts to military crimes by members of the military, and in 2017, further amendments to the constitution abolished military courts completely.[83]

Beyond Latin America and Europe, the only notable case of international court rulings effecting change is the International Criminal Court's (ICC) investigation into genocide, war crimes, and crimes against humanity committed in

Sudan's Darfur region, which triggered a brief period of reform in the country from military overreach to jurisdictional contestation.[84] The United Nations Security Council's referral of the case to the court in 2005 was part of a broader international campaign against Sudan, with many states, NGOs, and IOs united against Sudan's commission of genocide (Grono 2006). Sudan stopped trying civilians in military courts in 2003 (USDS 2004) and in response to the ICC's indictments enacted the 2007 Armed Forces Act, which reinforced this position and went out of its way to incorporate international law (Nouwen 2013, 284–87).[85] The reform was short-lived, however, with the National Assembly amending the act in 2013, granting military courts jurisdiction over civilians suspected to be members of rebel or paramilitary groups (HRW 2013; Radio Dabanga 2013). The failure to bring reform in Sudan is not surprising given the lack of meaningful engagement between the government and what it considers to be "just another international political instrument that Western powers in the Security Council use selectively to topple regimes of which they do not approve" (Nouwen 2013, 308).

Overall, international court rulings are an important external influence on the fight for military legal subordination. They serve as a catalyst for domestic action. They put direct pressure on governments to implement new policies or enact new legislation. Where a government resists international court rulings, they still provide indirect pressure for reform by establishing jurisprudence that domestic courts can use in their own rulings and that domestic civil society actors can use as a mobilizing tool to pursue change.

International influences: Human rights NGOs, IOs, and external states

As we discuss in Chapter 2, military justice is intrinsically linked to human rights. Military justice systems can be used to perpetuate a culture of impunity for human rights violations or even used as a tool of repression against the civilian population. Consequently, international human rights NGOs, IOs, and external states apply direct and indirect pressure on countries to reform their laws and practices.

International actors primarily pressure domestic actors on human rights issues through what Keck and Sikkink (1998) describe as a "boomerang model." Domestic actors who are unable to effect change themselves raise awareness about an issue and reach out to international NGOs, IOs, and external states in what coalesces into a transnational advocacy network. Those international actors in turn pressure the government to improve its human rights practices, principally through information politics and "naming and shaming" (Franklin 2015). Prominent NGOs and the UN in particular produce regular reports and condemn state behavior (DeMeritt and Conrad 2019; Ron, Ramos, and Rogers 2005).

The evidence of the effectiveness of international human rights advocacy is mixed. Some studies have found that advocacy can improve human rights practices (Murdie 2014) and reduce violence (DeMeritt 2012). Others, however, have found that effects are heavily contingent on other conditions, such as the strength of domestic human rights NGOs (Murdie and Davis 2010). Still others have found a negative effect, with advocacy causing a backlash and an increase in some types of repression (Hafner-Burton 2008, 705–13).

While military justice is under-examined compared to other human rights issues, reporting is prominent in some cases. Coverage is greater of systems of military overreach in which civilians are frequently being tried. In addition, where the military is committing high levels of human rights violations with impunity, due to protections from their own court systems, international actors take notice. The practice of military justice around the world is well documented by many organizations.

Human Rights Watch (HRW) and Amnesty International are the foremost global human rights organizations and note abuses of military justice in their annual reports as well as their coverage of individual countries. HRW in particular focuses on this issue and, in recent years, has come out strongly against the use of military courts in Lebanon (HRW 2017b), Tunisia (HRW 2018), and Israel (HRW 2019), among others. Military justice is also a point of emphasis of the International Commission of Jurists, which has focused its efforts in recent years on exposing abuses in military justice systems in Pakistan (ICJ 2019a) and Thailand (ICJ 2019b), among others. Its most recent global report on the topic presented in-depth case studies on Brazil, Guinea, Mexico, Portugal, Tunisia, and Venezuela (Andreu-Guzmán 2018).

Among IOs the UN has long articulated a position that full subordination is the only type of military justice system compatible with international law and necessary for the protection of human rights and democracy. This began with a major report in 2002 (Joinet 2002), the creation of draft principles in 2006 (United Nations Commission on Human Rights 2006), and a set of recommendations combined with a state questionnaire in 2013 (United Nations Office for the High Commissioner for Human Rights 2013). Reports on human rights and the rule of law in individual countries by various offices within the UN also incorporate assessments of military justice.

While we do not find any cases of governments making changes to their military justice systems as a direct result of international reporting, the presence of such information represents an important condition in which government decision-making occurs. We rarely see reform when abuses are not known to the general public. These organizations thus play an important role in providing information, exposing abuses, and amplifying the voices of domestic actors.

The ultimate goal of international human rights activists is to spur direct action by states and international organizations against the target state. These efforts may include restrictions on trade and foreign direct investment, economic sanctions, and, in extreme cases, even military or humanitarian intervention. Here again, the evidence of effectiveness is mixed. Most studies of economic sanctions, even targeted ones, have found that they increase repression rather than reduce it (Peksen 2009; Wood 2008). Humanitarian and peacekeeping interventions may stop killing and prevent the recurrence of war, but they may actually have a negative effect on human rights conditions going forward (Peksen 2012). We find very little evidence that direct international action significantly influences military justice, other than cases of direct foreign imposition by external actors as we discuss earlier in the chapter.[86] In a similar scenario, in Timor-Leste the UN helped transform the guerrilla army into a new state military, accompanied by a military justice system in the full subordination category (International Crisis Group 2008, 10; McClelland 2002). The UN also had a role in shaping militaries as part of its heavy involvement in the successful peace negotiations to end the Central American wars in the early 1990s, particularly El Salvador (Karl 1992). The country shifted from military overreach to full subordination with a constitutional amendment negotiated during the peace process.[87]

Other IOs have influenced military justice in more bureaucratic ways. The Council of Europe's European Commission for Democracy through Law (the Venice Commission), for example, has worked closely with many countries to improve their constitutions and judicial systems. In some cases, military justice reform has been a part of those processes. In Ukraine, for example, military justice was a specialized component of the regular civilian justice system from 1993 to 2010 (Vashakmadze 2018, 1), until a judicial reform package in 2010 abolished military courts entirely.[88]

Overall, international human rights NGOs, IOs, and external states play an important role in raising awareness about the issue of military justice. They enhance understandings of military court systems and draw attention to specific abuses. While they cannot effect change on their own, they provide valuable information to reform-minded actors in the domestic political arena.

Conclusion

The politics of military justice in the modern world is poorly understood, suffering from the lack of systematic research across cases and time. Using our new dataset, we set out in this chapter to present a clear picture of how states established military justice systems, identifying several key patterns in adoption. The nature of the origin of a system has a considerable impact on the trajectory of military justice in many cases. In our process of theory-building, we use evidence drawn from the dataset to develop a model explaining change over time. We articulate a set of principal actors and domestic and international influences that we argue shape military justice. In the following chapters, we apply our model to seven case studies to illustrate the relative importance of each factor and how the interactions between them play out. We first identify the nature of the establishment of military justice in each and then apply our model of change to explain reform and backsliding (or system continuity) over time. In Chapter 4, we present Portugal and Colombia as cases that reached the full subordination category immediately at a critical juncture and incrementally due to shifts in the influences and principal actors over time, respectively. Chapter 5 analyzes Indonesia and Fiji, both of which are mired in the jurisdictional contestation category. Indonesia is an example of stalled reform, while Fiji is an example of backsliding. We discuss Brazil and Pakistan in Chapter 6 to highlight the military overreach category. Brazil is a case of persistent overreach, having never successfully reformed. Pakistan is emblematic of countries that ebb and flow between jurisdictional contestation and military overreach. Finally, in Chapter 7, we present the United States, which has consistently been in the full subordination category since its founding, with the exception of several years punctuated by internal and external threats in which the system temporarily shifted to the military overreach category.

Notes

1 Regeringsform 1809, Article 20, https://sv.wikisource.org/wiki/Regeringsform_1809. Sweden's Constitution of 1974 with Amendments through 2012, https://www.constituteproject.org/constitution/Sweden_2012.pdf?lang=en.
2 Brottsbalk (1962: 700), 1962-12-21, http://rkrattsbaser.gov.se/sfst?bet=1962:700.
3 The constitution did allow for the King to appoint two military officers to join the High Court of Justice for cases of court martial "concerning either life or honour or the loss of freedom for more than three months." See the Constitution of the Kingdom of Norway of 1814, Article 90, https://en.wikisource.org/wiki/Constitution_of_Norway_(Unamended). This was repealed in 1996 (Andreu-Guzmán 2004, 295).
4 Loi du 16 février 1881 sur l'organisation de la force armée, http://legilux.public.lu/eli/etat/leg/loi/1881/02/16/n1/jo.
5 Law of 28 June 1889.
6 By 1768, Spain would enter the military overreach category when the Army Ordinances granted military courts jurisdiction over civilians for many crimes, including "insulting a member of the military" (Andreu-Guzmán 2004, 321).
7 Alvará de Lei, July 15, 1763, O Governo dos Outros, Imaginários Políticos no Império Portugês (1496-1961), http://www.governodosoutros.ics.ul.pt/index.php?menu=consulta&id_partes=115&accao=ver&pagina=300.
8 Portugal regressed into military overreach in 1895 when the government empowered councils of war to try civilians for crimes against national security (Andreu-Guzmán 2018, 145).
9 Law of July 10, 1791.
10 *The Petition of Right*, 1628, https://www.legislation.gov.uk/aep/Cha1/3/1/data.pdf.
11 *Naval Discipline Act 1866*, 28 & 29 Vict, c 109, https://www.pdavis.nl/NDA1866.htm; *Army Act 1881*, 44 & 45 Vict, c 58.
12 *Defence Force Discipline Act 1982*, No. 152, 1982, Part VII, https://www.legislation.gov.au/Details/C2016C00811.
13 Australia's Constitution of 1901 with Amendments through 1985, Article 51(vi), https://www.constituteproject.org/constitution/Australia_1985?lang=en.
14 *The Military Penal Code and Procedure of 1964* (Law 40/1964), http://www.cylaw.org/nomoi/indexes/1964_1_40.html.
15 *1964 Defence Act*, http://www.parliament.gov.zm/sites/default/files/documents/acts/Defence%20Act.pdf.
16 *Armed Forces Discipline Act 1971*, Public Act 1971 No 53, 12 November 1971, http://legislation.govt.nz/act/public/1971/0053/52.0/DLM401063.html.
17 *Armed Forces Act 1972* [Act 77], as at 15 June 2016, http://www.agc.gov.my/agcportal/uploads/files/Publications/LOM/EN/Armed%20Forces%20Act%201972%20%20second%20draft%20as%20at%2011%206%202016.pdf.

18 *Internal Security Act 1960* [Act 82], http://www.agc.gov.my/agcportal/uploads/files/Publications/LOM/MY/Act%2082%20(repealed).pdf; *Security Offences (Special Measures) Act 2012* [Act 747], http://www.agc.gov.my/agcportal/uploads/files/Publications/LOM/EN/Act%20747%20-%20Security%20Offences%20(Special%20Measures)%20Act%202012.pdf.

19 Act 13 of 1977, *Botswana Defence Force Act*, Chapter 21:05, Article 66, http://www.elaws.gov.bw/law.php?id=900.

20 Act 7 of 1962, *Defence Act*, Chapter 14:01, https://rgd.legalaffairs.gov.tt/laws2/Alphabetical_List/lawspdfs/14.01.pdf.

21 The Islamic State (IS) is also known as the Islamic State of Iraq and the Levant (ISIL), the Islamic State of Iraq and Syria (ISIS), and Daesh.

22 For example, see "Soldiers to face Court-Martial for alleged assault of civilians during the 2011 State of Emergency," December 3, 2013, Ministry of Communications, Government of the Republic of Trinidad and Tobago, http://www.news.gov.tt/content/soldiers-face-court-martial-alleged-assault-civilians-during-2011-state-emergency#.XTnbCehKjIV.

23 *Códigos Militares para el Ejército y Armada de la República Argentina*, Febrero 28 de 1895, http://www.bibliotecadigital.gob.ar/files/original/13/1102/edicion-oficial_codigos-militares-ejercito-armada-republica-argentina_1895.1.pdf.

24 Ley de 24 de Noviembre de 1904, *Códigos de Organización.—Militar, de Procedimientos y Penal*, http://www.gacetaoficialdebolivia.gob.bo/normas/buscarg/codigo%20militar.

25 Ley de 3 de Octubre de 1910, *Fuero Militar.—Queda Abolido en la República*, http://www.gacetaoficialdebolivia.gob.bo/normas/buscarg/fuero%20militar.

26 *Bases de Organización Política de la República de Mexico*, 1843, http://www.ordenjuridico.gob.mx/Constitucion/1843.pdf.

27 *Ordenanza Militar y Código Penal y de Procedimientos de la República del Paraguay 1887*, https://babel.hathitrust.org/cgi/pt?id=hvd.32044061555272&view=1up&seq=7.

28 Acta N.º 63, 10 de Marzo de 1831.

29 Ordinance No. 021/PRG/88.

30 Ordinance No. 71-28 (April 22, 1971).

31 As we outline in Chapter 2, we examine only countries that Polity5 codes as at least a partial democracy in at least one year from 1974 to 2017. Therefore, we exclude Bosnia and Herzegovina, Kazakhstan, Tajikistan, Turkmenistan, and Uzbekistan. Serbia and Montenegro experienced significant conflict and instability in the decade following the breakup of Yugoslavia. We exclude it from our analysis here, but we examine military justice systems in the separate countries of Serbia and Montenegro after they split in 2006. Kosovo is not a part of our study either given the significant role the international community has played in governing the country since its independence in 2008.

32 Article 82, Latvia's Constitution of 1922, Reinstated in 1991, with Amendments through 2016, https://www.constituteproject.org/constitution/Latvia_2016.pdf?lang=en.

33 *Law on Judicial Power*, http://www.vvc.gov.lv/export/sites/default/docs/LRTA/Likumi/Judicial_Power.pdf; *Law on Military Courts*, https://likumi.lv/doc.php?id=104829.

34 Republic of Moldova, *Decision No. 1150* (August 4, 1992). http://lex.justice.md/viewdoc.php?action=view&view=doc&id=306458&lang=1.

35 Constitution of the Republic of Georgia 1995 with Amendments through 2018, https://www.constituteproject.org/constitution/Georgia_2018.pdf?lang=en.

36 Organic Law of Georgia on Common Courts, Law No. 767-IIs, June 13, 1997, https://www.refworld.org/cgi-bin/texis/vtx/rwmain/opendocpdf.pdf?reldoc=y&docid=548f0a9c4.

37 The World Bank, "Judicial Modernization Project (JMP) for Azerbaijan," http://projects.worldbank.org/P099201/judicial-modernization-project?lang=en&tab=overview.

38 "On improving the judicial system of the Republic of Belarus," Decree of the President of the Republic of Belarus No. 6, November 20, 2013, http://www.pravo.by/document/?guid=3871&p0=Pd1300006&p1=1.

39 Federal Constitutional Law of 23.06.1999 N 1-FKZ (as amended on 27.12.2019) "On the military courts of the Russian Federation," http://www.consultant.ru/document/cons_doc_LAW_23479/adea892fc593c4cb48072c783c15c861eb269a33/.

40 Article 126, Constitution of Slovenia 1991, https://www.constituteproject.org/constitution/Slovenia_2016?lang=en.

41 United Nations Peacekeeping, "North Macedonia: Fact Sheet," April 25, 2019, https://peacekeeping.un.org/sites/default/files/north-macedonia-factsheet_20190425.pdf.

42 Article 96, paragraph 2, Basic Law for the Federal Republic of Germany, 23 May 1949, last amended on 13 July 2017, https://www.btg-bestellservice.de/pdf/80201000.pdf.

43 Permanent Mission of Germany to the United Nations, "Response to Questionnaire on Military Justice," Office of the United Nations High Commissioner for Human Rights, https://www.ohchr.org/Documents/Issues/IJudiciary/MilitaryCourts/Germany.doc.

44 The Constitution of Japan, https://japan.kantei.go.jp/constitution_and_government_of_japan/constitution_e.html.

45 The National Police Reserve, created in 1950, was a forerunner to the GSDF, see French 2014.

46 Constitución Política de la República de Panamá de 1972 reformada por los actos reformatorios de 1978, por el acto constituciónal de 1983 y los actos legislativos 1 de 1983 y 2 de 1994, https://pdba.georgetown.edu/Constitutions/Panama/panama1994.html.

47 The forces were under the Ministry of Government and Justice until 2010 when it was transformed into the Ministry of Public Security. Information on the organization of the Ministry of Public Security can be found here: https://www.minseg.gob.pa/.

48 POLITY5 defines a major democratic transition as "six points or greater increase in POLITY score over a period of three years or less including a shift from an autocratic POLITY value (–10 to 0) to a partial democratic POLITY value (+1 to +6) or full democratic POLITY value (+7 to +10) or a shift from a partial democratic value to a full democratic value." We also include new states that transitioned to a democracy from an authoritarian predecessor state.

49 Constitution of the Federal Republic of Nigeria 1999, https://www.wipo.int/edocs/lexdocs/laws/en/ng/ng014en.pdf.

50 Modificaciones al Código de Justicia Militar, Ley No. 23.049, February 9, 1984, http://servicios.infoleg.gob.ar/infolegInternet/anexos/25000-29999/28157/norma.htm.

51 Turkey's Constitution of 1982 with Amendments through 2017, Article 142, https://www.constituteproject.org/constitution/Turkey_2017?lang=en.

52 Ecuador's Constitution of 2008 with Amendments through 2015, Article 188, https://www.constituteproject.org/constitution/Ecuador_2015?lang=en.

53 Common Statute of Civil Servants of the Kingdom of Cambodia, NS-RKM-1094-006, October 26, 1994, https://www.ilo.org/dyn/natlex/docs/ELECTRONIC/63405/61076/F1970123888/KHM63405.pdf.

54 In 1999, the National Assembly amended Article 51, but there was no substantive change to its application, see Chandara and Meixner 1999.

55 The names of high courts vary by country, with supreme and constitutional courts being the most common.

56 Article 117.5, Spain's Constitution of 1978 with Amendments through 2011, https://www.constituteproject.org/constitution/Spain_2011?lang=en.

57 The Temporary Provisions Effective During the Period of National Mobilization for Suppression of the Communist Rebellion, 1948, https://www.eapasi.com/uploads/5/5/8/6/55860615/appendix_8_%E2%80%93_temporary_provisions_effective_during_the_period_of_the_communist_rebellion.pdf.
58 Taiwan Code of Criminal Procedure, January 15, 2020, https://law.moj.gov.tw/ENG/LawClass/LawAll.aspx?pcode=C0010001.
59 Estados Unidos Mexicanos, June 21, 2018, Código de Justicia Militar, http://www.diputados.gob.mx/LeyesBiblio/pdf/4_210618.pdf.
60 *Armed Forces (Special Powers) Act, 1958* (Act No. 28 of 1958) [11th September, 1958], http://legislative.gov.in/sites/default/files/A1958-28.pdf. The AFSPA has its origins in the 1942 Lord Linlithgow ordinance used by the British to suppress the 1942 Quit India Movement.
61 Funcionarios Militares y Policiales Se Reconoce Que Ha Caducado El Ejercicio De La Pretension Punitiva del Estado Respecto de Los Delitos Cometidos Hasta El 1 de Marzo de 1985, Ley N° 15.848 de 22 diciembre de 1986, https://legislativo.parlamento.gub.uy/temporales/leytemp5691949.htm.
62 Código Procesal Penal de la República Dominicana, Ley No. 76-02, July 19, 2002, https://docs.republica-dominicana.justia.com/nacionales/leyes/ley-76-02.pdf. The new law came into effect on September 27, 2004.
63 Article 252, Dominican Republic's Constitution of 2010, http://pdba.georgetown.edu/Constitutions/DomRep/vigente.html.
64 Decreto Legislativo N° 1097, September 1, 2010, http://www2.congreso.gob.pe/sicr/cendocbib/con2_uibd.nsf/B21025900B6DB3ED05257B6D006740E9/$FILE/DECR_LEGISLATIVO_1097.pdf.
65 Report No. 15/10, Petition 11.758, Rodolfo Correa Belisle, http://www.cidh.oas.org/annualrep/2010eng/ARSA11758EN.DOC.
66 *Código de Justicia Militar*, Ley 26.394, Agosto 26 de 2008, http://servicios.infoleg.gob.ar/infolegInternet/anexos/140000-144999/143873/norma.htm.
67 *Palamara Iribarne* v. *Chile*, Inter-Am. Ct. H.R. (ser. C). 135, (November 22, 2005), http://www.corteidh.or.cr/docs/casos/articulos/seriec_135_esp.pdf.
68 Ley no. 20.477, Modifica Competencia de Tribunales Militare, 30 diciembre 2010, https://www.leychile.cl/Navegar?idNorma=1021613.
69 The two most prominent rulings were: *Barrios Altos* v. *Peru*, Reparations and Costs, Inter-Am. Ct. H.R. (ser. C) No. 87 (November 30, 2001), http://www.corteidh.or.cr/docs/casos/articulos/Seriec_87_esp.pdf; *La Cantuta* v. *Peru*, Merits, Reparations and Costs, Inter-Am. Ct. H.R. (ser. C) No. 162 (November 29, 2006), http://www.corteidh.or.cr/docs/casos/articulos/seriec_162_esp.pdf.
70 *Marcelino Tineo Silva y Más de 5,000 Ciudadanos*, Tribunal Constitucional, EXP. N.° 010-2002-AIITC, 3 de enero de 2003, https://tc.gob.pe/jurisprudencia/2003/00010-2002-AI.pdf.
71 *Radilla Pacheco* v. *Mexico*, Preliminary Exceptions, Merits, Reparations and Costs, Inter-Am. Ct. H.R. (ser. C) No. 209 (November 23, 2009), http://www.corteidh.or.cr/docs/casos/articulos/seriec_209_esp.pdf.
72 *Expediente Varios* 912/2010 (Sup. Ct. Mex. [SCJN] 4 de octubre de 2011), http://dof.gob.mx/nota_detalle.php?codigo=5212527&fecha=04/10/2011.
73 Amparo Review No. 133/2012 (Sup. Ct. Mex. [SCJN] 21 de agosto de 2012), https://www2.scjn.gob.mx/AsuntosRelevantes/pagina/SeguimientoAsuntosRelevantesPub.aspx?Id=136182&SeguimientoId=478. A writ of *amparo* is a guarantee of individual rights. For a history of the *amparo*, see Zamudio 1979.
74 "Decreto por el que se reforman, derogan y adicionan diversas disposiciones del Código de Justicia Militar, del Código Federal de Procedimientos Penales y de la Ley que Establece las Normas Mínimas sobre Readaptación Social de Sentenciados," Diario Oficial de la Federación 13/06/2014, http://www.dof.gob.mx/nota_detalle.php?codigo=5348649&fecha=13/06/2014.

75 *El Amparo* v. *Venezuela*, Reparations and Costs, Inter-Am. Ct. H.R. (ser. C) No. 28 (September 14, 1996), http://www.corteidh.or.cr/docs/casos/articulos/seriec_28_ing.pdf.

76 *Montero-Aranguren et al (Detention Center of Catia)* v. *Venezuela*, Preliminary Objection, Merits, Reparations and Costs, Inter-Am. Ct. H.R. (ser. C) No. 150 (July 5, 2006), http://www.corteidh.or.cr/docs/casos/articulos/seriec_150_ing.pdf; *Usón Ramírez* v. *Venezuela*, Preliminary Objections, Merits, Reparations, and Costs, Inter-Am. Ct. H.R. (ser. C) No. 207 (November 20, 2008), http://www.corteidh.or.cr/docs/casos/articulos/seriec_207_ing.pdf.

77 *Gomes Lund et al. ("Guerrilha do Araguaia")* v. *Brazil*, Preliminary Objections, Merits, Reparations, and Costs, Inter-Am. Ct. H.R. (ser. C) No. 219 (November 24, 2010), http://www.corteidh.or.cr/docs/casos/articulos/seriec_219_ing.pdf.

78 Most notably, *Findlay* v. *United Kingdom*, European Court of Human Rights, Application no. 22107/93, Judgment of 25 February 1997, http://hudoc.echr.coe.int/eng?i=001-58016.

79 10 AVRIL 2003.—Loi 10 avril 2003, réglant la suppression des juridictions militaires en temps de paix ainsi que leur maintien en temps de guerre, 2003-05-07, 2003009370, http://www.ejustice.just.fgov.be/cgi/article_body.pl?language=fr&caller=summary&pub_date=03-05-07&numac=2003009370.

80 Constitution of the Turkish Republic, 1961, http://www.anayasa.gen.tr/1961constitution-text.pdf; Turkey: Law No. 353 of 1963 on Establishment of Military Courts and Tribunal Procedure, https://www.refworld.org/docid/3ae6b4d12c.html.

81 Most notably *Incal* v. *Turkey*, European Court of Human Rights, Application no. 22678/93, Judgment of 9 June 1998, http://hudoc.echr.coe.int/eng?i=001-58197.

82 *Ergin* v. *Turkey* (No. 6), European Court of Human Rights, Application no. 47533/99, Judgment of 4 May 2006, http://hudoc.echr.coe.int/eng?i=001-75327.

83 Turkey's Constitution of 1982 with Amendments through 2017, Article 142, https://www.constituteproject.org/constitution/Turkey_2017?lang=en.

84 For more details on the ICC's case against Sudan, see: https://www.icc-cpi.int/darfur.

85 *Armed Forces Act, 2007*, https://www.refworld.org/pdfid/4c037f1d2.pdf.

86 The impact of states on military justice is not always unidirectional. The United States, for example, has rewarded countries for enacting stronger anti-terrorism legislation in recent years (Whitaker 2007), providing an environment in which turning to military courts is perhaps more acceptable.

87 Mexico Agreement, April 27, 1991, https://peacemaker.un.org/sites/peacemaker.un.org/files/SV_910427_MexicoAgreement.pdf. The constitutional amendment was officially made with Article 7 of Decree No. 152, January 30, 1992. See Article 216, El Salvador's Constitution of 1983 with Amendments through 2014, https://www.constituteproject.org/constitution/El_Salvador_2014?lang=en.

88 Verkhovna Rada of Ukraine, Law No. 2453-VI, "On the Judicial System and Status of Judges," July 7, 2010, https://zakon.rada.gov.ua/laws/show/en/2453-17/ed20100707. The Venice Commission commented on draft versions, see: https://www.venice.coe.int/webforms/documents/default.aspx?country=47&year=all&other=true.

References

Adhoc, Licadho, and Human Rights Watch. 1999. "Impunity in Cambodia: How Human Rights Offenders Escape Justice." https://www.hrw.org/reports/1999/cambo2/.

Albritton, Robert B. 2005. "Thailand in 2004: The 'Crisis in the South.'" *Asian Survey* 45 (1): 166–73.

Amnesty International. 1999. "Kingdom of Cambodia: No Solution to Impunity: The Case of Ta Mok." ASA/23/05/99. https://www.amnesty.org/en/documents/ASA23/005/1999/en/.

Amnesty International. 2014. "Taiwan Government Must Ensure the Reform of Military Criminal Procedure Legislation Lives Up to Its Promise of Greater Accountability." ASA 38/001/2014. January 13. https://www.amnesty.org/en/documents/asa38/001/2014/en/.

Andreu-Guzmán, Federico. 2004. *Military Courts and Gross Human Rights Violations. Vol. 1. of Military Jurisdiction and International Law*. Geneva: International Commission of Jurists. https://www.icj.org/military-jurisdiction-and-international-law-military-courts-and-gross-human-rights-violations-vol-1/.

Andreu-Guzmán, Federico. 2018. *Fuero militar y Derecho internacional: Los civiles ante los tribunales militares. Vol 2. of Military Jurisdiction and International Law*. Geneva: International Commission of Jurists. https://www.icj.org/wp-content/uploads/2018/05/Universal-Tribunales-Militares-Vol-II-Publications-Reports-Thematic-reports-2018-SPA.pdf.

Andrews, George Reid. 1985. "Spanish American Independence: A Structural Analysis." *Latin American Perspectives* 12 (1): 105–32. DOI: 10.1177/0094582X8501200106.

Andújar Castillo, Francisco. 1996. "El Fuero Militar en el Siglo XVIII. Un Estatuto de Privilegio." *Chronica Nova* 23: 11–31.

Badri-Maharaj, Sanjay. 2017. "Globalization of the Jihadist Threat: Case Study of Trinidad and Tobago." *Strategic Analysis* 41 (2): 173–89.

Ball, Nicole, and Len le Roux. 2006. "A Model for Good Practice in Budgeting for the Military Sector." In *Budgeting for the Military Sector in Africa: The Processes and Mechanisms of Control*, eds. Wuyi Omitoogun and Eboe Hutchful. Oxford: Oxford University Press, 14–37.

Ballbé, Manuel. 1983. *Orden público y militarismo en la España constitucional (1812–1983)*. Madrid: Alianza Universidad.

Barany, Zoltan. 2007. *Democratic Breakdown and Decline of the Russian Military*. Princeton: Princeton University Press.

Barany, Zoltan. 2012. *The Soldier and the Changing State: Building Democratic Armies in Africa, Asia, Europe, and the Americas*. Princeton: Princeton University Press.

BBC News. 2013. "Taiwan Protest Over Hung Chung-chiu Death," August 3. https://www.bbc.com/news/world-asia-23561244.

bdnews24.com. 2014. "Military Clears Police to Arrest Three Ex-RAB Men," May 16. http://bdnews24.com/bangladesh/2014/05/16/military-clears-police-to-arrest-three-ex-rab-men.

Beissinger, Mark. 2002. *Nationalist Mobilization and the Collapse of the Soviet State*. Cambridge: Cambridge University Press.

Bennett, Valerie Plave. 1975. "Military Government in Mali." *The Journal of Modern African Studies* 13 (2): 249–66. DOI: 10.1017/S0022278X00053064.

Berman, Harold J., and James W. Spindler. 1972. *Soviet Criminal Law and Procedure: The RSFSR Codes*. Cambridge: Harvard University Press.

Betts, Raymond F. 2004. *Assimilation and Association in French Colonial Theory, 1890–1914*. Lincoln: University of Nebraska Press.

Bove, Vincenzo, Mauricio Rivera, Chiara Ruffa. 2020. "Beyond Coups: Terrorism and Military Involvement in Politics." *European Journal of International Relations* 26 (1): 263–88. DOI: 10.1177/1354066119866499.

Brubaker, Rogers. 2020. "Populism and Nationalism." *Nations and Nationalism* 26 (1): 44–66. DOI: 10.1111/nana.12522.

Capoccia, Giovanni, and R. Daniel Kelemen. 2007. "The Study of Critical Junctures: Theory, Narrative, and Counterfactuals in Historical Institutionalism." *World Politics* 59 (3): 341–69.

Casey, Nicholas. 2017. "Venezuela Tries Protesters in Military Court 'Like We Are in a War.'" *The New York Times*, May 12. https://www.nytimes.com/2017/05/12/world/americas/venezuela-protests-maduro.html?_r=0.

Castro, Gustavo Fabián, and Dolores Bermeo Lara. 2008. "*Justicia Militar, Códigos Disciplinarios y Reglamentos Generales Internos*." Buenos Aires: Red de Seguridad y Defensa de América Latina.

Central Intelligence Agency. 1948. "Development and Organization of the Judiciary in Yugoslavia" [Informativni prirucnik o Jugoslaviji, Book 1, 1948].

Chandara, Lor, and Seth Meixner. 1999. "Article 51 Amended, But Remains 'Unclear.'" *The Cambodian Daily*, August 18. https://www.cambodiadaily.com/news/article-51-amended-but-remains-unclear-89409/.

Clark, Andrew F. 1995. "From Military Dictatorship to Democracy: The Democratization Process in Mali." *Journal of Third World Studies* 12 (1): 201–22.

Collier, David, Jody LaPorte, and Jason Seawright. 2008. "Typologies: Forming Concepts and Creating Categorical Variables." In *Oxford Handbook of Political Methodology*, eds. Janet M. Box-Steffensmeier, Henry E. Brady, and David Collier. Oxford: Oxford University Press, 152–73.

Collier, Ruth Berins, and David Collier. 1991. *Shaping the Political Arena: Critical Junctures, the Labor Movement, and Regime Dynamics in Latin America*. Princeton: Princeton University Press.

Contesse, Jorge. 2019. "Resisting the Inter-American Human Rights System." *Yale Journal of International Law* 44 (2): 179–238.

Cook, Steven A. 2007. *Ruling but Not Governing: The Military and Political Development in Egypt, Algeria, and Turkey*. Baltimore: Johns Hopkins University Press.

Corner, Paul, ed. 2009. *Popular Opinion in Totalitarian Regimes: Fascism, Nazism, Communism*. New York: Oxford University Press.

Cottey, Andrew, Timothy Edmunds, and Anthony Forster. 2006. "Civil-Military Relations in Postcommunist Europe: Assessing the Transition." In *Civil-Military Relations in Post-Communist Europe: Reviewing the Transition*, eds. Timothy Edmunds, Andrew Cottey, and Anthony Forster. New York: Routledge, 1–16.

Curtis, Glenn E. 1992. *Yugoslavia: A Country Study*. Washington, DC: Library of Congress.

d'Argent, Pierre. 2003. "Military Law in Belgium." In *European Military Law Systems*, ed. Georg Nolte. Berlin: De Gruyter Recht, 183–231.

Dahl, Robert A. 1956. *A Preface to Democratic Theory*. Chicago: University of Chicago Press.

Dahl, Robert A. 1971. *Polyarchy: Participation and Opposition*. New Haven: Yale University Press.

Dahl, Robert A. 1998. *On Democracy*. New Haven: Yale University Press.

Daniels, Ronald J., Michael J. Trebilcock, and Lindsey D. Carson. 2011. "The Legacy of Empire: The Common Law Inheritance and Commitments to Legality in Former British Colonies." *The American Journal of Comparative Law* 59 (1): 111–78. DOI: 10.5131/AJCL.2010.0015.

Davis, Darren W., and Brian D. Silver. 2003. "Civil Liberties vs. Security: Public Opinion in the Context of the Terrorist Attacks on America." *American Journal of Political Science* 48 (1): 28–46. DOI: 10.1111/j.0092-5853.2004.00054.x.

DeMeritt, Jacqueline H. R. 2012. "International Organizations and Government Killing: Does Naming and Shaming Save Lives?" *International Interactions* 38 (5): 597–621. DOI: 10.1080/03050629.2012.726180.

DeMeritt, Jacqueline H. R., and Courtenay R. Conrad. 2019. "Repression Substitution: Hiding Human Rights Violations in Response to UN Naming and Shaming." *Civil Wars* 21 (1): 128–52. DOI: 10.1080/13698249.2019.1602805.

Denton, David H. 2016. "The Australian Military Justice System: History, Organisation and Disciplinary Structure." *Victoria University Law and Justice Journal* 6 (1): 26–35.

Depósito de la Guerra. 1873. *Memoria sobre la Organización Militar de España en 1871, Tomo III.* Madrid: Depósito de la Guerra.

Desch, Michael C. 1999. *Civilian Control of the Military: The Changing Security Environment.* Baltimore: Johns Hopkins University Press.

Dwyer, Maggie. 2017. *Soldiers in Revolt: Army Mutinies in Africa.* New York: Oxford University Press.

Epperly, Brad, and Jacqueline Sievert. 2019. "Conflict and Courts: Civil War and Judicial Independence across Democracies." *Political Research Quarterly* 72 (3): 700–13. DOI: 10.1177/1065912918803200.

Farrelly, Nicholas. 2013. "Why Democracy Struggles: Thailand's Elite Coup Culture." *Australian Journal of International Affairs* 67 (3): 281–96.

Firmin-Sellers, Kathryn. 2000. "Institutions, Context, and Outcomes: Explaining French and British Rule in West Africa." *Comparative Politics* 32 (3): 253–72. DOI: 10.2307/422366.

Fishel, John T. 2000. "The Institutional Reconversion of the Panamanian Defense Forces." In *Post-Invasion Panama: The Challenges of Democratization in the New World Order*, ed. Orlando J. Pérez. Lanham, MD: Lexington, 11–27.

Fisher, Roger. 1981. *Improving Compliance with International Law.* Charlottesville: University of Virginia Press.

Franklin, James C. 2015. "Human Rights Naming and Shaming: International and Domestic Processes." In *The Politics of Leverage in International Relations: Name, Shame and Sanction*, ed. H. Richard Friman. New York: Palgrave Macmillan, 43–60.

Freedom House. 2010. "Repeal of Decree Law in Peru a Win for Human Rights," September 17.

French, Thomas. 2014. *National Police Reserve: The Origin of Japan's Self Defense Forces.* Leiden, the Netherlands: Brill.

Gammelgaard, Karen, and Eirik Holmøyvik. 2014. *Writing Democracy: The Norwegian Constitution 1814–2014.* New York: Berghahn.

Geddes, Barbara, and John Zaller. 1989. "Source of Popular Support for Authoritarian Regimes." *American Journal of Political Science* 33 (2): 319–47.

Gershovich, Moshe. 2000. *French Military Rule in Morocco: Colonialism and its Consequences.* London: Frank Cass.

Gibler, Douglas M., and Kirk A. Randazzo. 2011. "Testing the Effects of Independent Judiciaries on the Likelihood of Democratic Backsliding." *American Journal of Political Science* 55 (3): 696–709. DOI: 10.1111/j.1540-5907.2010.00504.x.

Gilissen, John. 1963. "Military Justice in Belgium." *Military Law Review* (Department of the Army Pamphlet 27-100-20): 83–105.

Ginsburg. Tom. 2003. *Judicial Review in New Democracies: Constitutional Courts in Asian Cases.* New York: Cambridge University Press.

Golovko, Léonid. 2008. "Les cours militairs russes: juridictions de droit commun, juridictions spécialisées ou juridictions d'exception?" *The Journal of Power Institutions in Post-Soviet Societies* 8. http://journals.openedition.org/pipss/1173. DOI: 10.4000/pipss.1173.

González-Ocantos, Ezequiel A. 2016. *Shifting Legal Visions: Judicial Change and Human Rights Trials in Latin America*. New York: Cambridge University Press. DOI: 10.1017/CBO9781316535509.

Greer, Steven. 2013. "Exceptional Courts and the European Convention of Human Rights." In *Guantanamo and Beyond: Exceptional Courts and Military Commissions in Comparative Perspective*, eds. Fionnuala Ní Aoláin and Oren Gross. New York: Cambridge University Press, 341–60.

Grono, Nick. 2006. "Briefing—Darfur: The International Community's Failure to Protect." *African Affairs* 105 (421): 621–31. DOI: 10.1093/afraf/adl036.

Grzybowski, Kazimierz. 1960. "Soviet Criminal Law Reform of 1958." *Indiana Law Journal* 35 (2): 125–42.

Hafner-Burton, Emilie M. 2008. "Sticks and Stones: Naming and Shaming the Human Rights Enforcement Problem." *International Organization* 62 (4): 689–716. DOI: 10.1017/S0020818308080247.

Hafner-Burton, Emilie M. 2013. *Making Human Rights a Reality*. Princeton: Princeton University Press.

Hafner-Burton, Emilie, and Kiyoteru Tsutsui. 2005. "Human Rights in a Globalizing World: The Paradox of Empty Promises." *American Journal of Sociology* 110 (5): 1373–1411. DOI: 10.1086/428442.

Haglund, Jillienne. 2020. "Domestic Politics and the Effectiveness of Regional Human Rights Courts." *International Interactions* 46 (4): 551–78. DOI: 10.1080/03050629.2020.1751624.

Hall, Matthew E. K. 2011. *The Nature of Supreme Court Power*. Cambridge: Cambridge University Press.

Haltiner, Karl W. 2003. "Tradition as a Political Value—The Public Image of Security, Defense and Military in Switzerland." In *The Public Image of Security, Defence and the Military in Europe*, ed. Marie Vlachová. Belgrade, Serbia: Center for Civil-Military Relations.

Hanson, Mark. 1974. "Organizational Bureaucracy in Latin America and the Legacy of Spanish Colonialism." *Journal of Interamerican Studies and World Affairs* 16 (2): 199–219. DOI: 10.2307/174737.

Harsch, Ernest. 2017. *Burkina Faso: A History of Power, Protest and Revolution*. London: Zed.

Herspring, Dale R. 1992. "Civil-Military Relations in Post-Communist Eastern Europe: The Potential for Praetorianism." *Studies in Comparative Communism* 25 (2): 99–122. DOI: 10.1016/0039-3592(92)90001-Z.

Hillebrecht, Courtney. 2014. *Domestic Politics and International Human Rights Tribunals: The Problem of Compliance*. Cambridge: Cambridge University Press. DOI: 10.1017/CBO9781139628747.

Houngnikpo, Mathurin C. 2000. "The Military and Democratization in Africa: A Comparative Study of Benin and Togo." *Journal of Political and Military Sociology* 28 (2): 210–29.

Huddy, Leonie, Stanley Feldman, and Christopher Weber. 2007. "The Political Consequences of Perceived Threat and Felt Insecurity." *The Annals of the American Academy of Political and Social Science* 614 (1): 131–53. DOI: 10.1177/0002716207305951.

Human Rights Watch. 1995. "Former Yugoslavia: War Crimes Trials in the Former Yugoslavia." https://www.hrw.org/reports/1995/yugoslavia/.

Human Rights Watch. 2013. "Sudan: New Law Allows Military Trials of Civilians," July 9. https://www.hrw.org/news/2013/07/09/sudan-new-law-allows-military-trials-civilians#.

Human Rights Watch. 2017a. "Chile: Events of 2016." https://www.hrw.org/world-report/2017/country-chapters/chile#8586c1.

Human Rights Watch. 2017b. "'It's Not the Right Place for Us': The Trial of Civilians by Military Courts in Lebanon," January 26. https://www.hrw.org/report/2017/01/26/its-not-right-place-us/trial-civilians-military-courts-lebanon.

Human Rights Watch. 2018. "Tunisia: Parliament Member Prosecuted for Insulting Army," January 14. https://www.hrw.org/news/2018/01/24/tunisia-parliament-member-prosecuted-insulting-army.

Human Rights Watch. 2019. "Born Without Civil Rights: Israel's Use of Draconian Military Orders to Repress Palestinians in the West Bank," December 17. https://www.hrw.org/report/2019/12/17/born-without-civil-rights/israels-use-draconian-military-orders-repress.

Human Rights Watch. 2020. "Russia: Harsh Verdicts in Controversial Terrorism Cases," February 12. https://www.hrw.org/news/2020/02/12/russia-harsh-verdicts-controversial-terrorism-cases.

Huneeus, Alexandra. 2011. "Courts Resisting Courts: Lessons from the Inter-American Court's Struggle to Enforce Human Rights." *Cornell International Law Journal* 44 (3): Article 2. https://scholarship.law.cornell.edu/cilj/vol44/iss3/2/.

Hunter-Chester, David. 2016. *Creating Japan's Ground Self-Defense Force, 1945–2015: A Sword Well Made*. Lanham, MD: Lexington Books.

Huntington, Samuel. 1957. *The Soldier and the State: The Theory and Politics of Civil-Military Relations*. Cambridge: Belknap. DOI: 10.2307/j.ctvjf9wx3.

International Commission of Jurists. 2005. "Attacks on Justice—People's Democratic Republic of Algeria." https://www.icj.org/wp-content/uploads/2012/04/Algeria-Attacks-on-Justice-2005-Publications-2008.pdf.

International Commission of Jurists. 2013. "Authority without Accountability: The Struggle for Justice in Nepal." https://www.icj.org/wp-content/uploads/2013/10/ICJ-AUTHORITY-WITHOUT-ACCOUNTABILITY-final-1.pdf.

International Commission of Jurists. 2019a. "Military 'Justice' System: A Glaring Surrender of Human Rights," January 16. https://www.icj.org/military-justice-system-a-glaring-surrender-of-human-rights/.

International Commission of Jurists. 2019b. "Thailand: End Prosecution of Civilians in Military Courts," April 22. https://www.icj.org/thailand-end-prosecution-of-civilians-in-military-courts-and-repeal-or-amend-head-of-the-ncpo-and-ncpo-orders-and-announcements-in-line-with-international-human-rights-law/.

International Crisis Group. 2008. "Timor-Leste: Security Sector Reform." Asia Report No. 143. https://www.crisisgroup.org/asia/south-east-asia/timor-leste/timor-leste-security-sector-reform.

Janowitz, Morris. 1960. *The Professional Soldier: A Social and Political Portrait*. New York: Free Press.

Jenkins, Craig. 1983. "Resource Mobilization Theory and the Study of Social Movements." *Annual Review of Sociology* 9: 527–53.

Joinet, Louis. 2002. "Issue of the Administration of Justice through Military Tribunals." UN Sub-Commission on the Promotion and Protection of Human Rights. E/CN.4/Sub.2/2002/4. https://undocs.org/pdf?symbol=en/E/CN.4/Sub.2/2002/4.

Joireman, Sandra Fullerton. 2001. "Inherited Legal Systems and Effective Rule of Law: Africa and the Colonial Legacy." *Journal of Modern African Studies* 39 (4): 571–96. DOI: 10.1017/S0022278X01003755.

Kahle, Louis G. 1951. "The Spanish Colonial Judiciary." *The Southwestern Social Science Quarterly* 32 (1): 26–37.

Karl, Terry Lynn. 1992. "El Salvador's Negotiated Revolution." *Foreign Affairs* 71 (2): 147–64.

Keck, Margaret E., and Kathryn Sikkink. 1998. *Activists beyond Borders: Advocacy Networks in International Politics.* Ithaca: Cornell University Press.

Keith, Linda Camp. 2002. "Judicial Independence and Human Rights Protection around the World." *Judicature* 85 (4): 195–200.

Korea Herald. 2018. "[Editorial] Military Judicial Reform: Independence from Influence of Commanders Will Strengthen Trust in Military," February 13. http://www.koreaherald.com/view.php?ud=20180213000561.

Kosař, David. 2017. "Nudging Domestic Judicial Reforms from Strasbourg: How the European Court of Human Rights Shapes Domestic Judicial Design." *Utrecht Law Review* 13 (1): 112–23. DOI: 10.18352/ulr.368.

Kovalev, Nikolai P. 2008. "Trial by Jury in Russian Military Courts." *The Journal of Power Institutions in Post-Soviet Societies* 8. https://journals.openedition.org/pipss/1533. DOI: 10.4000/pips.1533.

Kuehn, David, and Harold Trinkunas. 2017. "Conditions of Military Contestation in Populist Latin America." *Democratization* 24 (5): 859–80. DOI: 10.1080/13510347.2017.1293659.

Kunz, Raffaela. 2020. "Judging International Judgments Anew? The Human Rights Courts before Domestic Courts." *European Journal of International Law* 30 (4): 1129–63. DOI: 10.1093/ejil/chz063.

Kutnjak Ivkovich, Sanja. 2001. "Mixed Tribunals in Croatia." *Revue Internationale de Droit Pénal* 72: 57–85. DOI: 10.3917/redp.721.0057.

Kyle, Brett J., and Andrew G. Reiter. 2013. "Militarized Justice in New Democracies: Explaining the Process of Military Court Reform in Latin America." *Law & Society Review* 47 (2): 375–407. DOI: 10.1111/lasr.12019.

Kyle, Brett J., and Andrew G. Reiter. 2019. "A New Dawn for Latin American Militaries." *NACLA Report on the Americas* 51 (1): 18–28. DOI: 10.1080/10714839.2019.1593684.

Lambert Abdelgawad, Elisabeth. 2007. "Juridictions militaires et tribunaux d'exception en mutation: perspectives comparees et internationales." UMR de droit compare (Universite Paris 1—CNRS), rapport final, http://www.gip-recherche-justice.fr/wp-content/uploads/2014/07/04-40-RF.pdf.

Lasswell, Harold D. 1941. "The Garrison State." *American Journal of Sociology* 46 (4): 455–68.

Lee, Therese. 2002. "Malaysia and the Internal Security Act: The Insecurity of Human Rights after September 11." *Singapore Journal of Legal Studies* (July): 56–72.

Levitsky, Stephen, and Lucan A. Way. 2010. *Competitive Authoritarianism: Hybrid Regimes after the Cold War.* Cambridge: Cambridge University Press.

Lindeblad, Benct. 1963. "Swedish Military Jurisdiction." *Military Law Review* (Department of the Army Pamphlet 27-100-19): 123–28.

Linz, Juan J. 2000. *Totalitarian and Authoritarian Regimes.* Boulder: Lynne Rienner.

Linz, Juan J., and Alfred Stepan. 1996. *Problems of Democratic Transition and Consolidation.* Baltimore: Johns Hopkins University Press.

Lipset, Seymour Martin, Kyoung-Ryung Seong, and John Charles Torres. 1993. "A Comparative Analysis of the Social Requisites of Democracy." *International Social Science Journal* 45 (2): 155–75.

Loveman, Brian. 1993. *The Constitution of Tyranny: Regimes of Exception in Spanish America*. Pittsburgh: University of Pittsburgh Press.

Luckham, Robin. 1982. "French Militarism in Africa." *Review of African Political Economy* 24: 55–84. DOI: 10.1080/03056248208703499.

Lynch, John. 1992. "The Institutional Framework of Colonial Spanish America." *Journal of Latin American Studies* 24: 69–81. DOI: 10.1017/S0022216X00023786.

Manukyan, Hovhannes. 2011. "Judicial and Legal Reform in the Republic of Armenia: Progress, Challenges, and Lessons Learned." Presented at the World Bank Conference "Empowerment, Security and Opportunity Through Law and Justice," Saint Petersburg, Russia.

Marshall, Monty G., and Ted Robert Gurr. 2018. "Polity5 Project: Political Regime Characteristics and Transitions, 1800-2018." http://www.systemicpeace.org/polityproject.html.

Mason, T. David, and Dale Krane. 1989. "The Political Economy of Death Squads: Toward a Theory of the Impact of State-Sanctioned Terror." *International Studies Quarterly* 33 (2): 175–98.

Matei, Florina Cristiana. 2013. "A New Conceptualization of Civil-Military Relations." In *The Routledge Handbook of Civil-Military Relations*, eds. Thomas C. Bruneau and Florina Cristiana Matei. New York: Routledge, 26–47.

McAdam, Doug, John McCarthy, and Mayer Zald, eds. 1996. *Comparative Perspectives on Social Movements: Political Opportunities, Mobilizing Structures, and Cultural Frames*. Cambridge: Cambridge University Press.

McAlister, Lyle N. 1957. *The "Fuero Militar" in New Spain: 1764–1800*. Gainesville: University of Florida Press.

McClelland, Justin. 2002. "Starting from Scratch: The Military Discipline System of the East Timor Defence Force." *Journal of Conflict and Security Law* 7 (2): 253–73. DOI: 10.1093/jcsl/7.2.253.

Menard, Orville D. 1967. *The Army and the Fifth Republic*. Lincoln: University of Nebraska Press.

Miller, Steven V. 2017. "The Effect of Terrorism on Judicial Confidence." *Political Research Quarterly* 70 (4): 790–802. DOI: 10.1177/1065912917716337.

Müller, Ingo. 1991. *Hitler's Justice: The Courts of the Third Reich*. Trans. Deborah Lucas Schneider. Cambridge: Harvard University Press.

Murdie, Amanda. 2014. *Help or Harm: The Human Security Effects of International NGOs*. Stanford, CA: Stanford University Press.

Murdie, Amanda, and David R. Davis. 2010. "Problematic Potential: The Human Rights Consequences of Peacekeeping Interventions in Civil Wars." *Human Rights Quarterly* 32 (1): 49–72.

Neild, Rachel. 2012. "Human Rights NGOs, Police and Citizen Security in Transitional Democracies." *Journal of Human Rights* 2 (3): 277–96.

Nouwen, Sarah M. H. 2013. *Complementarity in the Line of Fire: The Catalysing Effect of the International Criminal Court in Uganda and Sudan*. New York: Cambridge University Press. DOI: 10.1017/CBO9780511863264.

O'Donnell, Guillermo. 1998. "Horizontal Accountability in New Democracies." *Journal of Democracy* 9 (3): 112–26.

Osuna, José Javier Olivas. 2014. *Iberian Military Politics: Controlling the Armed Forces during Dictatorship and Democratisation.* New York: Palgrave Macmillan.

Peksen, Dursun. 2009. "Better or Worse? The Effect of Economic Sanctions on Human Rights." *Journal of Peace Research* 46 (1): 59–77. DOI: 10.1177/0022343308098404.

Peksen, Dursun. 2012. "Does Foreign Military Intervention Help Human Rights?" *Political Research Quarterly* 65 (3): 558–71. DOI: 10.1177/1065912911417831.

Pérez, Orlando J. 2015. *Civil-Military Relations in Post-Conflict Societies: Transforming the Role of the Military in Central America.* New York: Routledge.

Phillips, Dion. 1997. "The Trinidad and Tobago Defence Force: Origin, Structure, Training, Security and Other Roles." *Caribbean Quarterly* 43 (3): 13–33.

Phiri, B. J. 2001. "Civil Control of the Zambian Military Since Independence: Implications for Democracy." *African Security Review* 10 (4): 125–34.

Pollis, Adamantia. 1987. "The State, the Law, and Human Rights in Modern Greece." *Human Rights Quarterly* 9 (4): 587–614.

Posner, Eric A., and Adrian Vermeule. 2007. *Terror in the Balance: Security, Liberty, and the Courts.* New York: Oxford University Press.

Prizzia, Ross. 1985. *Thailand in Transition: The Role of Oppositional Forces.* Honolulu: University of Hawaii Press.

Radin, Max. 1942. "Martial Law and the State of Siege." *California Law Review* 30 (6): 634–47.

Radio Dabanga. 2013. "'Amendments to Sudan's Armed Forces Act Unconstitutional': Opposition," July 4. https://www.dabangasudan.org/en/all-news/article/amendments-to-sudan-s-armed-forces-act-unconstitutional-opposition.

Red de Seguridad y Defensa de América Latina. 2016. *A Comparative Atlas of Defence in Latin America.* Buenos Aires: RESDAL.

Reenock, Christopher, Jeffrey K. Staton, and Marius Radean. 2013. "Legal Institutions and Democratic Survival." *The Journal of Politics* 75 (2): 491–505. DOI: 10.1017/S0022381613000169.

Reuters. 2019. "Burkina Army Investigating Claims its Troops Carried Out Executions." *Reuters*, March 14. https://www.reuters.com/article/us-burkina-security/burkina-army-investigating-claims-its-troops-carried-out-executions-idUSKCN1QV2EL.

Ríos-Figueroa, Julio. 2016. *Constitutional Courts as Mediators: Armed Conflict, Civil-Military Relations, and the Rule of Law in Latin America.* Cambridge: Cambridge University Press. DOI: 10.1017/CBO9781139942157.

Ríos-Figueroa, Julio, and Jeffrey K. Staton. 2014. "An Evaluation of Cross-National Measures of Judicial Independence." *Journal of Law, Economics, & Organizations* 30 (1): 104–37. DOI: 10.1093/jleo/ews029.

Roeder, Philip G. 2004. "The Triumph of Nation-States: Lessons from the Collapse of the Soviet Union, Yugoslavia, and Czechoslovakia." In *After the Collapse of Communism: Comparative Lessons of Transition*, eds. Michael McFaul and Kathryn Stoner-Weiss. Cambridge: Cambridge University Press, 21–57.

Romero, Simon. 2008. "Ecuador's Leader Purges Military and Moves to Expel American Base." *The New York Times*, April 21. https://www.nytimes.com/2008/04/21/world/americas/21ecuador.html.

Ron, James, Howard Ramos, and Kathleen Rogers. 2005. "Transnational Information Politics: NGO Human Rights Reporting, 1986-2000." *International Studies Quarterly* 49 (3): 557–88. DOI: 10.1111/j.1468-2478.2005.00377.x.

Rosenn, Keith S. 2014. "Recent Important Decisions by the Brazilian Supreme Court." *The University of Miami Inter-American Law Review* 45 (2): 297–334.

Rossiter, Clinton L. 1948. *Constitutional Dictatorship: Crisis Government in Modern Democracies.* Princeton: Princeton University Press.

Rueda, Manuel, and Natalia Viana. 2017. "Maduro Justice: Secret Evidence and Military Courts for Venezuela's Protesters." *America's Quarterly*, June 26. https://www.americasquarterly.org/content/venezuelas-government-case-prison.

Salgado, José. 1905. *Historia de la República Oriental del Uruguay.* Montevideo: Talleres A. Barreiro y Ramos.

Samuel, E. 1816. *An Historical Account of the British Army, and of the Law Military.* London: William Clowes.

Schiff, Rebecca. 2009. *The Military and Domestic Politics: A Concordance Theory of Civil-Military Relations.* London: Routledge.

Schmidt, Elizabeth. 2009. "Anticolonial Nationalism in French West Africa: What Made Guinea Unique?" *African Studies Review* 52 (2): 1–34.

Schmitt, Michael N., and James E. Moody. 1991. "The Soviet Military Justice System." *Air Force Law Review* 34: 1–108.

Serra, Narcís. 2010. *The Military Transition: Democratic Reform of the Armed Forces.* Trans. Peter Bush. New York: Cambridge University Press.

Shapiro, Martin. 1963. "Political Jurisprudence." *Kentucky Law Journal* 52 (2): 294–345.

Sherman, Edward F. 1973. "Military Justice without Military Control." *The Yale Law Journal* 82 (7): 1398–1425.

Sidibe, Ibrahima. 2018. "Guinean Legal System and Research." GlobalLex. https://www.nyulawglobal.org/globalex/Guinea1.html#militarytribunal.

Simmons, Beth A. 1998. "Compliance with International Agreements." *Annual Review of Political Science* 1 (1): 75–93.

Simmons, Beth A. 2012. *Mobilizing for Human Rights: International Law in Domestic Politics.* Cambridge: Cambridge University Press.

Sives, Amanda. 2010. *Elections, Violence, and the Democratic Process in Jamaica, 1944–2007.* Kingston: Ian Randle.

Skaar, Elin. 2011. *Judicial Independence and Human Rights in Latin America: Violations, Politics, and Prosecution.* New York: Palgrave Macmillan.

Skaar, Elin. 2015. "Uruguay: Reconstructing Peace and Democracy Through Transitional Justice." In *After Violence: Transitional Justice, Peace, and Democracy*, eds. Elin Skaar, Camila Gianella Malca, and Trine Eide. New York: Routledge, 67–90.

Smith, Ryan. 2018. "The Trouble with Bangladesh's Military." *The Diplomat*, March 10. https://thediplomat.com/2018/03/the-trouble-with-bangladeshs-military/.

Souza, Adriana Barreto. 2015. "The Governance of the Military Justice between Lisboa and Rio de Janeiro (1750-1820)." *Almanack* 10: 368–408. DOI: 10.1590/2236-463320151009.

Sputnik. 2016. "Cost Optimization: Military Courts Abolished in Kyrgyzstan," December 12. https://ru.sputnik-tj.com/asia/20161227/1021398078/kyrgyzstan-sud.html.

Stepan, Alfred. 1986. "Paths toward Redemocratization: Theoretical and Comparative Considerations." In *Transitions from Authoritarian Rule: Comparative Perspectives*, eds. Guillermo O'Donnell, Philippe C. Schmitter, and Laurence Whitehead. Baltimore: Johns Hopkins University Press, 64–84.

Suárez-Enríquez, Ximena. 2017. "Overlooking Justice: Human Rights Violations Committed by Mexican Soldiers against Civilians Are Met with Impunity." Research Report, Washington Office on Latin America. https://www.wola.org/wp-content/uploads/2017/11/WOLA_MILITARY-CRIMES_REP_ENGLISH.pdf.

United Nations Commission on Human Rights. 2006. "Draft Principles Governing the Administration of Justice Through Military Tribunals." E/CN.4/2006/58 at 4. https://undocs.org/pdf?symbol=en/E/CN.4/2006/58.

United Nations Office for the High Commissioner for Human Rights. 2013. "Report of the Special Rapporteur on the Independence of Judges and Lawyers." A/68/285. https://undocs.org/pdf?symbol=en/A/68/285.

United States Department of State. 2001. "Dominican Republic: Country Reports on Human Rights Practices 2000." https://2009-2017.state.gov/j/drl/rls/hrrpt/2001/wha/8345.htm.

United States Department of State. 2004. "Sudan: Country Reports on Human Rights Practices 2003." https://2009-2017.state.gov/j/drl/rls/hrrpt/2003/27753.htm.

United States Department of State. 2011. "Cambodia: Country Reports on Human Rights Practices 2010." https://2009-2017.state.gov/j/drl/rls/hrrpt/2011humanrightsreport/index.htm?dlid=186266#wrapper.

Vashakmadze, Mindia. 2018. "Military Justice in Ukraine: A Guidance Note." Geneva Centre for the Democratic Control of Armed Forces, Security Sector Reform Working Group 1. https://www.dcaf.ch/sites/default/files/publications/documents/Military_Justice_Guidance_Note_eng.pdf.

von Soest, Christian, and Julia Grauvogel. 2017. "Identity, Procedures and Performance: How Authoritarian Regimes Legitimize Their Rule." *Contemporary Politics* 23 (3): 287–305. DOI: 10.1080/13569775.2017.1304319.

Washington Office on Latin America. 2010. "Nuevo Decreto en Perú llevará a una impunidad legitimada por el estado," September 9. https://www.wola.org/es/2010/09/nuevo-decreto-en-peru-llevara-a-una-impunidad-legitimada-por-el-estado/.

Weeks, Gregory. 2008. "A Preference for Deference: Reforming the Military's Intelligence Role in Argentina, Chile and Peru." *Third World Quarterly* 29 (1): 45–61.

Whitaker, Beth Elise. 2007. "Exporting the Patriot Act? Democracy and the 'War on Terror' in the Third World." *Third World Quarterly* 28 (5): 1017–32.

Wiener, Frederick Bernays. 1967. *Civilians under Military Justice: The British Practice since 1689 Especially in North America*. Chicago: University of Chicago Press.

Wiseman, John A. 1996. "Military Rule in The Gambia: An Interim Assessment." *Third World Quarterly* 17 (5): 917–40. DOI: 10.1080/01436599615182.

Wood, Reed M. 2008. "A Hand Upon the Throat of the Nation? Economic Sanctions and State Repression, 1976-2001." *International Studies Quarterly* 52 (3): 489–513. DOI: 10.1111/j.1468-2478.2008.00512.x.

Young, Thomas-Durell. 2006. "Military Professionalism in a Democracy." In *Who Guards the Guardians and How: Democratic Civil-Military Relations*, eds. Thomas C. Bruneau and Scott D. Tollefson. Austin: University of Texas Press, 17–33.

Zamudio, Hector Fix. 1979. "A Brief Introduction to the Mexican Writ of *Amparo*." *California Western International Law Journal* 9 (2): 306–48.

Zimbabwe Independent. 2016. "Military Takes Over Prosecuting Authority," October 28. https://www.theindependent.co.zw/2016/10/28/military-takes-prosecuting-authority/.

4 Full subordination in Portugal and Colombia: Playing by civilian rules

Introduction

To have a truly democratic regime with the rule of law, protections for human rights, and stable civil-military relations, military courts must be fully subordinated to civilian authority. In systems of full subordination, military courts are either abolished completely or operate for a narrow set of military crimes, internal to the institution and vital to maintain the good order and discipline necessary for effective command. In addition, there are no serious disputes between civilian and military courts regarding the jurisdiction of cases. There are two distinct pathways by which countries arrive at this type of system. First, full subordination may be realized immediately at a critical juncture in the country's politics. This is most often the case during transitions to democracy when institutions are redesigned. We begin this chapter with a discussion of Portugal to illustrate this pathway. Under the dictatorship of António de Oliveira Salazar (1932–68), Portugal used military courts as an instrument of repression against civilians while also retaining them as a privileged venue of justice for members of the armed forces. Once it consolidated its rule, the regime reduced the role of military courts in trying civilians, but when an army faction seized power in a coup in 1974, military courts once again became a tool to punish the government's opponents. A democratic transition and new constitution in 1976 limited military courts to disciplinary offenses of military personnel. Court cases in the ensuing years further refined the role of military justice in Portugal and deepened the legal subordination over time.

The second pathway countries undergo to achieve full subordination is through a protracted struggle among the military, politicians, human rights activists, external states, and the courts. It may take many years for reformers to win-out over resisters, and progress is often not linear. We present Colombia as an emblematic case of this type of long, gradual reform. Military courts initially played a prominent role in the government's fight against rebels during its long civil war. In the 1980s, however, a series of reforms took away the power of military courts to try civilians. Additional court rulings and political reforms over the next 15 years eventually restricted military courts to military-specific crimes. We conclude with important lessons learned on how reform succeeds and why it sticks in some cases and not in others.

Portugal: Immediate reform through democratization

The transformative event of democratization in Portugal (1974–76) brought with it reform of the country's military courts. Portuguese military justice was an entrenched parallel legal system that set military personnel beyond the reach of civilian courts. For much of the twentieth century, military courts also prosecuted civilians to stifle dissent and eliminate opponents of the authoritarian regime. Not until after the transition to democracy in 1976, following the Carnation Revolution, did a civilian government fully subordinate the military justice system.

Military privileges in early modern to nineteenth-century Portugal

As with many European states, the Portuguese military and its justice system evolved over time. The first formal system was established in 1763, but its precursors began in the 1600s. In its early history, Portugal relied largely on militias raised for temporary duty to maintain security. The government created a regular standing army during the Portuguese Restoration War (1640–68) and along with it military legal institutions to govern these troops (Tengwall 2010, 182). In 1640, Portugal established the Lisbon Council of War (*Conselho de Guerra*), which functioned as an administrative and advisory body to the Portuguese monarchy on military affairs ranging from consulting on promotions to management of fortresses and arsenals. It also served as the venue in which military crimes were tried (Dores Costa 2009, 385–92; Souza 2015, 370; Tengwall 2010, 144). Much like the *fuero militar* of neighboring Spain, being subject to military jurisdiction in Portugal and its empire was a personal privilege considered to be a benefit of the job (Andreu-Guzmán 2018, 145; Tengwall 2010, 212). This use of *in personam* jurisdiction reflected the stratification of European society of the time. A person's status, more so than the crime committed, determined where and how they would be judged. The application of military law to Portuguese soldiers extended beyond criminal charges to many civil matters such as contracts (Souza 2015).

Portugal focused its martial efforts on its navy and struggled to maintain sizable land forces; rates of desertion were high. Thus, extending legal privileges to army regulars (*exército da linha*) was a useful tool for recruitment and retention (Tengwall 2010, 200–1). These legal privileges often put the centralized authority of the Lisbon Council of War in conflict with the provincial governors (*governador das armas*), who were responsible for local military affairs (Tengwall 2010, 190). Military justice was integral to Portugal's empire at the time. It was common practice to transport convicted military personnel to Portuguese colonies, which undermined discipline and effectiveness there and increased the need for further military-based law and punishment (Coates 2014, 79–80). Moreover, the fusion of military and civilian authority in the empire meant the frequent use of martial law to govern the colonies (Benton 2010).

Mobilizing for the Seven Years War (1756–63) lent new urgency to military affairs across Europe. Portugal's experience in the conflict was only a brief defensive war with neighboring Spain, known as the *Guerra Fantástica*, but it demonstrated the need to modernize military practices (Speelman 2012). Through a series of royal decrees in 1763, Portugal consolidated its system of militias and reserve troops into a modern land army (Hayes 1976, 8); established councils of war for the army, navy, and overseas domains; and adopted its first code of military justice (Andreu-Guzmán 2018, 145; Souza 2015, 374).[1] The 1763 military code updated offenses and punishments, and the lower-level councils of war served as courts of first instance for military cases. These courts continued to act as a parallel, privileged forum for military members, responsible for trying a wide range of crimes, making Portugal a case of jurisdictional contestation. Additionally, the reforms eliminated the general auditor, who mediated between army units and the Lisbon Council of War, replacing the position with auditors tied to each regiment. This change made auditors a part of the units they were meant to oversee, compromising any legal independence that might have previously existed (Souza 2015, 371–76).

Portugal made a variety of changes to structures and practices in its military in the nineteenth century, including the creation of a general staff corps in 1834 to handle strategic planning (Loi 2018). Yet, apart from ending the death penalty for convicted soldiers and eliminating "the punishment of public works" in 1867 (Coates 2014, 28), military justice remained largely unchanged for more than a century (Brilhante 2017). The next code of military justice, adopted in 1875, was similar to the previous one. It made a distinction between strictly military crimes such as disciplinary offenses and common crimes committed by military personnel, but both types of offenses were still considered military crimes to be handled by the military justice system.

The end of the monarchy and rise of Republican Portugal, 1890–1926

The Portuguese monarchy faltered at the end of the nineteenth century and eventually ended in 1911 when a new republican constitution came into effect. King Carlos I took the throne in 1889, and the following year Portugal backed down from a feud with the United Kingdom over rival claims to territory in Africa. Nationalist republicans capitalized on the perceived humiliation to condemn the king's actions. A financial crisis in 1891 fed a republican revolt involving civilians and soldiers in the city of Oporto, followed by additional upheavals. The monarchy relied on the Municipal Guard (*Guarda Municipal*) and the army to put down these rebellions and to maintain order (Wheeler 1978, 41). In 1895, the monarchist government took a two-pronged approach to holding on to their power—significantly reducing the number of citizens eligible to vote in elections (Almeida 2018, 10–11) and giving councils of war jurisdiction over civilians accused of crimes against national security (Andreu-Guzmán 2018, 145). This change shifted Portugal from jurisdictional contestation to military overreach. Backsliding occurred in the context of a sitting government using military legal instruments to counter political opposition and internal security threats.

Intense anti-monarchist sentiment, political instability, and military agitation continued to roil Portugal at the turn of the century. In 1907, Carlos I gave Prime Minister João Franco the power to rule by decree. The military attempted a coup in response; it failed, but the turmoil led to the cancellation of the upcoming elections. In February 1908, two disgruntled republicans assassinated Carlos I and his youngest son, Luis Philipe. In the wake of the king's death, the prime minister resigned. Attempts to hold elections and form a new government failed. Finally, in October 1910, two naval units mutinied, and the army refused to stop the rebellion. Having clearly lost control over the military, King Manuel II, who had assumed the throne following the assassination, fled the country, and two days later a new republican government was formed (Opello 1991, 53–54).

Military justice was unchanged in the early republican era, continuing a state of military overreach. The 1911 constitution did not address military justice, in keeping with the constitutions of the monarchy that preceded it (Andreu-Guzmán 2018, 146). Portugal's young republic was characterized by continued political instability, economic hardship, and an ill-fated decision to enter World War I. The abrupt end to the monarchy in 1910 neither settled the numerous political conflicts in the country nor unified the republican forces. The new regime lacked a "foundational consensus" that would have enabled factions to work together in a coherent policy program (Madureira 2010, 648). During the republican era (1910–26), Portugal had 45 governments (Wheeler 1978), and "no parliament served a full term" (De Meneses 2004, 212). Moreover, the military routinely involved itself in politics, and the political fights of the time factionalized the institution (Opello 1991, 56–57; Osuna 2014a, 216).

Portugal's involvement in World War I fractured the military further and increased civil-military conflict. Portugal entered the war in 1916, which proved to be a mistake for the country and for the survival of the new regime (Payne 2011, 91). While the republican government saw joining the Allied war effort as an important step toward establishing its national leadership, defending democracy, and asserting Portugal's international position, its failures in the conflict ultimately undermined the legitimacy of the regime (De Meneses 2004). The war drained the Portuguese economy, inflation grew, and the cost of basic goods including foodstuffs increased dramatically (De Meneses 2004, 97; Osuna 2014a, 218). Meanwhile, battlefield losses took their toll on the military and deepened its discontent. Soldiers had been sent to war "poorly trained and equipped" (Opello 1991, 57). In the final years of the republic, military agitation produced a brief civil war and led to repeated coup attempts. On May 25, 1926, the military overthrew the republic, installing General Manuel Gomes da Costa as the new leader of Portugal (Opello 1991, 56–57; Payne 2011, 92).

Military overreach: Military rule and the Estado Novo, *1926–45*

The new military regime proved no more stable than the parliamentary government that preceded it. Conflicting ideological groups jockeyed for control (Pinto 1986) and rebellions within the military continued (Osuna 2014b, 50). Only months after taking power, a military faction removed General da Costa from office, and General Óscar Fragoso Carmona took over. Carmona became president in a non-competitive election in 1928 and appointed António de Oliveira Salazar, an economics professor, Finance Minister (Opello 1991, 59–61). Salazar held far more power than an ordinary minister: as a condition of taking the position, he insisted upon having control over the entire government's budget and expenditures (Kay 1970, 42–43; Opello 1991, 61). Salazar's competent management of Portugal's finances over the following years won him allies in the armed forces and among intellectuals and wealthy landowners, positioning him as a natural political leader (Opello 1991, 64).

In 1932, Salazar established the *Estado Novo*, an authoritarian regime that sought to depoliticize the country by subsuming nascent party competition into corporatist institutions that could channel demands through the state (Cruz 1988). While the regime was founded in the era in which fascism was taking hold in Italy, Germany, and Spain, the Portuguese regime was not explicitly fascist. It lacked the constant state-party mobilization and demagoguery seen in those nearby totalitarian states (Kay 1970, 3; Linz and Stepan 1996, 117). There was "no dominant ideology" associated with the regime (Wheeler 1978, 251). Salazar worked to balance the many competing political tendencies against each other in order to present an image of political unity. The National Union (*União Nacional*), for example, functioned as the "nonpartisan association" that served as the electoral vehicle for approved candidates in non-competitive elections (Kay 1970, 48; Opello 1991, 69). Salazar's power rested on elite and military support. While Salazar served as prime minister, the presidency was held by the military for the entire 1926–74 period (Opello 1991, 73). In this relationship, military justice played a prominent role in protecting those in the military and aiding the civilian government in repressing its opposition.

The government had updated the military code of justice in 1925, just before the beginning of the *Estado Novo*, and retained the special military legal privileges from the 1875 code. This code remained in place during the entire Salazar regime. Among other prerogatives, military personnel enjoyed "immunity to civilian arrest" (Osuna 2014b, 65).[2] Moreover, the military played an overt role in policing and public security. Army officers led the Public Security Force (*Polícia de Segurança Pública*) and the Republican National Guard (*Guarda Nacional Repúblicana*) (Opello 1991, 69–70). In 1927, the government of General Carmona established a new secret police—the "Vigilance and Defense section" of the Ministry of Interior (*Polícia de Vigilância e Defesa do Estado*, PVDE)—which was key to the Salazar regime's program of political repression (Harvey 1978, 11; Wheeler 1983, 3). The PVDE worked in conjunction with the military to imprison civilian rivals, prosecute them in political trials held in special military tribunals, and dole out harsh punishments, including deportation to faraway colonies (Opello 1991, 69–70; Osuna 2014b, 63; Pereira 2005, 181). Portugal in the first decade under the *Estado Novo* was a clear case of military overreach.

Jurisdictional contestation: Civilianization of Estado Novo *repression, 1945–74*

In 1945, with the Allied victory in World War II, Salazar implemented reforms to "improve Portugal's image" within an increasingly liberal, democratic Western Europe (Opello 1991, 71–72). Portugal had remained neutral during the war, and the authoritarian character of the *Estado Novo* was clear, giving Salazar reason to signal change to the international community. Each of the major reforms was a half-measure that may have served its purpose on the international stage but did little to change the level of repression. For example, Salazar allowed limited political competition in elections, but still restricted political organizing (Opello 1991, 71–72). Similarly, the government reformed and renamed the PVDE to be the International Police for the Defense of the State (*Polícia Internacional e do Defesa do Estado*, PIDE) but actually gave it more powers, notably the legal ability to detain people for years for political reasons (Osuna 2014b, 59; Pereira 2005, 182). Beginning in 1945, the Salazar regime also replaced the special military tribunals that had been in place since 1933 with Plenary Criminal Courts (*Tribunais Criminais Plenarios*), "special civilian courts located in Lisbon and Porto … presided over by judges trained in the law" (Pereira 2005, 181–82). This change represented a move toward civilianization of political repression, shifting the case from military overreach to jurisdictional contestation in the context of a new international political environment that was favorable to reform. Nevertheless, repression continued. The new civilian courts maintained jurisdiction over political and national security crimes (Andreu-Guzmán 2018, 146; Rosas et al. 2009). Similar to the conduct of the 1964–85 military regime in Brazil described in Chapter 5, Salazar's government engaged in a "highly legalistic form of repression" (Pereira 2005, 183).

The PIDE was effective at suppressing political activity in society at large, but it was not able to prevent dissent within the military (Harvey 1978). Civil-military relations under Salazar were complicated. In terms of reducing the direct presence of the military in government, the *Estado Novo* established civilian control over the military within the first two decades of the regime (Opello 1991, 69–70; Osuna 2014b), but there was considerable opposition to the Salazar regime within the military, including revolutionary factions who carried out armed revolts and others who plotted coups (Osuna 2019; Raby 1988; Silva and Ferreira 2019). Military intervention in government was a long-standing feature of Portuguese politics from the nineteenth century onward (Osuna 2014a), and "Salazar experienced at least 15 military coup attempts between 1931 and 1965" (Osuna 2019, 226). Such events were often the work of figures from the republican era seeking to oust Salazar and later from disaffected junior officers (Opello

1991, 72). Ultimately, it was a military intervention that brought an end to the *Estado Novo*.

Military overreach: The Carnation Revolution, 1974–76

In 1968, Salazar fell ill. His role as prime minister was over, and for the first time in over 35 years, Portugal was without his leadership. The military president chose Marcello Caetano, who had headed up a variety of ministries in the preceding decades, to be the new prime minister. Growing opposition to the regime, economic troubles, and the quagmire of colonial wars led Caetano to institute a program of political liberalization: he reduced media censorship, extended the franchise to all literate adults, and reformed the PIDE, which was renamed the General Directorate of Security (*Direcção-Geral de Segurança*, DGS) (Opello 1991, 77–79; Osuna 2014b, 52). The liberalization effort also included holding less restrictive elections to the National Assembly in 1969. The next round of elections in 1973, however, was "a throwback to those held when Salazar was alive" with opposition candidates barred from running on "technicalities" (Opello 1991, 79).

Managing the political opening was especially costly for the survival of the regime, because the country was simultaneously facing economic decline and the damaging effects of more than a decade of war against independence movements in the colonies. At the beginning of the *Estado Novo*, Salazar saw maintaining the empire as a useful, unifying tool of nationalism in Portugal and as a way of consolidating military support for his rule (Wheeler 1978, 249). By the 1960s, however, armed movements in the Portuguese colonies of Angola, Guinea-Bissau, and Mozambique were asserting their desire for independence, and carrying out colonial wars undermined the Portuguese economy and eroded military support for the regime. Over a decade of fighting, without a clear victory over independence movements, demonstrated that a political solution was necessary, yet the civilian government did not undertake such efforts while the military bore the brunt of the wars. Soldiers in the field were not well equipped (Osuna 2014a, 220), and personnel shortages forced the Portuguese government to recruit more broadly, including drafting student activists, which brought ardent anti-regime individuals into the military where they carried out acts of sabotage and encouraged desertion (Accornero 2013, 1045; Osuna 2014b, 38).

The colonial wars also fractured the military. Junior officers experienced the hardship of deployment to war zones while senior officers enjoyed privileged positions in Lisbon (Gill 2000, 160–61). The conduct of the war exacerbated the disconnect within the chain of command. Small units commanded by those of a rank no higher than captain carried out much of the fighting, and due to lack of routine communication, they did not always answer to a regular chain of command in the field (Osuna 2014a, 222; Osuna 2014b, 38).[3] Corporate grievances, combined with the hardship of the wars, led to increased political agitation within the military (Osuna 2014b, 40), especially among junior officers who feared being blamed for the eventual military defeat against the breakaway colonies (Gill 2000, 162; Opello 1991, 83).

On April 25, 1974, the Armed Forces Movement (*Movimento das Forças Armadas*, MFA), a group of reformist mid-level officers, removed Caetano from power in a coup (Rezola 2008). The MFA established new institutions, including the Assembly of the Armed Forces Movement and the Revolutionary Council, to implement a revolutionary socialist program and to guide a transition to civilian rule (Fishman 2011, 247; Gill 2000, 277; Serra 2010, 16). The new government sought to break with the war policies of the *Estado Novo*—"finding a political solution rather than a military one" (Fields 1976, 242)—and to institute significant reforms in government and the military. The MFA issued the *Proclamation of the Armed Forces Movement*, signaling short- and long-term changes the government would seek to make.[4] Among the short-term measures was the move to "insure the independence and dignity of the judicial power," which included "the extinction of special tribunals" and placing "crimes committed against the state" in the regular civilian court system (Fields 1976, 242). Additionally, the MFA called for the "immediate suspension of the DGS" (Porch 1977, 244). Civil society was still relatively weak at this moment in the transition (Hamann and Manuel 1999, 71) and the MFA saw itself as the one institution to provide a revolutionary break with the policies and repressive apparatus of the *Estado Novo* (Rezola 2008).

At the same time, however, it sought to establish firm military supervision over the transition and to maintain other institutional prerogatives (Gill 2000, 164–65; Serra 2010, 59). Despite its promise to eliminate special tribunals, the military did not trust the existing judicial system (despite undertaking a widespread purge) and therefore "became the principal force for public order" (Cerezales 2007, 161). The MFA government thus used military courts to put civilian members of the former government and of the secret police on trial (Pinto 2008, 313; Pinto 2010, 396–404).[5] This state of affairs shifted Portugal from jurisdictional contestation in the final years of the *Estado Novo* to military overreach under direct military rule from 1974 to 1976.

The period between the 1974 MFA coup and the establishment of the 1976 constitution was chaotic: Portugal went through six provisional governments. The MFA faced factionalism within its movement, governing partners who sought to moderate their plans for the country, a right-wing coup attempt in March 1975, and a left-wing coup attempt in November 1975 (Osuna 2019, 228–31). A moderate faction of the MFA eventually emerged as the dominant military and government actor, "which reasserted traditional military discipline and brought to power a group intent on the early passing of power to the civilians" (Gill 2000, 167).

Full subordination: Democracy and military justice reform, 1976–present

Portugal established its new civilian-led democracy in April 1976 through the approval of a new constitution and elections to the Legislative Assembly. While the military maintained a tutelary role through the Council of the Revolution until 1982 (Gill 2000, 167; Osuna 2014b, 9), the 1976 constitution broke with the past and began a new democratic era in which civilian government asserted control over the armed forces, including its justice system (Castaño 2017; Pinto 2010).[6] The 1976 transition was a critical juncture in Portugal's political history. It transformed the country, ushering in democracy and a commitment to the rule of law that did not exist in either the *Estado Novo* or the interim military rule of the MFA. The new government brought military justice under civilian control for the first time in Portugal's history, in an immediate change from military overreach to full subordination. The 1976 constitution upholds the principle of equality before the law (Article 13), rather than allowing people to be judged differently because of their status, such as service in the military. Article 218 defined the jurisdiction of military courts (*tribunais militares*) as limited to essentially military crimes (*crimes essencialmente militares*). Furthermore, Article 213, in a clear break with the institutions and practices of the *Estado Novo*, prohibited any special tribunals that would have jurisdiction over special categories of crimes. There would be no return to the political tribunals such as the Plenary Criminal Courts used by the Salazar regime. In a further demonstration of the importance of reforming military justice as part of the new era, Article 293 singled out the 1925 Code of Military Justice, which was still in effect, to be "harmonized with the constitution" within one year.

The transformative event of the transition to democracy moved Portugal directly from military overreach to full subordination, with the country achieving immediate and consistent compliance with civilian control. The democratic government worked to further refine the laws on the books over time. In 1977, the administration of Prime Minister Mário Soares successfully met the goal laid out in the 1976 constitution of establishing a new Code of Military Justice that followed the new constitutional principles, limiting military justice to "essentially military crimes."[7] The new code still described crimes beyond simple disciplinary offenses, which echoed the common crimes committed by personnel included in the country's previous codes of military justice. This contradiction led the Constitutional Court to rule in 1986 that an offense could not be defined as a military crime, subject to military justice, solely on the basis of the military status of the accused or the offense having taken place on military property (Andreu-Guzmán 2018, 147). Further Constitutional Court rulings in the 1990s declared more provisions of the 1977 Code of Military Justice unconstitutional, deepening legal subordination of the armed forces. For example, Article 207 of the 1977 Code of Military Justice provided for homicide and other corporal offenses committed by military personnel in the course of their duties to be adjudicated by military courts. The Court ruled that this provision extended military jurisdiction over a non-military crime in which the only reason the defendant would be treated differently was his connection to the armed forces.[8] The Court argued against the provision specifically on the grounds that it violated the constitutional principle of equality before the law (Article 13). Allowing for any extension of military jurisdiction beyond punishment of violations of military duty would be a reversal to military justice as a personal forum, which the 1976 Constitution prohibited. Notably, the Constitutional Court also justified its ruling on the grounds that military criminal law must pass the "test of its democratic legitimacy" by being clearly connected to the unique function of the military. Thus, in Portugal the high court is a principal actor in upholding democratic values in military legal affairs and reinforcing full subordination status.

In 1997, Portugal revised its constitution further to specify that military tribunals are allowed to exist only during a state of war and to have jurisdiction over "crimes of strictly military nature" (*crimes de natureza estritamente militar*) (Article 213).[9] In doing so, the old language of "accidental" military crimes and "essentially" military crimes ended. Following the constitutional reform, the government began drafting a new military code to harmonize the system with the new constitution.

The Portuguese legislature approved the new Code of Military Justice on November 15, 2003, and it went into effect on September 14, 2004.[10] It acknowledged the new constitutionally defined scope of military justice as limited to wartime and to judge only crimes of a strictly military nature (Article 128). Along with legislation that reorganized judicial bodies and provided for "military judges and military advisors in the Public Ministry" (Andreu-Guzmán 2018, 148), the new code reinforced civilian control of military justice. Today, regular civilian courts adjudicate cases involving armed forces personnel, which eliminates the potential for military justice to serve as a personal forum or privilege of service that undermines the rule of law and individual accountability. Furthermore, in cases in which the offense is "strictly military," military officers and civilian judges serve together to hear cases in chambers reserved for this purpose (Andreu-Guzmán 2018, 149). The system allows for the punishment of disciplinary offenses while ensuring that military law is not used to shield members of the armed forces from ordinary criminal prosecution and punishment.

Figure 4.1 illustrates reform through the critical juncture of democratization. Among the principal actors, the military had the strongest initial role in setting

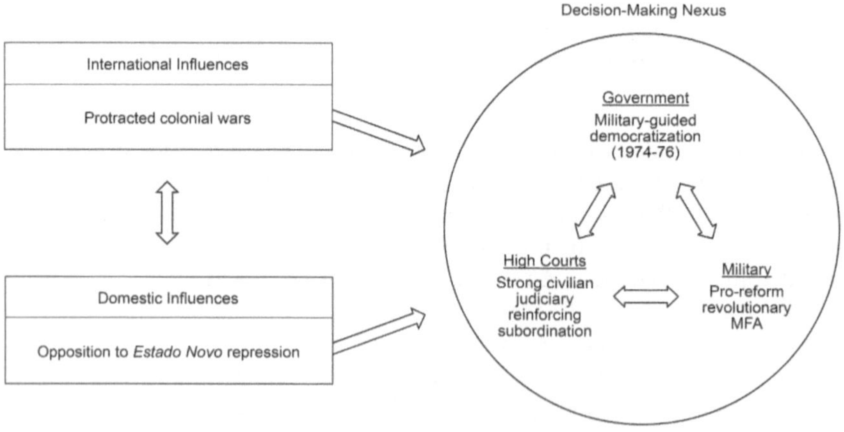

Figure 4.1 Full subordination in Portugal: Immediate reform

the course for reform. The revolutionary MFA faction that seized control of government in 1974 was committed to eliminating special courts, even those of the military. An active domestic civil society, strongly opposed to the decades of repression under the *Estado Novo*, helped set the political conditions for sweeping reform. International developments similarly set favorable conditions for a dramatic break with the past; namely the quagmire of failed military campaigns to hold on to colonies in Africa. After democratization, the high courts have been key players in reinforcing the system of full subordination by upholding democratic principles in military justice.

Colombia: Incremental reform

Colombia successfully subordinated its military to civilian control in its early post-independence history, but the onset of armed conflicts in the late-nineteenth century fundamentally altered the political landscape. Civilian governments routinely invoked states of emergency and extended military powers, including in the judicial arena. Military justice was an integral part of security operations against rebels and civilians alike, while the military simultaneously asserted authority over its personnel to avoid accountability for abuses. From 1886 to 1986, Colombia was firmly a case of military overreach. In 1987, a Supreme Court ruling prohibited military courts from trying civilians, shifting the country to the jurisdictional contestation category. This was reaffirmed in a new military code of justice and a new constitution shortly after. Military courts, however, continued to have extensive jurisdiction over military personnel, and the military frequently clashed with civilian authorities, making Colombia a case of jurisdictional contestation. In 2010, with a new military code of justice and increased cooperation between civilian and military courts, the country achieved full subordination.

Colonialism, independence, and civilian subordination of the military

In the Spanish empire, the military held significant power and the Crown granted its members extensive *fueros* (or privileges), including the right to maintain its own judicial system.[11] The high level of political and legal power of the military persisted in most of Spanish America after independence, but Colombia was an exception to the trend of colonial continuity. Stemming from the unique nature of its independence, the new government quickly exerted control over the military and eliminated most of its prerogatives, including those in the legal realm.

The war of independence against Spain was led by a small group of patriots, most prominently Simón Bolívar. By the end of the war, there were 30,000 enlisted men under Bolívar's control, and he attempted to create the highly centralized state of Gran Colombia with their support (Osterling 1989, 57). Colombian leaders, however, openly opposed his attempt to seize power and were antagonistic toward his Venezuelan army. This opposition contributed to the breakup of Gran Colombia in 1830 (Ruhl 1980b, 182), and the new Colombian government subsequently expelled over 200 military officers, including 13 generals, to Venezuela, along with the bulk of the army (Maingot 1970, 140).

Colombia's first constitution in 1832 limited the military to just 2,300 men, turned over control of its promotions to Congress, and eliminated its *fueros*.[12] The government placed all crimes committed by members of the military under the jurisdiction of civilian courts (Maingot 1970, 165). Due to fears over the legacy of Bolívar, the constitution also limited the extraordinary powers of the president. While he could order arrests during crises, detainees had to be turned over to a judge within 72 hours, and the constitution expressly prohibited the suspension of civil liberties and declarations of martial law (Loveman 1993, 163–64). The Colombian military and its legal power were fully subordinated to the civilian government after independence.

Surprisingly, this would persist for much of the remainder of the nineteenth century, despite the country being embroiled in violence for almost its entirety. Over the next 50 years, there were at least seven major civil wars and more than 60 regional wars, which killed over 20,000 people (Hartlyn 1988, 20–24; Osterling 1989, 47). There was ample opportunity for the government to empower the military and re-establish military courts to be used in its offensive against various opposition movements. The national Colombian military, however, played very little role, and these conflicts were mainly fought by "amateur officer-politicians" from the opposing Conservative and Liberal parties, who assembled their own militias and granted their own military titles (Osterling 1989, 47; Ruhl 1980a, 18). Colombia thus demonstrates how the nature of state formation, the creation of the military, and the establishment of military justice can persist far into the future.

The emergence of the military as a political actor

It was not until the end of the nineteenth century that a shift in military power occurred. Civilian politicians, for the first time, began using the military as a tool to achieve their goals. In turn, they made an effort to strengthen the institution. This included extending it more legal powers. The new constitution of 1886 reinstated some of the military *fueros*, including the right of military courts to try cases involving active military personnel.[13] The constitution also granted the president the ability to declare a state of siege during which he had sweeping powers to arrest and detain individuals suspected of committing a crime against the public order. Such crimes were then under the jurisdiction of military courts (Ruhl 1980a, 31). States of siege were common in subsequent decades and Colombia became a clear case of military overreach.

Tensions continued to grow between the Liberal and Conservative parties, leading to the outbreak of the War of a Thousand Days in 1899. By the time it ended in 1903 it had claimed approximately 100,000 lives. In prosecuting the war, the Conservative government issued a series of decrees that shifted trials of suspected rebels from civilian to military courts (Loveman 1993, 178). Over the coming decades, both parties would continue to use the military to support their aims. In power from 1930 to 1946, the Liberal party regularly employed the state of siege and military courts to confront Conservative resistance (Loveman 1993, 179). It was also during this period that legislation formally defined the military justice system for the first time (Maingot 1970, 166).[14]

Military overreach: La Violencia *and a permanent state of siege*

Colombia would become fully entrenched in the military overreach category when it became embroiled in a civil war that threatened its internal security for more than 70 years. In the 1946 presidential election, the Liberal vote was split between Jorge Eliécer Gaitán and Gabriel Turbay, allowing Conservative Mariano Ospina Pérez to take office. Rural violence increased between Liberals and Conservatives, and on April 9, 1948, Gaitán, who was widely expected to win the 1950 presidential election, was assassinated, which led to massive riots in Bogotá (the *Bogotazo*). Violence soon spread across the country, ushering in *La Violencia*, a 10-year civil war that would kill an estimated 200,000 people and displace more than a million.[15] The Conservative party formed an alliance with the military during the conflict and purged it of Liberal sympathizers (Ruhl 1980a, 22). In 1949, Pérez dissolved Congress, banned the Liberal party, and declared a state of siege (Loveman 1993, 179; Ríos-Figueroa 2016, 51–52).

When new Conservative president Laureano Gómez took office in 1950, he became a *de facto* dictator and launched a full-scale military operation into the Llanos Orientales region, in which the military exercised sweeping judicial powers. Any individuals over age 16 who fled from the military, violated the imposed curfew, or carried guns without authorization, could be executed without trial (Fluharty 1957, 119). Following a clash with Gómez, General Gustavo Rojas Pinilla, the commander-in-chief of the military, launched a bloodless coup on June 13, 1953. Rojas de-escalated the conflict significantly during his term through the use of a series of amnesties and pardons that enticed many of the larger, more organized armed groups to demobilize. Fears of his growing power, however, led the major political parties and the military to pressure Rojas to step down in 1957. A military junta served as a caretaker government while elections could be held. The country transitioned to democracy in 1958, ushering in a period known as the National Front in which the Liberal and Conservative parties agreed to rotate power (Hartlyn 1984).

The beginning of the National Front was conciliatory in nature, and the government extended an amnesty to any remaining armed actors in 1958.[16] Yet the state of siege was still in force in the departments of Caldas, Cauca, Huila, Tolima, and Valle del Cauca, and once the amnesty deadline passed on July 26, 1959, repression increased. The military imposed curfews and restricted movement within areas it controlled, and it was authorized to summarily execute those who attempted to flee (Sánchez and Meertens 2001, 152–57). The military grew from 20,800 in 1957 to 64,000 in 1968 (Ruhl 1980b, 187), and by 1964, only 22 of the estimated 129 guerrilla and bandit groups operating since 1949 were still active (Maullin 1973, 8). At the same time, a number of larger more organized guerilla groups in far flung areas remained intact, began to consolidate their power, and grew into *de facto* governments.[17] The two most prominent were the Revolutionary Armed Forces of Colombia—People's Army (*Fuerzas Armadas Revolucionarias de Colombia—Ejército del Pueblo*, FARC-EP), a Marxist-Leninist group, and the Army of National Liberation (*Ejército de Liberación Nacional*, ELN), a pro-Castro group.

To combat the larger groups, the government used the state of siege extensively (Ríos-Figueroa 2016, 54–56), during which the government could decree that military courts try civilians accused of any security-related crimes. Over time, decrees expanded the jurisdiction considerably, to cover the crimes of kidnapping, extortion, and bank robbery.[18] By the end of the 1970s, nearly one-third of all crimes in the Penal Code fell under the jurisdiction of military courts (Uprimny 2003, 52). Decree 2578 of 1976 gave the military the ability to impose a recognizance of good behavior on civilians if it was even suspected that they might commit a crime.[19]

Military courts also retained complete jurisdiction over their forces, and Decree 70 of 1978 excluded its members from all civilian criminal investigation for any crime committed in operations against kidnapping, extortion, or drug trafficking (Uprimny 2003, 54).[20] A Supreme Court ruling on March 9, 1978 reaffirmed the decree's constitutionality as long as the crimes took place during a planned operation (Cepeda 2004, 543).[21]

The FARC-EP and ELN continued to grow and by the mid-1970s were active in 91 municipalities. In response, new President Julio César Turbay (1978–82) issued Decree 1923, known as the Security Statute, in September 1978.[22] It expanded the jurisdiction of military courts over civilians to include any protests, demonstrations, or disruptions of public order. It also authorized the military to detain individuals for up to ten days without bringing charges against them, and it was not uncommon for the military to bring civilians hooded, without lawyers, to be held incommunicado at one of its secret interrogation centers. The decree also authorized the highest military court to decide conflicts of jurisdiction between civilian and military courts (Hartlyn 1988, 217–18; Steele 2017, 83).

In sum, through the mid-1980s, Colombia was firmly in the military overreach category: military courts retained complete jurisdiction over members of the military and had jurisdiction over civilians for a wide range of crimes. Their authority to try civilians particularly grew during states of siege, which presidents invoked frequently. From 1949 to 1991 Colombia was under a state of siege for 30 of the 42 years. Presidential decrees expanded the military's legal powers and Congress later approved them.

Moreover, the Supreme Court supported the military's position throughout this period. The military was involved in the selection of the first judges during the transition to the National Front and the process for appointing new judges shifted from one of executive and congressional approval to self-appointment (referred to as the co-optation system). This ensured that the Supreme Court remained loyal to the military (Uprimny 2003, 57–59). It considered states of siege and the decrees enacted within them to be political questions: it reviewed and verified the legality of the process of their declaration, but it did not weigh in on their content (Uprimny 2003, 54). In countless cases it upheld the jurisdiction of military courts over members of the military and civilians (Ríos-Figueroa 2016, 59–61). In sum, all three principal actors were united in their support of using military courts broadly to confront the security threat posed by the guerrillas.

Jurisdictional contestation: Political and judicial reform

The first reforms to the military justice system occurred in the 1980s, driven by changes in the civil war and Colombian politics more broadly. The illegal drug trade intensified throughout the decade, increasing the number of armed actors and exacerbating corruption within the government. The military used increasingly repressive tactics and turned even more to paramilitary groups to combat guerrillas and narco-traffickers. Human rights violations were widespread and began to draw international attention. Colombia's foreign and economic relations suffered in turn. As a reaction, three key developments occurred during the decade that would change Colombian politics, and the military's legal powers, dramatically.

First, the administrations of Belisario Betancur (1982–86) and Virgilio Barco (1986–90) broke with their predecessors and made a concerted effort to negotiate an end to the civil war. Shortly after taking office, Betancur declared a ceasefire, extended amnesties to armed groups, and granted the guerrillas belligerent status in accordance with the Geneva Conventions. The efforts culminated in the landmark 1984 La Uribe Agreement (*Acuerdos de la Uribe*) with the FARC-EP, which paved the way for the guerrillas to participate in legitimate politics.[23] In a sign of increased civilian authority over the military, Betancur fired the Minister of Defense and the heads of the army, air force, and Joint Chiefs of Staff on January 18, 1984, after they openly opposed the negotiations with the guerrillas (Martz 1997, 219). While the FARC-EP and ELN would eventually return to war, Barco engaged in peace processes with many smaller guerrilla groups.[24] They were not without setbacks, but the negotiations laid the groundwork for the groups' participation in the new constitution-writing process, as we discuss below. Changes in administrations thus played a major role in shifting the debate over the military and military justice.

Second, the Supreme Court shifted its position and took a stand against excessive executive power and the overreach of military courts. While it still refrained from ruling on states of siege themselves, the Court voided nearly 10% of all decrees enacted during them (Uprimny 2003, 55–56). A turning point came in 1985 when an armed group, the 19th of April Movement (*Movimiento 19 de Abril*, M-19), took over the Palace of Justice in Bogotá and held the Supreme

Court Justices hostage. The military's assault to retake the building killed over 100 people, including 11 of the Court's 25 justices. The judiciary's view of the military turned increasingly negative (Ríos-Figueroa 2016, 61). In 1987, new revelations of torture and disappearances at the hands of the military led to heightened international pressure and in March the Supreme Court ruled that military courts could no longer try civilians.[25] With the abolition of the ability of military courts to try civilians, and full compliance thereafter, Colombia shifted firmly into the jurisdictional contestation category. A new military code of justice in 1988 codified this change.[26] The Supreme Court also made its view clear that ordinary crimes committed by members of the military not directly related to military activities should be tried in civilian courts, but the military resisted such an encroachment on its power and compliance on this point was poor.

The third key development during this period was the growth of a strong human rights movement within the country, heavily supported by a network of international allies, including the International Commission of Jurists, Center for Justice and International Law, and Americas Watch (later named Human Rights Watch [HRW]) (Fox, Gallón-Giraldo, and Stetson 2010, 470). In 1981, a large number of diverse groups organized the Second National Forum for Human Rights and laid out a vision for a more open political system, and in 1987 a coalition of civil society organizations formed a national commission to push for a new constitution. The turning point came after the assassination of popular Liberal presidential candidate Luis Carlos Galán on August 18, 1989 and the subsequent rise of a large student movement that eventually coalesced into an even larger grassroots movement. They encouraged Colombians to cast an extra-legal ballot in favor of a National Constituent Assembly during the upcoming March elections. Over five million Colombians voted in favor. Elections for the assembly were held in December 1990. It began operating in February 1991 and produced a new constitution in July (Fox, Gallón-Giraldo, and Stetson 2010).[27]

The 1991 constitution included explicit protections for a wide range of rights and allowed for the *acción de tutela*, which gives citizens recourse to the courts when they believe public officials have violated or failed to protect their constitutional rights. It then established a new Constitutional Court to rule on constitutional issues and to conduct the final review of all *tutelas.* While the constitution permitted several states of exception, including the "state of internal commotion" that presidents can declare to deal with violence, they were far more restrictive than the preceding states of siege—the president was not allowed to suspend any branches of government or human rights and fundamental civil liberties, the Constitutional Court was authorized to automatically review all decrees passed during states of exception in a fast-track process, and states of siege expire when the exception ends. In addition, the constitution reaffirmed the 1987 Supreme Court ruling and expressly forbade military courts from trying civilians.

At the same time, however, the new constitution did not restrict the legal power of the military over its own forces. Article 221 granted military tribunals jurisdiction over crimes committed by the military and expanded that jurisdiction to include members of the police. Article 91 explicitly granted immunity for soldiers whose violations were the result of obeying superior orders. While there were discussions during the drafting of restricting the military's privileges, the military lobbied hard against such a move and made its acceptance of the new constitution "conditional" on its legal powers remaining intact (Avilés 2006, 94–95; Richani 2013, 40).

Colombia's transition to the jurisdictional contestation category was the result of a dramatic increase in domestic and international pressures for reform, a shift in the government's approach to the conflict, and a major change in the position of the Supreme Court. A strong domestic civil society movement worked closely with international NGOs. The military was implicated in human rights violations and public sentiment began to turn against it. Under international pressure and in response to a catalyzing event (the Palace of Justice Siege), the Supreme Court changed from supporting the government's use of military courts to directly challenging it.

The battle for control and compliance

Over the next two decades, Colombia would eventually move into the full subordination category, but it was a long battle between the military, politicians, courts, and activists, and the result was not inevitable. In fact, the successful reform is remarkable, given that during this period the internal security threat increased considerably. By 1994, the FARC-EP had over 10,000 combatants and 105 fronts operating in almost all of the country's territory. By 2006, there were an estimated 16,600 combatants, with another 8,000–10,000 active in local militias (Steele 2017, 96).

President César Gaviria (1990–94) drove the early efforts to rein in military judicial power. International pressure was a key factor. He was being considered for the position of Secretary General of the Organization of American States (and he would assume that role after his presidency) and needed to show commitment to democracy and human rights to secure the nomination, in particular to gain support from the United States (Avilés 2006). Gaviria appointed a civilian defense minister, created the Presidential Council on National Security to put military strategies under civilian control, and established the Justice and Security Unit in the National Planning Department to determine the military's budget (Avilés 2006, 64). He also implemented a number of initiatives to improve human rights training throughout the armed forces. In early 1994, Gaviria collaborated with the military to create a commission to reform the military justice system, though the military failed to take the effort seriously (Avilés 2006, 98).

Most importantly during this period, the Constitutional Court quickly asserted itself as the ultimate check on state power. Between 1992 and 1996 the Court voided over 30% of executive decrees (Uprimny 2003, 55–56). In a 1992 ruling, it went further and declared itself the authority to decide the legality of states of exception, rather than just the decrees enacted within them, and laid out a rigorous standard of review.[28] At the same time, however, it upheld the declaration in question, engaging in a strategy whereby it avoided "shaming the actors or producing outright non-compliance," while giving the actors time to "adapt and prepare for what was coming" (Ríos-Figueroa 2016, 73). It was not until 1994 that the Court struck down a state of internal commotion in its entirety.[29]

The Court's efforts were not unopposed. In 1995, it boldly declared that active military personnel could not preside as judges on military courts, arguing that this could affect their impartiality.[30] The military and its political allies called for the Constitutional Court's abolishment and, in June 1995, Congress almost approved a measure to curtail the Court's powers (Cepeda 1998, 89–90). Within a few months, Congress passed a constitutional amendment explicitly stating that military courts would be composed of active or retired members of the state's armed forces.[31]

Still, the Court continued to be assertive. In a landmark case in 1997, the Court struck down several key aspects of the 1988 military code of justice.[32] In its ruling, it laid out a very restrictive interpretation of the jurisdiction of military courts, limited to acts committed by members of the armed forces while carrying out their duties. Moreover, those acts need to have a close and direct relationship to a legitimate task. Because military courts are by their nature exceptional courts, in situations where there is any doubt, the case should be heard in the civilian court system. The court also dealt directly with human rights violations, arguing that crimes against humanity go against the constitutional function of the armed forces and can never be considered legitimate behavior in performing its duties. In turn, such crimes must be tried in civilian courts. Over the next few years the Court continued to define the conditions more narrowly and to further shift the jurisdiction of non-military crimes to civilian courts (Ríos-Figueroa 2016, 74).[33]

The early assertiveness and success of the Constitutional Court has several explanations. First, the Court benefited from a long history of judicial review in Colombia and thus did not have to build those norms from scratch as might new courts in other countries (Cepeda 2004, 537–45). The Court was also able to rule on a range of cases early on, given the constitutional requirement that it review all decrees during states of exception and due to the extensive use of the *tutela* by the population—between 1991 and 1994 there were more than 60,000 *tutelas* decided across the country (Cepeda 1998, 76). The new constitution and creation of the Constitutional Court was a critical juncture in Colombian politics with significant ramifications for military justice. Second, its work was aided by international pressure and jurisprudence. In 1995, the Inter-American Court of Human Rights (IACtHR) issued its first judgment against Colombia, in a case in which the military was accused of capturing, detaining, and disappearing two individuals in 1989.[34] Finally, individual, progressive judges mattered. Some of their nominations were barely approved by Congress and many of the votes in the Court on these important issues were close. Thus, in some ways, the Constitutional Court simply got lucky (Uprimny 2003, 63–64).

Despite these developments in jurisprudence, little changed on the ground during these years. The military became increasingly interconnected with paramilitaries, now organized in a larger umbrella organization called the United Self-Defense Forces of Colombia (*Autodefensas Unidas de Colombia*, AUC), in a brutal war in rural areas where there was little oversight and extrajudicial executions were common (HRW 1995, 65–106). Now implicated in human rights violations, the military made keeping its legal privileges a core interest and resisted attempts at reform. The Colombian government had a wide range of institutions designed to protect citizens from abuses, including the Office of the Inspector General (*Procuraduría General*), the Specialized Director against Human Rights Violations (*Directora Especializada contra las Violaciones a los Derechos Humanos*) in the Office of the Attorney General (*Fiscalía General de la Nación*), and the Ombudsman's Office (*Defensoría del Pueblo*). Yet the military and paramilitaries attacked and intimidated government investigators and citizens who tried to bring cases. The Attorney General had the right to bring charges against members of the military, but the military's delegate to the Office—the highest supervisory authority for the state's security forces—consistently delayed and closed cases. One former delegate stated publicly in 1993 that "his term had been successful in that only 1.7 percent of the cases resulted in military discipline" (HRW 1995, 19). Moreover, when cases did move forward, the Jurisdictional Disciplinary Chamber (*Sala Jurisdiccional Disciplinaria*) of the Superior Judicial Council (*Consejo Superior de la Judicatura*, CSJ) determined which court had jurisdiction and consistently ruled in favor of transferring cases to military courts, which subsequently almost always acquitted those on trial (Avilés 2006, 95–96). While there was some improvement, and military courts transferred over 500 cases to civilian courts from 1997 to 1999 (United States Department of State [USDS] 2000), it was not until the subsequent administrations of Andrés Pastrana (1998–2002) and Álvaro Uribe (2002–10) that compliance would significantly improve and full subordination would be reached.

Full subordination: Stronger courts and a stronger military

In 1999, Congress enacted a new military code of justice, which took effect in August 2000.[35] Once again, it prohibited military courts from trying civilians, and Article 3 explicitly required that all cases of torture, genocide, and enforced disappearance be tried in civilian courts. It also precluded unit commanders from judging their subordinates and included protections for soldiers who refused to carry out illegal orders to commit human rights violations. Moreover, it gave the Supreme Court, comprised of entirely civilian magistrates, the final review over all cases.

Aspects of the new code were quickly challenged, and in 2000 the Constitutional Court upheld the law but, quoting its 1997 judgment extensively, made it clear that those crimes were not the only three excluded from military court jurisdiction.[36] It concluded that "all criminal conduct that is openly contrary to the constitutional function of the security forces and that by its sole commission breaks the agent's functional link with the service, must be excluded from the field of competence of military criminal justice."[37] At the same time, the CSJ reversed its position and began to comply with the 1997 and 2000 Constitutional Court decisions and transferred appropriate cases to civilian courts (Andreu-Guzmán 2004, 246–47). Pastrana bolstered these rulings with a presidential decree in August 2000 that stated clearly that serious human rights violations should be tried in civilian courts, elevating the 1997 Constitutional Court ruling to the category of law (USDS 2001). In 2000, in cases of jurisdictional disputes, only 15% of cases were transferred to military courts, down from 50% in 1992 (USDS 2002).

The impact of the Constitutional Court was paramount, but initial compliance was poor. It would take increased judicial assertiveness over the coming decade to change this, facilitated by rising international and domestic pressure and a shift in the military's position on this issue as it collaborated with the government for increased power in other areas. The bargaining between the government and the military began under Pastrana. His approach to the conflict was conciliatory. He did not declare a state of emergency during his time in office and entered into formal peace negotiations with the FARC-EP and ELN, which included granting them a large demilitarized zone. This angered the military. Dozens of high-ranking officers, including 16 generals and 30 colonels, openly objected, and Defense Minister Rodrigo Hernán Lloreda resigned in protest in May 1999 (Richani 2013, 39). At the same time, however, the military's power increased. In 1999–2000, the United States and Colombia agreed on Plan Colombia, a $1 billion mostly military aid package to combat guerrillas and drug traffickers. This US support increased the capacity of and brought more prestige to the military, absorbing some of the frustration from the government curtailing its power in other areas. In addition, the heightened involvement of the United States brought increased scrutiny on the human rights practices of the Colombian military, leading it to become more willing, at least on paper, to comply with international standards.

Pastrana's peace process ultimately failed, and in 2002 Colombian voters elected independent candidate Álvaro Uribe, a hardliner who ran on a promise for a renewed military approach to confront the country's violence, to the presidency. Upon taking office, Uribe instituted a "war tax" on the wealthiest taxpayers and used the funds to further expand and professionalize the military. Combined with continued support from the United States, Uribe was able to increase the strength of the military dramatically. Over the first four years of his term, he expanded the armed forces by nearly 100,000 troops, and by the end of his second term in 2010, the government had gained effective control over most of the state for the first time in its history (Kline 2009, 5). In addition, Uribe facilitated the demobilization of the AUC in 2006, providing the military with an increased degree of monopoly on state power.[38]

Throughout this period, Uribe would make many attempts to expand the legal prerogatives of the military, but a united opposition, supported by an assertive Constitutional Court, stymied these efforts. A coalition of the Alternative

Democratic Pole (*Polo Democrático Alternativo*) party, labor unions, and human rights non-governmental organizations employed creative procedural strategies to slow down and obstruct legislation and challenged those laws that were enacted in the courts.

Within two weeks of his inauguration, Uribe declared a state of internal commotion and established "Rehabilitation and Consolidation Zones" in dangerous areas in which the military was granted judicial and police functions. In April 2003, however, the Constitutional Court declared the additional security procedures in these zones unconstitutional.[39] The most emblematic case was the response to Uribe's proposed Anti-Terrorist Statute in March 2004.[40] The constitutional reforms would have authorized military personnel to arrest, detain, and interrogate suspects without a court order. It would also create special units of "judicial military police" to operate in areas where other judicial authorities were not present (Kline 2009, 44). The opposition, however, created a procedural irregularity, which the Court used to strike down the statute in August 2004 (De Gamboa Tapias and Díaz Pabón 2018, 470).[41]

Given the military's increased power and prestige, it chose not to wage a public battle over its legal prerogatives. On June 14, 2006, the Minister of National Defense (*Ministro de Defensa Nacional*) and the Attorney General released a joint directive that reiterated the restrictive nature of the military criminal justice system and instructed all relevant parties to respect the constitutional jurisprudence (United Nations Human Rights Council [UNHRC] 2007). Another series of Ministry of National Defense directives in 2007 reinforced the need to respect the rule of law and protect human rights (UNHRC 2008). In September 2006, for the first time, a civilian became head of the military justice system. In subsequent years, military courts willingly transferred hundreds of cases to civilian courts. In 2006, civilian courts investigated over 100 members of the armed forces and convicted more than a dozen for murder or kidnapping and sentenced them to prison terms ranging from 20 to 38 years (USDS 2007). Where jurisdictional disputes arose, civilian courts were increasingly awarded the case. In the first half of 2005, for example, of 31 cases of jurisdictional dispute, only one case was transferred to military courts (United Nations Commission on Human Rights 2006).

Pressure to reform accelerated after 2008 when it was discovered that between 2002 and 2008 the military had killed more than 3,000 civilians and disguised them as guerrillas to boost their body counts (HRW 2015). The "false positives" scandal shifted public sentiment and brought intense international and domestic pressure for reform. Going forward there were more investigations and convictions of members of the military, and military courts increased their willingness to transfer cases to civilian courts (Ríos-Figueroa 2016, 77).[42] Additional measures to improve monitoring of units in 2008, new rules of engagement, and an Operational Law Handbook in 2009 also led to a dramatic decrease in human rights violations attributed to the military (UNHRC 2010).[43]

The Constitutional Court once again protected these gains. In 2008, it reviewed a draft bill for a new code of military justice and declared it unconstitutional, because it strayed too far from the restrictions laid out in the 1997 and 2000 court rulings.[44] The final code, passed in 2010, contained language that clearly limited the scope of military courts to a narrow set of crimes committed by members of the military in the course of carrying out their constitutionally defined duties.[45] While the civilian and military justice systems still have significant shortcomings and compliance is not absolute, it is at this point that we consider Colombia to have reached the full subordination category.

The Constitutional Court has continued to play the primary role in preventing backsliding. In 2012, Congress passed legislation to make several amendments to the constitution regarding military justice.[46] The law required crimes against humanity, and the crimes of genocide, enforced disappearance, extrajudicial execution, sexual violence, torture, and forced displacement to be tried in civilian courts, but left all other infractions related to international humanitarian law under the jurisdiction of military courts. Shortly thereafter, the Constitutional Court declared the entire law unconstitutional on procedural grounds.[47] Civilian courts continued to assert jurisdiction over members of the military, and in February 2011, officials from the military justice system and the Attorney General's Office developed a plan to meet regularly and attempt to transfer cases amicably rather than resort to the lengthy review by the CSJ (USDS 2012). In another positive sign, a magistrate of the CSJ was forced to resign in 2013 after it was discovered that he had promised a member of the military that he would ensure the transfer of his case to the military justice system (UNHRC 2014).

The military has attempted to regain some of its legal powers, in an effort to ensure it has a sufficient say in how conduct in armed operations is reviewed. From 2013 to 2014, the Ministry of National Defense submitted five proposals to Congress to expand military justice, and the Center Democratic (*Centro Democrático*) party submitted two more (UNHRC 2015). Legislative Act 01 of 2015 declared that the military should be judged under international humanitarian law given its role in engaging in armed combat.[48] Shortly thereafter, the Constitutional Court ruled that military behavior must also be judged under international human rights law, in line with obligations in the constitution and international treaties to which Colombia is a party.[49] In July 2015, Congress enacted legislation to restructure the military justice system.[50] Another ruling by the Constitutional Court reiterated the application of international human rights law to the behavior of the armed forces.[51]

Issues surrounding accountability for human rights violations continue to play a prominent role in Colombian politics. President Juan Manuel Santos (2010–18) successfully negotiated a peace agreement to end the civil war with the FARC-EP in 2016 (Nasi 2018).[52] The agreement created a Special Jurisdiction for Peace (*Jurisdicción Especial para la Paz*) to investigate and prosecute those involved in the conflict, allowing for potential reduced sentences for those who participate in its truth-telling and reparations components. As of this writing, debates continue about what crimes should be included and how command responsibility should be interpreted. The transitional justice process, however, only applies to past crimes, and the government continues to emphasize that current cases

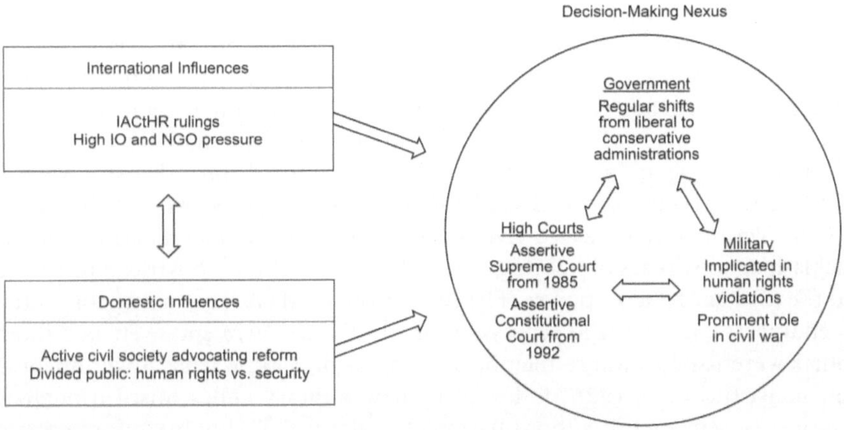

Figure 4.2 Full subordination in Colombia: Incremental reform

involving human rights violations are tried in civilian courts (Inter-American Commission on Human Rights 2017).

The case of Colombia is emblematic of how changes in domestic and international influences combined with gradual shifts in the positions of the principal actors can lead to successful reform. Colombia was once an entrenched system of military overreach, with the military having expansive legal powers. The government was willing to use all means at its disposal to confront guerrillas in its long, bloody civil war. The Supreme Court supported the government's position. As illustrated in Figure 4.2, however, as human rights violations escalated, public sentiment shifted and domestic human rights organizations launched a concerted effort to rein in the military's legal power. While there was no regime change in Colombia, the process of promulgating a new constitution and creating a Constitutional Court was a watershed moment in Colombian history. The shift in the role of the courts in the decision-making nexus dramatically shaped the trajectory of military justice, leading to reform. It would, however, require the military to change its own position for compliance to be realized. As it grew in size, and became better funded and increasingly professionalized, the military was more willing to acquiesce to efforts by the government and courts to limit its legal powers.

Conclusion

In systems of full subordination, military legal powers are limited. Military court jurisdiction extends only to military personnel to punish offenses contrary to good order and discipline in the armed forces. This system is most compatible with respecting the command imperative and facilitating military effectiveness, while also upholding the rule of law, democracy, and accountability for human rights violations. As with civilian control of the armed forces in other domains, military legal institutions and practices must ultimately answer to civilian authorities for a country to be ensured of good civil-military relations.

We identify two key pathways by which countries achieve full subordination—immediate reform at a critical juncture and incremental improvement over time in a dynamic process of change in laws and practices. Portugal illustrates a case of immediate reform in the context of regime change. Prime Minister António de Oliveira Salazar, who had held the post for over 35 years, fell ill and the *Estado Novo* faltered. Active civil society pressure for liberalization and the backlash against years of fighting colonial wars to hold on to African territories led the military to seize power. The revolutionary MFA faction was committed to ending the judicialized repression of the *Estado Novo* era, even as military courts were used to purge members of the prior regime from government. A new constitution in 1976, followed by new military codes, institutionalized the new system of full subordination. In contrast, Colombia reformed over many decades and in the context of an intense civil war. The internal security threat had justified exceptional executive and military power for long periods, but the election of reformers to the presidency, a Supreme Court ruling against military jurisdiction over civilians, and the growth of the human rights movement shifted the country from military overreach to jurisdictional contestation. Continued domestic and international pressure for reform and an assertive Constitutional Court further eroded military legal prerogatives, eventually completing the reform process by moving Colombia into full subordination in 2010.

These two pathways illustrate an important point about achieving reform and maintaining full subordination. Democratization is a transformative political event that presents opportunities to construct new institutions. Multiple sources of pressure, a cooperative or neutralized military, strong courts, and a lack of security threats help to erode potential legacies of the authoritarian regime and safeguard the achievement of full subordination in the long-term. Meanwhile, the lengthy process of reform that involves assertive civilian actors is most effective when it plays out as it did in Colombia with a negotiated process of reform of legal prerogatives coupled with attention to other areas of military interest such as pay, training, and procurement. This approach gives due consideration to the material and intangible corporate needs of the military while reining in legal power.

Notes

1 Alvará de Lei, July 15, 1763, O Governo dos Outros, Imaginários Políticos no Império Portugês (1496–1961), http://www.governodosoutros.ics.ul.pt/index.php?menu=consulta&id_partes=115&accao=ver&pagina=300.

2 Decreto n.° 11:292, (Codigo de Justiça Militar), Diário da República, Série I Numero 258, 28 November 1925, https://dre.pt/application/conteudo/203586.

3 For accounts of the conduct of Portugal's colonial wars in Africa and their impact on Portugal, see Cann 2012 and Venter 2013.

4 Lei n.° 3/74 de 14 de Maio, https://dre.pt/application/file/a/623309.

5 *Conselho da Revolução*, Lei n.° 8/75 de 25 de Julho, https://dre.pt/application/conteudo/336482.
6 Constituição da República Portuguesa, Decreto de aprovação Constituição de 10 de Abril, Diário da República n. 86/1976, Série I de 1976-04-10, https://dre.pt/application/conteudo/502635.
7 *Código de Justiça Militar*, Decreto-Lei n.° 141/77 de 9 de Abril, Diário da República, Série I—Número 83, https://dre.pt/application/conteudo/139922.
8 Acórdão 271/97 Tribunal Constitucional, May 15, 1997, Diário da República n.° 112/1197, Série I-A de 1997-05-15, https://dre.tretas.org/dre/81765/acordao-271-97-de-15-de-maio.
9 Assembleia da República, Lei Constitucional n.° 1/97, Diário da República Série-A N.° 218, September 20, 1997, https://dre.pt/application/conteudo/653562.
10 Assembleia da República, Lei Constitucional n.° 100/2003, Diário da República Série-A N.° 265, November 15, 2003, https://dre.pt/application/conteudo/446475.
11 For more on Spain's military *fueros*, see McAlister 1957.
12 Constitución Política del Estado de Nueva Granada 1 de 1832 (1 de Marzo de 1832), https://www.funcionpublica.gov.co/eva/gestornormativo/norma.php?i=13694.
13 Constitución Política de Colombia de 1886, Articulo 170, https://www.funcionpublica.gov.co/eva/gestornormativo/norma.php?i=7153.
14 Ley 3 de 1945 (febrero 19), "Sobre código de justicia penal military," http://www.suin-juriscol.gov.co/viewDocument.asp?ruta=Leyes/1557685.
15 The foundational work on *La Violencia* is Guzmán Campos, Fals Borda, and Umaña Luna 1963. The total of 200,000 dead is the most commonly cited, though estimates vary by source. This is also complicated by some disagreement on the end date of *La Violencia*. Most consider it ending in 1958 with the advent of the National Front, but others consider it lasting until 1964. Still others suggest that the period 1954–64 should be viewed as a distinct phase, bridging *La Violencia* to the Cold War-fueled guerrilla war. Abbey Steele (2017, 69) estimates that two million people fled their homes between 1951 and 1964, though acknowledges that an accurate number is difficult to determine.
16 Decreto Ley 328 de 1958 (noviembre 28), "por el cual se dictan unas disposiciones tendientes a facilitar el afianzamiento de la paz en los Departamento en donde subsiste el estado de sitio," http://www.suin-juriscol.gov.co/viewDocument.asp?ruta=Decretos/1075173.
17 For a concise overview of the emergence and decline of armed actors during the civil war, see Díaz Pabón 2018, in particular Figure 1 on page 17.
18 For example, Decreto Ley 593 de 1970 (abril 21), "Por el cual se atribuye a la Justicia Penal Militar el conocimiento de algunas infracciones previstas en las leyes penales communes," http://www.suin-juriscol.gov.co/viewDocument.asp?id=1855688; Decreto Ley 636 de 1970 (abril 30), "Por el cual se adiciona el Decreto número 593 de 1970 y se dictan otras disposiciones," http://www.suin-juriscol.gov.co/viewDocument.asp?id=1856764.
19 Decreto Ley 2578 de 1976 (diciembre 08), "Por el cual se dictan medidas conducentes al restablecimiento del orden público," http://www.suin-juriscol.gov.co/viewDocument.asp?ruta=Decretos/1918495.
20 Decreto Ley 70 de 1978 (enero 20), "Por el cual se dictan medidas conduncentes al restablecimiento del orden público," http://www.suin-juriscol.gov.co/viewDocument.asp?ruta=Decretos/1833239.
21 Corte Suprema de Justicia, Sentencia del 9 de marzo de 1978, MP Guillermo González Charry, http://www.suin-juriscol.gov.co/viewDocument.asp?id=30008927.
22 Decreto Ley 1923 de 1978 (septiembre 06), "Por el cual se dictan normas para la protección de la vida, honra y bienes de las personas y se garantiza la seguridad de los asociados," http://www.suin-juriscol.gov.co/viewDocument.asp?ruta=Decretos/1870140.

23 Acuerdos de la Uribe, 28 de marzo de 1984, https://peacemaker.un.org/colombia-acuerdouribe84.
24 The most prominent were the Popular Liberation Army (*Ejército Popular de Liberación*); Quintín Lame Armed Movement (*Movimiento Armado Quintín Lame*), an indigenous self-defense organization; Workers' Revolutionary Party (*Partido Revolucionario de los Trabajadores de Colombia*); Socialist Renewal Movement (*Corriente de Renovación Socialista*), a dissident faction of the ELN; Free Fatherland (*Patria Libre*); the Ricardo Franco Front, a 200-man hardline dissident faction of the FARC; and the Ernesto Rojas Commandos (*Comandos Ernesto Rojas*).
25 Corte Suprema de Justicia, Sentencia 20 del 5 de marzo de 1987, MP Jesús Vallegjo Mejía, http://www.suin-juriscol.gov.co/viewDocument.asp?id=30014948.
26 Decreto Ley 2550 de 1988 (diciembre 12), "Por el cual se expide el nuevo Código Penal Militar," http://www.suin-juriscol.gov.co/viewDocument.asp?id=1463049.
27 Constitución Política de República de Colombia 1991, http://pdba.georgetown.edu/Constitutions/Colombia/colombia91.pdf.
28 Corte Constitucional de Colombia, Sentencia C-004/92, https://www.corteconstitucional.gov.co/Relatoria/1992/C-004-92.htm.
29 Corte Constitucional de Colombia, Sentencia C-300/94, https://www.corteconstitucional.gov.co/Relatoria/1994/C-300-94.htm.
30 Corte Constitucional de Colombia, Sentencia C-141/95, https://www.corteconstitucional.gov.co/Relatoria/1995/C-141-95.htm.
31 Acto Legislativo 2 de 1995 (diciembre 21), "Por medio del cual se adiciona el artículo 221 de la Constitución Política," http://www.suin-juriscol.gov.co/viewDocument.asp?id=1825511.
32 Corte Constitucional de Colombia, Sentencia C-358/97, https://www.corteconstitucional.gov.co/Relatoria/1997/C-358-97.htm.
33 At the same time, it gained some support within the military by making other rulings in favor of benefits for the institution, including a special retirement system and control over promotions (Ríos-Figueroa 2016, 75–76).
34 *Caballero Delgado and Santana* v. *Colombia*, Merits, Inter-Am. Ct. H.R. (ser. C) No. 22 (December 8, 1995), https://www.corteidh.or.cr/docs/casos/articulos/seriec_22_ing.pdf.
35 Ley 522 de 1999, "por medio de la cual se expide el Código Penal Militar," http://www.suin-juriscol.gov.co/viewDocument.asp?ruta=Leyes/1661251.
36 Corte Constitucional de Colombia, Sentencia C-878/00, http://www.suin-juriscol.gov.co/viewDocument.asp?id=20042864.
37 Our translation.
38 The process included an eight-year cap on prison terms for demobilized paramilitaries provided that they faithfully engaged in a complex truth and reparations process, see Ley 975 de 2005 (julio 25), "Por la cual se dictan disposiciones para la reincorporación de miembros de grupos armados organizados al margen de la ley, que contribuyan de manera efectiva a la consecución de la paz nacional y se dictan otras disposiciones para acuerdos humanitarios," http://www.secretariasenado.gov.co/senado/basedoc/ley_0975_2005.html.
39 Corte Constitucional de Colombia, Sentencia C-327/03, https://www.corteconstitucional.gov.co/Relatoria/2003/C-327-03.htm.
40 Acto Legislativo 2 de 2003 (diciembre 18), "Por medio del cual se modifican los artículos 15, 24, 28 y 250 de la Constitución Política de Colombia para enfrentar el terrorismo," https://www.funcionpublica.gov.co/eva/gestornormativo/norma.php?i=11151.
41 Corte Constitucional de Colombia, Sentencia C-816/04, https://www.corteconstitucional.gov.co/Relatoria/2004/C-816-04.htm.
42 Some of the international pressure came from the IACtHR, which ruled against Colombia twice in 2007, see *Escué-Zapata* v. *Colombia*, Merits, Reparations and Costs, Inter-Am. Ct. H.R. (ser. C) No. 165 (July 4, 2007), http://www.corteidh.

or.cr/docs/casos/articulos/seriec_165_ing.pdf; *Rochela Massacre* v. *Colombia*, Merits, Reparations and Costs, Inter-Am. Ct. H.R. (ser. C) No. 163 (May 11, 2007), http://www.corteidh.or.cr/docs/casos/articulos/seriec_163_ing.pdf.

43 The dramatic drop in human rights violations and the increase in accountability beginning in 2009 is evident in the annual reports of the United Nations High Commissioner for Human Rights, Human Rights Watch, Amnesty International, and Freedom House, and in the United States Department of State's Country Reports on Human Rights Practices.

44 Corte Constitucional de Colombia, Sentencia C-533/08, http://www.suin-juriscol.gov.co/viewDocument.asp?id=20030849#ver_20030855.

45 Ley 1407 de 2010, http://www.suin-juriscol.gov.co/viewDocument.asp?id=1678866.

46 Acto Legislativo 2 de 2012 (diciembre 27), "Por el cual se reforman los artículos 116, 152 y 221 de la Constitución Política de Colombia," http://www.suin-juriscol.gov.co/viewDocument.asp?id=1810178.

47 Corte Constitucional de Colombia, Sentencia C-740/13, http://www.suin-juriscol.gov.co/viewDocument.asp?id=20038688.

48 Acto Legislativo 1 de 2015 (junio 25), "Por el cual se reforma el artículo 221 de la Constitución Política de Colombia," http://www.suin-juriscol.gov.co/viewDocument.asp?id=30019907.

49 Corte Constitucional de Colombia, Sentencia C-084/16, https://www.corteconstitucional.gov.co/RELATORIA/2016/C-084-16.htm.

50 Ley 1765 de 2015 (julio 23), "Por la cual se reestructura la Justicia Penal Militar y Policial, se establecen requisitos para el desempeño de sus cargos, se implementa su Fiscalía General Penal Militar y Policial, se organiza su cuerpo técnico de investigación, se señalan disposiciones sobre competencia para el tránsito al sistema penal acusatorio y para garantizar su plena operatividad en la Jurisdicción Especializada y se dictan otras disposiciones," http://www.suin-juriscol.gov.co/viewDocument.asp?id=30019977.

51 Corte Constitucional de Colombia, Sentencia C-326/16, https://www.corteconstitucional.gov.co/relatoria/2016/c-326-16.htm.

52 Final Agreement to End the Armed Conflict and Build a Stable and Lasting Peace, November 24, 2016, http://especiales.presidencia.gov.co/Documents/20170620-dejacion-armas/acuerdos/acuerdo-final-ingles.pdf.

References

Accornero, Guya. 2013. "Contentious Politics and Student Dissent in the Twilight of the Portuguese Dictatorship: Analysis of a Protest Cycle." *Democratization* 20 (6): 1036–55. DOI: 10.1080/13510347.2012.674367.

Almeida, Pedro Tavares de. 2018. "Elections and Parliamentary Recruitment in Portugal." In *The Politics of Representation: Elections and Parliamentarism in Portugal and Spain, 1875–1926*, eds. Pedro Tavares de Almeida and Javier Moreno Luzón. Brighton, UK: Sussex Academic Press, 7–38.

Andreu-Guzmán, Federico. 2004. *Military Courts and Gross Human Rights Violations. Vol. 1. of Military Jurisdiction and International Law*. Geneva: International Commission of Jurists. https://www.icj.org/military-jurisdiction-and-international-law-military-courts-and-gross-human-rights-violations-vol-1/.

Andreu-Guzmán, Federico. 2018. *Fuero militar y Derecho internacional: Los civiles ante los tribunales militares. Vol. 2 of Military Jurisdiction and International Law*. Geneva: International Commission of Jurists. https://www.icj.org/wp-content/uploads/2018/05/Universal-Tribunales-Militares-Vol-II-Publications-Reports-Thematic-reports-2018-SPA.pdf.

Avilés, William. 2006. *Global Capitalism, Democracy, and Civil-Military Relations in Colombia*. Albany: State University of New York Press.

Benton, Lauren. 2010. *A Search for Sovereignty: Law and Geography in European Empires, 1400–1900*. Cambridge: Cambridge University Press. DOI: 10.1017/CBO9780511988905.

Brilhante, Rodrigues Neuma. 2017. "Resultados parciais e expectativas frustradas: os Cunha Mattos sob as reformas de Lippe." *Almanack* 16: 309–42. DOI: 10.1590/2236-463320171606.

Cann, John P. 2012. *Counterinsurgency in Africa: The Portuguese Way of War 1961–1974*. Solihull, UK: Helion & Company.

Castaño, David. 2017. "To the Barracks: The President, the Military and Democratic Consolidation in Portugal (1976–1980)." *European Review of History* 24 (1): 1–16. DOI: 10.1080/13507486.2016.1155541.

Cepeda, Manuel José. 1998. "Democracy, State and Society in the 1991 Constitution: The Role of the Constitutional Court." In *Colombia: The Politics of Reforming the State*, ed. Eduardo Posada-Carbó. New York: St. Martin's, 71–95. DOI: 10.1007/978-1-349-26050-9_4.

Cepeda, Manuel José. 2004. "Judicial Activism in a Violent Context: The Origin, Role, and Impact of the Colombian Constitutional Court." *Washington University Global Studies Law Review* 3 (4): 529–700.

Cerezales, Diego Palacios. 2007. "'Fascist Lackeys'? Dealing with the Police's Past during Portugal's Transition to Democracy (1974–1980)." *Portuguese Journal of Social Science* 6 (3): 155–69. DOI: 10.1386/pjss.6.3.155_1.

Coates, Timothy J. 2014. *Convict Labor in the Portuguese Empire, 1740–1932: Redefining the Empire with Forced Labor and New Imperialism*. Leiden, the Netherlands: Brill. DOI: 10.1163/9789004254312.

Cruz, Manuel Braga da. 1988. *O partido e o estado no Salazarismo*. Lisbon: Editorial Presença.

De Gamboa Tapias, Camila, and Fabio Andrés Díaz Pabón. 2018. "The Transitional Justice Framework agreed between the Colombian Government and the FARC-EP." In *Truth, Justice and Reconciliation in Colombia: Transitioning from Violence*, ed. Fabio Andrés Díaz Pabón. New York: Routledge, 66–84.

De Meneses, Felipe Ribeiro. 2004. *Portugal 1914–1926: From the First World War to Military Dictatorship*. Bristol, UK: Hispanic, Portuguese, and Latin American Monographs.

Díaz Pabón, Fabio Andrés. 2018. "Conflict and Peace in the Making: Colombia from 1948–2010." In *Truth, Justice and Reconciliation in Colombia: Transitioning from Violence*, ed. Fabio Andrés Díaz Pabón. New York: Routledge, 15–33.

Dores Costa, Fernando. 2009. "O Conselho de Guerra como lugar de poder: a delimitação da sua autoridade." *Análise Social* 44 (191): 379–414.

Fields, Rona M. 1976. *The Portuguese Revolution and the Armed Forces Movement*. New York: Praeger.

Fishman, Robert M. 2011. "Democratic Practice after the Revolution: The Case of Portugal and Beyond." *Politics & Society* 39 (2): 233–67. DOI: 10.1177/003239211405439.

Fluharty, Vernon Lee. 1957. *Dance of the Millions: Military Rule and the Social Revolution in Colombia 1930–1956*. Pittsburgh: University of Pittsburgh Press.

Fox, Donald T., Gustavo Gallón-Giraldo, and Anne Stetson. 2010. "Lessons of the Colombian Constitutional Reform of 1991: Toward the Securing of Peace and Reconciliation?" In *Framing the State in Times of Transition: Case Studies in Constitution Making*, ed. Laurel E. Miller. Washington, DC: United States Institute of Peace Press, 467–82.

Gill, Graeme. 2000. *The Dynamics of Democratization: Elites, Civil Society, and the Transition Process.* New York: Palgrave Macmillan.

Guzmán Campos, Germán, Orlando Fals Borda, and Eduardo Umaña Luna. 1963. *La Violencia en Colombia: Estudio de un proceso social.* 2nd ed. Bogotá: Ediciones Tercer Mundo.

Hamann, Kerstin, and Paul Christopher Manuel. 1999. "Regime Changes and Civil Society in Twentieth-Century Portugal." *South European Society & Politics* 4 (1): 71–96. DOI: 10.1080/13608740408539560.

Hartlyn, Jonathan. 1984. "Military Governments and the Transition to Civilian Rule: The Colombian Experience of 1957–1958." *Journal of Interamerican Studies and World Affairs* 26 (2): 245–81. DOI: 10.2307/165470.

Hartlyn, Jonathan. 1988. *The Politics of Coalition Rule in Colombia.* New York: Cambridge University Press.

Harvey, Robert. 1978. *Portugal: Birth of a Democracy.* London: Macmillan.

Hayes, Robert A. 1976. "The Formation of the Brazilian Army and the Military Class Mystique, 1500–1853." In *Perspectives on Armed Politics in Brazil*, eds. Henry H. Keith and Robert A. Hayes. Tempe: Arizona State University Press, 1–26.

Human Rights Watch. 1995. *State of War: Political Violence and Counterinsurgency in Colombia.* New York: Human Rights Watch.

Human Rights Watch. 2015. "On Their Watch: Evidence of Senior Army Officers' Responsibility for False Positive Killings in Colombia." https://www.hrw.org/report/2015/06/24/their-watch/evidence-senior-army-officers-responsibility-false-positive-killings.

Inter-American Commission on Human Rights. 2017. "Annual Report 2017: Follow-Up to Recommendations Made by The IACHR in its Report Truth, Justice, and Reparation: Fourth Report on the Situation of Human Rights in Colombia." http://www.oas.org/en/iachr/docs/annual/2017/docs/IA2017cap.5CO-en.pdf.

Kay, Hugh. 1970. *Salazar and Modern Portugal.* New York: Hawthorn.

Kline, Harvey F. 2009. *Showing Teeth to the Dragons: State-building by Colombian President Álvaro Uribe Vélez 2002–2006.* Tuscaloosa: University of Alabama Press.

Linz, Juan, and Alfred Stepan. 1996. *Problems of Democratic Transition and Consolidation: Southern Europe, South America, and Post-Communist Europe.* Baltimore: Johns Hopkins University Press.

Loi, Stefano. 2018. "The Creation of the Portuguese General Staff: Origins, Reasons and Results, 1834–1911." *Portuguese Journal of Social Science* 17(3): 255–71. DOI: 10.1386/pjss.17.3.255_1.

Loveman, Brian. 1993. *The Constitution of Tyranny: Regimes of Exception in Spanish America.* Pittsburgh: University of Pittsburgh Press.

Madureira, Nuno Luís. 2010. "Revolution and Policy Failure: The 1910s Portuguese Republic." *European Review of History* 17 (4): 647–63. DOI: 10.1080/13507486/2010.495767.

Maingot, Anthony P. 1970. "Colombia." In *The Military in Latin American Socio-Political Evolution: Four Case Studies*, eds. Lyle N. McAlister, Anthony P. Maingot, and Robert A. Potash. Washington, DC: Center for Research in Social Systems, 127–95.

Martz, John D. 1997. *The Politics of Clientelism: Democracy and the State in Colombia.* New Brunswick, NJ: Transaction. DOI: 10.1007/s12117-997-1145-5.

Maullin, Richard. 1973. *Soldiers, Guerrillas, and Politics in Colombia.* Lexington, MA: Lexington.

McAlister, Lyle N. 1957. *The "Fuero Militar" in New Spain: 1764–1800.* Gainesville: University of Florida Press.

Nasi, Carlo. 2018. "The Peace Process with the FARC-EP." In *Truth, Justice and Reconciliation in Colombia: Transitioning from Violence*, ed. Fabio Andrés Díaz Pabón. New York: Routledge, 34–49. DOI: 10.4324/9781315148373-3.

Opello, Walter C., Jr. 1991. *Portugal: From Monarchy to Pluralist Democracy*. Boulder: Westview.

Osterling, Jorge P. 1989. *Democracy in Colombia: Clientelist Politics and Guerrilla Warfare*. New Brunswick, NJ: Transaction.

Osuna, José Javier Olivas. 2014a. "The Deep Roots of the Carnation Revolution: 150 Years of Military Interventionism in Portugal." *Portuguese Journal of Social Science* 13 (2): 215–31. DOI: 10.1386/pjss.13.2.215_1.

Osuna, José Javier Olivas. 2014b. *Iberian Military Politics: Controlling the Armed Forces During Dictatorship and Democratisation*. New York: Palgrave Macmillan.

Osuna, José Javier Olivas. 2019. "Revolutionary versus Reactionary: Contrasting Portuguese and Spanish Civil-Military Relations during Democratisation." *War & Society* 38 (3): 225–48. DOI: 10.1080/07292473.2019.1517663.

Payne, Stanley G. 2011. *Civil War in Europe, 1905–1949*. Cambridge: Cambridge University Press. DOI: 10.1017/CBO9780511820465.

Pereira, Anthony W. 2005. *Political (In)Justice: Authoritarianism and the Rule of Law in Brazil, Chile, and Argentina*. Pittsburgh: University of Pittsburgh Press.

Pinto, António Costa. 1986. "The Radical Right and the Military Dictatorship in Portugal: The National May 28 League (1928–1933)." *Luso-Brazilian Review* 23 (1): 1–15.

Pinto, António Costa. 2008. "The Legacy of the Authoritarian Past in Portugal's Democratisation, 1974–6." *Totalitarian Movements and Political Religions* 9 (2–3): 265–91. DOI: 10.1080/14690760802094891.

Pinto, António Costa. 2010. "Coping with the Double Legacy of Authoritarianism and Revolution in Portuguese Democracy." *South European Society and Politics* 15 (3): 395–412. DOI: 10.1080/13608746.2010.513601.

Porch, Douglas. 1977. *The Portuguese Armed Forces and the Revolution*. Stanford: The Hoover Institution Press.

Raby, D. L. 1988. *Fascism and Resistance in Portugal: Communists, Liberals and Military Dissidents in the Opposition to Salazar, 1941–1974*. Manchester, UK: Manchester University Press.

Rezola, Maria Inácia. 2008. "The Military, 25 April and the Portuguese Transition to Democracy." *Portuguese Journal of Social Science* 7 (1): 3–16. DOI: 101386.pjss.7.1.3_1.

Richani, Nazih. 2013. *Systems of Violence: The Political Economy of War and Peace in Colombia*, 2nd ed. Albany: State University of New York Press.

Ríos-Figueroa, Julio. 2016. *Constitutional Courts as Mediators: Armed Conflict, Civil-Military Relations, and the Rule of Law in Latin America*. New York: Cambridge University Press. DOI: 10.1017/CBO9781139942157.

Rosas, Fernando, Irene Flunser Pimentel, Maria Inácia Rezola, João Madeira, and Luís Farinha. 2009. *Tribunais Políticos: Tribunais Militares Especiais e Tribunais Plenários durante a Ditadura e o Estado Novo*. Lisbon: Temas e Debates.

Ruhl, J. Mark. 1980a. *Colombia: Armed Forces and Society*. Syracuse: Maxwell School of Citizenship and Public Affairs, Syracuse University Press.

Ruhl, J. Mark. 1980b. "The Military." In *Politics of Compromise: Coalition Government in Colombia*, eds. R. Albert Berry, Ronald G. Hellman, and Maurcio Solaún. New Brunswick, NJ: Transaction, 181–206.

Sánchez, Gonzalo, and Donny Meertens. 2001. *Bandits, Peasants, and Politics: The Case of "La Violencia" in Colombia*. Trans. Alan Hynds. Austin: University of Texas Press.

Serra, Narcís. 2010. *The Military Transition: Democratic Reform of the Armed Forces.* Cambridge: Cambridge University Press.

Silva, Raquel, and Ana Sofia Ferreira. 2019. "The Post-Dictatorship Memory Politics in Portugal which Erased Political Violence from the Collective Memory." *Integrative Psychological and Behavioral Science* 53 (1): 24–43. DOI: 10.1007/s12124-018-9452-8.

Souza, Adriana Barreto. 2015. "The Governance of the Military Justice between Lisboa and Rio de Janeiro (1750–1820)." *Almanack* 10: 368–408. DOI: 10.1590/2236-463320151009.

Speelman, Patrick J. 2012. "Strategic Illusions and the Iberian War of 1762." In *The Seven Years' War: Global Views*, eds. Mark H. Danley and Patrick J. Speelman. Leiden, the Netherlands: Brill, 429–60. DOI: 10.1163/9789004236448_017.

Steele, Abbey. 2017. *Democracy and Displacement in Colombia's Civil War.* Ithaca: Cornell University Press. DOI: 10.7591/9781501709753.

Tengwall, David Lewis. 2010. *The Portuguese Revolution (1640–1668): A European War of Freedom and Independence.* Lewiston, NY: Edwin Mellen.

United Nations Commission on Human Rights. 2006 "Report of the United Nations High Commissioner for Human Rights on the Situation of Human Rights in Colombia." E/CN.4/2006/9. https://digitallibrary.un.org/record/572003?ln=en.

United Nations Human Rights Council. 2007. "Report of the United Nations High Commissioner for Human Rights on the Situation of Human Rights in Colombia." A/HRC/4/48. https://digitallibrary.un.org/record/595276?ln=en.

United Nations Human Rights Council. 2008. "Report of the United Nations High Commissioner for Human Rights on the Situation of Human Rights in Colombia." A/HRC/7/39. https://digitallibrary.un.org/record/624685?ln=en.

United Nations Human Rights Council. 2010. "Report of the United Nations High Commissioner for Human Rights on the Situation of Human Rights in Colombia." A/HRC/13/72. https://digitallibrary.un.org/record/678713?ln=en.

United Nations Human Rights Council. 2014. "Annual Report of the United Nations High Commissioner for Human Rights: Addendum: Situation of Human Rights in Colombia." A/HRC/25/19/Add.3. https://digitallibrary.un.org/record/766691?ln=en.

United Nations Human Rights Council. 2015. "Annual Report of the United Nations High Commissioner for Human Rights: Addendum: Report of the United Nations High Commissioner for Human Rights on the Situation of Human Rights in Colombia." A/HRC/28/3/Add.3. https://digitallibrary.un.org/record/788949?ln=en.

United States Department of State. 2000. "Colombia: Country Reports on Human Rights Practices 1999." https://2009-2017.state.gov/j/drl/rls/hrrpt/1999/380.htm.

United States Department of State. 2001. "Colombia: Country Reports on Human Rights Practices 2000." https://2009-2017.state.gov/j/drl/rls/hrrpt/2000/wha/741.htm.

United States Department of State. 2002. "Colombia: Country Reports on Human Rights Practices 2001." https://2009-2017.state.gov/j/drl/rls/hrrpt/2001/wha/8326.htm.

United States Department of State. 2007. "Colombia: Country Reports on Human Rights Practices 2006." https://2009-2017.state.gov/j/drl/rls/hrrpt/2006/78885.htm.

United States Department of State. 2012. "Colombia: Country Reports on Human Rights Practices 2011." https://2009-2017.state.gov/j/drl/rls/hrrpt/2011humanrightsreport/index.htm.

Uprimny, Rodrigo. 2003. "The Constitutional Court and Control of Presidential Extraordinary Powers in Colombia." *Democratization* 10 (4): 46–69. DOI: 10.1080/13510340312331294027.

Venter, Al J. 2013. *Portugal's Guerrilla Wars in Africa: Lisbon's Three Wars in Angola, Mozambique and Portuguese Guinea 1961–74*. Solihull, UK: Helion & Company.

Wheeler, Douglas L. 1978. *Republican Portugal: A Political History 1910–1926*. Madison: University of Wisconsin Press.

Wheeler, Douglas L. 1983. "In Service of Order: The Portuguese Political Police and the British, German and Spanish Intelligence, 1932–1945." *Journal of Contemporary History* 18 (1): 1–25.

5 Jurisdictional contestation in Indonesia and Fiji: Competing for control of military justice

Introduction

In systems of jurisdictional contestation, civilian and military authorities regularly clash over legal powers. While militaries do not have jurisdiction over civilians, they claim almost total legal control over their own personnel. Members of the armed forces are subject to military justice, even for crimes that exist in civilian criminal law. This state of affairs may be the result of statutes that explicitly vest military courts with these powers or from the military's consistent refusal to cooperate with the transfer of relevant cases to civilian courts when the civilian and military codes overlap. Such an enclave of military power represents a dangerous rupture in civilian control of the military and a threat to the rule of law. Soldiers are beyond the reach of civilian legal authority, turning the parallel system of military justice into a mechanism of impunity for human rights violations, past and present. Militaries may fight to retain judicial powers specifically to avoid scrutiny for human rights abuses committed during previous eras of military dictatorship or to shield their personnel from the law when deployed in ongoing domestic missions such as combatting an insurgency or engaging in policing duties.

There are two pathways by which countries arrive in the jurisdictional contestation category. First, a country may move up from military overreach through the successful reform of its system by wresting jurisdiction over civilians from the hands of military courts. While this is a significant accomplishment, the reforms stall and remain incomplete. The military continues to assert control over its personnel and routinely refuses to comply with civilian jurisdiction. We illustrate this pathway of stalled reform with Indonesia, where the country made progress during a period of general political liberalization but internal conflict and threats of terrorism have given the military enough leverage to prevent further changes to military justice. By contrast, a country may backslide from full subordination to jurisdictional contestation. In this pathway, the growth of a severe internal security threat or other major disruption to normal democratic politics leads to an expansion of military power, including the ability to dictate terms on military courts or to resist civilian efforts to restrain them. We illustrate this category with Fiji, where the initial post-colonial system of full subordination regressed into jurisdictional contestation after a military coup.

Indonesia: From independence to guided democracy

In 1800, the Netherlands established the Dutch East Indies colony in present-day Indonesia. The military and military justice were vital to Dutch control over the territory, and the government enacted a number of emergency measures, including the 1939 Regulation on State of War and Siege (*Regeling Staat van Oorlog en van Beleg*, SOB). The Dutch government regularly imposed martial law in various parts of the colony throughout its rule (1800–1949) (Kurniawan 2018, 47). Where contact with the central government was difficult, regional military commanders could impose martial law themselves. When the Japanese invaded and occupied the region during World War II, Indonesians initially welcomed them as liberators, but Japan soon imposed a repressive regime of its own, with laws mirroring the martial law of the Dutch period (Kurniawan 2018, 48).

Following the defeat of Japan in 1945, Indonesia waged a four-year guerrilla war before the Dutch recognized its sovereignty in 1949 (though the Netherlands kept the region of West Papua until 1963). The nature of the military's formation during this period heavily influenced civil-military relations in the decades to follow. The government initially chose not to create a national army, instead establishing the small People's Security Body (*Badan Keamanan Rakyat*, BKR). It quickly realized it needed a larger force to secure its sovereignty and less than two months later transformed the BKR into the larger People's Security Army (*Tentara Keamanan Rakyat*, TKR). A year later, the TKR incorporated irregular militias and became the Army of the Republic of Indonesia (*Tentara Republik Indonesia*, TRI) and then finally the Indonesian National Army (*Tentara Nasional Indonesia*, TNI).

The TNI began as a "loose assemblage of commanders and their followers with little central coordination" (Bourchier 2015, 101). There was a major schism between Japanese-trained officers and the former Royal Netherlands East Indies Army officers, and regional military commanders effectively became warlords, engaging in illegal trade with little oversight. The preceding guerrilla war also meant that the military was involved in many non-military affairs and viewed itself as the guardian of the nation, laying the groundwork for its continued engagement in politics after independence (Honna 2009, 227). The military's role expanded significantly over the next two decades (Sundhaussen 1982).

The revolutionary period also established Indonesia's practice of using emergency laws and military courts to govern. Law No. 6/1946 established the State of Emergency and Law No. 7/1946 granted military courts jurisdiction over members of the military for all crimes.[1] The government declared martial law to deal with communist uprisings countrywide in 1946 and in East Java in 1948. In 1948, facing a well-entrenched Dutch occupation in the major cities, the

Military Commander of Java Command issued a decree declaring a state of "war emergency" in the entire territory of Indonesia. The military took over all aspects of civilian government, with civilian officials functioning as military advisors (Kurniawan 2018, 50). This arrangement continued following independence, with the government declaring states of emergency in South Sulawesi; North and South Maluku; West, Central, and East Java; Yogyakarta; and the Seram Islands, at various times between 1950 and 1956 (Kurniawan 2018, 51–52). In addition, the government replaced SOB 1939 with new legislation multiple times during the decade, culminating in Law No. 23 of 1959, which regulated states of emergency thereafter.[2] The nature of the creation of the military and the establishment of the military justice system had long lasting effects, setting the country on a path of military overreach from the start.

In February 1957, Sukarno, who had been president since 1945, declared Indonesia to be a "Guided Democracy" (*Demokrasi Terpimpin*), whereby a National Council and Cabinet representing the major parties and interest groups in society replaced the Western-style electoral system. In March, the military convinced Sukarno to declare martial law to quash revolts by local military commanders and political parties who had resisted his plan.[3] Sukarno and the military formed an alliance whereby the military suppressed Sukarno's opposition in exchange for control over economic resources and the exclusion of the Communist Party of Indonesia (*Partai Komunis Indonesia*, PKI) from Sukarno's cabinet (Bourchier 2015, 115).

Throughout this period the military became more professional and overtly political. In November 1958, the military declared a doctrine known as the "Middle Way" (*Jalan Tengah*), in which it would neither govern directly nor be subordinate to civilian rule and disengage from politics. The United States, the most important international influence at the time, provided counterinsurgency training and the military focused its mission on internal security (Wandelt 2007, 271). In 1962, the TNI became the Republic of Indonesia Armed Forces (*Angkatan Bersenjata Republik Indonesia*, ABRI), incorporating the police as a fourth force.

Suharto and the rise of the new order

Over time, Sukarno increasingly moved to the left, providing more support to the PKI and announcing an alliance with China. On October 1, 1965, an ABRI faction, calling itself the Thirtieth of September Movement (*Gerakan 30 September*), assassinated six Indonesian Army generals and occupied strategic buildings in an attempted coup. With the top-level generals dead, Suharto, a major-general in charge of the Strategic Reserve Command (*Komando Strategic Nasional*), assumed control of the army and crushed the movement. Sukarno gave Suharto the authority to restore order. He responded by declaring a state of emergency and creating the Operational Command for the Restoration of Security and Order (*Komando Operasi Pemulihan Keamanan dan Ketertiban*, Kopkamtib) (Sebastian and Gindarsah 2013, 32). A presidential order in

December expanded the mission of Kopkamtib to include the "restoration of the authority and integrity of the government through military and non-military operations" (Honna 2003, 91).[4] Kopkamtib would serve as the regime's principal intelligence agency for the next three decades.

Suharto blamed the coup on the PKI, and the armed forces used this security threat to engage in a massive crackdown against communists (Melvin 2018; Robinson 2018). In the next two years, ABRI and its civilian allies killed an estimated 500,000 supporters of the PKI and imprisoned over 100,000 more (Cribb 2001, 233). Over the next decade, the government arrested between 600,000 and 700,000 people for alleged links to the coup (Fealy 1995). It was still holding at least 30,000 in the mid-1970s and did not release the last untried detainees until 1979 (Crouch 1988, 354).

Viewing the civilian judicial system and police as unreliable, the military took control of the legal elements of the repression from the start. Suharto quickly created central and regional investigation teams within the military that controlled the "entire process of identifying, interrogating, classifying and physically managing prisoners" (Bourchier 2015, 129). Military courts did not have jurisdiction over civilians, but Suharto issued a special directive declaring that these cases were best handled in military courts and gave himself the ultimate power to decide on individual cases.[5] In December, Sukarno, under pressure, gave Suharto the authority to establish an Extraordinary Military Tribunal (*Mahkamah Militer Luar Biasa*, Mahmillub), based on a 1963 decree, and the power to decide on the court's composition and jurisdiction.[6] It began operating in February 1966 and held over 200 trials in the next four years (Bourchier 2015, 129).

Suharto and ABRI quickly solidified their grip on the country. In 1966, ABRI formalized a new "dual function" (*dwifungsi*) doctrine, whereby it proclaimed a legitimate role in national defense as well political, cultural, and economic affairs. To do so, it implemented an elaborate territorial command structure that mirrored the civilian government at every level. The commanders of each Regional Military Command (*Komando Daerah Militer*, KODAM) outranked provincial governors and the military was able to intervene in the day-to-day affairs of the government at will (Aspinall 2010, 22). The military also staffed most of the State Intelligence Coordinating Agency (*Badan Koordinasi Intelijen Negara*) in addition to operating its own intelligence agencies (Sebastian and Gindarsah 2013, 32). In 1967, Suharto replaced Sukarno as president, ushering in what he termed the New Order (*Orde Baru*). This regime change would consolidate the military's role as a dominant political player, sidelining courts and the legislative branch.

In suppressing opposition to its rule, the regime used the 1963 Anti-Subversion Law (*Pemberantsan Kegiatan Subversi*), which Sukarno had issued in the context of Indonesia's confrontation with Malaysia.[7] The decree was formally incorporated into law in 1969 (Hosen 2010, 270). While most cases eventually shifted to civilian courts, the military, not the police, conducted the investigations and carried out the detentions, and the Highest Ranking Military

Prosecutor had the right to authorize the detention of any civilian for up to one year without trial. In practice, detention was renewable indefinitely (Amnesty International [AI] 1997, 5). The regime arrested and detained anyone it deemed as subversive, including student activists, journalists, academics, Muslim leaders, suspected communists, and dissident military officers (Honna 2003, 91). The military also used violence to quell any large protests, as occurred with anti-Japanese demonstrations in 1974 and the Islamist Tanjung Priok riots in 1984 (Lee 2005, 92).

In addition, the government faced intermittent violence from separatist movements in West Papua after it came under Indonesian control in 1963. It also launched large-scale military operations to counter separatist movements in East Timor after its occupation following the Portuguese withdrawal in 1976, and in Aceh beginning in the 1970s against the Free Aceh Movement (*Gerakan Aceh Merdeka*, GAM). The government did not declare martial law during those operations (Kurniawan 2018, 59), but military courts still prosecuted civilians. In addition, military courts did not hold members of the military accountable for their actions. Impunity was almost absolute. Throughout the 1980s, the military regularly rewarded officers for using force to respond to national threats, and they "were frequently honored with medals, promoted in rank, and appointed to prestigious posts" (Kammen and Chandra 1999, 10). These types of low-level security threats and separatist wars have persistently plagued Indonesia and have been used as a justification for the expansion of the military's legal power.

The beginnings of military reform

International and domestic pressure against the armed forces for its violent repression grew in the 1980s, influencing decisions about the appropriate scope of military justice. As early as 1983, the military began to shift cases against civilians from military to civilian courts in East Timor in an attempt to normalize and legitimize its rule over the region.[8] In 1988, Suharto disbanded Kopkamtib and emphasized the need to shift governance from a security approach to a "prosperity approach" (*pendekatan kesejahteraan*) (Honna 2003, 90).[9] This change accelerated in the 1990s. A turning point came in 1991 when the military fired on a crowd of pro-independence demonstrators in the Santa Cruz cemetery in Dili, the capital of East Timor, killing at least 250 people. The Santa Cruz massacre (or Dili massacre) garnered widespread international coverage and condemnation.

Under this pressure, Suharto quickly established the National Commission of Inquiry (*Komisi Penyelidik Nasional*, KPN) to investigate the incident and dismissed two officers for their roles in the massacre. He also ordered the military to create the Military Honor Council (*Dewan Kehormatan Militer*, DKM), which ultimately dismissed 19 additional officers (Honna 2003, 92). In 1993, Suharto created the permanent National Human Rights Commission (*Komisi Nasional untuk Hak Asasi Manusia*, Komnas HAM), modeled after the KPN, to investigate human rights violations in the country.[10] Civil society actors, including "legal aid institutes, student activists and Muslim leaders," used the commissions to demand further inquiry into the military's behavior (Honna 2003, 94). In response, ABRI created its first guidebook on human rights and began to discipline some officers for using excessive force in breaking up protests and riots (Kammen and Chandra 1999, 10). The army also encouraged the national police to take on more of a role in internal security. In this case, human rights activists—domestic and international—were influential in pushing the military to engage in some reform.

The one exception to this trend was in Aceh. After a relatively long pause since its defeat in 1979, GAM began to show signs of revival in 1989, following the return of around 1,000 fighters who had received military training in Libya, the Philippines, and Afghanistan (Schultze 2004). GAM carried out attacks against the Indonesian police and army, civil authorities, and suspected government informers (Kell 1995). In 1990, ABRI deployed 6,000 additional troops to the province, including units of the Red Beret special forces (*Kapassus*), bringing the total number to 12,000. "Summary execution, arbitrary arrest, torture, rape, and disappearance" became commonplace (Sukma 2004, 10). Between 1989 and 1993, an estimated 2,000 civilians died as a result of the fighting (AI 1994, 3). While the military was willing to moderate its behavior to some extent in internal policing, the severity of the security situation in Aceh demonstrated that it was unwilling to do so when the territorial integrity of the nation was threatened.

The collapse of the new order

Years of growing tensions between Suharto and the military brought an abrupt end to the New Order in 1998. The military was dedicated to the preservation of the secularist national ideology of Pancasila and remained vigilant against communism on the extreme left and Islam on the extreme right (Lee 2005, 95).[11] In 1990, Suharto founded the Association of Indonesian Muslim Intellectuals (*Ikatan Cendekiawan Muslim Indonesia*) and began to Islamicize the military. The military gradually developed secular-nationalist and pro-Islam factions (Lee 2005, 96–97). In addition, Suharto began to feel that ABRI was the only real threat to his power and placed loyalists and family members in top positions, including his son-in-law, Prabowo Subianto, who became the commander of the Strategic Reserve Command (Honna 2009, 233). Prabowo clashed with General Wiranto, the commander of ABRI. Indonesia's democratization grew out of this conflict (Lee 2009, 655–60).

The ascent of Megawati Sukarnoputri, the daughter of Sukarno, to become leader of the Indonesian Democracy Party (*Partai Demokrasi Indonesia*, PDI) in 1993 brought this division to a head. Faced with a real challenger in the lead-up to the 1998 presidential elections, Suharto increased his repression of opposition parties and the media, and on July 27, 1996, the military attacked the offices of the PDI. Megawati's supporters responded by rioting for two days, and the general population lost trust in the military, viewing it as a tool of Suharto (Honna 2009, 234). Many in the military opposed the overt political use of the institution, and the anti-Prabowo faction grew.

The Asian Financial Crisis hit Indonesia hard in mid-1997, prompting mass protests, especially by university students, over soaring prices and unemployment. Despite having a mild stroke in December, Suharto won the presidential elections in March 1998, but protests against his rule grew, especially after he removed fuel subsidies in early May. On May 12, police shot and killed four students demonstrating peacefully at Trisakti University. More riots ensued. Prabowo engineered some of the violence himself by using forces loyal to him outside of the chain of command. He urged Suharto to dismiss Wiranto and declare a state of emergency (Honna 2009, 235).

Wiranto, however, stated publicly that the military would not suppress the student protests. He staged a series of open dialogues with them and allowed them to move from university campuses to do a sit-in at the Parliament building where the military officers' wives club handed out snacks (Lee 2009, 654–55). Wiranto asked Suharto to resign and he did so on May 21. Vice President B. J. Habibie became president, discharged Prabowo, and publicly backed Wiranto. The New Order was over. While the military lost a great deal of the public's respect by abandoning its apolitical nature and participating in the violence, it regained some support by being on the right side of history and helping to oust Suharto. This mirrors the military's position in Indonesia since the transition: it has been forced to accept significant limitations on its power but has remained influential enough to resist reform of its core interests, including military justice.

Reformasi *and reimagining civil-military relations*

Like many countries, a democratic transition in Indonesia represented a critical juncture in national politics that led to significant military justice reform. The fall of Suharto ushered in a period of reform known as *Reformasi* in which Indonesia made sweeping changes to its laws and constitution to implement a democratic political system and increase human rights protections. The period is as much remarkable for the extent to which civilian leaders stripped the military of its powers as it is for the military's ability to hold on to them. In many ways, "almost everything conspired to produce military acquiescence to reform of the political position of the armed forces in the early post-Suharto period" (Horowitz 2013, 211). The military was discredited for human rights abuses and its leadership was internally split, civilian leaders were focused on improving Indonesia's standing internationally, a robust civil society pressed for reform, and a newly created Constitutional Court provided the first independent judicial oversight of the government's affairs.[12] In this environment, the military was forced to cede significant political power to civilians. Overall, the military has become much more subordinated to civilian leadership, and "military careers are no longer the central corridors to elite status and political power that they were in the early New Order period" (Poczter and Pepinsky 2016, 78).

At the same time, the military united around its core interests—namely its territorial system, military businesses, and immunity from prosecution for its actions—and as reforms moved toward those issues, "evasive techniques and even noncompliance grew" (Horowitz 2013, 213). The military still had enough power that it made civilian leaders reluctant to antagonize the institution, and in many ways the process was "marked by an urge to accommodate the military as much as to reform it" (Aspinall 2010, 24). Military reform still remains incomplete and Indonesia is in the jurisdictional contestation category. While military courts no longer try civilians, the 1997 Law on Military Justice, which re-codified Law Number 7 of 1946, grants military courts jurisdiction over members of the military for almost all crimes.[13]

The reform process went through three distinct stages. First, during the administrations of Habibie (1998–99) and Abdurrahman Wahid (1998–2001), civilian leaders were united against a military in disarray, particularly after its involvement in the violence surrounding the independence of East Timor, and were able to implement significant reforms. Under the Megawati administration that followed (2001–2004), reform stalled, not so much because she "opposed further reform of the military but rather that she revealed no indication of giving it much thought" (Crouch 2010, 141). In addition, during this period the military's prestige increased due to its role in combatting the secessionist movement in Aceh and new terrorist threats in the post-9/11 era. President Susilo Bambang Yudhoyono (2004–2014) resumed military reform when he took office, but progress since has been slow, with little success in reducing military power in core areas, particularly military justice.

The first wave of reform

After the fall of Suharto, the government embarked on an aggressive reform process. Within the next two years it ratified important international human rights treaties and the People's Representative Council (*Dewan Perwakilan Rakyat*, DPR) repealed the Anti-Subversion Law. A series of four constitutional amendments from 1999 to 2002 transformed the government into a democratic system.[14]

The Second Amendment to the constitution, enacted in August 2000, added an entire chapter (XA) on human rights protections modeled after the Universal Declaration of Human Rights. The DPR passed the Third Amendment to the constitution in November 2001, creating a new Constitutional Court (*Mahkamah Konstitusi*) (Article 24C) and an Independent Judicial Commission to oversee the integrity of the judicial system (Article 24B)—both necessary to break with the lack of judicial independence of the New Order and the Supreme Court's poor reputation following the transition (Pompe 2005). The Constitutional Court has the power to review all statutes that the DPR passes. In September 1999, the DPR enacted Law No. 39 on Human Rights, which set out a long list of internationally recognized human rights that Indonesia is obliged to protect.[15] It also required the government to create a new Human Rights Court (*Pengadilan Hak Asasi Manusia*), which it did in 2002.[16]

The government curtailed the military's power dramatically. The initial focus was on ending the military's direct involvement in politics and government, by first abolishing its Political and Social Affairs Branch. At the time of the transition, over 4,000 military officers held government positions, including 5 of 36 cabinet ministers, 10 of 27 provincial governors, and 128 of 306 district heads. From April 1, 1999 all would have to resign or retire from active service to keep their positions (Crouch 2010, 133). The military would also have to reduce and ultimately end its representation in legislatures—in 1998, 77 officers were in the DPR and 2,800 in the 27 provincial and 306 district parliaments (Crouch 2010, 133–34).

The military also used the opportunity to undertake internal reforms. In September 1998, Wiranto announced the military's New Paradigm, which stated support for the democratic transition and the abandonment of *dwifungsi* (Sebastian and Gindarsah 2013, 295). A legislative provision in 2000 separated the national police from the armed forces and gave police the role of internal security.[17] ABRI renamed itself the TNI, its name during the anti-colonial revolution, in an attempt to further distance itself from the practices of the New Order.

At the same time, however, the military has avoided any judicial oversight of its activities. Komnas HAM is in charge of the preliminary investigations for the new Human Rights Court, but public prosecutors have no obligation to move forward with cases and they often refuse to do so to protect those in the security forces. When cases have advanced to trial, almost all convictions have been of low-level soldiers and most of those were overturned on appeal (Lindsey and Butt 2018, 259–79).

Likewise, the Constitutional Court has not encroached on the military's legal power. The first generation of the Court, under Chief Justice Jimly Asshiddiqie, engaged in "strategic pragmatism" (Butt 2012), whereby it struck down many government policies, but often "delayed the implementation of its decisions, or it allowed the government to make practical adjustments to its policies" (Hendrianto 2018, 5). Yet one of the nine original judges, Ahmad Roestandi, was a retired military officer and a "fierce defender of military interests on the bench," and while he was usually outvoted "he was able to voice TNI's point of view on a number of important issues" (Mietzner 2010, 132). The Court largely refrained from directly confronting the military, and subsequent generations of the Court, beginning in 2008, have been "less robust and less innovative than the first" (Hendrianto 2018, 3). Outside of the Constitutional Court, the civilian judicial system is rife with corruption and has been referred to as a "mafia" (*mafia peradilan*) (Butt and Lindsey 2010). Overall, civilian courts have played no significant role in military justice issues following the transition.

The tensions between the civilian government and the military were best illustrated by the crisis in East Timor. In a surprise move, in January 1999, Habibie requested the UN hold a referendum in East Timor, allowing the citizens to choose between increased autonomy within Indonesia or independence. The military heavily criticized Habibie's decision and in the months leading up to the referendum armed pro-integration militias. On August 30, the citizens of East Timor overwhelmingly voted for independence (78.5% in favor). Immediately, the militias and military launched a scorched-earth campaign, killing at least 1,300 and displacing hundreds of thousands more (Robinson 2010). Habibie was unable to control the military and eventually accepted the deployment of a UN-backed international peacekeeping force led by Australia (International Force for East Timor), which arrived on September 20. By the end of October, all Indonesian troops had withdrawn from the region. The UN then established the United Nations Transitional Administration in East Timor (UNTAET), which governed the territory until it gained full independence on May 20, 2002.

As part of that process, the UN established the Commission for Reception, Truth and Reconciliation in East Timor (*Comissão de Acolhimento, Verdade e Reconciliação de Timor Leste*) to investigate human rights violations from 1974 to 1999.[18] It also set up the Special Panels of the Dili District Court to prosecute those responsible for violence in the months leading up to and after the referendum. By the time of its closure in May 2005, it had indicted 391 individuals, including 101 members of the Indonesian security forces. Indonesia, however, refused to cooperate with the trials and 339 of those indicted remained at large, outside of the court's jurisdiction (Reiger and Wierda 2006, 18). Indonesia set up is own Human Rights Court for East Timor in an attempt to demonstrate a willingness to hold perpetrators accountable. It indicted 18 military and civilian officials, but found only six guilty and all were exonerated on appeal (Cammack 2015). Large crowds of uniformed military personnel attended the trials in an effort to intimidate witnesses and the judges (Lindsey and Butt 2018, 275). In the end, the military was discredited domestically and internationally for its involvement in human rights violations, but few of its members were held accountable for their actions. International pressure was thus influential in generating debate and forcing the government and military to respond, but alone it was insufficient to effect any meaningful change in military justice.

Megawati and new security threats

Habibie and Megawati were rivals for the presidency in 1999, but divisiveness within the legislature, which still elected the president, led to a third-party candidate, Abdurrahman Wahid, winning. Wahid continued military reform, removing Wiranto from the cabinet, purging his supporters, and appointing reformers to important posts (Horowitz 2013, 215–16). His term was short-lived, however, and following several corruption scandals he was impeached in July 2001. Megawati, who was his vice president, took office in July 2001 and was immediately beset by two major security threats. First, after a period of relative calm, the separatist war in Aceh intensified. Second, the events of September 11, 2001 put Indonesia on the front lines of international efforts to combat Islamic terrorism. Both would lead to increased power and prestige for the military and in turn reform efforts stalled.

The conflict in Aceh had diminished following the military crackdown in the early 1990s. With the military on the defensive politically and encouraged by the recent independence of East Timor, however, GAM intensified its activities in late 1998. The military played a prominent role in counter-insurgency operations in response, but unlike in the New Order, the police retained operational authority, with the military now playing a supporting role (Crouch 2010, 155; Sukma 2004, 14).[19] Megawati was known to be sympathetic to patriotic military leaders, and soon after taking office in 2001 the military increased its operations in the region—sabotaging ongoing peace talks—and pressured her for more freedom in waging the war (Honna 2013, 188). In May 2003, she agreed to declare a state of military emergency in the region.[20] The military then launched Integrated Operations (*Operasi Terpadu*), the largest military offensive since the annexation of East Timor in 1975–76.

The military framed the conflict as an effort to prevent the disintegration or "Balkanization" of the nation, and its "aggressive approach was largely endorsed by civilian political elites in the DPR who feared being labeled unpatriotic" (Honna 2013, 189). The war brought the military greater prestige and less scrutiny as it attempted to reimagine itself in the new democratic era. In addition, the military had an economic incentive to keep the violence going. It made vast sums of money from operating checkpoints and engaging in illicit trade, including selling weapons to GAM (Barron 2019, 126), to the point that it may have wanted to continue the war simply because "disorder provided more fundraising possibilities" (Aspinall 2009, 183).[21]

Following the declaration of a state of military emergency, the military implemented a form of martial law in Aceh. Arbitrary arrests and detentions, torture, and extra-judicial killings were rampant. From 1998 to August 2005, when the war ended, an estimated 10,613 people lost their lives (Barron 2019, 126). During this time, the security forces brought many suspected GAM supporters to trial. They were mostly for show and in most cases, the "outcome of trials had been determined in advance by the martial law administrator" (Human Rights Watch [HRW] 2004, 38). At the same time, however, the military did not use its own court system. The trials remained in civilian courts with prosecutors and judges brought in from outside in six-month assignments by the Minister of Justice and Human Rights. The military did use military courts to protect its own forces. Most abuses went unpunished but the military court-martialed some soldiers who abused civilians to demonstrate a commitment to human rights. When stories were publicized in the foreign press, however, it imposed strict controls on the media and revealed no further evidence of abuses (Crouch 2010, 174–75).

Megawati's biggest challenge was responding to the rising threat of terrorism in Indonesia. In 2002, Jemaah Islamiyah (JI), an Indonesian terrorist group linked to al-Qaeda, carried out a suicide bombing in the tourist district of Bali, killing 202 people and injuring 209. Further suicide bombings occurred at a Marriott Hotel in August 2003 and the Australian embassy in September 2004. US President George W. Bush labeled Southeast Asia the second front in the "war on terror" (Gershman 2002) and pressured Indonesia to do more to combat terrorism (Hosen 2010, 287). Pressure also came from Australia, given that most of the victims in the Bali bombings were its citizens.

The DPR was drafting an anti-terrorism law but had not yet finished. The Bali bombings forced Megawati to act quickly on her own. She issued two government regulations in lieu of law (*Peraturan Pemerintah Pengganti Undang-Undang*, Perpu). Perpu No. 1/2002 expanded the government's powers to deal with terrorist threats and Perpu No. 2/2002, on the same day, made Perpu No. 1 retroactive to those accused of the Bali bombings.[22] The government is required to bring a Perpu before the DPR for approval and both were later incorporated into law.[23] The anti-terrorism decrees were "far less draconian" than those implemented by its neighbors Singapore and Malaysia, and they protected the basic right to a fair trial for those accused of terrorism (Jones 2013, 117).

During this period, a nearly unlimited stream of counter-terrorism aid came in from abroad, but the military received very little (Jones 2013, 115). Instead, the money went to the police and other entities in the civilian law enforcement and judicial systems. In addition, the National Defense Law, enacted in 2002, restricted the TNI's role to responding to military threats, replacing the 1982 version that had legalized the concept of *dwifungsi*.[24] At the same time, however, the TNI published its first post-Suharto White Book, articulating a new "gray zone" or "security-as-part-of-defense" doctrine meant to ensure national unity. Resentful of the flow of anti-terrorism funding to the police, the TNI also successfully pushed Megawati to use its forces in anti-terrorism operations and was able to eventually secure its units a role in a new National Anti-Terrorism Agency controlled directly by the president (Honna 2013, 192). The presence of security threats re-emboldened the military and prevented any further reforms to military justice during this period.

Renewed efforts at military reform

By the end of her term in office, Megawati had become increasingly unpopular because of her unwillingness to take on controversial issues and challenge those who resisted continued reform. In the 2004 presidential election, Susilo Bambang Yudhoyono defeated her in a run-off election with 60% of the vote. Yudhoyono was a well-respected politician who also had a distinguished 27-year military career during which he rose to the rank of general. This background gave him more legitimacy in the eyes of the military, enabling him to resume reform efforts. He reassigned hardline commanders who Megawati had appointed and removed a number of extremists from the armed forces.

Yudhoyono also oversaw the end of the conflict in Aceh. Following a devastating tsunami on December 26, 2004, GAM declared a ceasefire to allow aid to enter the region and restarted talks with the government in February. While most observers credit the tsunami as the catalyst for peace, back channel negotiations had been going on well before and larger dynamics pushed the sides toward a negotiated settlement. The government's security operations convinced GAM that it could not win. In early 2005, there were 50,000 Indonesian security personnel stationed in Aceh, the most since 1998 (Kurniawan 2018, 113). GAM also realized that the international community would not allow the creation of a small Muslim state along the Straits of Malacca in the post-9/11 world (Barron 2019, 128). With Yudhoyono more interested in peace and having more respect from the military, he was able to seize on the moment to secure a comprehensive peace agreement in August 2005 (Aguswandi and Large 2008).[25]

In the last days of Megawati's administration, the DPR had passed the Law on the Indonesian Military.[26] It emphasized that the military would be neutral in politics, ordered it to surrender all of its business interests by 2009, and moved military courts under the supervision of the Supreme Court.[27] In practice, however, the law had little effect. The Supreme Court provides little oversight of the military justice system and the military "continues to control the composition, organization, procedure, and administration" of the courts (HRW 2013). Military police conduct the investigations and military prosecutors try the cases in front of military judges, who are active service members, in charge of adjudicating the cases.

The military also failed to comply with the order to eliminate its self- and off-budget financing. The TNI owned "large foundations, hotels, shopping malls, and tracts of land," and was "engaged in a host of other semi-legal and illegal enterprises, all of which has been justified as filling budgetary gaps" (Davidson 2018, 12–13). It took a presidential decree by Yudhoyono in 2009, which ordered the transfer of remaining businesses to the Ministry of Defense, to push the process forward (Horowitz 2013, 211).[28]

After Yudhoyono was elected, the DPR also turned its attention to reforming the military justice system. The military staunchly resisted any effort to shift crimes committed during operations to civilian courts, arguing that military secrets could be revealed. The DPR hoped to at least shift cases of off-duty crimes to civilian courts. This proposal had widespread support. Many members of the military were moonlighting as bodyguards, security staff, and assassins, and "the local sections of the popular tabloids were regularly filled with stories of soldiers beating up clients of bars or discotheques over minor quarrels or, alternatively, using their guns to settle traffic disputes" (Mietzner 2009, 310). The military, however, refused to accept its members being investigated by the police (Horowitz 2013, 218). The army and police have never gotten along, in part due to the territorial system that led to both having units in every city, town, and township in the country. The bill eventually died. In the 2008 and 2012 United Nations Universal Periodic Reviews of Indonesia's human rights, the government promised to reform its military justice system, but no changes have occurred. In 2014, the DPR passed a new law on military discipline, but it did not reform the court system (Reza 2014). The 1997 law still regulates military courts and they continue to protect members of the military by refusing to prosecute them for human rights violations or meting out lenient sentences

(HRW 2013). While many of the factors necessary for reform were present during this period—a reform-minded government with high popularity, domestic civil society and international human rights pressure, and a notable decline in security threats—the military's power was still well entrenched and domestic high courts were not strong enough to change its behavior.

Terrorism and the risk of military resurgence

In recent years, terrorism has become an even more dangerous threat to Indonesian security and there is a real risk that the military will become more political and involved in domestic policing once again. JI carried out another major suicide bombing at the Ritz-Carlton and JW Marriott hotels in Jakarta in 2009. In addition to JI still being active, Jamaah Ansharut Daulah and a number of smaller groups linked to ISIS began operating in 2015.[29] The TNI pushed to become more involved in domestic policing following the January 14, 2016 bombings near the Sarinah shopping mall in Jakarta, for which ISIS claimed responsibility. Current president Joko Widodo, who assumed office in 2014, proposed a new anti-terrorism bill shortly after, but it languished in the DPR for two years, held up in part by opposition to granting the military a greater role in internal security (Diela 2018).

Following a new series of bombings in May 2018 in three churches, an apartment complex, and a police headquarters in the city of Surabaya, Widodo gave the DPR an ultimatum to pass new legislation before the end of June or he would use his executive powers to do so via a Perpu (Nabbs-Keller 2018). It enacted the revised law just nine days later.[30] The new law makes the military part of the country's anti-terrorism force, though it is only allowed to participate in domestic activities when requested to do so by the police and with the approval of the President. Despite this expansion of military power, military justice still remains in the jurisdictional contestation category. The civilian judicial system continues to handle terrorism cases. In June 2018, for example, the South Jakarta District Court handed down a death sentence to a cleric linked to ISIS for inciting sympathizers to carry out terrorist attacks (Rohmah 2018).

In sum, the practice of military courts trying civilians ended after the transition to democracy, but as illustrated in Figure 5.1, military justice in Indonesia remains stalled in the jurisdictional contestation category. International and domestic actors have advocated for reform. Many politicians in the legislature and the presidency have desired to increase the legal subordination of the military. The military, however, retains a significant amount of political and economic power, holds influence because of pervasive security threats, and has the support of some international actors who are allies in fighting Islamic terrorism. In the 2017 United Nations Universal Periodic Review of Indonesia's human rights, the government once again promised to reform its military justice system, but as of this writing it has not taken any action in doing so and human rights abuses continue (HRW 2018).

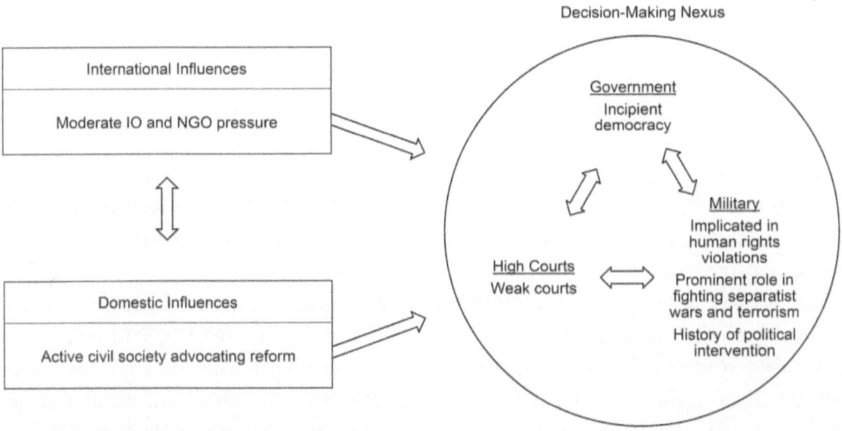

Figure 5.1 Jurisdictional contestation in Indonesia: Stalled reform

Fiji: Backsliding into jurisdictional contestation through military coup

Fiji represents a case of backsliding from full subordination to jurisdictional contestation. In 1987, the military intervened in the country's democratic government, upending the system of minimal military legal power left over from the British colonial era. The military claimed for itself a direct role in shaping the political institutions to favor native Fijian dominance in the ethnically divided society. The military's newfound political function also included carving out reserve powers and guarantees of immunity for its actions in the coup. Subsequent coups in 2000 and 2006 followed this familiar pattern—military intervention followed by writing military immunity into the post-coup legal order. Moreover, the military has expanded its praetorian role by breaking down barriers between military and police, giving the military policing duties and bringing the police under military control. Military authorities also have used force and threats of force to prevent civilian courts from functioning freely, because an unfettered civilian judiciary would challenge military impunity.

Colonialism, ethnicity, and civil-military relations

Fiji became a British colony in 1874. The British divided Fijian politics, economics, and society between indigenous Fijians (Melanesians or ethnic Fijians) and Indo-Fijians, the descendants of Indian indentured laborers who the British brought to the colony to work on commercial sugar plantations (Lal 1992, 38–39). British authorities established a political system for the indigenous Fijians based on communal representation through a series of hierarchical councils. The political system for the European population was based on representative electoral institutions. Indo-Fijians were initially completely excluded from government and only marginally incorporated into the European system in the mid-twentieth century. Economically, the populations occupied different spheres of activity—the indigenous had guaranteed communal land rights and engaged in subsistence farming while Indo-Fijians became part of the commercial sector. The populations were largely physically separated as well (Lawson 1991). These political, economic, and social divisions translated to indigenous control of the Royal Fiji Military Forces (RFMF). The British colonial authority, with the help of New Zealand, formalized the RFMF during World War II. British prejudices and imperial considerations had a significant influence on the ethnic composition of the institution in its formative years.

The RFMF was made up almost entirely of ethnic Fijians. Britain perceived ethnic Fijians to have a strong warrior tradition while viewing Indo-Fijians as unsuitable soldiers. Britain also distrusted Indo-Fijians due to their participation in labor strikes in the 1920s and 1930s and for their fraternal connection to South Asia where a growing independence movement threated British control over the subcontinent. British authorities in Fiji were convinced that Indo-Fijians were similarly opposed to the empire and feared their presence in the RFMF would be a threat to British control over Fiji. Britain discriminated against Indo-Fijian soldiers by paying them a fraction of normal wages, and they bristled at Indo-Fijian demands for pay equal to that of ethnic Fijian and European military personnel (Lal 1992, 117–23). Meanwhile, ethnic Fijians had an "affinity and admiration for the British and did not look upon them as colonial oppressors," making them willing to fight for the British Empire far from home (Scobell 1994, 188). Ethnic Fijians also saw a close relationship with Britain as their best bulwark against the Indo-Fijian population gaining political and economic equality. All of these factors led Britain to recruit ethnic Fijians into their ranks in large numbers while frequently rejecting Indo-Fijians who tried to join the Allied cause (Naidu 2019, 119). In 1940, the British even disbanded the Indo-Fijian volunteer unit that had been established in 1934. Over 11,000 men from Fiji served during the course of World War II, but only 264 of these were Indo-Fijian (Lal 1992, 110–23). The size of the RFMF declined significantly after the war, but it remained the domain of Europeans and indigenous Fijians. In the lead-up to independence in 1970, Britain favored abolishing the RFMF altogether, but ethnic Fijians "argued that the army was needed to protect native Fijian interests against Indo-Fijians" and insisted on keeping it (Howard 1991, 143).

Full subordination: Military justice from colonial rule to independence

Based on British law and practice, the RFMF was subordinated to civilian control, including in the legal sphere. Military courts had no jurisdiction over civilians, and jurisdiction over military personnel was limited to disciplinary offenses. Article 27 of the 1949 Royal Fiji Military Forces Act stated it did not "exempt any person from being prosecuted, tried and convicted before the ordinary tribunals of Fiji for any felony, misdemeanour or offence against any law."[31]

Article 133 of the 1955 UK Army Act similarly articulated that military justice could not be "construed as restricting the jurisdiction of any civil court" to try military personnel.[32] As a British colony, Fiji was in the full subordination category.

Upon independence in 1970, Fiji was a case of colonial continuity. Fiji remained within the British Commonwealth, allowing it to maintain its existing institutional framework for military justice. Even as an independent state, Fiji still followed the military justice rules laid out in the 1955 UK Army Act. Moreover, the RFMF had only 358 members in its ranks, and it was not active in politics (Howard 1991, 143). The first post-independence government, led by Prime Minister Ratu Sir Kamisese Mara, increased the size of the RFMF by a few hundred members when it tasked the military with an economic development mission and added naval forces. In 1978, RFMF ranks grew again when the Fijian government agreed to contribute 500 personnel to the United Nations Interim Force in Lebanon (UNIFIL), the peacekeeping mission established to monitor Israel's withdrawal from Lebanon. Contributions in 1982 to the Multinational Force & Observers (MFO) mission in the Sinai Peninsula increased the RFMF to 1,800, followed by additional commitments that brought total Fijian military numbers to over 2,000 by the mid-1980s (Firth and Fraenkel 2009, 118–19).

Fiji's participation in overseas peacekeeping operations not only increased the size of the armed forces but also enhanced the institution's prestige and altered senior officers' view of their role in their home country. These deployments contributed to military autonomy by providing educational and training opportunities on the international stage, which boosted officers' roles as national leaders. In peacekeeping operations, Fijian military forces found themselves in mediating and governing roles, which the institution came to adopt as its professional outlook (Baledrokadroka 2012; Firth 2012, 581). Furthermore, because the RFMF was paid for its contributions to peacekeeping forces, the military "became a significant source of foreign exchange," additionally enhancing the military's importance in Fijian politics (Scobell 1994, 190). By 1987, the dramatic growth and distinct outlook of the RFMF collided with the political problems born of the ethnically divided society, which set the stage for a military coup that would cause Fiji's military justice system to backslide from full subordination to jurisdictional contestation.

Jurisdictional contestation: The 1987 coups and their aftermath

Britain left behind an electoral system that reified ethnic divisions by having separate communal electoral rolls guaranteeing parliamentary seats for the two major populations and a national roll allowing open competition for a smaller number of seats (Firth 2012; Lawson 1991). Fiji held routine free and fair elections in the 1970s and 1980s, and the parties that developed in this time were defined largely on the basis of ethnicity. The Alliance Party (AP) mostly earned the votes of ethnic Fijians; the National Federation Party (NFP) mostly earned the votes of Indo-Fijians (Lawson 1991, 195–96). The AP held power through multiple election cycles and Indo-Fijians were "grossly under-represented in Alliance cabinets" (Lawson 1991, 220). In 1985, the Fiji Labour Party (FLP) emerged, organizing along class lines, prompted in part by economic decline and the government's imposition of a year-long wage freeze (Sharma 1987, 2097). The multi-racial Fiji Trade Union Congress (FTUC) constituted the FLP electoral base. It was a democratic socialist party, which at times advocated revolutionary policies such as nationalization of key industries (Lawson 1991, 234–35). Growing FLP popularity partly came from party members and average citizens defecting from the NFP. Thus, by the time of the 1987 general elections, the FLP was viewed as an Indo-Fijian-oriented party, despite being led by Timoci Bavadra, an indigenous Fijian (Sharma 1987, 2098). The FLP and NFP formed a coalition to contest the April 1987 general elections and won the largest number of seats, ending 17 years of Alliance government under Prime Minister Ratu Mara.

By including seven Indo-Fijians in his 14-member cabinet, Bavadra's incoming government was racially balanced as no previous one had been (Lawson 1991, 253). Indigenous elites, including military leaders, perceived the FLP victory as an unacceptable shift in ethnic power, and it overlapped with military fears of its corporate interests being under attack. The RFMF, 98% ethnic Fijian in 1987 (Lawson 2004, 142), was still very much "an ethnic institution in a multiethnic society" (Naidu 2019, 119), and on top of this ethnic fault-line, the RFMF viewed Bavadra as inherently anti-military. In the electoral campaign, Bavadra advocated reducing the size of the military, feeling that Fijian involvement in overseas peacekeeping operations had grown the RFMF far beyond the size and cost necessary for the defense of Fiji. The military thus feared that it would face budget and personnel cuts or even total dismantling if Bavadra were able to carry out his policies unimpeded (Scobell 1994, 191–92).[33] On May 14, 1987, just over a month after the election, while the RFMF commander, Brigadier General Ratu Epeli Nailatikau, was in Australia (Brown 1989, 111), Lieutenant Colonel Sitiveni Rabuka and 10 other soldiers carried out a bloodless coup against the government.

A period of political turmoil followed the May coup. The Governor-General, Ratu Sir Penaia Ganilau, as head of state under the Commonwealth system, declared a state of emergency and granted the police and military extraordinary powers to maintain public order.[34] Political leaders began working toward a solution to the crisis, including convening an interim government in which Bavadra would serve with the former prime minister, Ratu Mara. They agreed to this arrangement, but it prompted Rabuka to stage a second coup on September 25, 1987. Days later, he annulled the 1970 constitution, briefly took full control of government, and declared Fiji a republic (Sharma 1987, 2099).[35] Breaking ties with the Commonwealth meant re-styling the military as the Republic of Fiji Military Forces (also abbreviated RFMF) and disrupting the British-based rules of civil-military relations and military justice. Decree No. 3 (Article 5) initiated the shift in legal power by proclaiming, "no question as to the validity of this or any other Decree shall be entertained by any Court of Law in Fiji." Rabuka put the acts of his military dictatorship beyond the scrutiny of civilian legal authorities. Through a new Internal Security Decree in 1988, Penaia Ganilau (now president and commander-in-chief in the new republican order) granted the RFMF sweeping powers of "preventive detention." The decree permitted the military to hold detainees for up to two years without charges or trial.[36] The regime used these practices routinely to intimidate political opposition (MacDermot 1988, 12). Furthermore, this decree gave security forces the power to dismiss inquiries into civilian deaths, in effect guaranteeing impunity even in the most egregious cases of abuse. These security measures, however, did not empower military courts to prosecute civilians. The military used its brute force, but not its judicial instruments, in its repression of the civilian population.

Fiji established a new constitution in 1990, which again put in place a political system based on ethnically defined representation, and one in which the electoral rules guaranteed that ethnic Fijians would control a majority of seats in the legislature.[37] Chapter XIV of the 1990 constitution also codified civil and criminal immunity for Rabuka, the RFMF, the Police Force, and the Prison Services. No high court would have the authority to challenge the military for its abuses, firmly reinforcing Fiji's position in the jurisdictional contestation category in the post-coup era. As an additional point of continuity with the events of the coup, Rabuka was elected prime minister after the 1992 general election.

Fiji faced international criticism for its new racially discriminatory constitution, which made constitutional reform a domestic and international political issue the country would deal with for much of the 1990s. Fiji eventually approved a more multi-ethnic constitution in 1997 (Alley 1997). The new constitution made little mention of military issues but gave the Commander of the Military Forces responsibility for disciplinary action and specified that the court proceedings outlined in the constitution did not apply to courts martial, thereby allowing military justice to continue to protect members of the military from accountability for their actions.[38]

Jurisdictional contestation: The 2000 coup and its aftermath

The size of the RFMF dropped slightly in the 1990s and the military generally stayed out of politics (Fraenkel 2013, 331), but nationalist mobilization and political violence following the 1999 general election again brought the RFMF to the forefront of Fijian politics and resulted in a new round of abuses followed by impunity. The elections in May 1999 were the first held under the new constitution. Fiji's economic decline and growing unemployment under Rabuka's civilian government put economic issues front and center in the campaign. The FLP won a majority of seats in parliament and the FLP leader, Mahendra Chaudhry, became the first prime minister of Indian descent in Fiji's history. The FLP enjoyed a multi-racial base of support, and Chaudhry assembled the broad-based "People's Coalition" that included cabinet ministers from multiple parties and ethnic backgrounds (Seth 1999, 1413). While the administration began on solid footing, Chaudhry's economic reforms, including reversing the privatization of the 1990s, threatened elite interests (Field, Baba, Nabobo-Baba 2005, 63–68; Lal 2008b, 11–12). Moreover, ethno-nationalism (the *Taukei* movement) was still a powerful mobilizing tool, and soon nationalist politicians who had lost the 1999 election were stoking dissent against the Chaudhry government (Ramesh 2008). Marches took place in April 2000, with a much larger protest scheduled for May 19. In the weeks leading up to it, the protest was rumored to be a violent attempt to oust Chaudhry. In reality, a coup—planned in secret and executed the same day—would be the end of the civilian government (Field, Baba, Nabobo-Baba 2005, 70–71).

George Speight was a "failed businessman" who the Chaudhry government had fired from his position as chairman of a Fijian state-owned enterprise (Field, Baba, Nabobo-Baba 2005, 64; Lal 2008a, 4). On May 19, he entered the parliament building with six other armed men, proclaiming a "civil coup" (Field, Baba, Nabobo-Baba 2005, 82). He had obtained weapons in coordination with the military, and his group included members of the RFMF special forces Counter Revolutionary Warfare Unit (CRWU) (Field, Baba, Nabobo-Baba 2005, 74–76) and Metuisela Mua, the former head of the Intelligence Service, which Chaudhry's government had disbanded the previous year (Pacific Islands Report 1999; Robertson and Sutherland 2001, 8).[39] The necessary military support to complete the coup, however, seemed to elude Speight when the operation was underway, and the situation devolved into a prolonged hostage crisis in which dozens of parliamentarians and staff were held captive for almost two months (Robertson and Sutherland 2001, 15–16). In the days after the failed coup, Speight's supporters attacked Indo-Fijians and clashed with security forces while negotiations for a solution to the siege dragged on (Dobell 2008; Field, Baba, Nabobo-Baba 2005, 85).

In the midst of this turmoil, the RFMF Commander, Commodore Josaia Voreqe (Frank) Bainimarama, assumed control. On May 29, 2000, he abrogated the 1997 constitution and named himself head of government.[40] On June 2, he declared a state of emergency.[41] The decree gave police and military personnel broadly defined powers to maintain public order, including arresting and detaining people without charge or trial, and authorizing the use of force to break up gatherings and enforce curfews. Written into the state of emergency was a guarantee of immunity. Civilian high courts would not be able to hold security forces accountable for their actions. Furthermore, the decree granted the military the power to assume all duties normally carried out by civilian police and prison authorities. This erosion of the normal barrier between police and military would come to be a regular feature of Fijian security policy, which would further insulate the RFMF from civilian legal authority. As with the events of 1987, the military did not extend the power of its courts or give them jurisdiction over civilians. The measures used military legal power defensively rather than offensively.

On July 4, Bainimarama established an interim civilian administration led by Laisenia Qarase and other ethnic Fijian politicians.[42] Bainimarama continued to exercise power after this change, however, as evidenced by the fact that he continued issuing decrees, including one granting the security forces immunity from prosecution.[43] The parliamentary siege also ended in July through a negotiated settlement with Speight, which included an amnesty for his actions.[44] The conflict was not yet over, however; the military arrested Speight and many of his supporters on the grounds they had violated the terms of the amnesty, eventually charging them with treason (Field, Baba, Nabobo-Baba 2005, 248–49). On November 2, members of the CRWU, still sympathetic to Speight, staged a mutiny at the Queen Elizabeth Barracks (Fraenkel 2013, 333). Forces loyal to Bainimarama put down the rebellion. In an episode illustrative of the hermetic nature of military justice in Fiji at this point, the military handled the aftermath of the revolt entirely as an internal matter. Ultimately, over 150 rebel soldiers were court-martialed in secret proceedings over the next few years (AI 2003, 104; Bhim 2007, 126–27; International Commission of Jurists [ICJ] 2008, 5). Meanwhile, military court jurisdiction shielded loyalist forces from punishment for abuses inflicted on the rebels. After the fighting was over, five mutineers "were beaten to death by soldiers loyal to the military commander. The military refused to cooperate with police investigations into the extrajudicial executions" (AI 2003, 104). A presidential proclamation in 2001 reinforced the immunity specifically related to the events of the mutiny.[45]

More political instability followed the 2000 coups. The civilian interim government under Prime Minister Qarase was on questionable legal footing from the beginning, and the High Court ruled in November 2000 that his administration was illegitimate and the 1997 Constitution was still in effect.[46] The Court of Appeal upheld the ruling the following year, which led to resignations and reappointments for a caretaker government to manage the fragile situation until new elections could be held in August 2001 (Jowitt 2009).[47] Qarase's United Fiji Party (*Soqosoqo Dauvata ni Lewenivenua*, SDL) won the elections, making him the elected prime minister and returning Fiji to democratic government. The relationship between the Qarase administration and the RFMF deteriorated in the coming years, in part due to clashes over judicial powers and efforts to open the military to legal scrutiny.

Jurisdictional contestation: The 2006 coup and its aftermath

In the years leading up to the December 2006 coup, civil-military relations broke down due to "ideological difference, power contestation and personality clashes" (Ratuva 2011, 111). In 2004, the Qarase government reduced the sentences of the soldiers convicted for the November 2000 mutiny. Bainimarama opposed this intervention in military affairs and reversed Qarase's decision. The clash led the government to look for ways to replace Bainimarama, but it failed and he stayed in his position (Bhim 2007, 126; Lal 2007, 136–37).

In 2005, the government was considering numerous pieces of legislation that the RFMF opposed, particularly the Promotion of Reconciliation, Tolerance, and Unity Bill.[48] The proposed legislation included new amnesty provisions for

Speight and others involved in the May 2000 coup and its aftermath. It also would have established a Reconciliation and Unity Commission with an Amnesty Committee "empowered not simply to release prisoners, but also to nullify the original convictions" (Bhim 2007, 112–13). Indo-Fijian politicians voiced their opposition to the bill. Chaudhry went so far as to demand Qarase's resignation. Civil society, especially human rights and legal organizations, opposed the bill on the grounds that it would undermine the judiciary. Public opinion was split, but more opposed than in favor (Bhim 2007, 124–25). The police and military opposed the bill because they saw it as likely to stoke further violence, which would undermine their efforts to maintain order, and the amnesty in particular would "legitimize terrorism" (Bhim 2007, 125). In addition to the ideological and security concerns, the military saw the bill as an attack on its corporate interests. The Amnesty Committee's proposed powers would intrude on military justice (Bhim 2007, 128). Bainimarama spoke out publicly against the bill and military personnel attended the parliamentary readings of the bill in an apparent show of force (Bhim 2007, 129–30; United States Department of State [USDS] 2006). Amid parliamentary opposition, popular protest, military threats, and a pressing electoral calendar, the government withdrew the bill in February 2006. The May 2006 elections returned Qarase to power, but they did not resolve the tensions between the government and the RFMF, which came to a head at the end of the year. Qarase again sought to replace Bainimarama, but the RFMF leadership backed the commander (Fraenkel 2009). In late November, Bainimarama threatened a coup against the government (ICJ 2006), and he carried it out on December 5.

Immediately following the takeover, Bainimarama declared a state of emergency.[49] As with previous states of emergency, it tasked the military with maintaining public order, gave it expansive powers to do so, and granted legal immunity from consequences of use of force against the population. The military routinely carried out arbitrary arrests and took people to military facilities where they were detained and threatened. Security forces targeted pro-democracy activists in particular and subjected them to torture and degrading treatment while in detention (USDS 2007). RFMF powers did not include the use of military courts against civilians. Fiji continued to experience military repression through physical violence rather than through its judicial mechanisms. The state of emergency ended in May 2007, but Bainimarama later issued a new state of emergency that was in effect from September to October 2007.[50]

Bainimarama installed a civilian-military government in January 2007. He took the position of prime minister while remaining an active-duty officer, thereby fusing his military and governing powers (Fraenkel 2013, 335). Numerous military officers led government ministries, including the police and prison services. Military personnel were routinely part of police patrols, and military control of prisons furthered its ability to interfere with civilian justice. In early 2007, in multiple incidents, RFMF personnel beat several civilians, killing two. Civilian prosecutors charged soldiers with murder in these instances, and the military sought to obstruct civilian legal processes to shield their personnel from accountability. The government went as far as to attempt to "sen[d] the suspects ... out of the country on UN peacekeeping details" in order to prevent them from being subject to civilian trials (USDS 2008). Furthermore, the military head of the police attempted to interfere with judicial proceedings by prevailing upon the Ministry of Justice in a letter in which he accused two civilian High Court judges of anti-military bias (USDS 2008). Neither of these attempts at perverting the course of justice succeeded, and after years of delay, nine soldiers (and one police officer) finally were convicted in civilian court in early 2009. The military again asserted its institutional powers to impede civilian accountability. The army officer serving as commissioner of prisons, Brigadier General Iowane Naivalurua, had the convicted soldiers released within weeks and returned to their military duties (AI 2009; USDS 2010). This kind of brazen military impunity underscores the importance of military personnel being subject to justice that is not decided by their own commanders.

The military came into conflict with the civilian judiciary most directly in 2008. After being ousted from power, Qarase disputed the coup in court. While the High Court dismissed the case in October 2008, the Court of Appeal ruled in April 2009 that Bainimarama's takeover was illegal.[51] In response, Bainimarama's government issued Public Emergency Regulations and revoked the 1997 constitution.[52] In addition, Bainimarama issued the Administration of Justice Decree, which removed civilian judges from their posts and allowed his government to replace them.[53] Amendments to the Administration of Justice Decree granted immunity for the government's actions since the 2006 coup and canceled any court cases against the regime that were underway (USDS 2010).[54] Bainimarama further codified sweeping military immunity from prosecution in the 2010 Limitation of Legal Liability Decree.[55] The measure "irrevocably" granted "absolute and unconditional immunity ... from any criminal prosecution or any other liability in any court or tribunal." The military regime used its power to ensure ongoing exemption from civilian legal oversight even upon re-democratization in 2014.

Bainimarama issued a new constitution for Fiji in August 2013 and scheduled general elections for September 2014 (Angelo 2014).[56] Chapter 10 of the 2013 constitution reinforced past immunities, including re-stating those granted in the 1990 constitution. Frank Bainimarama founded the FijiFirst party in 2014 and ran for office as a civilian in the election. His party won a majority of seats in parliament, and he became prime minister (Firth 2015).

Jurisdictional contestation: Contemporary Fiji

Military judicial powers are an ongoing source of impunity in Fiji. Under the Public Order Amendment Decree (POAD), which replaced the Public Emergency Regulations in 2012, broad powers are granted to the RFMF to maintain public order, and restrictions remain on civilian court jurisdiction.[57] Military court jurisdiction, however, is limited to military personnel. The POAD does not give military courts the ability to put civilians on trial. POAD measures continue to give the military the authority to carry out the duties of police and prison services, which means military personnel are regularly in contact with civilians and there are reports of widespread abuses, including the routine use of torture against civilians in police and military custody (AI 2016). The military does not take action against its personnel, and to the extent that civilian courts have attempted to challenge RFMF impunity, the military is uncooperative and has used its ability to appoint leaders of the police and prisons to stifle legal action against it (Radio New Zealand [RNZ] 2015; USDS 2016).

Figure 5.2 illustrates the dynamics of Fiji backsliding into jurisdictional contestation in 1987 and remaining in that category since. The end of the full subordination system came in the context of a military coup against the sitting government, motivated simultaneously by perception of an unacceptable shift in the ethnic balance of political power as well as threats to the corporate interests of the armed forces. Guarding against accountability for the coup itself led the military to marginalize the civilian high courts by issuing a self-amnesty. This was followed by a perpetual need for the RFMF to defend its legal powers. Subsequent military interventions in government followed this same dynamic. Notably, the high court pushed back in 2009 by ruling that Bainimarama's takeover in 2006 was illegal, but this only led him to interfere with the civilian judiciary even more. Domestic and international influences indirectly pushed against reform of military justice. As an external state whose negative colonial legacy would linger long after independence, British rule established the social, political, and economic institutions that made Fiji an ethnically divided society. The expansion of RFMF power and prestige through participation in international peacekeeping missions similarly indirectly influenced the conditions for civil-military conflict. Meanwhile, ethno-nationalist party mobilization created political conditions in which extremist violence was used, including by the state.

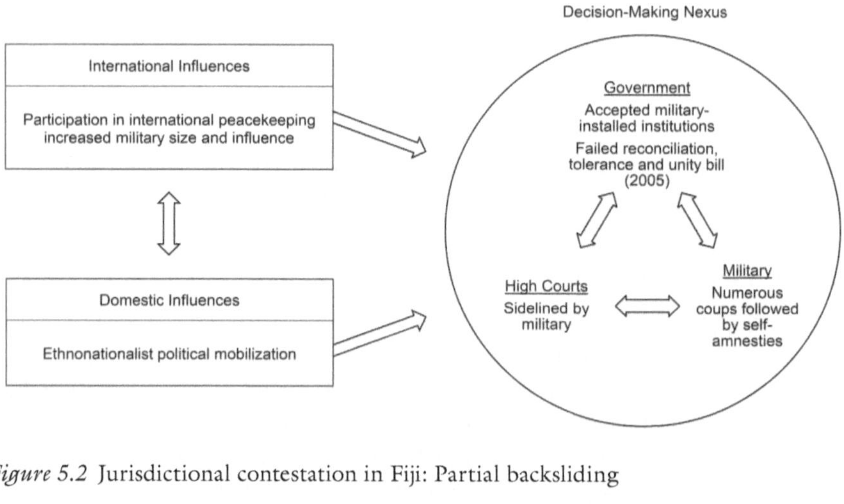

Figure 5.2 Jurisdictional contestation in Fiji: Partial backsliding

Conclusion

In systems of jurisdictional contestation, civilian and military legal authority conflict with one another. Military courts assert jurisdiction over their personnel for almost all crimes, including those beyond disciplinary offenses. This expansive view of military legal power impedes civilian justice and allows military courts to serve as a shield of impunity. Jurisdictional contestation undermines democracy, because the armed forces are not fully under civilian control. Additionally, the uncertainty of not being able to see justice done when the perpetrator of a crime is a member of the military subverts the rule of law by undermining the fundamental principal that everyone is equal under the law. In jurisdictional contestation, militaries use their exceptional status to achieve exceptional outcomes. Indonesia and Fiji illustrate the problems of jurisdictional contestation and how difficult it can be to achieve reform when mired in this system.

Indonesia represents a case of stalled reform. A democratic transition represented a critical juncture in national politics that improved the country's human rights protections, created a new constitutional court, and curtailed many aspects of the military's power. Unlike other countries that fully reformed in similar situations, Indonesia still faced pervasive security threats and confronted a military with significant political power dating back to its founding. Moreover, while promising at first, the Constitutional Court failed to reach the level of independence and authority of those in many other countries, making it a weak actor with little influence over military justice decision-making.

Finally, as Fiji demonstrates, a country with a military justice system of full subordination is not immune to backsliding. The military legal instruments left behind by the British permitted continuity of a system in which the RFMF was subject to civilian legal authority. Yet the legacy of ethnic division that British colonialism also produced set the stage for civil-military conflict that led to numerous coups. The abuses committed in those rounds of intervention in politics became the rationale for the military to expand its legal power in order to avoid potential accountability. Challenging this impunity is itself fraught with the danger of only provoking another cycle of intervention, abuse, and impunity. There is one sign of hope, however, which underscores the importance of seeing the potential for reform in a holistic manner. Since re-democratization in 2014, Fiji has attempted to normalize its international relationships, particularly with its most important historical partners, Australia and New Zealand, including strengthening defense ties and engaging in senior military visits (Powles and Sousa-Santos 2016). Included in this process is a review of Fiji's military justice system. New Zealand's Ministry of Defence is assisting Fiji in updating its military justice system, with a new code anticipated by 2022 (RNZ 2019). This international influence from fellow states, in partnership with the government and RFMF, may provide what is necessary to achieve reform.

Notes

1 Peraturan Pemerintah (PP) Nomor 6 Tahun 1946: Mengadakan Mahkamah Tentara Agung Luar Biasa, https://peraturan.bpk.go.id/Home/Details/62757/pp-no-6-tahun-1946; Undang-undang (UU) No. 7 Tahun 1946: Pengadilan Tentara, https://peraturan.bpk.go.id/Home/Details/25080/uu-no-7-tahun-1946.
2 Peraturan Pemerintah Pengganti Undang-Undang (Perpu) No. 23 Tahun 1959: Pencabutan Undang-Undang NO. 74 Tahun 1957 (Lembaran-Negara NO. 160 Tahun 1957) Dan Penetapan Keadaan Bahaya, https://peraturan.bpk.go.id/Home/Details/53973/perpu-no-23-tahun-1959.
3 Undang-undang (UU) No. 74 Tahun 1957: Pencabutan "Regeling Po De Staat Van Oorlog En Beleg" Dan Penetapan "Keadaan Bahaya," https://peraturan.bpk.go.id/Home/Details/52827/uu-no-74-tahun-1957.
4 Keputusan Presiden/Panglima Tertinggi No. 179/KOTI/1965.
5 PANGOPKAMTIB KEP-1196/10/1965 (Bourchier 2015, 129).
6 The Extraordinary Military Court was created by PENPRES-16/1963 on December 24, 1963. Sukarno authorized Suharto to use Mahmillub to try the September 30th Movement conspirators with Kepres 370/1965 of December 4, 1965. For both see Kopkamtib 1970.
7 Penetapan Presiden Nomor 11 Tahun 1963, "Pemberantasan Kegiatan Subversi," http://hukum.unsrat.ac.id/pres/penpres1963_11.pdf.
8 See Chapter 7.6 in "Chega! The Report of the Commission for Reception, Truth and Reconciliation in Timor-Leste," released in 2005, http://www.cavr-timorleste.org/en/chegaReport.htm.
9 It was disbanded with Presidential Instruction No. 29/1988 issued on 5 September and implemented in November. Keputusan Presiden (KEPPRES) No. 29 Tahun 1988: Badan Koordinasi Bantuan Pemantapan Stabilitas Nasional, https://peraturan.bpk.go.id/Home/Details/64298/keppres-no-29-tahun-1988.
10 Keputusan Presiden (KEPPRES) No. 50 Tahun 1993: Komisi Nasional Hak Asasi Manusia, https://peraturan.bpk.go.id/Home/Details/62324/keppres-no-50-tahun-1993.
11 Pancasila is the philosophical foundation of Indonesia comprised of five principles: belief in one god, a just and civilized humanity, the unity of Indonesia, citizens led by collective wisdom derived from deliberation, and social justice.
12 Many organizations were autonomous from the New Order regime and when Indonesia transitioned to democracy it already had a "robust associational life" (Lussier 2016, 174). The most influential civil society organizations following the transition were the Legal Aid Foundation (*Lembaga Bantuan Hukum*), Commission for the Disappeared and Victims of Violence (*Komisi untuk Orang Hilang dan Studi dan Advokasi Masyarakat*), Imparsial: The Indonesia Human Rights Monitor, the Setera Institute for Democracy and Peace, and the Human Rights Working Group.
13 Undang-undang (UU) No. 31 Tahun 1997: Peradilan Militer, https://peraturan.bpk.go.id/Home/Details/46050/uu-no-31-tahun-1997.
14 Indonesia's Constitution of 1945, Reinstated in 1959, with Amendments through 2002, https://www.constituteproject.org/constitution/Indonesia_2002.pdf?lang=en. The symbolic nature of the 1945 constitution led the government to heavily revise it rather than replacing it.
15 Undang-undang (UU) No. 39 Tahun 1999: Hak Asasi Manusia, https://peraturan.bpk.go.id/Home/Details/45361/uu-no-39-tahun-1999.
16 Undang-undang (UU) No. 26 Tahun 2000: Pengadilan Hak Asasi Manusia, https://peraturan.bpk.go.id/Home/Details/44993/uu-no-26-tahun-2000.
17 Ketetapan MPR Nomor VI/MPR/2000 Tahun 2000: Pemisahan Tentara Nasional Indonesia Dan Kepolisian Negara Republik Indonesia, https://www.hukumonline.com/pusatdata/detail/lt4ffe8d256bf00/node/657/tap-mpr-no-vi_mpr_2000-

tahun-2000-pemisahan-tentara-nasional-indonesia-dan-kepolisian-negara-republik-indonesia; Ketetapan MPR Nomor VII/MPR/2000 Tahun 2000, Peran Tentara Nasional Indonesia Dan Peran Kepolisian Negara Republik Indonesia, https://www.hukumonline.com/pusatdata/detail/lt4ffe81e8bf92e/node/657/tap-mpr-no-vii_mpr_2000-tahun-2000-peran-tentara-nasional-indonesia-dan-peran-kepolisian-negara-republik-indonesia.

18 Chega! The Report of the Commission for Reception, Truth and Reconciliation in Timor-Leste (CAVR), 2005, https://www.etan.org/news/2006/cavr.htm.

19 Under Law on the Police No. 28/1997 and Law No. 2/2002, regional police chiefs had the ability to request military assistance, with the military then operating under its command, though in practice the military had a high degree of autonomy, see Undang-undang (UU) No. 28 Tahun 1997: Kepolisian Negara Republik Indonesia, https://peraturan.bpk.go.id/Home/Details/46044/uu-no-28-tahun-1997; Undang-undang (UU) No. 2 Tahun 2002: Kepolisian Negara Republik Indonesia, https://peraturan.bpk.go.id/Home/Details/44418/uu-no-2-tahun-2002.

20 Keputusan Presiden (KEPPRES) No. 28 Tahun 2003: Pernyataan Keadaan Bahaya Dengan Tingkatan Keadaan Darurat Militer Di Provinsi Nanggroe Aceh Darussalam, https://peraturan.bpk.go.id/Home/Details/56113/keppres-no-28-tahun-2003.

21 The military was active in combatting violence in a number of other locations in the years immediately after the transition. Communal violence in Maluku killed approximately 5,000 people and displaced 500,000 between 1999 and 2001 (Bhakti, Yanuarti, and Nurhasim 2009, 25). The government deployed 5,000 additional troops to the region (Kurniawan 2018, 168–69). There were other extended episodes of communal violence in Central Sulawesi, Central Kalimantan, and West Kalimantan, and large scale riots throughout the country (Barron 2019, 50–63). In many cases, security forces "provided weaponry and ammunition to combatants" and "stood idly by as belligerents engaged in combat" (Davidson 2009, 302).

22 Peraturan Pemerintah Pengganti Undang-Undang (Perpu) No. 1 Tahun 2002: Pemberantasan Tindak Pidana Terorisme, https://peraturan.bpk.go.id/Home/Details/53104/perpu-no-1-tahun-2002; Peraturan Pemerintah Pengganti Undang-Undang (Perpu) No. 2 Tahun 2002: Pemberlakuan Peraturan Pemerintah Pengganti Undang-Undang Republik Indonesia Nomor 1 Tahun 2002 Tentang Pemberantasan Tindak Pidana Terorisme, Pada Peristiwa Peledakan BOM Di Bali Tanggal 12 Oktober 2002, https://peraturan.bpk.go.id/Home/Details/53110/perpu-no-2-tahun-2002.

23 Undang-undang (UU) No. 15 Tahun 2003 Penetapan Peraturan Pemerintah Pengganti Undang-Undang Nomor 1 Tahun 2002 Tentang Pemberantasan Tindak Pidana Terorisme, Menjadi Undang-Undang, https://peraturan.bpk.go.id/Home/Details/43015/uu-no-15-tahun-2003; Undang-undang (UU) No. 16 Tahun 2003: Penetapan Peraturan Pemerintah Pengganti Undang-Undang Nomor 2 Tahun 2002 Tentang Pemberlakuan Peraturan Pemerintah Pengganti Undang-Undang Nomor 1 Tahun 2002 Tentang Pemberantasan Tindak Pidana Terorisme, Pada Peristiwa Peledakan Bom Di Bali Tanggal 12 Oktober 2002, Menjadi Undang-Undang, https://peraturan.bpk.go.id/Home/Details/43016/uu-no-16-tahun-2003. Law No. 16, which codified Perpu No. 2/2002, however, was declared invalid by the Constitutional Court because of its retroactivity, see Putusan Perkara Nomor 013/PUU-I/2003, https://mkri.id/public/content/persidangan/putusan/putusan_sidang_Putusan013PUUI2003.pdf.

24 Undang-undang (UU) No. 3 Tahun 2002: Pertahanan Negara, https://peraturan.bpk.go.id/Home/Details/44421/uu-no-3-tahun-2002.

25 Memorandum of Understanding between the Government of the Republic of Indonesia and the Free Aceh Movement, August 15, 2005, https://peacemaker.un.org/indonesia-memorandumaceh2005.

26 Undang-Undang (UU) Nomor 34 Tahun 2004: Tentang Tentara Nasional Indonesia, http://www.dpr.go.id/dokblog/dokumen/F_20150616_4760.PDF.
27 In the original draft of the bill, the TNI inserted clause 19, which authorized it to act without presidential approval for up to 24 hours in "pressing circumstances," but it was removed from the final version (Crouch 2010, 146–47)
28 Peraturan Presiden (PERPRES) Nomor 43 Tahun 2009: Pengambilalihan Aktivitas Bisnis Tentara Nasional Indonesia, https://peraturan.bpk.go.id/Home/Details/42317/perpres-no-43-tahun-2009.
29 Several smaller groups, including Khatibul Iman in Solo and Jambi; Al-Hawariyun which is connected to ISIS and Syria; and Negara Islam Indonesia (NII) in Bandung, Makassar, and Riau; "all operate independently command-wise but are connected with Jamaah Ansharut Daulah through a shared ideological thread" (Renaldi 2018).
30 Undang-undang (UU) Nomor 5 Tahun 2018: Perubahan atas Undang-Undang Nomor 15 Tahun 2003 tentang Penetapan Peraturan Pemerintah Pengganti Undang Undang Nomor 1 Tahun 2002 tentang Pemberantasan Tindak Pidana Terorisme Menjadi Undang-Undang, https://peraturan.bpk.go.id/Home/Details/82689/uu-no-5-tahun-2018.
31 *An Act to Provide for the Establishment, Maintenance and Regulation of Military Forces and for Purposes Incidental Thereto*, Royal Fiji Military Forces, September 1, 1949, http://www.paclii.org/fj/legis/consol_act/rfmfa276/.
32 *Army Act, 1955*, United Kingdom Public General Acts 1955 3 & 4 Eliz. 2, Ch. 18, http://www.legislation.gov.uk/ukpga/1955/18/pdfs/ukpga_19550018_en.pdf.
33 Rabuka initially claimed he carried out the coup to protect the cabinet from threats from the Fijian ethno-nationalists but would later claim a racial motivation, saying he carried it out to ensure ethnic Fijian supremacy (Dean and Ritova 1988, 11; Sharma 1987, 2098).
34 *Proclamation (No. 2 of 1987)*, May 14, 1987, http://www.paclii.org/fj/legis/sub_leg/fiol970posoe480/; *Public Emergency Regulations, 1987*, May 14, 1987, http://www.paclii.org/fj/legis/sub_leg/cofper1987489/.
35 *Fiji Constitution 1970 Revocation Decree 1987*, Interim Military Government Decree No. 1, Sept. 25, 1987, http://www.paclii.org/fj/promu/promu_dec/fc1970rd1987343/; *Constitution Abrogation—Military Government and Finance Decree 1987*, Fiji Interim Military Government Decree No. 3, October 3, 1987, http://www.paclii.org/fj/promu/promu_dec/fmgafd1987606/; *Declaration—Republic of Fiji Decree 1987 No. 8*, Interim Military Government of Fiji Decree No. 8, October 7, 1987, http://www.paclii.org/fj/promu/promu_dec/drofd1987n8279/.
36 *Internal Security Decree 1988*, Decree No. 32, June 16, 1988, http://www.paclii.org/fj/promu/promu_dec/isd1988231/.
37 *Constitution of the Sovereign Democratic Republic of Fiji (Promulgation) Decree 1990*, July 25, 1990, http://www.paclii.org/fj/promu/promu_dec/cotsdrofd1990712/.
38 *Constitution (Amendment) Act 1997*, July 10, 1997, http://www.paclii.org/fj/legis/num_act/ca1997268/index.html.
39 Fiji established a National Security Council and Intelligence Services in 1990, see *Fiji Intelligence Service Decree 1990*, Decree No. 26, September 17, 1990, http://www.paclii.org/fj/promu/promu_dec/fisd1990241.pdf.
40 *Fiji Constitution Amendment Act 1997 Revocation Decree 2000*, May 29, 2000, http://www.paclii.org/fj/promu/promu_dec/rd2000146/; *Constitution Abrogation—Interim Military Government and Finance Decree 2000*, Fiji Interim Military Government Decree No. 3, May 29, 2000, http://www.paclii.org/fj/promu/promu_dec/camgafd2000657/.
41 *Emergency Decree 2000*, Interim Military Government Decree No. 4, June 2, 2000, http://www.paclii.org/fj/promu/promu_dec/ed2000120/.

42 *Interim Civilian Government (Establishment) Decree 2000*, Interim Military Government Decree No. 10, July 4, 2000, http://www.paclii.org/fj/promu/promu_dec/icgd2000443/.
43 *Immunity (Disciplined Forces) Decree 2000*, Interim Civilian Government Decree No. 17, July 12, 2000, http://www.paclii.org/fj/promu/promu_dec/ifd2000303/.
44 *Immunity Decree 2000*, Decree No. 18, July 9, 2000, http://www.paclii.org/fj/promu/promu_dec/id2000150/.
45 *Immunity of Disciplined Forces Proclamation 2001*, Proclamation No. 2, August 2, 2001, http://www.paclii.org/fj/legis/num_act/iodfp2001413/.
46 *Chandrika Prasad* v. *The Republic of Fiji*, High Court of Fiji at Lautoka Civil Jurisdiction, Action No. HBC0217.00L, November 15, 2000, http://www.paclii.org/fj/cases/FJHC/2000/121.html.
47 *The Republic of Fiji* v. *Chandrika Prasad*, Court of Appeal, Fiji Islands, on Appeal from the High Court of Fiji Islands, Civil Appeal No. ABU0078/2000S (High Court Civil Action No. 217/2000), March 1, 2001, http://www.paclii.org/fj/cases/FJCA/2001/2.html.
48 For the draft text of the proposed RTU bill, see "Unity—or more division?," *FijiTimes Online*, May 15, 2005, https://web.archive.org/web/20050525174452/http://www.fijitimes.com/unitybill.pdf.
49 *State of Emergency Regulation 2006*, Interim Military Government of Fiji, December 5, 2006, http://www.paclii.org/fj/legis/sub_leg/poasoer2006410/.
50 *Public Emergency (Maintenance of Public Safety) Regulations 2007*, September 6, 2007, http://www.paclii.org/fj/legis/sub_leg/psapeopsr2007655/.
51 *Qarase and Others* v. *Bainimarama and Others*, High Court of Fiji at Suva Civil Jurisdiction, Civil Action No. HBC60.07S HBC398.07S, October 9, 2008, http://www.paclii.org/fj/cases/FJHC/2008/241.html; *Qarase and Others* v. *Bainimarama and Others*, Court of Appeal of Fiji, Civil Appeal No. ABU0077 of 2008S, April 9, 2009, http://www.paclii.org/fj/cases/FJCA/2009/9.html.
52 *Public Safety Act—Public Emergency Regulations 2009*, April 10, 2009, http://www.paclii.org/fj/legis/sub_leg/psaper2009421/; *Fiji Constitution Amendment Act 1997 Revocation Decree 2009*, Decree No. 1, April 10, 2009, http://www.paclii.org/fj/promu/promu_dec/fcaa1997rd2009444/.
53 *Administration of Justice Decree 2009*, Decree No. 9, April 16, 2009, http://www.paclii.org/fj/promu/promu_dec/aojd2009285/.
54 *Administration of Justice (Amendment) Decree 2009*, Decree No. 10, May 12, 2009, http://www.paclii.org/fj/promu/promu_dec/aojd2009365/; *Administration of Justice (Amendment) (No. 2) Decree 2009*, Decree No. 25, July 17, 2009, http://www.paclii.org/fj/promu/promu_dec/aoj2d2009392/.
55 *Limitation of Legal Liability for Prescribed Political Events Decree 2010*, Decree No. 18, March 22, 2010, http://www.paclii.org/fj/promu/promu_dec/lolfpped2010547/.
56 *Constitution of the Republic of Fiji (Promulgation) Decree 2013*, Decree No. 24, September 6, 2013, http://www.paclii.org/fj/promu/promu_dec/cotrofd2013526/.
57 *Public Order (Amendment) Decree 2012*, Decree No. 1 of 2012, January 5, 2012, http://www.paclii.org/fj/promu/promu_dec/pod2012226/.

References

Aguswandi, and Judith Large, eds. 2008. "Reconfiguring Politics: The Indonesia-Aceh Peace Process." *Accord: An International Review of Peace Initiatives* 20. https://rc-services-assets.s3.eu-west-1.amazonaws.com/s3fs-public/20_Indonesia_2008_ENG_F.pdf.

Alley, Rod. 1997. "Fiji at the Crossroads?" *The Round Table: The Commonwealth Journal of International Affairs* 86 (342): 245–56. DOI: 10.1080/00358539708454360.

Amnesty International. 1994. "Indonesia and East Timor: Power and Impunity: Human Rights Under the New Order." ASA 21/17/1994. https://www.amnesty.org/en/documents/asa21/017/1994/en/.

Amnesty International. 1997. "Indonesia: The Anti-Subversion Law: A Briefing." ASA 21/03/97. https://www.amnesty.org/download/Documents/160000/asa210031997en.pdf.

Amnesty International. 2003. *Amnesty International Annual Report 2003.* London: Amnesty International.

Amnesty International. 2009. *Fiji: Paradise Lost: A Tale of Ongoing Human Rights Violations, April-July 2009.* London: Amnesty International.

Amnesty International. 2016. *Beating Justice: How Fiji's Security Forces Get Away with Torture.* London: Amnesty International.

Angelo, Tony. 2014. "Pacific Islands Review." *New Zealand Law Review* 3: 489–512.

Aspinall, Edward. 2009. *Islam and Nation: Separatist Rebellion in Aceh, Indonesia.* Stanford: Stanford University Press.

Aspinall, Edward. 2010. "Indonesia: The Irony of Success." *Journal of Democracy* 21 (2): 20–34. DOI: 10.1353/jod.0.0157.

Baledrokadroka, Jone. 2012. "The Unintended Consequences of Fiji's International Peacekeeping." *Security Challenges* 8 (4): 105–16.

Barron, Patrick. 2019. *When Violence Works: Postconflict Violence and Peace in Indonesia.* Ithaca: Cornell University Press. DOI: 10.7591/9781501735455.

Bhakti, Ikrar Nusa, Sri Yanuarti, and Mochamad Nurhasim. 2009. "Military Politics, Ethnicity and Conflict in Indonesia." Centre for Research on Inequality, Human Security and Ethnicity, Working Paper No. 62. https://assets.publishing.service.gov.uk/media/57a08b7bed915d3cfd000d4a/wp62.pdf.

Bhim, Mosmi. 2007. "The Impact of the Reconciliation, Tolerance and Unity Bill on the 2006 Election." In *From Election to Coup in Fiji: The 2006 Campaign and Its Aftermath*, eds. Jon Fraenkel and Stewart Firth. Canberra: Australian National University, 111–43. DOI: 10.22459/fecf.06.2007.10.

Bourchier, David. 2015. *Illiberal Democracy in Indonesia: The Ideology of the Family State.* New York: Routledge. DOI: 10.4324/9780203379721.

Brown, Carolyn Henning. 1989. "The Social Background of Fiji's 1987 Coup." *Sociological Bulletin* 38 (1): 95–117.

Butt, Simon. 2012. "Indonesia's Constitutional Court: Conservative Activist or Strategic Operation?" In *The Judicialization of Politics in Asia*, ed. Björn Dressel. New York: Routledge, 98–116. DOI: 10.4324/9780203115596.

Butt, Simon, and Tim Lindsey. 2010. "Judicial Mafia: The Courts and State Illegality in Indonesia." In *The State and Illegality in Indonesia*, ed. Edward Aspinall and Gerry van Klinken. Leiden, the Netherlands: KITLV, 189–213. DOI: 10.1163/9789004253681_011.

Cammack, Mark. 2015. "Crimes Against Humanity in East Timor." In *Trials for International Crimes in Asia*, ed. Kerstin Sellars. Cambridge: Cambridge University Press, 191–225. DOI: 10.1017/CBO9781316221754.010.

Cribb, Robert. 2001. "Genocide in Indonesia, 1965-1966." *Journal of Genocide Research* 3 (2): 219–32. DOI: 10.1080/713677655.

Crouch, Harold. 1988. "Military-Civilian Relations in Indonesia in the Late Soeharto Era." *Pacific Review* 4 (1): 353–62. DOI: 10.1080/09512748808718785.

Crouch, Harold. 2010. *Political Reform in Indonesia After Soeharto.* Singapore: Institute of Southeast Asian Studies. DOI: 10.1355/9789812309211.

Davidson, Jamie S. 2009. "Dilemmas of Democratic Consolidation in Indonesia." *The Pacific Review* 22 (3): 293–310. DOI: 10.1080/09512740903068354.

Davidson, Jamie S. 2018. *Indonesia: Twenty Years of Democracy*. New York: Cambridge University Press. DOI: 10.1017/9781108686518.

Dean, Eddie, and Stan Ritova. 1988. *Rabuka: No Other Way*. Moorebank, Australia: Doubleday.

Diela, Tabita. 2018. "Indonesia Toughens Up Anti-Terror Laws Days After Worst Attack in Years." *Reuters*, May 25. https://uk.reuters.com/article/uk-indonesia-security-bill-idUKKCN1IQ0KB.

Dobell, Graeme. 2008. "The Strange Saga of Speight's Siege in Suva." In *Coup: Reflections on the Political Crisis in Fiji*, eds. Brij V. Lal and Michael Pretes. Canberra: Australian National University, 126–36. DOI: 10.22459/c.12.2008.22.

Fealy, Greg. 1995. "The Release of Indonesia's Political Prisoners: Domestic versus Foreign Policy, 1975-1979." Working Paper 94. Melbourne: Monash University, Centre of Southeast Asian Studies.

Field, Michael, Tupeni Baba, and Unaisi Nabobo-Baba. 2005. *Speight of Violence: Inside Fiji's 2000 Coup*. Canberra: Pandanus.

Firth, Stewart. 2012. "Reflections on Fiji since Independence." *The Round Table: The Commonwealth Journal of International Affairs* 101 (6): 575–83. DOI: 10.1080/00358533.2012.749098.

Firth, Stewart. 2015. "The Fiji Election of 2014: Rights, Representation and Legitimacy in Fiji Politics." *The Round Table: The Commonwealth Journal of International Affairs* 104 (2): 101–12. DOI: 10.1080/00358533/2015/1017254.

Firth, Stewart, and Jon Fraenkel. 2009. "The Fiji Military and Ethno-Nationalism: Analyzing the Paradox." In *The 2006 Military Takeover in Fiji: A Coup to End All Coups?*, eds. Jon Fraenkel, Stewart Firth, and Brij V. Lal. Canberra: ANU Press, 117–37. DOI: 10.22459/mtf.04.2009.06.

Fraenkel, Jon. 2009. "Fiji's December 2006 Coup: Who, What, Where and Why." In *The 2006 Military Takeover in Fiji: A Coup to End All Coups?*, eds. Jon Fraenkel, Stewart Firth, and Brij V. Lal. Canberra: ANU Press, 43–66. DOI: 10.22459/mtf.04.2009.03.

Fraenkel, Jon. 2013. "The Origins of Military Autonomy in Fiji: A Tale of Three Coups." *Australian Journal of International Affairs* 67 (3): 327–41. DOI: 10.1080/10357718.2013.788125.

Gershman, John. 2002. "Is Southeast Asia the Second Front?" *Foreign Affairs* 81 (4): 60–74. DOI: 10.2307/20033240.

Hendrianto, Stefanus. 2018. *Law and Politics of Constitutional Courts: Indonesia and the Search for Judicial Heroes*. New York: Routledge. DOI: 10.4324/9781315100043.

Honna, Jun. 2003. *Military Politics and Democratization in Indonesia*. London: Routledge. DOI: 10.4324/9780203378861.

Honna, Jun. 2009. "From *Dwifungsi* to NKRI: Regime Change and Political Activism of the Indonesia Military." In *Democratization in Post-Suharto Indonesia*, eds. Marco Bübte and Adreas Ufen. New York: Routledge, 226–47. DOI: 10.4324/9780203934760.

Honna, Jun. 2013. "Security Challenges and Military Reform in Post-authoritarian Indonesia: The Impact of Separatism, Terrorism, and Communal Violence." In *The Politics of Military Reform Experiences from Indonesia and Nigeria*, eds. Jürgen Rüland, Maria-Gabriela Manea, and Hans Born. New York: Springer, 185–99. DOI: 10.1007/978-3-642-29624-6_9.

Horowitz, Donald L. 2013. *Constitutional Change and Democracy in Indonesia*. New York: Cambridge University Press. DOI: 10.1017/CBO9781139225724.

Hosen, Nadirsyah. 2010. "Emergency Power and the Rule of Law in Indonesia." In *Emergency Powers in Asia: Exploring the Limits of Legality*, eds. Victor V. Ramraj and Arun K. Thiruvengadam. Cambridge: Cambridge University Press, 267–93. DOI: 10.1017/CBO9780511770630.011.

Howard, Michael C. 1991. *Fiji: Race and Politics in an Island State*. Vancouver: University of British Columbia Press.

Human Rights Watch. 2004. "Aceh at War: Torture, Ill-Treatment, and Unfair Trials." Vol. 16, No. 11(C). https://www.hrw.org/reports/2004/indonesia0904/indonesia0904.pdf.

Human Rights Watch. 2013. "Indonesia: Civilian Courts Should Try Abusive Soldiers," April 23. https://www.hrw.org/news/2013/04/23/indonesia-civilian-courts-should-try-abusive-soldiers.

Human Rights Watch. 2018. "Indonesia: New Military Chief Should Tackle Abuses," January 25. https://www.hrw.org/news/2018/01/25/indonesia-new-military-chief-should-tackle-abuses.

International Commission of Jurists. 2005. "Attacks on Justice—Fiji." https://www.icj.org/wp-content/uploads/2012/04/Fiji-Attacks-on-Justice-2005-Publications-2008.pdf.

International Commission of Jurists. 2006. "ICJ Calls on Military to Withdraw Threat of Coup d'état and Respect the Rule of Law," December 4, 2006. https://www.icj.org/icj-calls-on-military-to-withdraw-threat-of-coup-detat-and-respect-the-rule-of-law/.

Jones, Sidney. 2013. "Indonesian Government Approaches to Radical Islam Since 1998." In *Democracy and Islam in Indonesia*, eds. Mirjam Künkler and Alfred Stepan. New York: Columbia University Press, 109–25. DOI: 10.7312/Columbia/9780231161916.003.0006.

Jowitt, Anita. 2009. "The Qarase v Bainimarama Appeal Case." *Journal of South Pacific Law* 13 (1): 24–31.

Kammen, Douglas, and Siddharth Chandra. 1999. *A Tour of Duty: Changing Patterns of Military Politics in Indonesia in the 1990s*. Ithaca: Cornell Southeast Asia Program.

Kell, Tim. 1995. *The Roots of Acehnese Rebellion, 1989-1992*. Cornell Modern Indonesia Project, No. 74. Ithaca: Cornell University Press.

Kopkamtib. 1970. "Himpunan surat2 keputusan/perintah jang berhubungan dengan Kopkamtib, 1965 s/d 1969." Sekretariat Kopkamtib.

Kurniawan, Yandry. 2018. *The Politics of Securitization in Democratic Indonesia*. Cham, Switzerland: Palgrave Macmillan. DOI: 10.1007/978-3-319-62482-2.

Lal, Brij V. 1992. *Broken Waves: A History of the Fiji Islands in the Twentieth Century*. Honolulu: University of Hawaii Press.

Lal, Brij V. 2007. "'Anxiety, Uncertainty, and Fear in Our Land': Fiji's Road to Military Coup, 2006." *The Round Table: The Commonwealth Journal of International Affairs* 96 (389): 135–53. DOI: 10.1080/00358530701292447.

Lal, Brij V. 2008a. "Fijicoup.com." In *Coup: Reflections on the Political Crisis in Fiji*, eds. Brij V. Lal and Michael Pretes. Canberra: Australian National University, 1–7. DOI: 10.26530/OAPEN_458920.

Lal, Brij V. 2008b. "The Sun Set at Noon Today." In *Coup: Reflections on the Political Crisis in Fiji*, eds. Brij V. Lal and Michael Pretes. Canberra: Australian National University, 8–17. DOI: 10.26530/OAPEN_458920.

Lawson, Stephanie. 1991. *The Failure of Democratic Politics in Fiji*. Oxford: Clarendon.

Lawson, Stephanie. 2004. "The Military Versus Democracy in Fiji: Problems for Contemporary Political Development." In *Military and Democracy in Asia and the Pacific*, eds. Ron May and Viberto Selochan. Canberra: Australia National University, 132–47.

Lee, Terence. 2005. "Military Cohesion and Regime Maintenance: Explaining the Role of the Military in 1989 China and 1998 Indonesia." *Armed Forces & Society* 32 (1): 80–104. DOI: 10.1177/0095327X05277906.

Lee, Terence. 2009. "The Armed Forces and Transitions from Authoritarian Rule: Explaining the Role of the Military in 1986 Philippines and 1998 Indonesia." *Comparative Political Studies* 42 (5): 640–69. DOI: 10.1177/0010414008328640.

Lindsey, Tim, and Simon Butt. 2018. *Indonesian Law*. Oxford: Oxford University Press. DOI: 10.1093/oso/9780199677740.003.0002.

Lussier, Danielle N. 2016. *Constraining Elites in Russia and Indonesia: Political Participation and Regime Survival*. New York: Cambridge University Press. DOI: 10.1017/cbo9781316026700.

MacDermot, Niall, ed. 1988. "Human Rights in the World: Fiji." In *The Review: International Commission of Jurists*. Geneva: International Commission of Jurists, 11–13.

Melvin, Jess. 2018. *The Army and the Indonesian Genocide: Mechanics of Mass Murder*. New York: Routledge. DOI: 10.4324/9781351273329.

Mietzner, Marcus. 2009. *Military Politics, Islam, and the State in Indonesia: From Turbulent Transition to Democratic Consolidation*. Singapore: Institute of Southeast Asian Studies. DOI: 10.1355/9789812308450.

Mietzner, Marcus. 2010. "The Political Marginalization of the Military in Indonesia: Democratic Consolidation, Leadership, and Institutional Reform." In *The Political Resurgence of the Military in Southeast Asia*, ed. Marcus Mietzner. New York: Routledge, 126–47. DOI: 10.4324/9780203810460.

Nabbs-Keller, Greta. 2018. "Indonesia's Anti-Terror Law: Crisis to Consensus." *The Interpreter*, October 25. https://www.lowyinstitute.org/the-interpreter/indonesia-anti-terror-law-crisis-consensus.

Naidu, Vijay. 2019. "Moving Towards a More Multiethnic Fiji Military Forces." In *Guns and Roses: Comparative Civil-Military Relations in the Changing Security Environment*, eds. Steven Ratuva, Radomir Compel, and Sergio Aguilar. Singapore: Palgrave Macmillan, 117–36. DOI: 10.1007/978-981-13-2008-8_7.

Pacific Islands Report. 1999. "Fiji Intelligence Service Is No More," August 27. http://www.pireport.org/articles/1999/08/27/fiji-intelligence-service-no-more.

Poczter, Sharon, and Thomas B. Pepinsky. 2016. "Authoritarian Legacies in Post–New Order Indonesia: Evidence from a New Dataset." *Bulletin of Indonesian Economic Studies* 52 (1): 77–100. DOI: 10.1080/00074918.2015.1129051.

Pompe, Sebastiaan. 2005. *The Indonesian Supreme Court: A Study of Institutional Collapse*. Ithaca: Cornell University Press. DOI: 10.7591/9781501718861.

Powles, Anna, and Jose Sousa-Santos. 2016. *Principled Engagement: Rebuilding Defence Ties with Fiji*. Sydney: Lowy Institute for International Policy.

Radio New Zealand. 2015. "Fiji Military Defied Police Arresting Wanted Officer, Court Told," November 4. https://www.rnz.co.nz/international/pacific-news/288840/fiji-military-defied-police-arresting-wanted-officer,-court-told.

Radio New Zealand. 2019. "Review of Fiji Military Laws to Resolve Human Rights 'Issues,'" February 26. https://www.rnz.co.nz/audio/player?audio_id=2018684065.

Ramesh, Sanjay. 2008. "The Race Bandwagon." In *Coup: Reflections on the Political Crisis in Fiji*, eds. Brij V. Lal and Michael Pretes. Canberra: Australian National University, 117–25. DOI: 10.26530/OAPEN_458920.

Ratuva, Steven. 2011. "The Military Coups in Fiji: Reactive and Transformative Tendencies." *Asian Journal of Political Science* 19 (1): 96–120. DOI: 10.1080/02185377/2011.568249.

Reiger, Caitlin, and Marieke Wierda. 2006. "The Serious Crimes Process in Timor-Leste: In Retrospect." International Center for Transitional Justice, Prosecutions Case Studies Series. https://www.ictj.org/sites/default/files/ICTJ-TimorLeste-Criminal-Process-2006-English.pdf.

Renaldi, Adi. 2018. "The Inside Story of JAD, Indonesia's Newest, and Deadliest, Terrorist Group." *Vice*, May 31, https://www.vice.com/en_asia/article/pav339/the-inside-story-of-jad-indonesias-newest-and-deadliest-terrorist-group.

Reza, Bhatara Ibnu. 2014. "Prevent New Military Discipline Law from Leading to Impunity." *The Jakarta Post*, October 6. https://www.thejakartapost.com/news/2014/10/06/prevent-new-military-discipline-law-leading-impunity.html.

Robertson, Robbie, and William Sutherland. 2001. *Government by the Gun: The Unfinished Business of Fiji's 2000 Coup*. Annandale, Australia: Pluto.

Robinson, Geoffrey B. 2010. "If You Leave Us Here, We Will Die": *How Genocide Was Stopped in East Timor*. Princeton: Princeton University Press. DOI: 10.1515/9781400831838.

Robinson, Geoffrey B. 2018. *The Killing Season: A History of the Indonesian Massacres, 1965-66*. Princeton: Princeton University Press. DOI: 10.23943/princeton/9780691196497.001.0001.

Rohmah, Ainur. 2018. "Indonesia Court Sentences ISIS-Linked Cleric Abdurrahman to Death for Inciting Terrorist Attacks." *The Defense Post*, June 22. https://thedefensepost.com/2018/06/22/indonesia-court-sentences-isis-cleric-abdurrahman-death/.

Schultze, Kirsten E. 2004. *The Free Aceh Movement (GAM): Anatomy of a Separatist Organization*. Policy Studies No. 2. Washington, DC: East-West Center.

Scobell, Andrew. 1994. "Politics, Professionalism, and Peacekeeping: An Analysis of the 1987 Military Coup in Fiji." *Comparative Politics* 26 (2): 187–201. DOI: 10.2307/422267.

Sebastian, Leonard C., and Iis Gindarsah. 2013. "Taking Stock of Military Reform in Indonesia." In *The Politics of Military Reform Experiences from Indonesia and Nigeria*, eds. Jürgen Rüland, Maria-Gabriela Manea, and Hans Born. New York: Springer, 29–56. DOI: 10.1007/978-3-642-29624-6_2.

Seth, S. P. 1999. "New Beginnings in Fiji." *Economic and Political Weekly* 34 (23): 1413.

Sharma, Shalendra. 1987. "The Politics of Race in Fiji." *Economic and Political Weekly* 22 (49): 2096–99.

Sukma, Rizal. 2004. "Security Operations in Aceh: Goals, Consequences, and Lessons." East-West Center, Policy Studies 3. https://www.eastwestcenter.org/publications/security-operations-aceh-goals-consequences-and-lessons.

Sundhaussen, Ulf. 1982. *The Road to Power: Indonesian Military Politics 1945-1966*. Kuala Lumpur: Oxford University Press.

United States Department of State. 2006. "Fiji: Country Reports on Human Rights Practices 2005." https://2009-2017.state.gov/j/drl/rls/hrrpt/2005/61608.htm.

United States Department of State. 2007. "Fiji: Country Reports on Human Rights Practices 2006." https://2009-2017.state.gov/j/drl/rls/hrrpt/2006/78773.htm.

United States Department of State. 2008. "Fiji: Country Reports on Human Rights Practices 2007." https://2009-2017.state.gov/j/drl/rls/hrrpt/2007/100520.htm.

United States Department of State. 2010. "Fiji: Country Reports on Human Rights Practices 2009." https://2009-2017.state.gov/j/drl/rls/hrrpt/2009/eap/135991.htm.

United States Department of State. 2016. "Fiji: Country Reports on Human Rights Practices 2015." https://2009-2017.state.gov/j/drl/rls/hrrpt/humanrightsreport/index.htm?year=2015&dlid=252763.

Wandelt, Ingo. 2007. "Security Sector Reform in Indonesia: Military vs. Civilian Supremacy." In *Democracy in Indonesia: The Challenge of Consolidation*, eds. Bob S. Hadiwinata and Christoph Schuck. Baden-Baden, Germany: Nomos, 269–95. DOI: 10.5771/9783845200484-267.

6 Military overreach in Brazil and Pakistan: When the generals become the judges

Introduction

In systems of military overreach, military courts have jurisdiction not only over their own personnel but also civilians. Extending jurisdiction in this manner allows military justice to shield soldiers from accountability while also infringing on the rights of the civilian population. Such systems undermine respect for human rights, subvert the rule of law, and threaten civilian control of the armed forces. Subjecting civilians to military punishment inherently deprives them of the right to a fair trial they would otherwise enjoy. Moreover, if military justice is largely a tool of command to ensure good order and discipline within the armed forces, there can be no reasonable justification for this standard to apply to civilians who have not signed up to follow military law. Extending military justice to civilians also raises the specter of outright political repression through punishment of political activity deemed contrary to national security. Due process and the rule of law are imperiled by military jurisdiction over civilians because military proceedings often take place away from public view, permit standards of evidence different from that of a civilian court, and are by definition not a trial by one's peers. Systems of military overreach represent a clear enclave of military power in which civilians answer to the military, rather than the other way around.

There are two distinct pathways by which democratic countries arrive at military overreach. First, military overreach may be the result of unreformed practices from a preceding period of authoritarian rule. We begin this chapter by discussing Brazil to illustrate this scenario. During the 1964–85 dictatorship, military courts were an expansive venue for military personnel and an instrument of repression against civilians. When Brazil democratized in the 1980s, military court jurisdiction remained largely unchanged. A variety of reform efforts attempted to redefine military legal powers, but in practice the military still exercises legal power over civilians, especially in the *favelas* (as the shantytowns are known in Brazil) of the city of Rio de Janeiro and other urban areas.

The second pathway by which countries arrive at military overreach involves backsliding after successful reform. In such scenarios, states enjoy greater degrees of legal subordination of the armed forces only to see those gains reversed as governments empower military courts to address large-scale, persistent domestic problems such as organized crime or terrorism. Electoral pressure to deliver results leads public officials to turn to military courts. We present Pakistan as an illustrative case of this pathway. While military rule and martial law have been common features of Pakistan's history, the Supreme Court declared the use of military courts to try civilians unconstitutional in 1999. This status held during the rule of General Pervez Musharraf (1999–2008), but a major terrorist attack in 2014 led a democratically elected civilian government to pass legislation extending military court jurisdiction to civilian suspects in terrorism cases, thereby reversing the previous check on the legal power of the armed forces and moving the country from jurisdictional contestation to military overreach. We conclude by reflecting on the warning signs for the protection of rights and quality of democracy these cases present.

Brazil: Intractable military overreach

In Brazil, the military justice system was an integral part of state repression during the 1964–85 military dictatorship, putting civilians on trial and shielding military personnel from accountability. After the long transition to democracy in the 1980s and subsequent reforms, many of Brazil's military prerogatives were increasingly brought into check, but military justice remained largely unreformed. The few moments of potential progress were stymied, and bad practices have been further codified with the passage of a new law in 2017 which gives military courts jurisdiction over cases of unlawful killings of civilians by military personnel. Brazil is a case of intractable military overreach.

The military retains jurisdiction over most potential cases against its personnel while also having the ability to subject civilians to military trial for crimes against the military or security-related crimes. These powers are increasingly pertinent to understanding human rights and the rule of law in Brazil because elected civilian governments have empowered the military to address sustained large-scale challenges such as drug trafficking and gang violence. Democracy itself incentivizes political leaders to achieve results—or at least to show they are "doing something"—in an effort to please voters and win elections. Turning to the military in this effort, however, short-circuits the process of building more effective civilian police and courts, thereby exacerbating the problem in the long-term. Such practices also threaten civil-military relations by granting the military a prominent role in the civilian government's political survival. Meanwhile, placing soldiers in a position where they are more likely to harm civilians, and simultaneously empowering military courts to judge alleged offenses, threatens the rule of law by enabling impunity.

Colonialism, independence, and contentious civil-military relations

Military justice in Brazil originates in colonialism. While a colony of Portugal, Brazil had a system of military justice similar to that of the mother country; military courts were privileged legal forums, making Brazil a case of jurisdictional contestation in this era.[1] Councils of War (*Conselhos de Guerra*) convened locally on an *ad hoc* basis to judge offenses, while regionally based Military Justice Councils (*Conselhos de Justiça Militar*) served as courts of appeal. The Governor or Captain General of the region would preside over the Military Justice Council alongside three military personnel of higher rank than the accused and three members of the local court (Andreu-Guzmán 2018, 127).

The first major changes to military justice in the Brazilian colony came at the beginning of the nineteenth century with the arrival of Prince Regent João VI. In 1808, he established a Ministry of Navy and Overseas (*Marinha e Ultramar*), a Ministry of War and Foreign Lands (*Guerra e Estrangeiros*), and the Supreme Military and Justice Council (*Conselho Supremo Militar e de Justiça*) (Hayes 1976, 10). The latter, based in Rio de Janeiro, replicated the administrative and judicial functions of the Lisbon Council of War and acted as a court of appeals for the entire territory of Brazil (G. Castro and Lara 2008, 15). Centralizing the military court function did not, however, address the civil-military conflicts that Portugal experienced at home and in its colonies. Military personnel saw themselves subject to their superiors rather than to the police, and neither body fully recognized the authority of the other (Souza 2015, 376).

João VI returned to Portugal in 1821 and left his son, Dom Pedro I, behind to rule. At the time, Brazil enjoyed kingdom status, equal with Portugal. When Portugal attempted to reestablish control, Dom Pedro I ordered Portuguese forces to leave and declared Brazil an independent constitutional monarchy. While Brazil's fight for independence was not entirely without bloodshed, it did not involve the widespread mobilizations and lengthy wars that rocked Spanish America, which meant the Brazilian armed forces were small and held little political influence (Nunn 1983, 56). The monarchy dealt with the routine mutinies in the army after independence by disbanding entire units (Hahner 1969; Haring 1958, 128). The military feared being made redundant by the newly created National Guard (*Guarda Nacional*), which took on internal policing duties and served as a counterweight to the army (Haring 1958, 46; Hayes 1976, 3).[2]

Upon independence, the colonial-era 1820 Military Penal Code remained in effect (Souza 2015), making Brazil a case of colonial continuity. Portugal had written the code only for its land army, and Brazilian navy commanders saw it as insufficient for the disciplinary issues they faced aboard ship.[3] In 1834, Minister of the Navy Rodrigo Torres called for a naval commission to produce a naval penal code. The commission formed, but it failed to develop a new code (Morgan 2014, 66–67).

The Paraguayan War (or the War of the Triple Alliance, 1864–70) led to a reassessment of military justice. During the conflict, military justice in the army and navy was harsh and uneven. Discipline consisted of routine corporal punishment meted out by immediate commanders (Haring 1958, 130) who could invoke the death penalty for almost half of the articles of war. The legislature appointed a commission in 1865 to draft new military codes, but the commission made little progress over the next decade and was abandoned entirely in 1878 (Souza 2012, 73). Constant turnover in government and political impasse between the opposing Liberal and Conservative parties on numerous issues facing the country hindered progress. Thus, despite decades of military appeals to update its legal system, a comprehensive military code of justice continued to elude the country.

Simultaneously, the Paraguayan War and its aftermath changed the military and its relationship to civilian leaders. The Brazilian army grew dramatically in size and importance. At the outset of the war, the army had approximately 18,000 personnel, but reached a war-time high of over 100,000 (Bethell 2018, 100). Battlefield successes in the war brought national attention to individual military leaders and imbued the officer corps with a new sense of identity and mission of national defense. Moreover, the government had struggled to supply the army in the field, which demonstrated to the Brazilian military the shortcomings of the country's economic and industrial base (Simmons 1976, 36–37). After the war, Dom Pedro II, who had inherited the throne from his father in 1831, attempted to reduce the army to its pre-war size and status, and by 1871 it had only 19,000 men. Having felt "victimized" by the civilian government's failures and ensuing attempts to diminish their standing (Hahner 1969, 9), the officer corps adopted an outlook focused on modernization and national progress (C. Castro 2001).

Civil-military relations deteriorated further in the 1880s. There were frequent public disagreements between senior officers and the civilian government, which led the Ministry of War in 1884 to prohibit officers from making public statements about government affairs, and required that "every article or speech had to be sent to the Minister of War for preliminary approval" (Haring 1958, 132). This measure was impractical and contradictory, given that officers served in the Senate and other government positions, which only intensified the conflict between civilian and military leaders. Brazilian officers in this era began to engage in fierce debate on "the military question" (*questão militar*)—to what degree should the military be involved in politics? (Nunn 1983, 60). In 1887, officers institutionalized their political voice with the founding of the Military Club (*Clube Militar*) in Rio de Janeiro, uniting around the idea that the military should have a role "in ensuring the progress of the nation" (Hahner 1969, 75). In November 1889, with the support of vocal anti-monarchist civilian elites, the military overthrew Pedro II and proclaimed Brazil a republic.

Military justice in republican Brazil, 1889 to mid-twentieth century

The military obtained significant political power in Republican Brazil. Marshal Manuel Deodoro da Fonseca became the leader of the provisional government, and at least one-quarter of the delegates to the new Constituent Assembly, convened to write a constitution for the republic, were military officers (Hahner 1969, 40). The Assembly was also responsible for electing the first president and chose Deodoro da Fonseca for the post, amid pressure from the military delegates within the Assembly (Haring 1958, 167) and from influential officers through the Military Club. The Assembly elected another military officer, Marshal Floriano Peixoto, as vice president. Furthermore, at the state level, half of the country's governors were officers, some of whom simultaneously held positions as legislators (Burns 1993, 233; Hahner 1969, 93).

President Deodoro began to use military justice to target remaining pro-monarchist factions. He issued Decree No. 85-A in December 1889, which created a military commission empowered to judge anyone, military or civilian, who conspired against the republic "in words or deeds to cause civil revolt or military indiscipline."[4] The decree remained in effect until November 1890 (Souza and Silva 2016, 369–71). Deodoro's decree shifted Brazil from jurisdictional contestation to military overreach, illustrating backsliding in the context of regime change.

In 1891, Brazil instituted a new constitution, addressing military justice.[5] Article 14 established the land and naval forces as "permanent national institutions" (in contrast to the 1824 constitution that did not) and described the armed forces as "essentially obedient, within the limits of the law," which the military interpreted as giving it justification to intervene "if the laws of the Republic were subverted" (Keith and Hayes 1976, xvii). Article 77 defined the Supreme Military Tribunal (*Supremo Tribunal Militar*, STM) as a forum for judging military offenses. Implementing legislation in 1893 brought the STM into effect, replacing the old Supreme Military and Justice Council as the military high court.[6] In 1890, Brazil finally established the Penal Code of the Navy and revised it the following year.[7] In 1899, this naval code expanded to include the army, placing the entire Brazilian military under the same system of military justice for the first time.[8] The division between civilian and military criminal law was apparent in Article 6 of the civilian 1890 Penal Code, which stated that it did not apply to "purely military crimes."[9] The new system effectively maintained the practice of military jurisdiction over military personnel in its form as a privilege, and it asserted jurisdiction over certain military crimes, whether committed by military personnel or by civilians (Andreu-Guzmán 2018, 127; G. Castro and Lara 2008, 15). For example, civilians engaging in espionage, encouraging desertion or aiding deserters in time of war, attacking military establishments, or committing a crime in "territory or waters subject to blockade or militarily occupied" were subject to the military code of justice.[10]

The government of Floriano Peixoto, who succeeded Deodoro da Fonseca as president, faced multiple revolts from within the military and from civilians. Peixoto responded by declaring states of siege and issuing decrees that put civilians under military justice.[11] Peixoto's actions overstepped the criminal codes, whose provisions had been interpreted as applying only in cases of external war, not internal rebellion. Consequently, a ruling by the Supreme Federal Tribunal (*Supremo Tribunal Federal*, STF) rebuked his decrees, declaring them unconstitutional.[12] This bold action by the STF set the stage for legislative reform, which came just days after Peixoto left office in November 1894. The new law clarified the provisions of the penal code and prevented military court jurisdiction over civilians (Lemos 2012, 70–72).[13] This episode shifted Brazil back to the jurisdictional contestation category and illustrates the importance of a high court challenging the government and serving as a catalyst for further reform.

The military strengthened its power and political influence in the early twentieth century. In the mid-1920s, the army "was only slightly larger than all state militias taken together" (Keith 1976, 64), but lessons learned from observing World War I, enhanced training from European military missions, and fears of a rising Argentina added urgency to Brazilian military expansion. The country implemented a draft lottery, increased in size to 30,000 in 1920 and 50,000 by 1930, and established an army unit in every state (McCann 1997, 46–47). Simultaneously, the French military mission in Brazil enhanced military professionalism and led to updated regulations in military organization, finance, and other areas (Nunn 1983, 194). In 1920, the government similarly reorganized the institutions of military justice with the Code of Judicial Organization and Military Procedure (*Codigo de Organização Judiciaria e Processo Militar*).[14] The same year, it established military courts of first instance in 12 administrative regions throughout Brazil.[15] The new system created the Military Public Ministry (*Ministério Público Militar*) and military auditors, replacing the Councils of War. The STM would handle appeals (Andreu-Guzmán 2018, 127; G. Castro and Lara 2008, 15; Souza and Silva 2016, 372).

This increased professionalization, however, pushed in multiple directions. For some, it underscored the need for the officer corps to be an apolitical force, while others took the lesson that European military training made them superior to the general public and the natural overseers of national politics (McCann 1997; Nunn 1983). Military factionalization proved detrimental to Brazil. It led to military revolts in the 1920s and a coup in 1930 that brought Getúlio Vargas to power, spelling the end of the Old Republic and the beginning of the New State (*Estado Novo*) (R. Schneider 1997, 75–82).

At this point, military judicial powers grew, moving Brazil into the military overreach category. As with the previous episode of backsliding in 1889, this regression came in the context of an authoritarian takeover of government and the use of military courts to target political opponents of the regime. Vargas issued Decree 20-656 in 1931, which allowed for military justice to be used against civilians for "attacks on the public order" (Souza and Silva 2016, 372).[16] This power was cemented in the 1934 constitution, which reaffirmed the existence of a separate military judiciary whose power extended to civilians for "crimes against the external security of the country or against military institutions" (Article 84).[17] Military justice over civilians expanded after communist uprisings in late 1935 led congress to declare a state of siege, which allowed Vargas to rule through the emergency powers established in Articles 159–167 of the 1934 Constitution. In 1936, the Vargas regime established the National Security Tribunal (*Tribunal de Segurança Nacional*, TSN), wielding it as a tool of repression against political opposition (Burns 1993, 353–54; Mathias and Guzzi 2010, 51–52). The TSN was originally under the auspices of the military justice system until it became an independent body in 1937. It continued operating until 1945 (Pereira 1998, 50; Souza and Silva 2016, 373).

The 1930s to the 1950s were decades of political tumult in Brazil. Vargas alternated between holding the presidency through force or by congressional election from 1930 to 1945, at which point the country experienced a brief period of democratization with the popular election of Eurico Gaspar Dutra to the presidency (1946–51). The military remained a central political actor in these decades, deciding the fate of presidencies and regimes. The new constitutions introduced in 1937 and 1946 also maintained the language of the 1934 constitution regarding military court powers and their jurisdiction over civilians for crimes involving national security.[18] Otherwise, there were only minor changes in court structures and the 1946 change in the name of the military high court from Supreme Military Tribunal (*Supremo Tribunal Militar*) to Superior Military Tribunal (*Superior Tribunal Militar*), which it retains.

Vargas returned to the presidency in 1951 through a democratic election. After his suicide in office in 1954, Brazil experienced a succession of brief presidencies, a period of political stability during the Juscelino Kubitschek administration (1956–61), and then years of economic decline under President João Goulart (1961–64), leading the military to remove him in a coup (Stepan 1978). The military's direct seizure of power represented a "boundary change" in which the military would now seek to be the "directors not the moderators of politics" (Stepan 1971, 124).

Military rule and legalized repression, 1964–85

The Brazilian military's politically empowered role, combined with the international environment of the Cold War, led it to develop a perspective of "new professionalism," in which it focused on internal threats, especially the fight against communist "subversion" (Stepan 1973). The military regime of 1964–85 would be guided by a mission of modernization and political re-ordering, seeking to reset politics in the country to reflect a military-approved democratic system (Bacchus 1990).

The military sought to maintain a façade of normal government. Even with the declaration in 1964 of Institutional Act No. 1, which superseded regular constitutional authority, the 1946 constitution remained in effect (Guerchon 1971, 258–62).[19] For most of the 1964–85 period, the government kept congress open and continued to hold elections for its seats, even as it used anti-democratic practices to manipulate its composition and functions. In 1965, Institutional Act No. 2, for example, created an artificial two-party system—the pro-regime National Renewal Alliance (*Aliança Renovadora Nacional*, ARENA) and the official opposition Brazilian Democratic Movement (*Movimento Democrático Brasileiro*, MDB)—in order to permit legal opposition while maintaining control over congress.[20]

The military dictatorship pursued a strategy of control that relied on a high degree of judicialization of the regime, in which punishment of political opponents through military courts was much more common than the widespread use of disappearances and extrajudicial murder in other Latin American countries during this same period (Pereira 2005b). The 1946 constitution, the 1938 Code of Military Justice, and the 1953 National Security Law all predated the military regime and enabled military courts to be the venue in which to judge crimes seen to affect the country's national security (Pereira 1998; 2005a; Souza and Silva 2016, 374).[21] In 1965, Institutional Act No. 2 extended military court jurisdiction to cover any matters of national security (Souza and Silva 2016). The 1967 military-written constitution codified these practices (Zaverucha 1999, 46).[22]

Institutional Act No. 1 suspended the political rights of thousands of civilians and purged members of congress. The military carried out an internal purge as well, removing hundreds of officers from it ranks (Chirio 2018, 55; Stepan 1971, 123). The Act specifically empowered the use of Military-Police Inquiries (*Inquérito Policial Militar*, IPM)—investigations carried out by the armed forces—as a legal mechanism of repression against tens of thousands of civilians and thousands of military personnel (Burns 1993, 451; Chirio 2018, 73).

Military courts and military investigatory powers—while clearly used to circumvent the protection of citizens' rights that would be expected in a democratic state under the rule of law—were more than window-dressing to cover up the regime's brutality. Meaningful decision-making did take place within the courts, and verdicts were not a foregone conclusion. Defense lawyers were able to make a difference for their clients, and the STM, in its capacity as an appeals court, "often overturned convictions and gave out shorter average sentences" than the lower military courts (Pereira 1998, 46). Furthermore, until 1968, individuals could appeal verdicts from the STM to the STF, the civilian high court, which sometimes overturned them. While the government quickly purged other institutions of anti-regime elements, the civilian judiciary was initially spared these intrusions (Chirio 2018, 70). In 1965, however, General Castelo Branco added five seats to the 11-member STF in a court-packing scheme. In 1968, Institutional Act No. 5 went further, forcibly retiring judges, ending the appellate role of the STF in national security cases or offenses against the military (Arceneaux 2001, 153), and effectively putting the actions of the dictatorship beyond the reach of any judicial review (Guerchon 1971, 269).[23]

During the dictatorship, the regime also extended the power of military courts to shield military and police personnel from accountability for abuses. The 1969 Military Penal Code (*Código Penal Militar*) granted Brazilian military courts jurisdiction over unlawful killings of civilians by military personnel and over civilians accused of crimes against military property and personnel, as well as any crime committed in an area under military administration.[24] The Military Criminal Process Code (*Código de Processo Penal Militar*) of 1969 also established military court jurisdiction over the Military Police (*Polícia Militar*), which was responsible for day-to-day policing and would now be prosecuted in state-level Military Police courts. This was reinforced through constitutional amendments in 1977 (Costa and Thompson 2011, 29), and the legal framework persisted after democratization (Cavallaro and Delgado 2012, 89; Zaverucha 1999, 47).[25]

Embedding military power in the transition to democracy, 1979–85

In the 1970s, the military regime initiated a long and gradual transition to democracy. While democratization is often an important critical juncture that affords a country the opportunity to rein in military judicial power, military control over the process in Brazil enabled the institution to hold on to this prerogative through the transition. The military government repealed Institutional Act No. 5 in 1978, ending "large-scale prosecutions of civilians in military courts," but the underlying Military Penal Code and National Security Law remained in effect (Pereira 2005b, 162–63; Zaverucha 2000, 21). Meanwhile, as the 1985 transition to a civilian president approached, the military revised the National Security Law's provision against "offenses to public authority" that it had used to stifle journalism and other criticism of the government.[26] The revised version placed such offenses in the hands of civilian courts, but cases of "defaming the president or heads of the legislative and judiciary bodies" remained under military jurisdiction (Bacchus 1990, 122).

The nature of the transition in Brazil ensured that the military's legal powers would endure in the new democracy. The worst of the regime's abuses took place in the 1968–74 period, allowing time for the military to improve its national image before the 1985 handover. Many in society also credited the military with the economic "miracle" of the 1970s (N. Schneider 2011). Military officers continued to serve in the presidential cabinet (Hunter 1997, 32–33), and the first two civilian presidents after 1985 had been involved in the military regime as politicians in ARENA and its successor, the Democratic Social Party (*Partido Democrático Social*) (Pereira 2005b, 162; Zirker 1993, 90). Finally, the military enacted the sweeping Amnesty Law (*Lei de Anistia*) in 1979 that protected police and military personnel from any legal accountability for abuses committed during the regime (N. Schneider 2011, 43).[27] The military left power in a position of political strength and maintained its standing after the transition.

Military overreach under constitutional democracy, 1988–present

The new democratic constitution of October 1988 reinforced the extensive reach of military justice.[28] It maintained military jurisdiction over non-military crimes committed by military personnel and over civilians in certain circumstances. Military courts "were primarily used defensively" after the transition (Pereira 2001, 561), but they were still competent to process and judge "military crimes defined in law" (Article 124), which allowed the prosecution of civilians for crimes committed in areas under military control or against the military itself, such as insults or contempt (*desacato*) against soldiers (Andreu-Guzmán 2018, 133–34).

The consequences of military judicial powers were immediately evident in the new constitutional era. In November 1988, the government called on the armed forces to handle a strike at the Volta Redonda steelworks. The army killed three striking workers. Civilian courts sought testimony from soldiers, but Minister of the Army General Leônidas Pires Gonçalves rejected civilian prosecution of his troops, and President José Sarney (1985–90) did not press the matter further. He left the issue in the hands of the military, and it took no action (Zaverucha 1993, 295–96; Zirker 1993, 100).

In addition to the continued judicial powers of the federal military, the 1988 constitution "permitted the creation of state military courts" to handle cases involving the Military Police (Costa and Thompson 2011, 29). In the new constitutional order, Military Police were placed under the control of the governor of each state, not the Brazilian Army (*Exército Brasileiro*), as it had been for most of the dictatorship (Human Rights Watch [HRW] 1997, 21; Hunter 1997, 35).[29] The Military Police would remain "auxiliary and reserve forces of the Army" (Article 144) that could be called into military service but would otherwise no longer be the national armed forces themselves, despite the military name and character of the forces. Separating the Military Police from the armed forces was itself an important reform (Pereira and Ungar 2004, 270), but the Military Police would remain subject to military justice, with crimes investigated and judged by their own Military Police Courts (*Auditorias Militares; Tribunais de Justiça Militar*) (Costa and Thompson 2011, 29; Hinton 2006, 125). Given the extraordinary levels of violence associated with policing in Brazil, this separate status has been a source of impunity for crimes against civilians.

Reduction of military political influence in the 1990s

Over the next decade, the civilian government gradually asserted its authority over the military and achieved important reforms to prerogatives other than the justice system. By the end of the 1990s, for example, Brazil terminated the practice of active-duty military officers serving in the cabinet (Hunter 1997; Hunter 2001, 37–38). While the military was willing to accommodate civilian reformers in many areas, it flatly "reject[ed] fundamentally the notion that civilians can bring officers to trial" (Hunter 2001, 47). Civilian pressure for reform in this area was relatively weak (Pereira 2001, 563), and the military saw maintaining its judicial system as a core interest, in part because it interpreted any change in military legal power as ultimately tied to the potential for accountability for human rights abuses committed during the dictatorship (Hunter 2001; Zirker 1993, 99). Amid other improvements in civil-military relations, military justice remained largely unreformed.

The most significant military justice reform effort came from 1995 to 1997 when President Fernando Henrique Cardoso announced a National Human Rights Plan of over 200 measures to address human rights issues (HRW 1997, 3; Pereira and Ungar 2004, 274).[30] Congressional Deputy Hélio Bicudo introduced legislation in 1995 that sought to give civilian courts jurisdiction in cases of crimes committed by military personnel against civilians (Pereira 2001, 563).

The military lobby and military allies in congress, however, successfully undermined the reform effort (Macaulay 2007, 35–36; Zaverucha 1999, 66–70). The eventual 1996 law only addressed cases of intentional homicide and only applied to the state-level military justice system, not the federal armed forces (Costa and Thompson 2011, 30; Pereira 2001, 563).[31] Nothing changed in practice, and "crimes classified as unintentional killings, severe non-lethal physical abuse and other, lesser offences continue[d] to be investigated and prosecuted within the specialized military courts" (Cavallaro and Delgado 2012, 109). The military retained the power to investigate and decide whether a killing was intentional or not, which reinforced impunity.

Similarly, in 1997, Brazil passed a new law criminalizing torture, particularly intended to curb the practice by police and prisons when holding suspects or convicts in custody.[32] Yet there was no jurisdictional reform. Military courts would still try torture cases (Costa and Thompson 2011, 29). Consequently, the law was "virtually ignored" and torture remained widespread (Hinton 2006, 128–29; International Commission of Jurists [ICJ] 2002b, 57–65; Rodley 2001). Another reform effort came with a 2004 amendment (included in the subsequent 2005 revision) to the 1988 constitution, which established the federal courts as the competent body to process and judge cases related to human rights with the rationale that this measure would enable the country to comply with its international treaty obligations (Article 109).[33] Practice, however, did not change. Transfers of such cases did not occur (HRW 2007b, 188), and the code of military justice, especially as it applies to the Military Police, remains a source of impunity (Amnesty International 2015; HRW 2009). The ability to subject civilians to military trial also remains unchanged.

The military still guards its legal prerogative because it fears that any reform could open it up to prosecution for abuses committed during the military dictatorship. The government created the National Truth Commission (*Comissão Nacional da Verdad*) in 2011 to investigate human rights violations from 1946 to 1988.[34] The 2014 final report provides detailed evidence of military complicity in a wide range of crimes and calls for an end to the 1979 amnesty.[35] The military has been defiant, however, and the Supreme Court upheld the amnesty in April 2010, putting the issue back in the legislature's hands by ruling, "only Congress could revoke the statute" (Rosenn 2014, 330).[36] Months later, the Inter-American Court of Human Rights (IACtHR) ruled against the amnesty law, but Brazil did not accept this decision and has taken no further action (Rosenn 2014, 331).[37] Moreover, the Supreme Court has stopped the few efforts to bring criminal charges against military personnel for their actions during the dictatorship (HRW 2018c, 97).

Military deployment for law and order

Maintaining its legal power has become even more important to the military in recent years as it takes on a greater responsibility for domestic policing. In November 1994, the government launched Operation Rio, which sent the military into the *favelas* of Rio de Janeiro to "restore public order," placing thousands of soldiers in a law enforcement role until the end of that year (Hinton 2006, 99). The deployment was ordered in response to a crime wave and a deteriorating security situation that the regular police forces seemed incapable of handling—or worse, were believed to be complicit in. Authorities turned to the military, which the public "viewed as more trustworthy and capable than the police" (Hunter 1997, 67). This dynamic would play out many times in the coming decades, and domestic deployments accelerated in the 2010s, with military occupation of particular *favelas* and other operations in advance of major events Brazil hosted, including the 2014 World Cup and 2016 Olympic Games (Fábio 2017; HRW 2012, 216; United States Department of State [USDS] 2016). In these instances, civilians were subject to military trial for disobeying orders of military personnel. The military justified this practice on the legal basis of military courts having authority in territory under military administration and the 1969 Military Penal Code's prohibitions on insults against or disobedience of the military (Andreu-Guzmán 2018, 134; Charleaux 2016; HRW 2018c, 92).[38] While the constitution allows for military deployments in emergency situations, the use of the armed forces in a policing role has become routine, as presidents have sought to respond to public pressure over high levels of crime and violence in Brazil's major cities.[39] A majority of the public views the armed forces favorably, rating them with higher confidence than the police and civilian judiciary (Corporación Latinobarómetro 2018c, 49–51). These attitudes, coupled with the government's reliance on the military for internal security, negatively impact any potential for reform.

In 2017, army commanders publicly advocated for legal changes that would give the military even more control over cases involving their personnel, on the grounds that answering to civilian courts could hinder policing operations (Charleaux 2017). Despite opposition from human rights groups and the Inter-American Commission on Human Rights, President Michel Temer (2016–18) signed into law a new measure in October 2017 that gave military courts jurisdiction over "human rights violations, including murder or attempted murder, committed by military personnel against civilians" (Amnesty International 2018, 98; Valente 2017).[40] The consequences of the new law became immediately clear. In November 2017, a joint military and police operation in Rio de Janeiro killed eight civilians. Civilian prosecutors were not able to investigate the military personnel involved, and the military took no action against them (HRW 2018b; 2019). The army additionally stonewalled to prevent any of its members from being interviewed as witnesses (HRW 2018a). A further case in April 2019 demonstrates acutely the stakes of putting the military on the streets while shielding its members from civilian justice. Soldiers on patrol in the Guadalupe neighborhood of Rio de Janeiro fired more than 80 rounds into the car of an innocent family after mistaking the vehicle for one used by gang members. The driver was killed and two others were injured. The Eastern Military Command arrested 10 soldiers for "noncompliance with rules of engagement," a minor military charge to be heard in a military court (Reuters 2019).

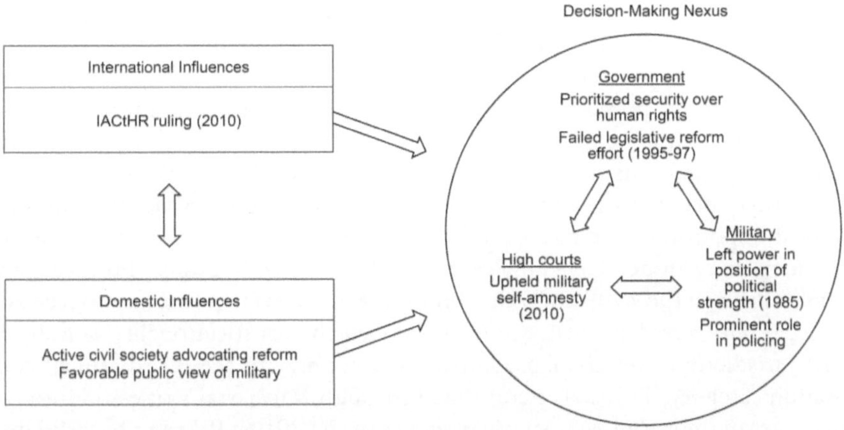

Figure 6.1 Military overreach in Brazil: Persistent military control

These developments underscore the danger of allowing security forces to sit in judgment of their own actions—they can operate a parallel legal system that shields their members from accountability for serious crimes, putting citizens at risk and undermining equality before the law. Brazil illustrates a case of intractable military overreach in the modern era. As we illustrate in Figure 6.1, the behaviors and interactions of the principal actors, as well as domestic conditions, have been unfavorable to military justice reform.

The military left power in a politically strong position in the 1980s, with a self-amnesty in place and continuity of the military justice system. Governments in the democratic era routinely have given the military a role in internal security, thereby increasing the institution's leverage in national politics and reinforcing its incentive to maintain control over its courts. The military successfully resisted a legislative reform effort in the 1990s. The high court upheld the military self-amnesty in a 2010 ruling, and international pressure in the form of the IACtHR ruling against the amnesty in the same year was ineffective. The government rejected the ruling, which underscores the practical limits of judgments by international human rights courts to effect change when the principal actors in the decision-making nexus are dismissive of such pressure. Public sentiment is favorable toward the military, minimizing electoral incentives to confront the armed forces and challenge its judicial prerogatives. We now turn to Pakistan as a case of incremental backsliding, illustrating how a military whose baseline legal power is strong enough to consistently contest civilian authority that it can repeatedly shift the country into military overreach.

Pakistan: Backsliding into military overreach

Pakistan has backslid from jurisdictional contestation to military overreach multiple times—most recently in 2015. Legal prerogatives have long been an element of the military's political power. The armed forces have been responsible for numerous interventions in politics since independence in 1947, determining the form and composition of government and ruling directly several times. It has been rare for a civilian government to complete its term in office and peacefully transfer power to another elected government. The many interruptions brought with them new constitutions and shifts in the reach of military justice. The numerous rounds of military rule in the latter half of the twentieth century included the use of military courts to assert control and suppress political opposition. The role of military courts in the most recent instance of non-democracy under General Pervez Musharraf (1999–2008), however, was limited. Prior to the 1999 coup that brought Musharraf to power, civilian courts and legal reformers had successfully challenged the constitutionality of military court jurisdiction over civilians, shifting the country to the jurisdictional contestation category. This status continued through Musharraf's rule and into the early years of improved democratic practices in the 2010s. Pakistan backslid into military overreach beginning in 2015. In response to a terrorist attack against the Peshawar Army Public School, the democratically elected government legalized the use of military courts against civilians in terrorism cases. The new law initially empowered military courts to serve this role for only two years, but the government then extended it for an additional two. This episode illustrates the conditions under which democracies, faced with pressing challenges such as terrorism, choose to grant the military more legal power.

Military justice in British India, 1757–1947

Pakistan's colonial experience had a profound impact on its post-independence development, namely the practice of ruling through the military-bureaucratic axis of the army and the civil service (Malagodi 2019; Talbot 2015, 455). Britain used military authority expansively during colonial rule, and maintaining order within its locally recruited forces—numbering in the tens of thousands (Lees 2010, 1–2)—required subjecting them to British military law, even beyond disciplinary offenses (Roy 2001). Civilians were not regularly subject to trial by military courts, making colonial-era Pakistan a case of jurisdictional contestation. Courts martial were used most commonly to deal with Indian soldiers' acts of insubordination against European officers, to crack down on drunkenness, and to punish deserters (Roy and Dasgupta 2006, 66–68). Punishments for offenses included flogging, dismissal, and even death, as was the case for desertion.

The British colony under the East India Company (EIC) was quick to use force to put down rebellions among the population and to quell mutinies within the Indian armies under its control (Lees 2010). Unrest within the forces at this time typically took the form of mutinies "aimed at the improvement of service conditions," rather than being politically motivated (Roy 2001, 961). In the 1850s, however, dissent grew due to a series of measures related to religious rights and practices as well as long-standing frustration over EIC tax collection and inept rural administration (Gilbert 2015, 292–93). Furthermore, new rifle cartridges issued to Indian troops were greased with beef and pig fat. The cartridges had to be bitten open before loading, and this offended the religious prohibitions of Hindu and Muslim soldiers' consumption of beef and pork, respectively. Soldiers refused to use the cartridges, and British commanders responded by "punish[ing] offenders with intentionally humiliating conditions of imprisonment or dismissal" (Gilbert 2015, 293) and using public hangings to deter further disobedience (Roy 2006, 20). British authorities badly miscalculated. Their response to dissent further inflamed the situation and led to the 1857 Great Mutiny, a major rebellion across northern India that lasted a year and a half. The British government in London saw the conflict as a disaster for its hold on the Indian colony, leading Parliament to relieve the EIC of its position and assert direct control, beginning the era of Crown rule (Gilbert 2015, 292–95). In the aftermath of the Great Mutiny, military justice became more lenient, motivated by a belief that the arbitrary, uneven, and excessively harsh pre-1857 system had contributed to the uprising. Punishments given in the decades after 1857 were typically lighter and more in keeping with professional military discipline, such as confinement to barracks (Roy 2001, 940; Roy 2006, 20–21).

While another widespread military rebellion did not occur, violent uprisings among the general population were still common after 1857 (Guha 1999). The British responded to these events quickly and violently, frequently using military personnel as additional police forces (Omissi 1994, 217). In policing and law, British India was characterized by a fusion of civilian and military authority (Rahman 2019). Military commanders assumed control over designated administrative areas, where their powers included the ability to direct the civilian courts to put subjects on trial for violations of military law (Dawson 1923, 141). Military forces were key to British rule, and this role continued after independence, effectively making the military a parallel state, ready to assume control when it perceived international threats or internal disorder to merit martial law. The persistence of expansive military jurisdiction over personnel after independence makes Pakistan a unique case of colonial continuity in jurisdictional contestation, unlike the continuity most British colonies experienced by retaining systems of full subordination.

Parliamentary democracy, 1947–58

After World War II, South Asian independence leaders, especially in the Muslim League and the Indian National Congress, successfully pressured British authorities to negotiate an end to colonial rule. The British departure brought not only independence but also the partition of territory into majority-Hindu India and majority-Muslim Pakistan (Gilbert 2015, 311). This traumatic division instigated large-scale violence and mass migrations, including the movement of millions of Muslims into Pakistan in a matter of months. The new state was unprepared to handle them (Talbot 2015, 455). Pakistan was itself geographically divided between West Pakistan (present-day Pakistan) and East Pakistan (present-day Bangladesh), which reflected and intensified ethnic and linguistic divisions as well as disagreements over the appropriate balance between the central government and provincial powers (Jalal 1990, 136–67; Talbot 2015, 462–73). Pakistan's early years after British rule were tumultuous. Muhammad Ali Jinnah, Pakistan's founding father, died in 1948. Liaquat Ali Khan, Jinnah's successor, was assassinated in 1951 (Talbot 2015, 454–57). These factors set the stage for overwhelming governance challenges and a military that would become more internally focused and politically active over time (A. Shah 2014, 10).

In March 1953, in response to religious riots, Prime Minister Kwhaja Nazimuddin imposed martial law in Punjab province (Malagodi 2019, 1243). The army militarized the city of Lahore, setting up defensive positions in public spaces and enforcing a curfew (Talbot 2015, 465–66). The military quickly put an end to the riots and then embarked on a program of civic improvement, laying new roads and sidewalks, and providing basic public services, such as health and sanitation (Cheema 2001, 125). Military control also involved "sprucing up public parks, cleaning up shops, and controlling the prices of essential goods" (A. Shah 2014, 68). The military previously put down riots in Bengal in 1952, but this was the first time it took on an extensive governing role (Talbot 2015, 466). The military's task as an "aid to the civil power"—which stemmed from the colonial era practice of using the military for internal law and order—was now interpreted much more broadly. The experience was a turning point in the military's role as a political actor and the first episode of backsliding into military overreach as a consequence of the security threat of public disorder. The public and the officer corps saw the military as succeeding where civilians had failed, which encouraged further involvement in civic and governing affairs (A. Shah 2014, 67–69).

In the midst of the 1953 martial law episode, Governor-General Ghulam Muhammad dismissed Khwaja Nazimuddin from his post as Prime Minister (Talbot 2015, 458). The move against Nazimuddin amounted to a coup against the normal order and ended any real attempt at democracy (Ayoob 1971, 199; Malagodi 2019, 1243). The military consolidated its power under General Ayub Khan and the Defense Secretary, General Iskander Mirza (Talbot 2015, 459), but martial law was brief. The country returned to its previous status of jurisdictional contestation. Mirza succeeded Muhammad as Governor-General in 1955 and became the first president of Pakistan under the new republican constitution in 1956 that formally ended Dominion status. Mirza continued to deploy the military for internal administrative functions, especially the anti-smuggling effort known as Operation Close Door. The military shut down East Pakistan's border with India, which reduced the loss of goods and revenue from illicit cross-border trade (Sayeed 1959, 73; A. Shah 2014, 86).

Military overreach: Martial law, 1958–62

By 1958, Pakistan's military had taken on a praetorian role in the country's politics. The officer corps had adopted a view of itself as the institution ultimately responsible for the survival of the Pakistani state. Moreover, they strongly considered civilian politicians to be the cause of the country's poor economic performance and political instability (Rizvi 1974, 87–88; A. Shah 2014, 85–87). President Mirza and high-ranking military figures saw the parliamentary government established by the 1956 constitution as unworkable and anticipated delaying the elections scheduled for early 1959. Junior officers who favored keeping to the election schedule were rumored to be plotting a coup, which prompted Mirza to declare martial law on October 8, 1958, ostensibly to prevent a direct military takeover.[41] The new martial law administration abrogated the 1956 constitution, dissolved parliament and provincial assemblies, banned political parties, and canceled the elections (Jalal 1990, 272–76). Within days, the military jailed most prominent politicians (Wilcox 1965, 143). In place of the constitution, the government ruled under the 1958 Laws (Continuance in Force) Order (Rizvi 1974, 98).[42] Within weeks, the Supreme Court legitimized martial law through its ruling in the case of *State* v. *Dosso*, which reasoned that the revolutionary nature of the military regime justified the new military-imposed legal order.[43] The same day, October 27, 1958, Chief Martial Law Administrator (CMLA) General Ayub Khan ousted Mirza and assumed control of the country (Mahmud 1993, 1245–47). Thus, the 1958 episode of backsliding came in the context of the marginalization of the other principal actors in the decision-making nexus regarding military legal power. The army seized control of government and the high court validated this move.

Under martial law from 1958 to 1962, Pakistan was a clear case of military overreach. Military courts prosecuted civilians in military courts for violations of martial law regulations addressing corruption and economic issues, including black marketeering, smuggling, and price gouging, as well as for criticism of the government or armed forces (Sayeed 1959, 74–77). Moreover, though the Laws (Continuance in Force) Order kept the civilian judiciary in place, its powers were highly restricted. Civilian courts were not permitted to challenge military authorities, martial law regulations, or military court judgments (Newberg 1995, 72; Sayeed 1959, 74).

The martial law administration began with a heavy-handed approach, including military searches of the homes of those suspected of smuggling and black-market activity (Rizvi 1974, 103). Ayub Khan, however, soon took a less aggressive posture, preferring instead to rule through the civil service while relying on the martial law regulations to deter illegal behaviors such as smuggling and tax avoidance. Just over one month into martial law, he "ordered the withdrawal of troops from martial law duties and declared that all standing Military Courts would be wound up immediately" (Sayeed 1959, 76), but this departure from martial law did not last. Weeks later, military courts were operating again. Military authorities justified their reinstatement on the grounds that military courts were more capable of carrying out trials given their familiarity with military law. Ultimately, martial law regulations under Ayub Khan were used to prosecute individuals and to institute wide-ranging national policies, from industrialization programs to land reform (Baxter 2015, 492; Sayeed 1959, 76–77).

In 1960, Ayub Khan established a new partyless political system known as Basic Democracy, which channeled participation and representation into a hierarchical system of councils (Sayeed 1961). The same year, he submitted his continuation in office to a pro forma referendum. Additionally, he retired from the army, thereby civilianizing his rule, even as martial law continued and he retained the CMLA title (Rizvi 1974, 139). This state of affairs marked the first instance, one to be repeated multiple times in Pakistani history, of a mismatch between civilian rule and civilian law. Not until 1962, with the introduction of a new constitution, did martial law formally end (Baxter 2015, 485), removing civilians from military courts and thereby shifting the country back to jurisdictional contestation. Ayub Khan won a competitive election for his office in 1965, but weak economic performance and growing opposition in the ensuing years undermined his hold on power. Military officials grew disaffected with his rule, leading him to resign in 1969 and to turn the presidency over to the Commander-in-Chief of the Army, General Agha Muhammad Yahya Khan, who again declared martial law and became the CMLA (Cheema 2001, 141–42).

Military overreach: A return to martial law, 1969–72

Martial law under Yahya Khan returned Pakistan to a status of military overreach. Much like the imposition of martial law a decade earlier, it annulled the constitution, shut down national and provincial legislatures, and banned political activity (Rizvi 1974, 209–10). Similar to the Laws (Continuance in Force) Order of the preceding martial law administration, the 1969 Provisional Constitutional Order (PCO) kept all other laws in effect, and the civilian judiciary remained intact even while sidelined by the parallel use of military courts.[44] As in the previous experience with martial law, military courts extended their jurisdiction over civilians, defendants could not appeal military court decisions to civilian courts, and civilian courts were not permitted to challenge martial law regulations (Newberg 1995, 112; Rizvi 1974, 216–17). Military courts initially only prosecuted violations of martial law regulations, but Martial Law Regulation 42, instituted in May 1969, "empowered martial law administrators to transfer to Military Courts any criminal case" (Dias 1970, 50). Thus, the military and civilian legal systems were directly in conflict with each other. In the 1969 case of *Hassan and Rasul* v. *The State*, the civilian district Rawalpindi Court ruled against the transfer of civilian cases to military courts on the grounds that martial law regulations contradicted the fundamental right of due process still guaranteed by the provisional constitution. Moreover, the civilian court asserted its power to interpret the meaning of martial law regulations, even though it was not allowed to challenge them. This dispute led Yahya Khan to issue the Jurisdiction of Courts (Removal of Doubts) Order in June 1969 to clarify that civilian courts were not free to interpret the regulations (Dias 1970, 49–51).[45]

In addition to these legal fights, Yahya Khan faced growing discontent in East Pakistan and large-scale open defiance of the martial law regulations, especially from student groups. Inconsistent enforcement only exacerbated the problem (Rizvi 1974, 218). The government allowed the return of political activity beginning in January 1970, even as martial law continued. In setting up a new framework for political competition, Yahya Khan scrapped Ayub Khan's complex Basic Democracy arrangement in favor of a system based on direct elections, universal suffrage, and legislative representation determined by population size, which naturally gave an advantage to the more populous East Pakistan.

Consequently, when elections were held in December 1970 to convene a National Assembly that would write a new constitution, the Awami League, a party advocating a high degree of provincial autonomy, won nearly all of the seats allocated to East Pakistan, and therefore held an almost two-thirds majority in the legislature (Rizvi 1974, 228–29). When Yahya Khan sought to postpone the anticipated March 1971 first session of the new National Assembly, East Pakistani leaders saw it as an attempt to deny their rightful place in government. The Awami League organized a general strike and demanded an end to martial law in East Pakistan. Widespread violence shook East Pakistan for weeks while negotiations between East and West failed to produce a settlement. By the end of March 1971, the Awami League effectively established an independent government and declared an end to martial law in East Pakistan. Yahya Khan responded by outlawing the Awami League and deploying the military to reassert control by force. The situation grew worse throughout 1971, eventually leading to war with India and independence for East Pakistan (Bangladesh) (Rizvi 1974, 238–44).

This traumatic defeat discredited military rule and, in December 1971, led Yahya Khan to cede power to Zulfikar Ali Bhutto, leader of the Pakistan People's Party (PPP), the largest party in government in what remained of Pakistan. Despite the fact that leadership passed to a civilian, martial law continued. Bhutto assumed the role of president and CMLA. Bhutto's government continued to use military courts to prosecute civilians and still did not permit civilian courts to review the decisions. This state of affairs was challenged, however, in the 1972 Supreme Court case *Asma Jilani* v. *Government of Punjab*, which involved two civilians' appeals against detention under Yahya Khan's martial law regulations.[46] Lower civilian courts had dismissed the case by concluding they did not have jurisdiction, but the Supreme Court took the case and condemned the use of martial law. In doing so, the Court also repudiated its previous ruling in the 1958 *Dosso* case that had legitimized martial law under Ayub Khan (Mahmud 1993, 1255–56; Yap 2017, 137). In *Asma Jilani*, the Court argued that Ayub Khan violated the 1962 constitution by handing power to Yahya Khan instead of following constitutional succession. Thus, Yahya Khan's government was illegitimate and its use of martial law illegal. This reasoning allowed the justices to draw a contrast between the two periods of martial law and to therefore account for the contradictory judgments about the legitimacy of its use. The Court pointed to the military's own rationale for intervention to challenge the logic of martial law. Both military rulers had claimed seizing control was necessary to restore law and order, prevent chaos, and protect democracy. In the eyes of the justices, subjecting the country to martial law was the antithesis of supporting the legal order of the state and therefore could not be part of the military's fundamental mission of protecting it.

In addition to the *Asma Jilani* ruling, the civilian provincial Lahore Court challenged martial law in the case of *Zia-ur-Rehman* v. *The State* by arguing that military jurisdiction over civilians was unjustifiable when civilian courts were still operating, as was the case during both of the preceding periods of martial law. The Supreme Court affirmed the lower court ruling and also struck down Article 281 of the 1972 interim constitution on the grounds that its powers were derived from the martial law regulations which were no longer in effect (Newberg 1995, 119–30).[47] Concurrent with the rulings in these cases, the government finally lifted martial law in April 1972 (Cheema 2001, 145; Yap 2017, 137), which moved Pakistan from military overreach to jurisdictional contestation. Military courts no longer put civilians on trial, but the military still claimed broad jurisdiction over its personnel, including retired members (Newberg 1995, 146). In this instance of positive change, civilian high courts asserted their authority in the context of a regime transition and a disastrous civil war that discredited military rule. Nevertheless, Pakistan did not see progress beyond jurisdictional contestation, which set the stage for yet another instance of backsliding to military overreach.

Military overreach: A third round of martial law, 1977–85

Zulfikar Ali Bhutto (1972–77) assumed the presidency as a popular figure but at a very difficult time in Pakistan's history. Chastened by the loss of Bangladesh and the failures of the Yahya Khan regime, the military was hesitant to insert itself into civilian politics, but relations between civilian leaders and the armed forces were nevertheless strained (Shafqat 1997). While Bhutto made progress in re-establishing civilian control over the armed forces, that control largely proved to be based on personal loyalty, rather than institutionalization, and even this had limits. For example, when Bhutto called on the army to respond to a police strike in Peshawar, Commander-in-Chief of the Army, General Gul Hassan, refused. Bhutto forced Hassan and others to resign and created the Federal Security Force (FSF) in October 1972, which became in effect a personal militia for him to use to attack his opposition. The army saw the FSF as a competing military force that threatened its institution (Jones 2015, 570–73). Bhutto's regime also engaged in legalized repression against political opponents through civilian courts, invoking the international threat of India and the domestic threat of terrorism as justifications (Newberg 1995, 138).

In 1973, Pakistan established a new constitution, which paved the way for elections in 1977—the country's first since the loss of Bangladesh.[48] A newly created opposition coalition, the Pakistan National Alliance (PNA), proved especially adept at uniting disparate groups of supporters and drawing attention to Bhutto's failures in governing. The March 1977 elections to fill the National Assembly were rigged in favor of the PPP, and the fraud was so blatant that the PNA called for the Election Commissioner to resign and declared that it would boycott the upcoming provincial elections. Violent protests followed, and the police were unable to control the situation (Ahmad and Sultan 1977, 14–15). Bhutto called on his FSF and the army to put down the riots, and he implemented martial law in the cities of Karachi and Lahore in April 1977 (Choudhury 1988, 25; Jones 2015, 590–93). Bhutto and the PNA engaged in negotiations over the next two months but failed to arrive at an agreement on new elections. At this point, the military stepped in. General Muhammad Zia-ul-Haq ousted Bhutto on July 5, 1977, held the constitution in abeyance, and extended martial law across Pakistan (Cheema 2001, 146; Yap 2017, 138).[49] This marked another instance in which the country shifted to military overreach in response to the threat of public disorder.

Zia initially promised to hold elections within 90 days of the coup, but as with previous interventions the military's goal of re-shaping politics took precedence over a quick resumption of democracy.[50] The Supreme Court would again serve a mediating role that ultimately upheld Zia's coup. The military regime argued in *Begum Nusrat Bhutto* v. *Chief of Army Staff and Federation of Pakistan* that the revolutionary legality for martial law had been established in *Dosso*.[51] The Court rejected this assertion because Zia claimed his rule would be temporary and that the constitution had only been suspended, not repealed outright. Instead, the Court ruled more narrowly that Zia was justified in seizing power due to the unique chaotic conditions in the country at the time. By resting the judgment on the doctrine of necessity, the Supreme Court avoided granting unchecked power to the military regime (Newberg 1995, 165–68). The Court ruled that the military's authority extended only to taking actions to get out of the emergency, which preserved the civilian courts' powers to subject martial law regulations and actions to judicial review on a continuing basis.

In principle, this ruling meant that civilian courts would be able to hear challenges to the martial law regime and to judge whether Zia's government was acting in accordance with what was truly necessary to serve the public interest, restore order, and return the country to democracy. They continued to rule on cases throughout the 1977–80 period of Zia's rule. In practice, however, the civilian high courts largely abandoned the potential restraint this could have provided, reasoning that once the doctrine of necessity legitimized the regime, the courts could rule only on procedure not substance of government actions (Mahmud 1993, 1274–82; Yap 2017, 138–39). Thus, while the civilian courts remained open and functional, as in the two prior rounds of martial law, they were ineffective in restraining military power (Newberg 1995, 174–78).

Throughout Zia's dictatorship, military courts put thousands of civilians on trial, including for ordinary crimes (Petrén et al. 1987, 70–72). In 1981, Zia revoked the 1973 constitution entirely and issued a new PCO, which put martial law beyond the reach of any civilian legal authority (Newberg 1995, 180–82).[52] Furthermore, it asserted control over the civilian courts by ordering judges to pledge their loyalty to his new provisional constitution. Zia removed judges who refused (Cheema 2001, 149; Mahmud 1993, 1282–83). Secure in his battle against the civilian judiciary, Zia sought popular legitimacy for his rule through a referendum in December 1984. The ensuing victory gave him five more years in office. He oversaw partyless elections for the National Assembly in February 1985. As a condition of ending martial law and reinstating the 1973 Constitution in December 1985, Zia forced parliamentary acceptance of numerous changes, including the Eighth Amendment, which amounted to an indemnity for all acts and regulations of the martial law administration retroactive to the 1977 coup (Yap 2017, 140).[53] The changes effectively prevented civilian challenges to the rules laid down by the military government, even after the end of martial law. It also meant civilians convicted in military trials, including those awaiting death sentences, had no new legal recourse (Petrén et al. 1987, 73–77).

The post-1985 system granted a praetorian role to the armed forces and reflected significant continuity with the martial law era. Zia remained in the presidency and retained control of the armed forces as Chief of Army Staff (COAS). The modified constitution codified sweeping presidential authority, including the power to remove the prime minister from office and dissolve the National Assembly (Rizvi 1986, 1071–73), which he did in May 1988. Zia had set new elections for November but did not live to see them; he was killed when his plane exploded in August 1988. The elections went forward, convening a new National Assembly and restoring a civilian executive, albeit one hobbled by the military's insistence that its internal affairs and budgets could not be touched by civilian decision making and that the president, Ghulam Ishaq Khan, and Zia's Minister of Foreign Affairs, Sahibzada Yaqub Khan, would remain in their positions (Mufti 2015, 634–36). The next decade was characterized as "military rule by other means" (Haqqani 2005). No government could survive without the support of the COAS. Acting through the reserve powers of the president, the military removed prime ministers and dissolved parliament multiple times from 1988 to 1999 (Croissant et al. 2013, 177).

Civil-military tensions and anti-terrorism courts

In 1997, Nawaz Sharif was elected prime minister with a two-thirds majority of the National Assembly behind him, which gave him the ability to push back against presidential and military political powers. Sharif's parliamentary support allowed him to amend the constitution to prevent a president from dismissing a prime minister. Thereafter, he proceeded to remove the president, the Chief Justice of the Supreme Court, and the COAS (Croissant et al. 2013, 183).

These moves helped Sharif consolidate his power, but the military retained a significant political presence due to its role in internal security. In the 1990s, insurgent groups and terrorism proliferated. Conditions deteriorated in Sindh province in southern Pakistan and the government deployed the military to combat terrorist organizations and general lawlessness (Cheema 2001, 132–34; Mufti 2015, 649–50). In addition, the government passed the Anti-Terrorism Act in 1997, which created new Anti-Terror Courts (ATCs) that existed separately from the regular civilian justice system.[54] The government deemed these special courts necessary to move trials more swiftly than they would in ordinary courts. The ATCs allowed just seven days for investigation and seven days for trial (Justice

Project Pakistan 2010, 7). In practice, however, trials often took longer than the permitted time, or experienced delays, leading to a case backlog similar to that of the regular courts. The ATCs remained in place but were generally seen as ineffective in combatting terrorism and have instead been associated with trials of common crimes and widespread rights abuses (Justice Project Pakistan 2010, 10; Zaidi 2016, 9).

In October 1998, the security situation in Sindh led Sharif to invoke Governor's Rule in the province, which removed the provincial government, installed an army general in its place, and gave military courts jurisdiction to prosecute civilians for numerous acts deemed to cause "civil commotion" (Rizvi 1999, 179).[55] By January 1999, the government extended military jurisdiction over civilians across the country.[56] Military jurisdiction was immediately challenged, leading to a landmark Supreme Court ruling in the case of *Sheikh Liaquat Hussain* v. *Federation of Pakistan* that declared military jurisdiction over civilians unconstitutional (Cheema 2001, 133–34; USDS 2000).[57] These cases were still cause for concern because the ruling mandated their transfer to the ATCs rather than to the regular judicial system (HRW 1999), but this was a significant instance of the high court successfully pushing back against the government and military to preserve citizens' rights.

Sharif had close ties with the military in its fight against domestic terrorism, but an ill-fated international military adventure spelled the end for Sharif's administration and civilian government. In May 1999, Pakistan initiated a limited conflict against India over Kashmir, but after profound international criticism, Sharif withdrew the military without its agreement and "publicly blamed the military for Pakistan's de facto defeat" (Croissant et al. 2013, 184). In October 1999, Sharif attempted to dismiss General Pervez Musharraf, the acting COAS. Musharraf, backed by the military, ousted Sharif, seized power, and suspended the constitution (Mufti 2015, 659–60).

Jurisdictional contestation: General Pervez Musharraf, 1999–2008

With respect to the military justice system, Musharraf's government was different from the previous rounds of military rule for three reasons. First, Musharraf declared a state of emergency rather than formally invoking martial law. This action still suspended the constitution, but it did not specifically empower military courts the way prior martial law administrations had done (Cheema 2001, 153; Yap 2017, 144). Second, in carrying out the coup and suppressing potential opposition immediately afterward, the new leaders opted to use military detention without trial rather than bringing their opponents in front of courts (ICJ 2002a; USDS 2000). Third, to the extent that the Musharraf dictatorship did pursue judicialized repression, it relied upon the 1997 Anti-Terrorism Act and its court system, which were not directly part of military justice. The Musharraf regime expanded ATC powers multiple times during his rule (Justice Project Pakistan 2010).

Despite these differences, Musharraf's regime was still characterized by military dominance of the legal sphere. The 1999 *Sheikh Liaquat Hussain* ruling only months prior to Musharraf's coup stood as an external check on military court jurisdiction over civilians, but the military regime again significantly undermined the civilian court system. Musharraf interfered directly and immediately with the membership of the superior courts. He forced them to "take an oath of allegiance to the military regime and those judges who refused were removed from office" (Yap 2017, 145). In an attempt to place limits on Musharraf's rule, the Supreme Court asserted its power of judicial review and required elections to be held within three years (Cheema 2001, 154; Yap 2017, 145).[58]

As with his military predecessors, Musharraf extended his time in office by subjecting his rule to a referendum. In April 2002, in a highly suspect vote, he secured for himself another five years as president (Siddiqa 2015, 702). Later that year, he oversaw elections to the National Assembly, ended the state of emergency, and reinstated the 1973 constitution. Much like the Eighth Amendment that was added in 1985, Musharraf added the Seventeenth Amendment to the constitution, which "validated all the laws and orders issued during the State of Emergency" (Yap 2017, 147), effectively putting Musharraf's takeover beyond any future judicial scrutiny and legalizing his fraudulent referendum victory.[59]

Musharraf's rule began to falter in 2007 as the end of his term approached. The Supreme Court, now led by Chief Justice Iftikhar Muhammad Chaudhry, investigated military detentions and other suspected abuses (Yap 2017, 148). Musharraf removed Chaudhry from his post, but it provoked widespread protests, particularly from what came to be known as the Lawyers' Movement, which condemned the blatant interference in the judiciary (Siddiqa 2015, 690). He was forced to reinstate Chaudhry. Musharraf secured re-election in October, but the Supreme Court "ordered the Election Commission not to certify the results" until it could rule on the legality of his potential third term (Yap 2017, 148). Musharraf declared a new state of emergency, which included an assertion of military court jurisdiction over civilians (HRW 2007a, 8), thereby briefly shifting Pakistan again into the military overreach category.[60] He issued a provisional constitution and demanded justices pledge to uphold it. Those who refused were dismissed (Ghias 2010). The military did not back Musharraf in this effort, however, and his power evaporated quickly (Croissant et al. 2013, 186; Siddiqa 2015, 699). He resigned his position as COAS in late November and ended the state of emergency the following month.[61] A major opposition victory in the general elections in 2008 changed the political landscape and led to legal pressure and threats of impeachment. Musharraf in turn resigned as president in August 2008 (Yap 2017, 149–50).

Military overreach: Terrorism and the civilian empowerment of military courts, 2015–19

After Musharraf's resignation, Pakistan returned to elected civilian government. Serious internal security challenges remained, and to make up for the slow proceedings of the regular judiciary the country increasingly turned to special courts to address the problem. In July 2014, parliament passed the Protection of Pakistan Act, which took a war footing, authorizing measures against the "waging of war or insurrection against Pakistan" (Zaidi 2016, 6).[62] The law established a new set of special courts, in addition to the ATCs still in operation, and expanded police and army powers for preventive detention. In December 2014, a terrorist attack at the Army Public School in Peshawar shocked the nation. Tehrik-i-Taliban in Pakistan, a militant group based along the Afghan–Pakistan border, killed 131 schoolchildren and wounded 121 more (Khan 2014). The government responded with the National Action Plan, a comprehensive approach to combatting terrorism, which included creating new counter-terrorism forces, tracking terrorist financing, and addressing extremism and hate speech (Zaidi 2016).[63] The plan also sought to expand military courts' role in the fight against terrorism. In January 2015, the government amended the 1952 Pakistan Army Act and added the Twenty-first Amendment to the 1973 constitution.[64] These measures eliminated terrorist suspects' right to a trial by civilian courts and empowered the military justice system to try cases involving individuals who are "claiming or are known to belong to any terrorist group or organization using the name of religion or sect and raise arms or wage war against Pakistan," thereby placing civilians under military jurisdiction yet again.[65] Some legislators expressed concern over the resort to military courts; others who found military courts acceptable were still opposed to the drastic step of incorporating the changes into the constitution (Dawn 2015b). Nevertheless, national unity and political expediency won out, and parliament passed the measures unanimously (ICJ 2015a). Civil society groups, especially Bar Associations across the country, protested the government's move and formally condemned it as an attack on the rule of law, with no effect (Dawn 2015a).

The new military judicial powers were tempered somewhat by the fact that, unlike some of the past instances of the use of military courts, they would in principle still be subject to civilian judicial review. In practice, however, this did not serve as an effective restraint. In August 2015, the Supreme Court upheld the use of military courts against civilian terrorism suspects and one year later rejected a challenge from families of 16 people sentenced to death in military courts, who had argued they were not fair trials (ICJ 2015b; ICJ 2016).[66] Though the precise numbers are unknown, from 2015 to 2019, military courts convicted at least 641 defendants on terrorism charges, sentencing at least 345 of them to death. The charges, evidence, and rulings were not made public, frequently making it impossible to appeal a ruling to a higher civilian court (ICJ 2019a, 3–7). Only in 2018 did the Peshawar High Court successfully challenge military court proceedings on the grounds of a lack of appropriate defense counsel, a failure to produce evidence against the defendants, and the arbitrary and secret nature of their operations. The Court forced military courts to release 70 defendants who were being held for trial (ICJ 2019a, 8–9).[67]

In addition, the 2015 law contained a two-year sunset clause, which was meant to constrain military courts. The government emphasized that the resort to military justice was due to the acute threat of terrorism and the shortcomings of the civilian system to deal with it effectively. Using military courts in the short term would be a stop-gap measure while the government could reform the civilian courts to improve their ability to prosecute terrorism. The two-year window ended, however, and the courts remained in place. In March 2017, the government passed the Twenty-third Amendment to the constitution, renewing the mandate for military courts and giving them retrospective legality to January 2017 when the previous amendment had expired (ICJ 2017; ICJ 2019a, 3).[68]

As the second two-year deadline approached in early 2019, politicians debated whether to support another extension. The governing party favored an extension but could not pass a new amendment to that effect without a two-thirds majority in the legislature. Nawaz Sharif's Pakistan Muslim League-Nawaz (PML-N) party was open to the idea, but the PPP firmly opposed it. The military, meanwhile, was also in favor of continuing the use of military courts (Syed 2019). Nevertheless, PPP opposition ensured the proposed second extension would not go forward (W. Shah 2019b; Wasim 2019a). Pakistan stopped using military courts as part of the National Action Plan against terrorism in March 2019 (Wasim 2019b). Though military courts ceased to function for this purpose, the ongoing consequences of their rulings remain contentious. Many defendants are serving sentences or awaiting execution based on decisions handed down by now-terminated military legal processes. Hundreds of petitions have been brought to the civilian high courts to challenge military court rulings, most commonly demanding documentation of the convictions (W. Shah 2020). These efforts have achieved some success in the courts, which have affirmed the right to bring such petitions, but government ministries and the military have been uncooperative, even claiming they did not keep records (Iqbal 2020a; Iqbal 2020b).

While dilemmas born of the 2015–19 use of military courts against civilians persist, Pakistan also faces enduring problems related to other military legal practices. The military maintains full legal control over its own personnel, conducting secretive, opaque trials and retaining its authority to put retired personnel on trial (Bhatti 2020). Additionally, while military courts do not have jurisdiction over civilians, the military continues to arrest and hold citizens without trial, notably those who have challenged military conduct (BBC News 2020). Military deployment in internal security missions remains especially dangerous in this regard. For example, the provincial government of Khyber Pakhtunkhwa empowered the military to carry out widespread internment of civilians as part of its security operations in the province (ICJ 2019b). Review of cases of internment is not referred to a normal court in either the civilian or military systems, but instead is conducted by a hybrid military-civilian oversight board with two military officers and two civilians (W. Shah 2019a).

In sum, the 2015–19 period of military overreach illustrates the troubling decision of an elected, civilian government turning to the military to deal with the large-scale, persistent problem of terrorism. As we illustrate with Figure 6.2, Pakistan has experienced backsliding into military overreach on multiple occasions through largely the same dynamics each time.

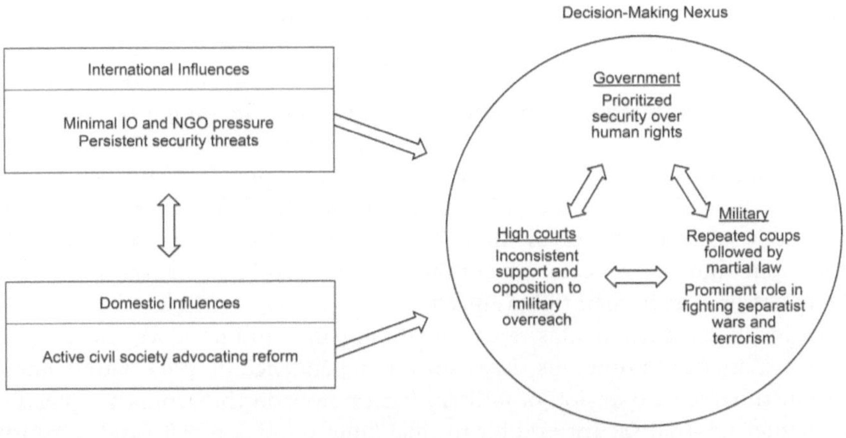

Figure 6.2 Military overreach in Pakistan: Repeated backsliding

The principal actors of the military and the civilian high courts have engaged in a battle over military legal powers, but the military has had the upper hand. Historically, the military's coups to implement martial law fused it with the government and left the civilian courts with few options to prevent backsliding into military overreach. Instead, they validated military takeovers. On the notable occasions when high courts took bold action to counter martial law, they did so when the military was not directly in control of government. Civilian and military governments have cited public disorder or other internal security threats, such as terrorism, as justification for invoking martial law and subjecting civilians to military justice. Meanwhile, domestic civil society actors have played an active role in protesting military overreach—most notably in 1971 when opposition to martial law coincided with the breakdown of state control and eventual independence for Bangladesh—but they have not been able to prevent backsliding. The principal actors in the decision-making nexus have been largely unmoved by civil society opposition. International influences have had little direct effect on Pakistan's backsliding into military overreach, though the international conditions of the Cold War and the War on Terror have been unfavorable to sustained democratic practices and civilian control of the armed forces.

Conclusion

In systems of military overreach, in addition to giving them legal authority over their personnel for almost all offenses, militaries also extend the jurisdiction of their courts to civilians. These conditions represent a breakdown of democracy and the rule of law. The military is not under the control of civilian leadership who ultimately answer to the voting public, thereby subverting an essential condition of democracy. Moreover, using military courts in this manner infringes upon civilians' rights and virtually guarantees military impunity for other abuses of power.

Brazil is a case that shows persistent military overreach in the modern era. Governments used military courts expansively during the twentieth century, especially during the military dictatorship from 1964 to 1985, and the practices of that period endured into the new democratic era. The military left power in a position of political strength and successfully resisted civilian efforts to reform military justice in the 1990s, even as other military prerogatives were brought under control. The Brazilian military views its legal power as a core interest because it not only preserves the ability to avoid potential accountability for misconduct but also restrains one of the most powerful mechanisms available to shed light on past human rights abuses.

Meanwhile, Pakistan illustrates backsliding into military overreach, which it has experienced numerous times since independence in 1947. Governments have justified the expansion of military legal power on the grounds of needing to counter internal security problems, including public disorder and terrorism. Notably, backsliding has occurred not only in the context of military intervention in politics that bring the generals directly to power but also through democratically elected governments choosing to empower military courts. Both countries illustrate the fraught reality that military legal subordination is a greater challenge where security issues dominate the national political debate. For Brazil and Pakistan, the intensity of the threats, combined with politically activated militaries, produced persistent military overreach and cycles of backsliding, respectively. In the next chapter, we turn to the United States as a case study of a country whose default position has been full subordination but that has empowered military courts in response to security threats.

Notes

1 We discuss the history of Portuguese military justice at length in Chapter 4.

2 Chapter VIII, Article 147 of the 1824 constitution did not define the army and navy as permanent institutions, giving the General Assembly the power to alter their status even to the point of dissolving them completely, see Federative Republic of Brazil, 1824 Constitution, http://pdba.georgetown.edu/Constitutions/Brazil/brazil1824.html. Military officers were thus concerned that the military would be replaced by the National Guard.

3 Alvará de 7 de Agosto de 1820, "Approva e confirma o novo Codigo Penal Militar," https://www2.camara.leg.br/atividade-legislativa/legislacao/colecao-anual-de-leis/copy_of_colecao1.html.

4 Decreto N. 85-A de 23 de dezembro de 1889, "Crêa uma commissão militar para o julgamento dos crimes de conspiração contra a Republica e seu governo, applicando-lhes as penas militares de sedição," https://www2.camara.leg.br/legin/fed/decret/1824-1899/decreto-85-a-23-dezembro-1889-543749-publicacaooriginal-54307-pe.html.

5 Federative Republic of Brazil, Constitution of 1891, http://pdba.georgetown.edu/Constitutions/Brazil/brazil1891.html.

6 Decreto N. 149, de 18 de julho de 1893, "Dá organisação ao Supremo Tribunal Militar," https://www2.camara.leg.br/legin/fed/decret/1824-1899/decreto-149-18-julho-1893-540930-publicacaooriginal-42460-pl.html. While the STM was a military court, its composition included three civilian lawyers in addition to the four navy and eight army members (G. Castro and Lara 2008, 15).

7 Decreto N. 949, de 5 novembro de 1890, "Estabelece um Codigo Penal para a Armada," https://www2.camara.leg.br/legin/fed/decret/1824-1899/decreto-949-5-novembro-1890-553428-publicacaooriginal-71316-pe.html; Decreto N. 18, de 7 de março de 1891, "Estabelece novo Codigo Penal para a Armada, de accordo com o decreto de 14 de fevereiro deste anno," https://www2.camara.leg.br/legin/fed/decret/1824-1899/decreto-18-7-marco-1891-526137-publicacaooriginal-1-pe.html.

8 Lei N. 612, de 29 de setembro de 1899, "Approva, e amplia ao Exercito nacional, o Codigo Penal para a Armada, que acompanhou o decreto n. 18, de 7 de março de 1891," https://www2.camara.leg.br/legin/fed/lei/1824-1899/lei-612-29-setembro-1899-540610-publicacaooriginal-41179-pl.html.

9 Decreto N. 847, de 11 de outubro de 1890, "Promulga o Codigo Penal," https://www2.camara.leg.br/legin/fed/decret/1824-1899/decreto-847-11-outubro-1890-503086-publicacaooriginal-1-pe.html.

10 Decreto N. 18, de 7 de março de 1891, "Estabelece novo Codigo Penal para a Armada, de accordo com o decreto de 14 de fevereiro deste anno," https://www2.camara.leg.br/legin/fed/decret/1824-1899/decreto-18-7-marco-1891-526137-publicacaooriginal-1-pe.html.

11 For example: Decreto N. 1681, de 28 de Fevereiro de 1894, "Declara sujeitos á jurisdicção do fôro militar os crimes que se relacionarem a rebellião que ora conflagra o Districto Federal e outros pontos do territorio da União," https://www2.camara.leg.br/legin/fed/decret/1824-1899/decreto-1681-28-fevereiro-1894-500201-publicacaooriginal-1-pe.html; Decreto N. 1685, de 5 de Março de 1894, "Amplia as disposições do decreto n. 1681, de 28 de fevereiro do corrente anno, quanto aos crimes sujeitos á jurisdicção do fôro militar," https://www2.camara.leg.br/legin/fed/decret/1824-1899/decreto-1685-5-marco-1894-507690-publicacaooriginal-1-pe.html.

12 Habeas Corpus 410, "Acórdão de 12 de Agosto," http://www.stf.jus.br/arquivo/cms/sobreStfConhecaStfJulgamentoHistorico/anexo/HC410.pdf.

13 Lei N. 221, de 20 de novembro de 1894, "Completa a organisação da Justiça Federal da Republica," https://www2.camara.leg.br/legin/fed/lei/1824-1899/lei-221-20-novembro-1894-540367-publicacaooriginal-40560-pl.html.

14 Decreto N. 14.450, de 30 de outubro de 1920, "Manda observar o Codigo de Organização Judiciaria e Processo Militar," https://www2.camara.leg.br/legin/fed/decret/1920-1929/decreto-14450-30-outubro-1920-502847-republicacao-95110-pe.html.

15 Decreto N. 14.544, de 16 de dezembro de 1920, "Designa as sédes de circumscripções de Justiça Militar em tempo de paz e estabelece a jurisdicção dos respectivos auditores," https://www2.camara.leg.br/legin/fed/decret/1920-1929/decreto-14544-16-dezembro-1920-517452-publicacaooriginal-1-pe.html.

16 Decreto N. 20.656, de 14 de novembro de 1931, "Determina que seja processado e julgado pela Justiça Militar todo aquele que, militar, assemelhado, ou civil, tomar parte por qualquer fórma, nos atentados contra a ordem pública ou contra os governos da União e dos Estados," https://www2.camara.leg.br/legin/fed/decret/1930-1939/decreto-20656-14-novembro-1931-518419-publicacaooriginal-1-pe.html.

17 Federative Republic of Brazil, Constitution of 1934, http://pdba.georgetown.edu/Constitutions/Brazil/brazil34.html.

18 Federative Republic of Brazil, Constitution of 1937, Article 111, http://pdba.georgetown.edu/Constitutions/Brazil/brazil37.html; Federative Republic of Brazil, Constitution of 1946, Article 108 § 1, http://pdba.georgetown.edu/Constitutions/Brazil/brazil46.html.

19 Ato Institucional N° 1, de 9 de abril de 1964, http://www.planalto.gov.br/ccivil_03/AIT/ait-01-64.htm.

20 Ato Institucional N° 2, de 27 de outubro de 1965, http://www.planalto.gov.br/ccivil_03/AIT/ait-02-65.htm.
21 Decreto-Lei N. 925, de 2 de dezembro de 1938, "Estabelece o Código da Justiça Militar," http://www.planalto.gov.br/ccivil_03/decreto-lei/1937-1946/Del0925.htm; Lei N.° 1.802, de 5 de janeiro de 1953, "Define os crimes contra o Estado e a Ordem Política e Social, e dá outras providências," https://www2.camara.leg.br/legin/fed/lei/1950-1959/lei-1802-5-janeiro-1953-367324-publicacaooriginal-1-pl.html.
22 Constitution of Brazil 1967 (As amended by Constitutional Amendment No. 1 of October 17, 1969), https://babel.hathitrust.org/cgi/pt?id=mdp.39015011287649&view=1up&seq=5.
23 Ato Institucional N° 5, de 13 de dezembro de 1968, https://www2.camara.leg.br/legin/fed/lei/1950-1959/lei-1802-5-janeiro-1953-367324-publicacaooriginal-1-pl.html.
24 Decreto-Lei N° 1.001, de 21 de outubro de 1969, "Código Penal Militar," http://www.planalto.gov.br/ccivil_03/decreto-lei/del1001.htm.
25 Decreto-Lei N° 1.002, de 21 de outubro de 1969, "Código de Processo Penal Militar," https://www.planalto.gov.br/ccivil_03/decreto-lei/del1002.htm.
26 Lei N° 7.170, de 14 de dezembro de 1983, "Define os crimes contra a segurança nacional, a ordem política e social, estabelece seu processo e julgamento e dá outras providências," http://www.planalto.gov.br/ccivil_03/leis/l7170.htm.
27 Lei N° 6.683, de 28 agosto de 1979, "Concede anistia e dá outras providências," http://www.planalto.gov.br/ccivil_03/leis/L6683.htm.
28 Federative Republic of Brazil, 1988 Constitution, http://pdba.georgetown.edu/Constitutions/Brazil/brazil88.html.
29 In January 1983, pressure from state governors led the federal government to "eliminate the requirement that state commanders come from the federal army," allowing governors to "choose the commander of the *polícia militar* from within the ranks of the *polícia militar*" (Hunter 1997, 51). Nevertheless, the president could still call them into federal military service, in which case they would be back under the command of the army.
30 Programa Nacional de Derechos Humanos, Presidência da República Governo Fernando Henrique Cardoso, Ministério da Justiça Brasília, 1996, http://www.biblioteca.presidencia.gov.br/publicacoes-oficiais/catalogo/fhc/programa-nacional-de-derechos-humanos-1996.pdf.
31 Lei 9.299, de 7 de agosto de 1996, "Altera dispositivos dos Decretos-leis n°s 1.001 e 1.002, de 21 de outubro de 1969, Códigos Penal Militar e de Processo Penal Militar, respectivamente," https://www.planalto.gov.br/ccivil_03/leis/l9299.htm.
32 Lei N° 9.455, de 7 de abril de 1997, "Define os crimes de tortura e dá outras providências," http://www.planalto.gov.br/ccivil_03/leis/L9455.htm.
33 Federative Republic of Brazil, 1988 Constitution, with 2005 Reforms, http://pdba.georgetown.edu/Constitutions/Brazil/brazil05.html.
34 Lei N° 12.528, de 18 de novembro de 2011, "Cria a Comissão Nacional da Verdade no âmbito da Casa Civil da Presidência da República," http://www.planalto.gov.br/ccivil_03/_Ato2011-2014/2011/Lei/L12528.htm.
35 *Relatório da Comissão Nacional da Verdade*, 10 de dezembro de 2014, http://cnv.memoriasreveladas.gov.br/index.php.
36 Informativo STF, Brasilia 26 a 30 de abril de 2010—N° 584, http://stf.jus.br/arquivo/informativo/documento/informativo584.htm.
37 *Gomes Lund et al. ("Guerrilha do Araguaia")* v. *Brazil*, Preliminary Objections, Merits, Reparations, and Costs, Inter-Am. Ct. H.R. (ser. C) No. 219 (November 24, 2010), http://www.corteidh.or.cr/docs/casos/articulos/seriec_219_ing.pdf.
38 Decreto-Lei N° 1.001, de 21 de outubro de 1969, "Código Penal Militar," Articles 298–302, http://www.planalto.gov.br/ccivil_03/decreto-lei/Del1001.htm.

39 Respondents to the Latinobarómetro survey in Brazil consistently rate crime as one of the most important problems facing the country (Corporación Latinobarómetro 2018b), and majorities respond that they are concerned about being a victim of violent crime all or almost all of the time (Corporación Latinobarómetro 2018a).
40 Lei N° 13.491, de 13 de outubro de 2017, http://www.planalto.gov.br/ccivil_03/_ato2015-2018/2017/lei/l13491.htm.
41 For Iskander Mirza's 1958 declaration of martial law, see Rizvi 1974, 285–94.
42 For the *Laws (Continuance in Force) Order, 1958*, see Hasan 1999, 31–33.
43 *State* v. *Dosso and Another*, PLD 1958 SC 533, https://pakistanconstitutionlaw.com/pld-1958-sc-533/.
44 For the *Provisional Constitutional Order (PCO), 1969*, see Hasan 1999, 64–67.
45 For *The Jurisdiction of Courts (Removal of Doubts) Order, 1969*, see Hasan 1999, 68–71.
46 *Asma Jilani* v. *Government of Punjab*, PLD 1972 SC 139, https://pakistanconstitutionlaw.com/pld-1972-sc-139-2/.
47 *State* v. *Zia-ur-Rehman and Others*, PLD SC 49, https://pakistanconstitutionlaw.com/pld-1973-sc-49/.
48 Pakistan's Constitution of 1973, Reinstated in 2002, with Amendments through 2018, https://www.constituteproject.org/constitution/Pakistan_2018.pdf?lang=en.
49 "Proclamation of Martial Law," Gazette of Pakistan, July 5, 1977, https://pakistanconstitutionlaw.com/proclamation-of-martial-law-gazette-of-pakistan-extraordinary-part-i-5th-of-july-1977/.
50 Local elections took place in 1979, 1983, and 1987, but Zia postponed indefinitely the national elections that had been scheduled for October 1977 and canceled the November 1979 national elections (Choudhury 1988, 51).
51 *Begum Nusrat Bhutto* v. *Chief of Army Staff and Federation of Pakistan*, PLD 1977 SC 657, https://pakistanconstitutionlaw.com/p-l-d-1977-sc-657/.
52 For the *Provisional Constitution Order, 1981*, see Hasan 1999, 312–32.
53 *The Constitution (Eighth Amendment) Act, 1985*, Act No. XVIII of 1985, The Gazette of Pakistan, November 11, 1985, http://na.gov.pk/uploads/documents/1485318332_808.pdf.
54 *The Anti-terrorism Act, 1997* (XXVII of 1997), https://nacta.gov.pk/wp-content/uploads/2017/08/Anti-Terrorism-Act-1997.pdf.
55 "Order imposing Governor's Rule in Sindh," No. 8 1/98-Min-I, October 30, 1998, http://www.pakistani.org/pakistan/legislation/1998/sindh_governors_rule_order_30oct1998.html.
56 "Pakistan Armed Forces (Acting in Aid of the Civil Power) Ordinance," Ordinance XII of 1998, http://www.pakistani.org/pakistan/legislation/1998/ord_XII.html.
57 *Sh. Liaquat Hussain and Others* v. *Federation of Pakistan*, PLD 1999 SC 504, https://pakistanconstitutionlaw.com/p-l-d-1999-sc-504-2/.
58 One external factor—increased pressure from the United States at the outset of the War on Terror—also pushed Musharraf to civilianize his dictatorship rather than pursuing the same military legal strategies as his predecessors (Mufti 2015).
59 *The Constitution (Seventeenth Amendment) Act, 2003*, Act No. III of 2003, The Gazette of Pakistan, December 31, 2003, http://na.gov.pk/uploads/documents/1321274383_862.pdf.
60 "Proclamation of Emergency," November 3, 2007, https://pakistanconstitutionlaw.com/proclamation-of-emergency/.
61 "Revocation of Proclamation of Emergency Order, 2007," December 15, 2007, https://pakistanconstitutionlaw.com/revocation-of-proclamation-of-emergency-order-2007/.
62 *The Protection of Pakistan Act, 2014*, Act No. X of 2014, The Gazette of Pakistan, July 14, 2014, http://na.gov.pk/uploads/documents/1409034186_281.pdf.

63 National Action Plan, 2014, National Counter Terrorism Authority (NACTA) Pakistan, https://nacta.gov.pk/nap-2014/.

64 *Pakistan Army (Amendment) Act, 2015*, Act No. II of 2015, The Gazette of Pakistan, January 7, 2015, http://na.gov.pk/uploads/documents/1420800454_327.pdf; *The Constitution (Twenty-first Amendment) Act, 2015*, Act No. I of 2015, The Gazette of Pakistan, January 7, 2015, http://na.gov.pk/uploads/documents/1420800195_264.pdf.

65 *Pakistan Army (Amendment) Act, 2015*, Act No. II of 2015, The Gazette of Pakistan, January 7, 2015, http://na.gov.pk/uploads/documents/1420800454_327.pdf.

66 *District Bar Association, Rawalpindi* v. *Federation of Pakistan*, Const. P. No. 12 of 2010 etc., https://www.supremecourt.gov.pk/downloads_judgements/Const.P.12of2010.pdf.

67 *Abdur Rashid et al.* v. *Federation of Pakistan*, High Court of Peshawar, Writ Petition 536-P of 2018, 18 October 2018, https://www.peshawarhighcourt.gov.pk/PHCCMS//judgments/wp536-2018-finaljudgemnt.pdf.

68 *The Constitution (Twenty-third Amendment) Act, 2017*, Act No. XII of 2017, March 31, 2017, http://na.gov.pk/uploads/documents/1491460727_515.pdf.

References

Ahmad, Nesar, and Fareena Sultan. 1977. "Popular Uprising in Pakistan." *MERIP Reports* 58: 14–18. DOI: 10.2307/3010840.

Amnesty International. 2015. "You Killed My Son: Homicides by Military Police in the City of Rio de Janeiro." https://www.amnesty.org/download/Documents/AMR1920682015ENGLISH.PDF.

Amnesty International. 2018. *Amnesty International Report 2017/18: The State of the World's Human Rights*. London: Amnesty International.

Andreu-Guzmán, Federico. 2018. *Fuero militar y Derecho internacional: Los civiles ante los tribunales militares. Vol. 2 of Military Jurisdiction and International Law*. Geneva: International Commission of Jurists. https://www.icj.org/wp-content/uploads/2018/05/Universal-Tribunales-Militares-Vol-II-Publications-Reports-Thematic-reports-2018-SPA.pdf.

Arceneaux, Craig L. 2001. *Bounded Missions: Military Regimes and Democratization in the Southern Cone and Brazil*. University Park: Pennsylvania State University Press.

Ayoob, Mohammed. 1971. "Pakistan's Political Development, 1947 to 1970: Bird's Eye View." *Economic and Political Weekly* 6 (3/5): 199–204.

Bacchus, Wilfred A. 1990. *Mission in Mufti: Brazil's Military Regimes, 1964–1985*. New York: Greenwood.

Baxter, Craig. 2015. "Muhammad Ayub Khan." In *A History of Pakistan*, ed. Roger D. Long. Karachi: Oxford University Press, 485–512.

BBC News. 2020. "Manzoor Pashteen: Activist Who Dared to Challenge Pakistan Army Held," January 27. https://www.bbc.com/news/world-asia-51262639.

Bethell, Leslie. 2018. *Brazil: Essays on History and Politics*. London: University of London Institute of Latin American Studies. DOI: 10.14296/618.9781908857613.

Bhatti, Haseeb. 2020. "Civilians Cannot Be Court-Martialed, SC Reminds Govt Lawyer." *Dawn*, March 4. https://www.dawn.com/news/1538352.

Burns, E. Bradford. 1993. *A History of Brazil*. 3rd ed. New York: Columbia University Press. DOI: 10.7312/burn07954.

Castro, Celso. 2001. "The Army as a Modernizing Actor in Brazil, 1870–1930." In *The Soldier and the State in South America*, ed. Patricio Silva. New York: Palgrave Macmillan, 53–70. DOI: 10.1057/9780333977972.

Castro, Gustavo Fabián, and Dolores Bermeo Lara. 2008. *Justicia Militar, Códigos Disciplinarios y Reglamentos Generales Internos*. Buenos Aires: Red de Seguridad y Defensa de América Latina.

Cavallaro, James L., and Fernando Delgado. 2012. "The Paradox of Accountability in Brazil." In *After Oppression: Transitional Justice in Latin America and Europe*, eds. Vesselin Popovski and Mónica Serrano. Tokyo: United Nations University Press, 86–115. DOI: 10.18356/b2c785fd-en.

Charleaux, João Paulo. 2016. "Por que civis ainda são julgados por militares no Brasil." *Nexo Jornal*, July 4. https://www.nexojornal.com.br/expresso/2016/07/03/Por-que-civis-ainda-s%C3%A3o-julgados-por-militares-no-Brasil.

Charleaux, João Paulo. 2017. "Por que o Exército quer mudar o jeito de julgar militar que mata civil." *Nexo Jornal*, August 16. https://www.nexojornal.com.br/expresso/2017/08/16/Por-que-o-Ex%C3%A9rcito-quer-mudar-o-jeito-de-julgar-militar-que-mata-civil.

Cheema, Pervaiz Iqbal. 2001. *The Armed Forces of Pakistan*. New York: New York University Press.

Chirio, Maud. 2018. *Politics in Uniform: Military Officers and Dictatorship in Brazil, 1960-1980*. Pittsburgh: University of Pittsburgh Press. DOI: 10.2307/j.ctv36zp5h.

Choudhury, Golam W. 1988. *Pakistan: Transition from Military to Civilian Rule*. London: Scorpion.

Corporación Latinobarómetro. 2018a. Análisis Online: Brasil/Series de tiempo. "Con qué frecuencia se preocupa de que pueda llegar a ser victim de un delito con violencia." http://www.latinobarometro.org/latContents.jsp.

Corporación Latinobarómetro. 2018b. Análisis Online: Brasil/Series de tiempo. "Problema más importante en el país." http://www.latinobarometro.org/latContents.jsp.

Corporación Latinobarómetro. 2018c. *Informe 2018*. Santiago, Chile: Corporación Latinobarómetro. http://www.latinobarometro.org/latContents.jsp.

Costa, Arthur Trindade Maranhão, and Timothy Thompson. 2011. "Police Brutality in Brazil: Authoritarian Legacy or Institutional Weakness?" *Latin American Perspectives* 38 (5): 19–32. DOI: 10.1177/0094582X10391631.

Croissant, Aurel, David Kuehn, Philip Lorenz, and Paul W. Chambers. 2013. *Democratization and Civilian Control in Asia*. New York: Palgrave Macmillan. DOI: 10.1057/9781137319272.

Dawn. 2015a. "Lawyers Vow to Resist Military Courts," January 30. https://www.dawn.com/news/1160372.

Dawn. 2015b. "PPP Lawmakers Unhappy Over Leadership's Decision on Military Courts," January 6. https://www.dawn.com/news/1155195.

Dawson, V. 1923. "British India." *Journal of Comparative Legislation and International Law*, Third Series, 5 (3): 133–41.

Dias, R. W. M. 1970. "The Grundnorm Again—Martial Law and Fundamental Rights in Pakistan." *The Cambridge Law Journal* 28 (1): 49–51. DOI: 10.1017/S0008197300011594.

Fábio, André Cabette. 2017. "Como as Forças Armadas se tornaram uma constante na segurança do RJ." *Nexo Jornal*, August 9. https://www.nexojornal.com.br/expresso/2017/08/09/Como-as-Forças-Armadas-se-tornaram-uma-constante-na-segurança-do-RJ.

Ghias, Shoaib A. 2010. "Miscarriage of Chief Justice: Judicial Power and the Legal Complex in Pakistan Under Musharraf." *Law & Social Inquiry* 35 (4): 985–1022. DOI: 10.1111/j.1747-4469.2010.01211.x.

Gilbert, Marc Jason. 2015. "The Era of British Rule." In *A History of Pakistan*, ed. Roger D. Long. Karachi: Oxford University Press, 283–313. DOI: 10.7916/D8M90JXF.

Guerchon, C. W. 1971. "Institutional Acts of the Brazilian Government." *International Journal of Politics* 1 (2/3): 258–69.

Guha, Ranajit. 1999. *Elementary Aspects of Peasant Insurgency in Colonial India*. Durham: Duke University Press.

Hahner, June E. 1969. *Civilian-Military Relations in Brazil: 1889–1898*. Columbia: University of South Carolina Press.

Haqqani, Husain. 2005. *Pakistan: Between Mosque and Military*. Washington, DC: Carnegie Endowment for International Peace.

Haring, C. H. 1958. *Empire in Brazil: A New World Experiment with Monarchy*. Cambridge: Harvard University Press.

Hasan, Abrar. 1999. *Constitutional and Extra-Constitutional (Martial Law-Emergency) Decisions of the Superior Courts of Pakistan*. Karachi: CreateSpace.

Hayes, Robert A. 1976. "The Formation of the Brazilian Army and the Military Class Mystique, 1500-1853." In *Perspectives on Armed Politics in Brazil*, eds. Henry H. Keith and Robert A. Hayes. Tempe: Arizona State University Press, 1–26.

Hinton, Mercedes S. 2006. *The State on the Streets: Police and Politics in Argentina and Brazil*. Boulder: Lynne Rienner.

Human Rights Watch. 1997. *Police Brutality in Urban Brazil*. New York: Human Rights Watch.

Human Rights Watch. 1999. "Shut-Down of Military Courts in Pakistan Hailed," February 17. https://www.hrw.org/news/1999/02/17/shut-down-military-courts-pakistan-hailed#.

Human Rights Watch. 2007a. "Destroying Legality: Pakistan's Crackdown on Lawyers and Judges," December 18. https://www.hrw.org/report/2007/12/18/destroying-legality/pakistans-crackdown-lawyers-and-judges.

Human Rights Watch. 2007b. *World Report 2007*. New York: Human Rights Watch.

Human Rights Watch. 2009. *Lethal Force: Police Violence and Public Security in Rio de Janeiro and São Paulo*. New York: Human Rights Watch.

Human Rights Watch. 2012. *World Report 2012*. New York: Human Rights Watch.

Human Rights Watch. 2018a. "Brazil: Army Stonewalls on Rio Killings," February 23. https://www.hrw.org/news/2018/02/23/brazil-army-stonewalls-rio-killings.

Human Rights Watch. 2018b. "Brutality in Uniform in Brazil," May 21. https://www.hrw.org/news/2018/05/21/brutality-uniform-brazil.

Human Rights Watch. 2018c. *World Report 2018*. New York: Human Rights Watch.

Human Rights Watch. 2019. *World Report 2019*. New York: Human Rights Watch.

Hunter, Wendy. 1997. *Eroding Military Influence in Brazil: Politicians Against Soldiers*. Chapel Hill: University of North Carolina Press.

Hunter, Wendy. 2001. "Reason, Culture, or Structure? Assessing Civil-Military Dynamics in Brazil." In *Civil-Military Relations: New Analytical Perspectives*, ed. David Pion-Berlin. Chapel Hill: University of North Carolina Press, 36–58.

International Commission of Jurists. 2002a. "Attacks on Justice–Pakistan." https://www.icj.org/wp-content/uploads/2002/08/pakistan_attacks_justice_27_08_20021.pdf.

International Commission of Jurists. 2002b. "Attacks on Justice–Brazil." https://www.icj.org/wp-content/uploads/2012/03/brazil_attacks_justice_27_08_2002.pdf.

International Commission of Jurists. 2015a. "Pakistan: ICJ Denounces Law Permitting Military Trials of Civilians," January 6. https://www.icj.org/pakistan-icj-denounces-law-permitting-military-trials-of-civilians/.

International Commission of Jurists. 2015b. "Pakistan: Supreme Court Decision Upholding 21st Amendment a Blow to Human Rights and Judicial Independence," August 7. https://www.icj.org/pakistan-supreme-court-decision-upholding-21st-amendment-is-a-blow-to-human-rights-and-judicial-independence/.

International Commission of Jurists. 2016. "Pakistan: Supreme Court Validation of Military Court Trials a Blow to the Rule of Law," August 29. https://www.icj.org/pakistan-supreme-court-validation-of-military-court-trials-a-blow-to-the-rule-of-law/.

International Commission of Jurists. 2017. "Pakistan: ICJ Denounces the Revival of Military Trials of Civilians," March 28. https://www.icj.org/pakistan-icj-denounces-the-revival-of-military-trials-of-civilians/.

International Commission of Jurists. 2019a. "Military Injustice in Pakistan," January. https://www.icj.org/wp-content/uploads/2019/01/Pakistan-military-courts-Advocacy-Analysis-brief-2018-ENG.pdf.

International Commission of Jurists. 2019b. "Pakistan: Immediately Revoke Oppressive Khyber Pakhtunkhwa Actions (In Aid of Civil Power) Ordinance," September 27. https://www.icj.org/pakistan-immediately-revoke-oppressive-khyber-pakhtunkhwa-actions-in-aid-of-civil-power-ordinance/.

Iqbal, Nasir. 2020a. "SC Asks Ministry to Give Details of Military Courts Sentences." *Dawn*, March 12. https://www.dawn.com/news/1540234.

Iqbal, Nasir. 2020b. "SC Rejects Govt Plea to Stay PHC Hearing Against Military Court Verdicts." *Dawn*, March 10. https://www.dawn.com/news/1539609.

Jalal, Ayesha. 1990. *The State of Martial Rule: The Origins of Pakistan's Political Economy of Defence*. Cambridge: Cambridge University Press.

Jones, Philip E. 2015. "Zulfikar Ali Bhutto: Triumph and Tragedy." In *A History of Pakistan*, ed. Roger D. Long. Karachi: Oxford University Press, 546–600.

Justice Project Pakistan. 2010. *Trial and Terror: The Overreach of Pakistan's Anti-Terrorism Act*. Lahore: Justice Project Pakistan.

Keith, Henry H. 1976. "Armed Federal Interventions in the States During the Old Republic." In *Perspectives on Armed Politics in Brazil*, eds. Henry H. Keith and Robert A. Hayes. Tempe: Arizona State University Press, 51–78.

Keith, Henry H., and Robert A. Hayes, eds. 1976. *Perspectives on Armed Politics in Brazil*. Tempe: Arizona State University Press.

Khan, Ismail. 2014. "Taliban Massacre 131 Schoolchildren: Principal Among 141 Dead in Attack on Army Public School, Peshawar." *Dawn*, December 17. https://www.dawn.com/news/1151361.

Lees, James. 2010. "A 'Tranquil Spectator': The District Official and the Practice of Local Government in Late Eighteenth-Century Bengal." *The Journal of Imperial and Commonwealth History* 38 (1): 1–19. DOI: 10.1080/03086530903538145.

Lemos, Renato Luís do Couto Neto e. 2012. "A Justiça Militar e a Implantação da Ordem Republicana no Brasil." *Topoi (Rio de Janeiro)* 13 (24): 60–72.

Macaulay, Fiona. 2007. "Justice-Sector and Human Rights Reform under the Cardoso Government." *Latin American Perspectives* 34 (5): 26–42. DOI: 10.1177/0094582X07306236.

Mahmud, Tayyab. 1993. "Praetorianism and Common Law in Post-Colonial Settings: Judicial Responses to Constitutional Breakdowns in Pakistan." *Utah Law Review* 4: 1225–303.

Malagodi, Mara. 2019. "Dominion Status and the Origins of Authoritarian Constitutionalism in Pakistan." *International Journal of Constitutional Law* 17 (4): 1235–57. DOI: 10.1093/icon/moz080.

Mathias, Suzeley Kalil, and André Cavaller Guzzi. 2010. "Autonomy in Law: The Armed Forces in Brazil's Constitutions." *Revista Brasileira de Ciências Sociais* 25 (73): 41–57. DOI: 10.1590/S0102-69092010000200003.

McCann, Frank D., Jr., 1997. "Origins of the 'New Professionalism' of the Brazilian Military." In *The Politics of Anti-Politics: The Military in Latin America*, eds. Brian Loveman and Thomas M. Davies, Jr. Wilmington, DE: Scholarly Resources, 41–51.

Morgan, Zachary R. 2014. *Legacy of the Lash: Race and Corporal Punishment in the Brazilian Navy and the Atlantic World.* Bloomington: University of Indiana Press.

Mufti, Mariam. 2015. "The Years of a Failed Democratic Transition, 1988-1999." In *A History of Pakistan*, ed. Roger D. Long. Karachi: Oxford University Press, 633–79.

Newberg, Paula R. 1995. *Judging the State: Courts and Constitutional Politics in Pakistan.* Cambridge: Cambridge University Press. DOI: 10.1017/CBO9780511563362.

Nunn, Frederick M. 1983. *Yesterday's Soldiers: European Military Professionalism in South America, 1890-1940.* Lincoln: University of Nebraska Press.

Omissi, David. 1994. *The Sepoy and the Raj: The Indian Army, 1860-1940.* London: Macmillan.

Pereira, Anthony W. 1998. "'Persecution and Farce': The Origins and Transformation of Brazil's Political Trials, 1964–79." *Latin American Research Review* 33 (1): 43–66.

Pereira, Anthony W. 2001. "Virtual Legality: Authoritarian Legacies and the Reform of Military Justice in Brazil, the Southern Cone, and Mexico." *Comparative Political Studies* 34 (5): 555–74. DOI: 10.1177/0010414001034005004.

Pereira, Anthony W. 2005a. "The Dialectics of the Brazilian Military Regime's Political Trials." *Luso-Brazilian Review* 41 (2): 162–83. DOI: 10.1353/lbr.2005.0013.

Pereira, Anthony W. 2005b. *Political (In)Justice: Authoritarianism and the Rule of Law in Brazil, Chile, and Argentina.* Pittsburgh: University of Pittsburgh Press.

Pereira, Anthony W., and Mark Ungar. 2004. "The Persistence of the *Mano Dura*: Authoritarian Legacies and Policing in Brazil and the Southern Cone." In *Authoritarian Legacies and Democracy in Latin America and Southern Europe*, eds. Katherine Hite and Paola Cesarini. Notre Dame: University of Notre Dame Press, 263–304.

Petrén, Gustaf, Helen Cull, Jeremy McBride, and D. Ravindran. 1987. *Pakistan: Human Rights After Martial Law.* Geneva: International Commission of Jurists.

Rahman, M. Raisur. 2019. "Religion, Law and State Policing: Accusations, Inquests and Arbitration of Religious Conflicts in Colonial India." *South Asian History and Culture* 10 (2): 187–98. DOI: 10.1080/19472498.2019.1609264.

Reuters. 2019. "Brazil Army Arrests 10 Troops After Botched Operation Kills Innocent Driver," April 8. https://www.reuters.com/article/us-brazil-violence/brazil-army-arrests-10-troops-after-botched-operation-kills-innocent-driver-idUSKCN1RK2A5.

Rizvi, Hasan-Askari. 1974. *The Military and Politics in Pakistan.* Lahore: Progressive.

Rizvi, Hasan-Askari. 1986. "The Civilianization of Military Rule in Pakistan." *Asian Survey* 26 (10): 1067–81. DOI: 10.2307/2644257.

Rizvi, Hasan-Askari. 1999. "Pakistan in 1998: The Polity Under Pressure." *Asian Survey* 39 (1): 177–84. DOI: 10.2307/2645607.

Rodley, Nigel S. 2001. *Civil and Political Rights, Including the Questions of Torture and Detention: Report of the Special Rapporteur [On Torture], Nigel Rodley, Submitted Pursuant to Commission on Human Rights Resolution 2000/43. Addendum: Visit to Brazil.* E/CN.4/2001/66/Add.2. https://digitallibrary.un.org/record/437371.

Rosenn, Keith S. 2014. "Recent Important Decisions by the Brazilian Supreme Court." *The University of Miami Inter-American Law Review* 45 (2): 297–334.

Roy, Kaushik. 2001. "Coercion through Leniency: British Manipulation of the Courts-Martial System in the Post-Mutiny Indian Army, 1859–1913." *The Journal of Military History* 65 (4): 937–64. DOI: 10.2307/2677624.

Roy, Kaushik. 2006. "Spare the Rod, Spoil the Soldier? Crime and Punishment in the Army of India, 1860-1913." *Journal of the Society for Army Historical Research* 84 (337): 9–33.

Roy, Kaushik, and Sabyasachi Dasgupta. 2006. "Discipline and Disobedience in the Bengal and Madras Armies, 1807–56." In *War and Society in Colonial India*, ed. Kaushik Roy. New Delhi: Oxford University Press, 55–81.

Sayeed, Khalid B. 1959. "Martial Law Administration in Pakistan." *Far Eastern Survey* 28 (5): 72–79. DOI: 10.2307/3024211.

Sayeed, Khalid B. 1961. "Pakistan's Basic Democracy." *Middle East Journal* 15 (3): 249–63.

Schneider, Nina. 2011. "Breaking the 'Silence' of the Military Regime: New Politics of Memory in Brazil." *Bulletin of Latin American Research* 30 (2): 198–212. DOI: 10.1111/j.1470-9856.2010.00448.x.

Schneider, Ronald M. 1997. "The Military and Brazilian Politics to World War II." In *The Politics of Anti-Politics: The Military in Latin America*, eds. Brian Loveman and Thomas M. Davies, Jr. Wilmington, DE: Scholarly Resources, 75–82.

Shafqat, Saeed. 1997. *Civil-Military Relations in Pakistan: From Zufikar Ali Bhutto to Benazir Bhutto*. Boulder: Westview.

Shah, Aqil. 2014. *The Army and Democracy: Military Politics in Pakistan*. Cambridge: Harvard University Press.

Shah, Waseem Ahmad. 2019a. "Ordinance Extends Actions in Aid of Civil Power to Entire KP." *Dawn*, September 18. https://www.dawn.com/news/1505809.

Shah, Waseem Ahmad. 2019b. "View from the Courtroom: Extension to Military Courts Difficult Without Opposition's Support." *Dawn*, January 7. https://www.dawn.com/news/1456020/view-from-the-courtroom-extension-to-military-courts-difficult-without-oppositions-support.

Shah, Waseem Ahmad. 2020. "View from the Courtroom: Petitions against Military Courts' Convictions Enter Decisive Stage." *Dawn*, February 24. https://www.dawn.com/news/1536280.

Siddiqa, Ayesha. 2015. "Pervez Musharraf: Yet Another Dictator." In *A History of Pakistan*, ed. Roger D. Long. Karachi: Oxford University Press, 680–705.

Simmons, Charles Willis. 1976. "Military Leaders in National Politics, 1853-1889." In *Perspectives on Armed Politics in Brazil*, eds. Henry H. Keith and Robert A. Hayes. Tempe: Arizona State University Press, 27–50.

Souza, Adriana Barreto. 2012. "Um edifício gótico entre instituições modernas: o debate parlamentar sobre o conselho supremo militar e de justiça (1822–1860)." *Acervo* 25 (2): 59–77.

Souza, Adriana Barreto. 2015. "The Governance of the Military Justice between Lisboa and Rio de Janeiro (1750–1820)." *Almanack* 10: 368–408. DOI: 10.1590/2236-463320151009.

Souza, Adriana Barreto, and Angela Moreira Domingues da Silva. 2016. "A Organização da Justiça Militar no Brasil: Império e República." *Revista Estudos Históricos* 29 (58): 361–80. DOI: 10.1590/S2178-14942016000200003.

Stepan, Alfred. 1971. *The Military in Politics: Changing Patterns in Brazil*. Princeton: Princeton University Press.

Stepan, Alfred. 1973. "The New Professionalism of Internal Warfare and Military Role Expansion." In *Authoritarian Brazil: Origins, Policies, and Future*, ed. Alfred Stepan. New Haven: Yale University Press, 47–65.

Stepan, Alfred. 1978. "Political Leadership and Regime Breakdown: Brazil." In *The Breakdown of Democratic Regimes: Latin America*, eds. Juan J. Linz and Alfred Stepan. Baltimore: Johns Hopkins University Press, 110–37.

Syed, Baqir Sajjad. 2019. "Govt Seeks Consensus on Military Courts Extension." *Dawn*, April 4. https://www.dawn.com/news/1473786/govt-seeks-consensus-on-military-courts-extension.

Talbot, Ian. 2015. "The Democratic Phase." In *A History of Pakistan*, ed. Roger D. Long. Karachi: Oxford University Press, 454–81.

United States Department of State. 2000. "Pakistan: Country Reports on Human Rights Practices 1999." https://2009-2017.state.gov/j/drl/rls/hrrpt/2000/sa/710.htm.

United States Department of State. 2016. "Brazil: Country Reports on Human Rights Practices 2015." https://www.state.gov/reports/2016-country-reports-on-human-rights-practices/brazil/.

Valente, Rubens. 2017. "Military Courts Given Jurisdiction over Crimes Against Civilians During Armed Forces Operations." *Folha de S. Paulo*, October 17. http://www1.folha.uol.com.br/internacional/en/brazil/2017/10/1927693-military-courts-given-jurisdiction-over-crimes-against-civilians-during-armed-forces-operations.shtml.

Wasim, Amir. 2019a. "Govt Decides to Extend Military Courts Term." *Dawn*, January 9. https://www.dawn.com/news/1456403.

Wasim, Amir. 2019b. "Military Courts Cease to Function Today." *Dawn*, March 31. https://www.dawn.com/news/1472947.

Wilcox, Wayne Ayres. 1965. "The Pakistan Coup d'Etat of 1958." *Pacific Affairs* 38 (2): 142–63. DOI: 10.2307/2753785.

Yap, Po Jen. 2017. *Courts and Democracies in Asia*. Cambridge: Cambridge University Press. DOI: 10.1017.9781108131513.

Zaidi, Syed Manzar Abbas. 2016. *Terrorism Prosecution in Pakistan*. Washington, DC: United States Institute of Peace Press.

Zaverucha, Jorge. 1993. "The Degree of Military Autonomy during the Spanish, Argentine and Brazilian Transitions." *Journal of Latin American Studies* 25 (2): 283–99. DOI: 10.1017/S0022216X0000465X.

Zaverucha, Jorge. 1999. "Military Justice in the State of Pernambuco after the Brazilian Military Regime: An Authoritarian Legacy." *Latin American Research Review* 34 (2): 43–73.

Zaverucha, Jorge. 2000. "Fragile Democracy and the Militarization of Public Safety in Brazil." *Latin American Perspectives* 27 (3): 8–31. DOI: 10.1177/0094582X0002700302.

Zirker, Daniel. 1993. "The Military Ministers and Political Change in Post-Authoritarian Brazil." *Canadian Journal of Latin American and Caribbean Studies* 18 (35): 87–110. DOI: 10.1080/08263663.1993.10816691.

7 From full subordination to military overreach and back again: Military justice in the United States

Introduction

The United States has a complicated history with military justice. During the American Revolutionary War, the Continental Army installed a system of military discipline with harsh punishments intended to maintain order in a patchwork of state militias. As the country became independent, it faced the challenge of creating a military for self-defense without replicating the centralized power and abusive standing army of the British that instigated the revolution. For the next half century, the US military remained surprisingly unprofessionalized and commanders often made up military justice along the way to deal with domestic and foreign threats. At the same time, the military justice system has remained fully subordinated to civilian leaders throughout the country's history. During periods when security threats are acute, however, the jurisdiction of military courts frequently expanded to cover civilians, shifting the country into the military overreach category temporarily. This pattern played out most dramatically during the US Civil War and its aftermath when the government gave military courts a prominent role in its strategy to defeat and reintegrate the Confederate states. Since then, the military justice system has had to adapt to the complexities of a military that has become increasingly involved in international wars, from the Spanish-American War to the ongoing War on Terror.

Full subordination: From colonialism to independence

The first experience that Americans had with military justice came during colonial rule, and like many other British colonies, the United States adopted the British system of full subordination upon independence. More than 8,000 Americans enlisted with British military units during the French and Indian War (1754–63), and thousands more served in provincial militias raised for individual campaigns (Ward 2006, 1). Initially, colonies regulated their own forces as they fought alongside British units. Virginia, for example, passed the Act against Mutiny and Desertion in 1755, which George Washington, then commander of the Virginia Regiment, ordered read aloud regularly to the troops (Ward

2006, 4–5). The British Mutiny Act of 1754, however, eliminated the need for local codes by declaring that all American colonial troops were under the same Articles of War as British soldiers, and this became reality in 1757 when units were integrated.[1] The ranks were full of criminals, debtors, and the jobless, and the officers installed a harsh system of military discipline on the enlisted men, who faced corporal punishments and the death penalty for a large number of crimes (Ward 2006, 3–6). The jurisdiction of military courts, however, was limited to military crimes committed by members of the military.

After the outbreak of the American Revolutionary War in 1775, colonies enacted their own military codes, beginning with Massachusetts in April and followed shortly by several other New England colonies.[2] These military codes were copied almost directly from the British Articles of War of 1765.[3] When the Second Continental Congress created the Continental Army on June 14, 1775, it appointed a five-man committee to draft a code of military justice. The subsequent code, enacted on June 30, was almost identical to the code of Massachusetts.[4]

After assuming the role of Commander-in-Chief of the Continental Army, Washington quickly came to believe that the existing code was too lenient. The troops were poorly maintained and ill-equipped, desertion rates were 20%–35% during the war, and mutinies were common (Ward 2006, 13–29). Washington met with a congressional committee in October to discuss revisions. In November, Congress amended the code to expand the list of capital crimes.[5] In a continued effort to control the undisciplined force, Congress created the Committee of Spies, which included John Adams and Thomas Jefferson, in June 1776, to draft a new code of military justice. Enacted in September, it expanded the list of capital offenses further and increased the maximum number of lashes allowed for other crimes.[6] Military courts, however, did not have jurisdiction over civilians, and the code explicitly ordered any capital crimes or incidents of violence by members of the military against civilians or their property to be adjudicated in civilian courts (Section X, Article 1). Military justice in the United States is a clear case of colonial continuity.

Establishing civilian control

Following independence, the new US government was hesitant to create a military and when it did so it firmly established civilian control over it. This also applied to the military justice system, which remained in the full subordination category. In 1783, Washington urged the Continental Congress to maintain a small standing army in peacetime, but it refused and the army was dissolved. By 1784, fewer than 100 soldiers remained in service at Fort Pitt and West Point (Britton 2005, 353). Opposition to a standing army was considerable. Seventeenth-century English military dictator Oliver Cromwell was still reviled in America, the forcible quartering of British soldiers in private homes was one of the grievances that led to the war, and British units had performed policing functions in New York and Boston leading to a number of clashes, including the

Boston Massacre in March 1770 (Britton 2005, 91; Ward 2006, 3–10). Even the Society of Cincinnati, an organization of veteran officers of the war led by Washington, was viewed with suspicion. Thomas Jefferson and others saw it as "a royalist cadre plotting to take over the government" and make Washington king (Britton 2005, 354). These anti-Federalists felt strongly that the central government's power should be limited and, as Samuel Adams wrote, "A standing Army, however necessary it may be at some times, is always dangerous to the Liberties of the People" (Cushing 1907, 250–51).

Federalists, led by Alexander Hamilton, James Madison, and John Jay, in contrast, advocated for a stronger federal government and argued that a standing army "is a dangerous, at the same time that it may be a necessary, provision" (Madison 1788). After a heated and drawn-out debate, Congress created the Regiment of Infantry on September 29, 1789.[7] The military was gradually expanded and reorganized in the coming decades, particularly after the Battle of the Wabash (also known as St. Clair's defeat) on November 4, 1791 in which the Western Confederacy of Native Americans routed US forces. In addition, Congress passed the First and Second Militia Acts in May 1792, authorizing the president to call up state militias to deal with internal or external threats.[8] Washington invoked the Militia Acts in 1794 to suppress the Whiskey Rebellion, a violent insurrection in Pennsylvania against an excise tax on distilled spirits. The Insurrection Act replaced the Militia Acts in 1807 and continues to be the basis for the use of the US military to intervene in domestic conflicts (Vladeck 2004), which it has done on a regular basis since its inception (Coakley 2011; Laurie and Cole 1997; Scheips 2012).[9]

The 1776 Articles of War continued to apply until 1806 when Congress passed a new, comprehensive military code.[10] There were few substantive differences, however, and this code would remain in place, largely unchanged, until the Civil War. The jurisdiction of military courts did not change, and Article 33 was almost exactly the same as Section X, Article 1 of the 1776 code. In addition, the nature of the US judicial system means that military courts never have exclusive jurisdiction over any crimes in the US criminal code. Civilian courts can prosecute members of the military regardless of whether military courts also do so, though there is a history of deference to military courts first, given that penalties for the same crimes are typically more severe. The United States established a strong civilian government and faced few serious security threats. In addition, while the US military itself was not implicated in past abuses against civilians, the British military was—and the memory of its behavior shaped the government's approach toward the military and military justice. These factors led to a system of full subordination with little tension between the principal actors.

Military overreach: Martial law in the War of 1812

Despite the United States being firmly in the full subordination category, the War of 1812 against Great Britain represented an acute security threat that dramatically shifted, albeit briefly, the country to military overreach. Major-General Andrew Jackson, the commander of the seventh military district, arrived in the city of New Orleans on December 1, 1814 and implemented martial law on December 16, 1814, moving the country into the military overreach category.[11] Governor William C. C. Claiborne had pleaded with Jackson months before he came to take over the city due to fears of the foreign-born population and its sympathies toward Britain and Spain (Warshauer 2006, 20–21). It was not simply the external security threat of a foreign war that drove the expansion of military justice, but the perceived internal dangers associated with it that led to the application of military law to civilians. After the dramatic defeat of the British on January 8, 1815, most in the city expected Jackson to lift martial law, but he continued to worry about invasion and chose to maintain it. He arrested and detained many civilians for weeks and tried them in military courts (Warshauer 2006, 30–31). In addition, many members of the militia now wanted out and Jackson jailed those who tried to desert. On March 13, Jackson finally received official notification of the *Treaty of Ghent* that ended the war, which had already been signed on December 24.[12] He immediately lifted martial law and released and pardoned all prisoners.[13] With military courts no longer trying civilians, the United States returned to a system of full subordination.

In a pattern that would repeat, there was a backlash after the fact. Federal District Court Judge Dominick Augustan Hall brought charges against Jackson for contempt of court for interfering with its operations during martial law and fined him $1,000 (Warshauer 2006, 38–39).[14] Secretary of War Alexander J. Dallas and President James Madison also criticized Jackson for going too far.[15] They dropped the issue, however, given Jackson's newfound status as a national war hero.[16] Overall, the government and courts retained strong control over the military and military courts, but the nature of the security threat led to a deference to the military—in this case one prominent commander—and the temporary expansion of the military's legal power.[17]

Military justice comes of age: The Mexican-American War

While the United States remained in the full subordination category in the coming decades, a foreign security threat, in the form of the Mexican-American War, led the military to professionalize its justice system and systematically apply it to civilians for the first time. While these civilians were not US citizens, and thus does not affect our coding, the operations in Mexico would lay the foundation for the use of military courts during the US Civil War that would come shortly after.

Following the War of 1812, military justice remained underdeveloped, and "officers, especially young subalterns, insecure in their new authority, tended to resort to force. For alleged acts of insubordination, soldiers were beaten with swords, confined in damp cells, branded, tied to trees, and in extreme cases, shot to death on the spot" (Peskin 2003, 121). General Winfield Scott attempted to reform the system when he became Commanding General in 1841. He issued a general order in 1842 for everyone to follow the articles of war and due process and for military courts to try those who committed abuses, but the officers sitting on those courts often protected each other. Scott resorted to intervening directly to reduce or overturn harsh sentences where he saw them (Peskin 2003, 122).

The poor state of military justice and lack of discipline within the forces would come to a head in the Mexican-American War (1846–48) and Scott was forced to make up his own system. In the early stages of the war, Major General Zachary Taylor struggled to maintain internal discipline and control of the population during his invasion of northern Mexico. Guerrillas used a strategy of kidnapping and killing US soldiers, "leaving their mutilated bodies for their comrades to find" which led to retaliatory massacres of Mexican civilians, which the guerrillas in turn used to recruit new members to their ranks (Myers 2008, 207). The military justice system was ill-prepared for handling an occupation of foreign territory. Courts martial only had jurisdiction over spies and members of the military for military offenses.

In 1847, Scott launched an invasion of Mexico just south of Veracruz. To avoid the problems Taylor faced, he wanted more authority to try Mexican citizens and US soldiers for crimes against the civilian population, such as murder. Scott asked Congress to amend the courts-martial system and it responded by neither authorizing nor rejecting his proposals (Myers 2008, 211–14). He thus took the initiative and declared martial law and created two new tribunals—councils of war and military commissions—with General Order 20 in February.[18] Councils of war tried guerrillas and recruiters who attempted to convince US troops to defect, treating them as enemy combatants. Military commissions tried any other crimes committed by or against US forces. Mexican courts were allowed to continue to adjudicate crimes committed by Mexicans against Mexicans.

Scott made a point to enforce discipline immediately. Following the occupation of Veracruz in March, one soldier was flogged and another hanged for offenses against Mexican civilians (Peskin 2003, 159–60). He continued this approach in his occupation of Mexico City. By keeping abuses by US soldiers in check and affording Mexicans the same procedural protections as US courts martial, the commissions aimed "to improve relations between American soldiers and the Mexican population, lessening support for guerrillas" and "were extremely successful at achieving these aims" (Myers 2008, 206). The US military thus gained experience using military justice to discipline its own forces during a major armed conflict and occupation, and applying military justice to civilians in areas of operation. The system created and implemented by Scott would form the foundation of military justice when the Civil War broke out.

Military overreach: The Civil War

The greatest expansion of the power of military justice in the United States occurred during the American Civil War (1861–65), which represented an existential security threat to the survival of the state. The Union government in the north granted the military significant authority and severely restricted civil liberties as it waged war against the Confederate States of America in the south. The war began on April 12, 1861 with a Confederate attack on Fort Sumter in Charleston, South Carolina. The US Army surrendered the fort two days later. The following day, US President Abraham Lincoln issued Proclamation 80 to call forth "the militia of the several States of the Union to the aggregate number of 75,000."[19] Over the next 11 weeks, he would assume more power than any other US president before or since in what some have termed the "Lincoln Dictatorship" (Rossiter 1948, 224–30).

Lincoln first ordered a blockade of southern ports, a move that many criticized for being unconstitutional and against international law given the lack of a declared war against a foreign adversary (Rossiter 1948, 226).[20] In response to attacks on railways by mobs in Baltimore, on April 27, Lincoln authorized the Commanding General of the Unites States Army to suspend the writ of habeas corpus wherever he deemed necessary on the military line between Philadelphia and Washington, DC.[21] In July, he extended this to New York City, and in October to Bangor, Maine.[22] On May 3, he took the dramatic step of calling forth volunteers to increase the size of the army and navy, despite the constitution vesting this power solely in Congress.[23] On May 10, Lincoln suspended the writ of habeas corpus for parts of Florida.[24] While the Supreme Court would eventually draw a legal distinction between the suspension of the writ of habeas corpus and martial law, at this point the terms were used interchangeably and both involved the use of military courts to try civilians (Neely 1991, 35–36).

As the war progressed, local military commanders regularly declared martial law in areas under their control. They did so in all or parts of New Mexico and Kentucky in 1861; Arizona, Florida, Georgia, Kentucky, and South Carolina in 1862; Delaware, Ohio, Indiana, and Texas in 1863; and Delaware, Kentucky, Maryland, and Tennessee in 1864 (Reed 2017, 66–68). With the nation's survival at stake, the military expanded military justice to deal with all types of internal threats. Local commanders declared martial law to deal with Native American uprisings in California in 1862 and Colorado in 1865. In the context of the Dakota War in Minnesota (1862–65), military commanders tried nearly 400 Native Americans and Lincoln approved the death sentence for 38.[25]

Martial law was at its most complicated in Missouri (Neely 1991, 32–50). As early as May 1861, local military commanders began arresting civilians without authorization and flatly denied a writ of habeas corpus issued by a civilian judge. On August 30, 1861, Major General John C. Frémont, the Commander of the Department of the West, declared martial law for all of Missouri. His orders went too far, however, by declaring the emancipation of any slaves held by those who had taken up arms against the Union.[26] Lincoln removed Frémont in November and replaced him with Major General Henry Halleck, and he imposed a less expansive martial law in January.[27] There were more arrests in Missouri than any other state during the war, with a conservative estimate placing the number at 5,000 (Neely 1991, 46).[28]

At the national level, on September 24, 1862, Lincoln issued a proclamation that declared "all rebels and insurgents, their aiders and abettors, within the United States, and all persons discouraging volunteer enlistments, resisting militia draft or guilty of any disloyal practice affording aid and comfort to rebels" were subject to martial law and trial by military courts.[29] The offenses in the proclamation were "vague enough, in effect, to have placed the whole of the United States under martial law" (Neely 1991, 65). In March 1863, Congress officially authorized the suspension of habeas corpus.[30] While expansive in scope, martial law and the reach of military courts was in practice more limited, with an estimated 25,000 people arrested during the war (Rossiter 1948, 236). The usual practice of the military was to arrest, detain, and release, and "only in locales where disorder and treason were rampant—Indiana, southern Ohio, and Missouri—did martial law and trial by military commission exist in any real sense" (Rossiter 1948, 236). During the war, the government also had the tacit support of the Supreme Court. On May 5, 1863, the military arrested and tried Clement Vallandigham of Ohio in a military court for treason. Vallandigham appealed the verdict to the Supreme Court, which unanimously ruled that it did not have the authority to hear appeals from military courts.[31] In sum, the nature of the security threat changed the behavior of all three principal actors. The government, at the federal and state/territory levels, aggressively expanded the jurisdiction of military courts to civilians. The military willingly used these new powers to carry out the war effort. The high courts supported the expansion of the military's legal powers.

Military overreach continued: The Reconstruction era

The Civil War ended with the surrender of the Confederate States on April 9, 1865, but the nature of the war's aftermath meant that the security threat persisted and military courts continued to play a prominent role. On April 14, Confederate sympathizer John Wilkes Booth shot Lincoln in Ford's Theatre in Washington, DC; Lincoln died the next day. The military hunted down and killed Booth 12 days later and rounded up dozens of people suspected to be involved in the conspiracy.[32] The government released most of them but continued to hold eight suspects for trial. Debate ensued about the venue, but Attorney General James Speed advised President Andrew Johnson that they should be tried in a military tribunal. He argued that martial law was still in effect in Washington, DC, the defendants were acting as enemy combatants, and Lincoln was assassinated as Commander-in-Chief, thus the crimes were violations of the laws of war and under jurisdiction of military rather than civilian courts.

On May 1, Johnson ordered the creation of a special military commission, composed of nine officers, to try the case.[33] After a seven-week trial, the commission found all eight guilty, and sentenced four to prison sentences and four to death, including Mary Surratt, who would become the first woman executed in the United States when she and the three others were hanged on July 7 (Steers

2003).[34] The government convened a similar military commission in August to try Henry Wirz, the commandant of an infamous Confederate prisoner-of-war camp near Andersonville, Georgia, known for its brutal conditions that led to the deaths of many Union troops. The commission convicted him in October 1865 and he was hanged on November 10 (Rutman 1960).[35]

Beyond those high-profile trials, military courts were still in use during the efforts to rebuild and reintegrate the Confederate states into the Union, known as Reconstruction. The army was involved in nearly every aspect of Reconstruction including appointing public officials, supervising elections, and managing property and labor disputes (Vagts 2008, 236). Its most important role was to maintain law and order in a region where lynchings and torture at the hands of groups such as the Ku Klux Klan were widespread. There was no expectation that civilian courts would hold whites who committed crimes against freed slaves accountable, so the military established its own commissions to render justice. From 1865 to 1870, these commissions heard approximately 1,400 cases (Neely 1991, 176–77). In addition, those in charge of the courts were not always clear on their mandates and, despite it being peacetime, tried soldiers for civilian crimes, such as burglary (Vagts 2008, 258). While the war was over, the government faced continued security threats from Confederate sympathizers and non-state actors in the South, justifying the continued expansion of military justice.

The government, however, faced a serious legal challenge to its continued use of military courts. On August 20, 1864, the military had raided the offices of Harrison H. Dodd in Indiana, finding guns, ammunition, and evidence of his involvement in a conspiracy to obstruct the war effort and incite a rebellion in the state. In subsequent weeks, the government arrested several other co-conspirators, including Lambdin Milligan, a lawyer from Huntington, Indiana. General Alvin Peterson Hovey, commander of the Military District of Indiana, authorized a military commission to try the accused. Dodd escaped and fled to Canada, but the commission found him guilty in absentia on October 10 and sentenced him to death. The commission convicted four others on December 10, sentencing one to hard labor and three, including Milligan, to death. In May 1865, Milligan's legal counsel filed a writ of habeas corpus with the US Circuit Court for the District of Indiana. The Court, unable to reach a decision, referred the case to the Supreme Court (Warren 1926, 425).

The Supreme Court thus found itself in the position of ruling on the use of military courts during the Civil War well after it was over. On April 3, 1866, in *Ex Parte Milligan*, it ruled unanimously that the military commission did not have jurisdiction to try and sentence Milligan, and it ordered his release.[36] The Court was split, however, on the use of military courts in general. The five-justice majority argued that military commissions could not try civilians, even during times of war, if civilian courts were operating. In this case, the civilian courts in Indiana were operating as normal. In a concurring opinion, the four other justices departed from the majority on the overall reach of military courts. They contended that the ruling should be limited to this case in which the president had authorized their use, but that Congress did have that power and could authorize the use of military courts for civilians if it deemed it necessary (Rehnquist 1997, 934–35). The Supreme Court thus asserted its authority over military courts, but was unwilling to do so while the war was ongoing, and in its ruling many of the justices demonstrated a clear deference to the government and military on this issue when dealing with threats to national security.

Shortly after this ruling, on May 1, 1866, Johnson issued General Order No. 26, which directed the end of all trials of civilians in military commissions where civilian courts were open.[37] In July, he ordered the release of all prisoners who had been tried by military commissions who had served at least six months, with the exception of those who had been convicted of murder, rape, and arson.[38] These policies were part of a larger initiative by Johnson to moderate Reconstruction, leading to clashes with Congress and his eventual impeachment. Johnson's orders and the *Milligan* ruling would seem to preclude the continued use of military commissions. On March 2, 1867, however, Congress passed (over Johnson's veto) the Act to Provide for the More Efficient Government of the Rebel States, which "empowered commanders of Southern military districts to use military commissions to prosecute offenders instead of local civil courts if necessary to protect persons and property, suppress insurrection, and punish criminals" (Neely 1991, 178).[39] In the face of challenges by civilian courts, the government held that the "links of allegiance that bound" the former Confederate states to the United States "had not been fully restored" and "*Milligan* therefore was not decisive" (Vagts 2008, 252). The issue was never fully resolved because the military dropped the last case that was being challenged before it reached the Supreme Court.

Ironically, the one Confederate who escaped trial was Jefferson Davis, the former president of the Confederate States. Shortly after the end of the war, on May 10, the US military captured him, and there was considerable debate within the government and among the public about what to try him for and in what venue (Mitchell 2012). Davis remained in military custody at Fort Monroe in Virginia until May 1867. While he was indicted for treason in federal court, the government, fearing a trial would open larger legal issues related to the war and Reconstruction, eventually dropped the case. Davis was released on December 25, 1868, when President Andrew Johnson issued a pardon for all Confederate soldiers who had fought in the conflict.[40]

Full subordination restored: From Reconstruction to World War II

The end of the Civil War ushered in what some refer to as the "golden age" of civil-military relations in the United States. There were no domestic security threats. The military was small and externally focused, and it professionalized largely without civilian interference (Huntington 1957, 222–69). As part of this process, military courts ceased trying civilians in the former Confederate states in 1870, shifting the United States back to the full subordination category, and Congress approved a completely revised Articles of War in 1874.[41] The code reinforced the jurisdiction of civilian courts over any capital crimes committed by members of the military in peacetime (Article 59). In addition, it banned various corporal punishments, such as flogging and branding, for the first time. It was also at this point that Congress passed the Posse Comitatus Act (1878), which remains in force in an amended version, giving itself the sole power to deploy federal military troops domestically, outside the limited situations articulated in the Insurrection Act (Congressional Research Service 2018).[42]

The United States embarked on its first overseas conflict in the Spanish-American War in 1898 and, much like in Mexico a half-century earlier, military justice would play an important role in curbing abuses by members of the military against the local population in the ensuing Philippine-American War (1899–1902) (Reed 1995, 33).[43] During World War I, Congress enacted a new military code of justice in 1916 to modernize the system.[44] Despite fears to the contrary, no significant domestic threats developed, and President Woodrow Wilson made it clear that he was against military trials for sedition and espionage. Congress passed the Espionage Act on June 15, 1917 and the Sedition Act on May 16, 1918.[45] The government used both to prosecute US civilians, but all were in civilian federal courts (Rossiter 1948, 252–53). Following a study of the military justice system during the war, Congress passed a revised Articles of War on June 4, 1920.[46] Article 74 closely mirrored Article 59 of the 1874 code in requiring the transfer of non-military crimes to civilian courts, and Article 92 specifically required that any cases of murder or rape committed in peacetime also be heard in civilian courts. Military courts thus remained fully subordinated to civilian rule. This status would change with the outbreak of World War II, the greatest threat to US security since the Civil War.

Military overreach: The home front in World War II

The military justice system would come into the spotlight again in World War II as the United States faced the dual problems of handling perceived domestic threats to the war effort and managing a force that included 16 million members. The government's use of military courts was tested in 1942 when eight Nazi saboteurs were captured in June attempting to destroy war industries. President Franklin Delano Roosevelt worried that civilian courts would be too lenient and quickly issued Proclamation 2561 to order the defendants be tried in a military tribunal and explicitly to bar them from pursuing relief in civilian courts.[47] He also directed Attorney General Francis Biddle to comply (Buttaro 2016, 44).

The defense in the case argued, citing *Milligan*, that the defendants—two of whom (Herbert Haupt and Ernst Burger) were US citizens—could not be tried in military courts because civilian courts were still operating. The government argued that the accused had violated the laws of war, which were not under the jurisdiction of civilian courts. The defense petitioned for a writ of habeas corpus and the Supreme Court convened a special session; its decision (*Ex parte*

Quirin) supported the government's position.[48] A special military tribunal of seven officers convicted all eight defendants on August 3 and sentenced them to death. Roosevelt spared two of them, including Burger, for cooperating with the prosecution, but the other six were executed by electrocution on August 8. Once again, in the face of a significant security threat, the government and the Supreme Court were quick to set aside concerns over civil liberties and broaden the power of military courts.

The expansion of the power of military courts was most extreme in Hawaii. Just hours after the Japanese attack on the US naval base at Pearl Harbor on December 7, 1941, Governor J. B. Poindexter declared martial law and turned over all functions of the government to the military. Army Lieutenant Colonel Thomas H. Green, the chief legal officer for the military command, had been preparing for martial law for months and already had a series of general orders ready to declare (H. Scheiber and J. Scheiber 1990, 346). Initially, every crime, "from the most serious violent crimes to curfew and dog-leash infractions, was prosecuted in military courts with no conformity to normal constitutional requirements of due process" (H. Scheiber and J. Scheiber 1990, 348). A month later, the army allowed civilian courts to operate for non-criminal cases, but their operations were significantly restricted. Military provost courts heard most cases; the average trial took less than five minutes and more than 99% resulted in convictions (H. Scheiber and J. Scheiber 1990, 352–53). There was no right to appeal.

Legal challenges began almost immediately. In February, Clara Zimmerman filed a writ of habeas corpus on behalf of her husband, Hans Zimmerman, a German-American citizen who the military had arrested and interned as a "loyalty risk." The case reached the Ninth Circuit Court where Zimmerman's counsel argued, again citing *Milligan*, that only an invasion that prevents civilian courts from operating can justify the suspension of the writ of habeas corpus. The court, however, argued that where martial law existed these rights could be suspended and that only the military could determine whether a military necessity existed to require martial law.[49] The plaintiffs planned to appeal to the Supreme Court, but the army released Zimmerman before that could happen to avoid a potentially unfavorable ruling.

In the ensuing years, opposition grew, particularly after the US victory in the Battle of Midway in June 1942 that made an invasion of Hawaii by Japan infeasible. In early 1943, martial law was moderated slightly but remained extremely restrictive (H. Scheiber and J. Scheiber 1990, 359–65). The conflict came to a head in summer 1943 when Judge Delbert Metzger of the US District Court in Hawaii heard two petitions for writs of habeas corpus and ordered General Robert C. Richardson Jr., who was then the military commander of Hawaii, to testify in court.[50] Richardson refused and his guards roughed up a deputy US marshal who was attempting to serve him papers. Metzger promptly declared him in contempt and fined him $5,000. Richardson responded by passing a general order prohibiting the case from going forward and threatening to bring Metzger before a military tribunal (H. Scheiber and J. Scheiber 1990, 359–68).

At that point, the Department of Justice intervened to resolve the quarrel and released the two prisoners involved in the cases.

Two additional cases would end up settling the debate over the application of military courts to civilians, but not until after the war ended. Military tribunals convicted Harry E. White for embezzlement in August 1942 and Lloyd Duncan for assault of two Marine sentries in the Pearl Harbor Navy Yard in February 1944. Both were civilians. Each filed a writ of habeas corpus in the Hawaii Federal District Court in 1944.[51] The Court ordered Duncan released in April and White released in May. In both cases, the Court challenged the constitutionality of martial law. The government appealed, and in a combined case, the Ninth Circuit Court reversed the decisions, reaffirming its position in the *Zimmerman* case.[52] The Supreme Court heard the appeal in one consolidated case: *Duncan* v. *Kahanamoku*.[53] In February 1946, it reversed the Ninth Circuit's decision by a vote of 6-2, arguing that the Organic Act of Hawaii, which governed the territory until it became a state in 1959, did not allow for military trials of civilians, and Congress had not expressly authorized it either.[54] Though it refrained from ruling on the constitutionality of martial law itself, Justice Hugo Black's majority opinion contained a "long discourse on the entire history of habeas corpus in Anglo-American law" and "eloquently represented the Army's rule as the very kind of tyranny that made the writ so vital to liberty" (H. Scheiber and J. Scheiber 1990, 377). The ruling, however, came too late to make much of a difference. The military had already lifted martial law in Hawaii in October 1944 and World War II ended in August 1945. Most of the prisoners held by the military had already been released. The federal government has not declared martial law since.[55] Once again, the courts largely supported the US government and the military during the war, only taking a firm stance against the expansion of military courts after the war was over and the security threat had subsided.

While not involving military trials, the military's legal powers were also expanded as it played a role in arresting and interning US citizens and residents whose loyalties the government questioned. Immediately after the Japanese attack on Pearl Harbor, Roosevelt used his powers under the Alien Enemies Act, which the government passed in 1798 during the Quasi-War with France (Halperin 2016), to issue a series of presidential proclamations to detain potentially dangerous enemy aliens in the United States.[56] By the end of the war, over 31,000 people had been interned at Immigration and Naturalization Services and military facilities, and the last were not released until 1948.[57] These included German and Japanese Americans, but also Italians and a handful of Bulgarians, Hungarians, and Romanians (Hayashi 2004, 77).

In addition, on February 19, 1942, Roosevelt issued Executive Order 9066 granting Secretary of War Henry Stimson the "power to exclude persons regardless of citizenship and without formal hearings from designated areas in the interest of national security."[58] On March 2, General John L. DeWitt, head of the Western Defense Command, issued Public Proclamation No. 1 to designate Military Areas 1 and 2 in Washington, Oregon, California, and Arizona.[59] In total, the military forcibly relocated over 110,000 individuals of Japanese ancestry (62% of whom were US citizens) to camps in Arizona, Arkansas, California, Colorado, Idaho, Utah, and Wyoming, which were controlled by military police (Hayashi 2004, 1).

Four Japanese-Americans—Gordon Hirabayashi, Minoru Yasui, Fred Korematsui, and Mitsuye Endo—all challenged various aspects of their internment. In June 1943, however, the Supreme Court unanimously upheld the criminal convictions of Hirabayashi and Yasui.[60] In December 1944, the Supreme Court also affirmed Korematsu's conviction in a 6-3 decision.[61] Yet on the same day, in *Ex parte Endo*, the Supreme Court ordered the government to grant Endo her liberty from the camps, arguing that the government had admitted that she was a loyal and law-abiding citizen and thus had no reason to detain her further.[62] When Roosevelt became aware of the ruling, the military issued Public Proclamation No. 21 to end internment.[63] Once again, the Supreme Court was supportive of the government's actions, only demonstrating any resistance near the end of the war.

Post-war reform

The United States quickly returned to full subordination after World War II, but the nature of the military justice system was still contentious. In addition to the serious issues related to prosecuting civilians during the war, many people criticized how the existing system dealt with members of the armed forces. There were more than 1.7 million courts martial during World War II and approximately 45,000 service members were still in prison at its conclusion. Separately, the US Navy conducted more than 600,000 courts martial and held approximately 15,000 individuals at war's end.[64] Dissatisfaction with the military justice system was widespread, with commanders viewed as unfairly influencing cases (Effron 2002, 169). In 1948, Congress passed the Elston Act to revise the military justice system for the army.[65] Shortly after, Secretary of Defense James Forrestal created a committee to draft a new code of military justice, which culminated in the Uniform Code of Military Justice that applied to all branches of the armed services.[66] It was signed into law in 1950 and entered into force in 1951.[67]

Over the next several decades, the Supreme Court would attempt to clarify the jurisdiction of military courts. In *Kinsella* v. *Krueger* (1956), the Supreme Court ruled that courts martial could prosecute civilian dependents of US service personnel stationed overseas.[68] In 1957, however, it reversed course in *Reid* v. *Covert*, ruling that civilian dependents could not be tried in military courts because it violated the constitutional right to trial by jury.[69] Regarding members of the military, in *O'Callahan* v. *Parker* (1969), the Supreme Court attempted to limit the jurisdiction of military courts, ruling that a "service connection" is required for them to prosecute members of the military, making most off-duty, off-post offenses outside of their jurisdiction. In *Relford* v. *Commandant* (1971), the Court created a checklist to evaluate which court had jurisdiction.[70] In 1987, however, the Supreme Court overruled those cases in *Solorio* v. *United*

States, discarding the "service connection" test and ruling instead that the accused "military status" is the determining factor in jurisdiction.[71] As noted above, however, civilian courts still have the power to prosecute members of the military for all crimes committed on US soil, regardless of whether military courts also take up the case or not. The United States thus remained in the full subordination category.

Military justice in the War on Terror

The role of military justice has become a prominent issue again for the United States as it faces a new security threat in the form of international terrorism. To avoid legal constraints, the government initially chose to capture, detain, and interrogate suspected terrorists outside of judicial oversight as much as possible. When it did attempt to use military courts to try them, its efforts were largely thwarted by an assertive Supreme Court. In the face of this judicial opposition and under intense international and domestic pressure for its practices, the government gradually shifted to trying suspected terrorists in civilian courts. At the same time, however, it has increased its targeting and killing of individuals on the battlefield to avoid complications of bringing them to trial.

Osama bin Laden founded the Islamic terrorist group al-Qaeda in 1988 and it became increasingly active throughout the 1990s (Gerges 2011).[72] Al-Qaeda bombed the World Trade Center in New York City in 1993; the US embassies in Dar es Salaam, Tanzania and Nairobi, Kenya in 1998; and the guided missile destroyer USS Cole in 2000. The turning point came on September 11, 2001 when al-Qaeda operatives hijacked four passenger planes, crashing two of them into the World Trade Center and another into the Pentagon; the fourth crashed into a field in Pennsylvania after passengers attempted to regain control of the aircraft. In total, nearly 3,000 people were killed and more than 25,000 injured.

As happened after the attack on Pearl Harbor, the government responded swiftly to the new security threat. Within days, Congress enacted the Authorization for Use of Military Force (AUMF), which granted the president expansive powers in using force to pursue terrorists.[73] The United States invaded Afghanistan less than a month later, after the Taliban government refused to surrender bin Laden. Domestically, the government enacted a wide range of legislation to expand its powers to fight terrorism, most prominently the USA PATRIOT Act, just 45 days after the attacks (Howell 2004).[74] It also established the Department of Homeland Security in 2003 (Chertoff 2009) and the National Counterterrorism Center in 2004, among other dedicated units in existing agencies (Kraft and Marks 2012).[75] To avoid legal limitations in its pursuit of suspected terrorists, the government under President George W. Bush took two different approaches. First, it chose to carry out its activities in secret and outside of the United States to the extent possible. The Central Intelligence Agency (CIA), in particular, took the lead in detaining and interrogating suspected terrorists at clandestine locations ("black sites") in other countries (Mudd 2019; Open Society Foundation 2013).

Second, it sought to reinterpret and revise existing law when it came to the detention, interrogation, and trial of detainees. With a Military Order on November 13, 2001, Bush granted the Secretary of Defense the power to detain suspected terrorists and authorized them to be tried by military tribunals rather than civilian courts.[76] The military imprisoned detainees in the Guantanamo Bay detention camp in the Guantanamo Bay Naval Base in Cuba. The government classified them as "unlawful enemy combatants," a category not delineated in any international treaty, and therefore argued that they were not afforded the rights granted to prisoners of war under the Geneva Conventions.[77] Led by Deputy Assistant Attorney General John Yoo, the Department of Justice articulated a limited interpretation of the meaning of torture under the Convention Against Torture and current US law.[78] Through a series of legal memos (referred to as the "torture memos"), it advised the CIA and the Department of Defense (DOD) on how to apply "enhanced interrogation techniques" that would be legal under their interpretation (Cole 2009). These practices have been widely condemned as constituting torture (e.g. Human Rights Watch 2011).[79]

The attempt to use military courts to try detainees, however, was fraught with problems and led to a contentious legal battle (Bravin 2013). The Supreme Court issued two landmark rulings on the same day in 2004 (*Rasul* v. *Bush* and *Hamdi* v. *Rumsfeld*), finding that all detainees—foreign nationals and US citizens—had the right to petition federal courts for writs of habeas corpus.[80] In addition, the Supreme Court argued that no competent tribunal had determined that the detainees were not POWs. In response, Congress passed the Detainee Treatment Act of 2005, which created new Combatant Status Review Tribunals (CSRTs) to review each case and determine if detainees were enemy combatants.[81] The Act also attempted to replace detainees' rights to habeas corpus with a more limited appeal process whereby the Court of Appeals for the District of Columbia would have jurisdiction to review the final decisions of the CSRTs, but would be significantly limited in its scope of that review.

In 2006, in *Hamdan* v. *Rumsfeld*, the Supreme Court ruled that the CSRTs were unconstitutional because they violated the UCMJ and Common Article 3 of the Geneva Conventions, which extends the coverage of all four Conventions to "conflicts not of an international character."[82] In response to the ruling, the Bush administration and Congress enacted the Military Commissions Act (MCA) of 2006, which clearly defined the category of unlawful enemy combatants, and declared that such individuals do not have the rights granted by the Geneva Conventions and are not entitled to file for writs of habeas corpus.[83] In 2008, however, in *Boumediene* v. *Bush*, the Supreme Court once again ruled that detainees had the right to the writ of habeas corpus and that the MCA was an unconstitutional suspension of that right.[84]

The Supreme Court has been the deciding factor in preventing backsliding, overruling attempts to expand the jurisdiction of military courts. The political environment was also less conducive to the expansion of the military's legal power. International and domestic human rights organizations had exposed the use of torture, which resonated with the public. Most importantly, there were no further high-profile attacks on US soil, reducing the sense of an imminent security threat. It should be noted, however, that even then the cases were decided by close margins in the Supreme Court, with liberal judges ruling against the government and more conservative judges in favor, indicating that shifts in individual judges and their ideological positions could easily reduce or even eliminate the check on military legal power in the future.

Full subordination was further secured with the election of President Barack Obama in 2008, a liberal president who promised to take a different approach from his conservative predecessor, including closing the detention center at Guantanamo Bay. In just his second day in office he signed an executive order directing that it be shut down within a year. The government also enacted the 2009 MCA, which provided for increased due process guarantees for detainees to bring practice in line with the Court's decision in *Boumediene*.[85] The Obama administration began to prosecute more captured terrorists in civilian courts. In 2011, for example, the military transferred a captured Somali accused of terrorism caught in the Gulf of Aden to a US federal court, though only after interrogating him for two months aboard a naval vessel (Weiser 2013). The government has released 731 Guantanamo detainees to 59 different countries; the center remains open, however, and, as of this writing, 40 "high-value" detainees remain (Hafetz 2016).[86]

As we have shown throughout this book, a system of full subordination is not always synonymous with human rights protections. In this case, while the government has backed away from its attempt to use military courts, it has significantly increased its use of long-range drone strikes to target suspected terrorists and militants, avoiding the legal complications of detaining and trying them.[87] The government has a complex internal process to approve a strike, involving legal counsel, but federal courts are not involved. The government argues that the power to carry out drone strikes comes from the 2001 AUMF, and that the country is in a perpetual state of international armed conflict with al-Qaeda and its affiliates and that each target poses an imminent threat of violent attack against the United States (D'Errico 2018). Drone strikes have killed US citizens abroad and the government has legally justified denying these individuals the due process rights guaranteed to them by the Fifth Amendment of the Constitution by arguing that the interest of national security and the infeasibility of capturing these individuals justify the targeting.[88] The process has received heavy criticism on legal and human rights grounds (e.g. United Nations Human Rights Council 2010). When apprehended, however, the government has tried individuals in civilian courts.

More recently, the United States has faced a new terrorist threat from the Islamic State (IS), which declared itself a global caliphate in 2014 and expanded to control significant territory in Syria and Iraq (Gerges 2016; Mohamedou 2018).[89] A number of affiliate groups have formed in countries around the world and many individuals have carried out IS-inspired attacks, including in the United States (Wilson Center 2019). Most perpetrators have committed suicide or have been killed by police; those who have been apprehended, however, have been tried in civilian courts. In the most high-profile case, Sayfullo Habibullaevic Saipov killed eight people and injured 11 when he drove a pickup truck into pedestrians near the World Trade Center in New York City in October 2017. He is currently being tried in federal court on a variety of charges, including providing material support for terrorism.[90] Likewise, Dzhokhar Tsarnaev, who collaborated with his brother to detonate two homemade pressure cooker bombs at the Boston Marathon in 2013, was convicted and sentenced to death in a civilian federal court.[91]

Conclusion

The history of military courts in the United States offers important insights into the evolution of military justice over time. In the eighteenth century, under British rule, military courts were restricted to judging military personnel for a limited set of offenses and did not have jurisdiction over civilians. As in many countries, colonial institutions and practices persisted into the post-independence era, maintaining a status of full subordination in the United States. The country quickly consolidated its democratic system of government, established clear civilian control over the military, and over time developed a strong court system to serve as a check on government power. For most of US history, those characteristics have endured and military justice has been in the full subordination category. We illustrate this in Figure 7.1.

This stable history of full subordination, however, has been punctuated by years of military overreach when the government has confronted acute security threats. During those periods, the positions of the principal actors shifted quickly and dramatically. Government leaders who had respected civil liberties became willing to roll them back. The military, accustomed to staying out of

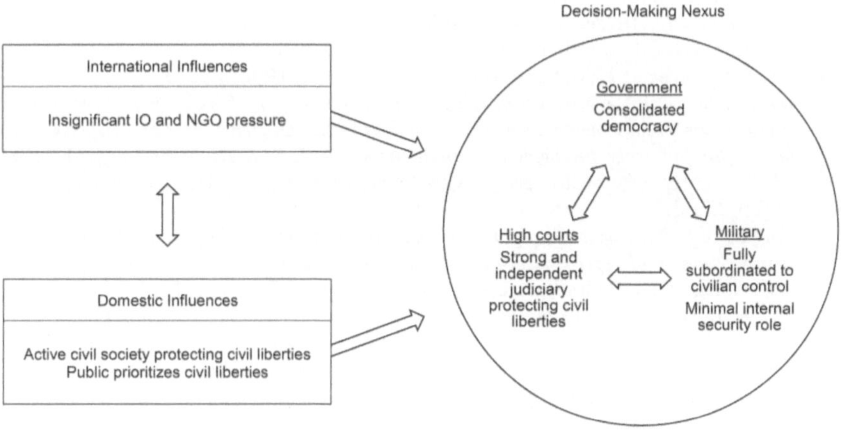

Figure 7.1 Full subordination in the United States: Low-threat environment

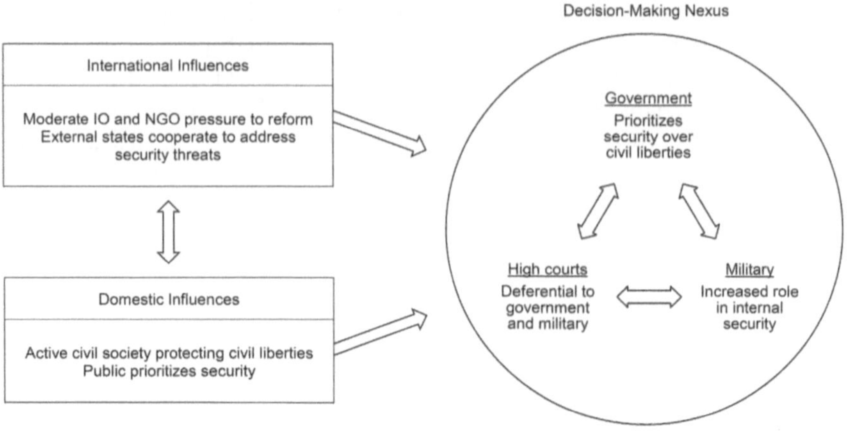

Figure 7.2 Military overreach in the United States: High-threat environment

domestic politics and policing, worked closely with government officials to expand its legal power. The courts, normally a strong barrier to prevent backsliding, deferred to the government to address the security threat with military justice if necessary. This relationship is illustrated in Figure 7.2.

Notes

1 *Sketch of an Order about the Rank &ca of the Provincial Troops in North America*, November 1754 (Pargellis 1936, 43–44).
2 *Rules and Regulations for the Massachusetts Army*, April 5, 1775 (Force 1833, 1350–56).
3 *Rules and Articles for the Better Government of Our Horse and Foot Guards, and All Other Our Forces in Our Kingdoms of Great Britain and Ireland, Dominions Beyond the Seas, and Foreign Parts*, 1765 (Winthrop 1920, 931–46).
4 *Rules and Regulations of the Continental Army*, June 30, 1775 (Ford 1905a, 111–23).
5 *Additions and Alterations or Amendments to the Rules and Regulations of the Continental Army*, November 7, 1775 (Ford 1905b, 331–34).
6 *Articles of War of 1776*, September 20, 1776 (Ford 1906, 788–807).
7 *An Act to recognize and adapt to the Constitution of the United States the establishment of the Troops raised under the Resolves of the United States in Congress assembled, and for other purposes therein mentioned*, *U.S. Statutes at Large* 1 (1789): 95–96, http://www.loc.gov/law/help/statutes-at-large/1st-congress/session-1/c1s1ch25.pdf.
8 *An Act to provide for calling forth the Militia to execute the laws of the Union, suppress insurrections and repel invasions*, *U.S. Statutes at Large* 1 (1792): 264–265, http://www.loc.gov/law/help/statutes-at-large/2nd-congress/session-1/c2s1ch28.pdf; *An Act more effectually to provide for the National Defence by establishing an Uniform Militia throughout the United States*, *U.S. Statutes at Large* 1 (1792): 271–274, http://www.loc.gov/law/help/statutes-at-large/2nd-congress/session-1/c2s1ch33.pdf.
9 *An Act authorizing the employment of the land and naval forces of the United States, in case of insurrection*, *U.S. Statutes at Large* 2 (1807): 443, http://www.loc.gov/law/help/statutes-at-large/9th-congress/session-2/c9s2ch39.pdf.

10 *An Act for establishing Rules and Articles for the government of the Armies of the United States*, *U.S. Statutes at Large* 9 (1806): 359–372, http://www.loc.gov/law/help/statutes-at-large/9th-congress/session-1/c9s1ch20.pdf.

11 "To New Orleans Citizens," December 16, 1814 (Feller 2015).

12 *Treaty of Peace and Amity between His Britannic Majesty and the United States of America*, December 24, 1814, https://avalon.law.yale.edu/19th_century/ghent.asp.

13 "Proclamation of Peace," March 13, 1815 (Feller 2015).

14 *United States* v. *Major General Andrew Jackson*, 791 (E.D. La. 1815), http://www.laed.uscourts.gov/sites/default/files/200th/interesting/doc32.pdf.

15 Despite the rebuke, Jackson continued to use military courts where needed. In April 1818, during the First Seminole War, he captured two British civilians—Alexander Arbuthnot and Robert Ambrister—accused of aiding the Seminoles in Spanish Florida. Jackson used a military tribunal to try, convict, and execute them (Rosen 2008).

16 The fine would be a sticking point for Jackson and in 1844, after a heated partisan debate, Congress honored his request and issued him a full refund, plus interest, shortly before his death (Warshauer 2006, 77–112), see *An Act to refund the fine imposed on General Andrew Jackson*, *U.S. Statutes at Large* 5 (1844): 651, http://www.loc.gov/law/help/statutes-at-large/28th-congress/session-1/c28s1ch2.pdf.

17 There was one additional attempt in the nineteenth century to extend military courts to US civilians, but it was done in Washington Territory, outside of the federal government's control and knowledge, see Lokken 1952.

18 [General Orders No. 20.] Headquarters of the Army, Tampico, February 19, 1847, "California and New Mexico, Message from the President of the United States, Transmitting Information in Answer to a Resolution of the House of the 31st of December, 1849, on the Subject of California and New Mexico," 353–54, https://books.google.com/books/about/California_and_New_Mexico.html?id=3kYOAAAAIAAJ. Taylor eventually adopted Scott's approach in September 1847 (Myers 2008, 226).

19 Proclamation 80, "Calling Forth the Militia and Convening an Extra Session of Congress," April 15, 1861, https://www.presidency.ucsb.edu/documents/proclamation-80-calling-forth-the-militia-and-convening-extra-session-congress.

20 Proclamation 81, "Declaring a Blockade of Ports in Rebellious States," April 19, 1861, https://www.presidency.ucsb.edu/documents/proclamation-81-declaring-blockade-ports-rebellious-states. The blockade was expanded to several other states just over a week later: Proclamation 82, "Extension of Blockade to Ports of Additional States," https://www.presidency.ucsb.edu/documents/proclamation-82-extension-blockade-ports-additional-states.

21 Executive Order of April 27, 1861, https://www.presidency.ucsb.edu/documents/executive-order-465.

22 Executive Order, "Authorizing General Winfield Scott to Suspend the Writ of Habeas Corpus," July 2, 1861, https://www.presidency.ucsb.edu/documents/executive-order-authorizing-general-winfield-scott-suspend-the-writ-habeas-corpus; Executive Order, "Suspension of the Writ of Habeas Corpus," October 14, 1861, https://www.presidency.ucsb.edu/documents/executive-order-suspension-the-writ-habeas-corpus.

23 Proclamation 83, "Increasing the Size of the Army and Navy," May 3, 1861, https://www.presidency.ucsb.edu/documents/proclamation-83-increasing-the-size-the-army-and-navy.

24 Proclamation 84, "Declaring Martial Law, and Suspending the Writ of Habeas Corpus in the Islands of Key West," May 10, 1861, https://www.presidency.ucsb.edu/documents/proclamation-84-declaring-martial-law-and-suspending-the-writ-habeas-corpus-the-islands.

25 A major uprising on August 17, 1862 led to the deaths of several hundred settlers, and the government was bent on revenge against captured Native American men. Colonel Henry Sibley created a five-member military commission that tried 391 men. It sentenced 303 of them to death, though Lincoln reviewed all of the cases and only approved the execution of 39 who he felt were proven to have been involved in rapes, murders, or massacres (Haymond 2016, 108). One received a last-minute reprieve, but the other 38 were hanged on December 26 in front of a sizeable crowd in what is the largest mass execution in US history. The trials were rife with prejudice, self-interest, and serious flaws in procedure and evidence (Chomsky 1990, 46–56).

26 General Frémont's Proclamation, Headquarters, Western Department, St. Louis, August 30, 1861 (Moore 1862 [Documents and Narratives], 33).

27 Executive Order, "Authorizing General H. W. Halleck to Suspend the Writ of Habeas Corpus," December 2, 1861, https://www.presidency.ucsb.edu/documents/executive-order-authorizing-general-hw-halleck-suspend-the-writ-habeas-corpus.

28 Later in the war, on August 25, 1863, Brigadier General Thomas Ewing, commanding the District of the Border, ordered the evacuation of four counties in western Missouri, creating as many as 20,000 refugees (Neely 1991, 46–47), see General Order No. 11, August 25, 1863, Headquarters District of the Border, https://civilwaronthewesternborder.org/content/general-order-no-11.

29 Proclamation 94, "Suspending the Writ of Habeas Corpus," September 24, 1862, https://www.presidency.ucsb.edu/documents/proclamation-94-suspending-the-writ-habeas-corpus.

30 *An Act relating to Habeas Corpus, and regulating Judicial Proceedings in Certain Cases, U.S. Statutes at Large* 12 (1863): 755–758, http://www.loc.gov/law/help/statutes-at-large/37th-congress/session-3/c37s3ch81.pdf.

31 *Ex parte Vallandigham*, 68 U.S. 243 (1863), https://casetext.com/case/ex-parte-vallandigham.

32 Another conspirator stabbed Secretary of State William H. Seward the same evening, but Seward lived. They had planned to assassinate Vice President Andrew Johnson as well, but failed to carry out the attack.

33 "Order of the President Establishing a Military Commission to Try the Lincoln Assassination Conspirators," May 1, 1965, https://famous-trials.com/lincoln/2157-commissionorder. This site also contains the "Opinion On the Constitutional Power of the Military to Try and Execute the Assassins of the President," Attorney General James Speed, Attorney General's Office, July 1865.

34 The work by Edward Steers Jr. (2003) is a commentary on the most complete transcript of the trials compiled by Ben Pitman published in 1865. The original work by Pitman is available here: http://hdl.loc.gov/loc.law/llds.00120275616.2.

35 The Trial of Henry Wirz, "Letter from the Secretary of War ad interim in answer to a resolution of the House of April 16, 1866, transmitting a summary of the trial of Henry Wirz," December 5, 1867, https://www.loc.gov/rr/frd/Military_Law/pdf/Wirz-trial.pdf.

36 *Ex parte Milligan*, 71 U. S. 2 (1866), https://casetext.com/case/ex-parte-milligan.

37 General Orders, No. 26, "Order in Relation to Trials by Military Courts and Commissions," War Department, Adjutant-General's Office, Washington, May 1, 1866 (Richardson 1897, 440–42).

38 General Orders, No. 46, "Release of Convicts," War Department, Adjutant-General's Office, Washington, July 13, 1866 (McPherson 1871, 198–99).

39 *Act to Provide for the More Efficient Government of the Rebel States, U.S. Statutes at Large* 14 (1867): 428–30, http://www.loc.gov/law/help/statutes-at-large/39th-congress/session-2/c39s2ch153.pdf.

40 Proclamation 179, "Granting Full Pardon and Amnesty to All Persons Engaged in the Late Rebellion," December 25, 1868, https://cdn.loc.gov/service/rbc/rbpe/rbpe23/rbpe236/23602600/23602600.pdf.

41 *Articles of War of 1874*, June 22, 1874 (Winthrop 1920, 986–96).

42 *An act making appropriations for the support of the Army for the fiscal year ending June thirtieth, eighteen hundred and seventy-nine, and for other purposes, U.S. Statutes at Large* 20 (1878): 145–152, http://www.loc.gov/law/help/statutes-at-large/45th-congress/session-2/c45s2ch263.pdf.

43 The major exception was the use of torture to interrogate captured guerrillas, most notably the "water cure" (Vestal 2017).

44 *A Manual for Courts-Martial, Courts of Inquiry and of other Procedure Under Military Law (Corrected to April 15, 1917)*, War Department Document No. 560, Office of the Judge Advocate General, https://www.loc.gov/rr/frd/Military_Law/pdf/manual-1917.pdf.

45 *An Act to punish acts of interference with the foreign relations, the neutrality, and the foreign commerce of the United States, to punish espionage, and better to enforce the foreign commerce of the United States, to punish espionage, and better to enforce the criminal laws of the United States, and for other purposes, U.S. Statutes at Large* 40 (1917): 217–231, https://www.loc.gov/law/help/statutes-at-large/65th-congress/session-1/c65s1ch30.pdf; *An Act To amend section three, title one, of the Act entitled "An Act to punish acts of interference with the foreign relations, the neutrality, and the foreign commerce of the United States, to punish espionage, and better to enforce the criminal laws of the United States, and for other purposes," approved June fifteenth, nineteen hundreds and seventeen, and for other purposes, U.S. Statutes at Large* 40 (1918): 553–554, https://www.loc.gov/law/help/statutes-at-large/65th-congress/session-2/c65s2ch75.pdf.

46 *An Act to amend an Act entitled "An Act for making further and more effectual provision for the national defense, and for other purposes," approved June 3, 1916, and to establish military justice, U.S. Statutes at Large* 41 (1920): 759–812, http://www.loc.gov/law/help/statutes-at-large/66th-congress/session-2/c66s2ch227.pdf.

47 Proclamation 2561, "Denying Certain Enemies Access to the Courts of the United States," July 7, 1942, http://cdn.loc.gov/service/ll/fedreg/fr007/fr007132/fr007132.pdf.

48 *Ex parte Quirin*, 317 U.S. 1 (1942), https://casetext.com/case/ex-parte-quirin-2.

49 *Ex parte Zimmerman*, 132 F.2d 442 (9th Cir. 1942), https://casetext.com/case/ex-parte-zimmerman.

50 *Ex parte Glockner*, 295 (D. Haw. 1943), and *Ex parte Seifert*, 296 (D. Haw. 1943) (H. Scheiber and J. Scheiber 1990, 439).

51 *Ex parte Duncan*, 66 F. Supp. 976 (D. Haw. 1944), https://casetext.com/case/ex-parte-duncan-2; *Ex parte White*, 66 F. Supp. 982 (D. Haw. 1944), https://casetext.com/case/ex-parte-white.

52 *Ex parte Duncan*, 146 F.2d 576 (9th Cir. 1945), https://casetext.com/case/ex-parte-duncan.

53 *Duncan* v. *Kahanamoku*, 327 U.S. 304 (1946), https://casetext.com/case/duncan-v-kahanamoku-whit-v-steer.

54 *An Act to provide a government for the Territory of Hawaii, U. S. Statutes at Large* 31 (1900): 141–162, http://www.loc.gov/law/help/statutes-at-large/56th-congress/session-1/c56s1ch339.pdf.

55 State governors also have the right to declare martial law. The last instance was in 1966 when the governor of California declared martial law to suppress an uprising in the Hunters Point neighborhood of San Francisco following the shooting of a black teenager by a white police officer, see State of California, Executive Department, "Proclamation of Extreme Emergency," September 27, 1966, https://www.library.ca.gov/Content/pdf/GovernmentPublications/executive-order-proclamation/5236.pdf; State of California, Executive Department, "Proclamation: Activation of the National Guard," September 27, 1966, https://www.library.ca.gov/Content/pdf/GovernmentPublications/executive-order-proclamation/2190.pdf; State of

California Executive Department, "Rules and Regulations," September 27, 1966, https://www.library.ca.gov/Content/pdf/GovernmentPublications/executive-order-proclamation/7137-7138.pdf; State of California, Executive Department, "Amended Rule No. 1," September 30, 1966, https://www.library.ca.gov/Content/pdf/GovernmentPublications/executive-order-proclamation/6699.pdf.

56 Presidential Proclamation Aliens No. 2525, "Alien Enemies—Japanese," https://gaic.info/proc_2525/; Presidential Proclamation Aliens No. 2526, "Alien Enemies—German," https://gaic.info/proc_2526/; Presidential Proclamation Aliens No. 2527, "Alien Enemies—Italian," https://gaic.info/proc_2527/. The Quasi-War was an undeclared naval war with France from 1798–1800. The government countered what it saw as domestic support for France by passing the Alien and Sedition Acts of 1798: *An act supplementary to and to amend the act, intituled "An act to establish an uniform rule of naturalization; and to repeal the act heretofore passed on that subject," U.S. Statutes at Large* 1 (1798): 566–569, http://www.loc.gov/law/help/statutes-at-large/5th-congress/session-2/c5s2ch54.pdf; *An Act concerning Aliens, U.S. Statutes at Large* 1 (1798): 570–572, http://www.loc.gov/law/help/statutes-at-large/5th-congress/session-2/c5s2ch58.pdf; *An Act respecting Alien Enemies, U.S. Statutes at Large* 1 (1798): 577–578, http://www.loc.gov/law/help/statutes-at-large/5th-congress/session-2/c5s2ch66.pdf; *An Act in addition to the act, entitled "An act for the punishment of certain crimes against the United States," U.S. Statutes at Large* 1 (1798): 596–597, http://www.loc.gov/law/help/statutes-at-large/5th-congress/session-2/c5s2ch74.pdf.

57 World War II Enemy Alien Control Program Overview, National Archives, https://www.archives.gov/research/immigration/enemy-aliens-overview.

58 Executive Order 9066, "Authorizing the Secretary of War to Proscribe Military Areas," February 21, 1942, https://catalog.archives.gov/id/5730250.

59 Headquarters of Western Defense Command and Fourth Army, Public Proclamation No. 1, March 2, 1942, https://evols.library.manoa.hawaii.edu/handle/10524/58963.

60 *Hirabayashi* v. *United States*, 320 U.S. 81 (1943) https://casetext.com/case/hirabayashi-v-united-states; *Yasui* v. *United States*, 320 U.S. 115 (1943), https://casetext.com/case/yasui-v-united-states-2.

61 *Korematsu* v. *United States*, 323 U.S. 214 (1944), https://casetext.com/case/korematsu-v-united-states-2.

62 *Ex parte Endo*, 323 U.S. 283 (1944), https://casetext.com/case/ex-parte-endo.

63 Headquarters of Western Defense Command, Office of the Commanding General, Public Proclamation No. 21, December 17, 1944, https://www.du.edu/behindbarbedwire/pp_21.html.

64 Report of the Military Justice Review Group, Part I: UCMJ Recommendations, December 22, 2015, https://www.jag.navy.mil/documents/NJS/MJRG_Report_PartI_22Dec15.pdf.

65 *An Act to provide for the common defense by increasing the strength of the armed forces of the United States, including the reserve components thereof, and for other purposes, U.S. Statutes at Large* 62 (1948): 604–644, http://www.loc.gov/law/help/statutes-at-large/80th-congress/session-2/c80s2ch625.pdf.

66 Prior to this, the Navy was under its own regulations, first established by Congress in 1799, see *An act for the Government of the Navy of the United States, U.S. Statutes at Large* 1 (1799): 709–717, http://www.loc.gov/law/help/statutes-at-large/5th-congress/session-3/c5s3ch24.pdf. The Coast Guard also had a separate set of regulations. The Marine Corps was under the Navy code unless it was detached for service with the Army.

67 *An Act to unify, consolidate, revise, and codify the Article of War, the Articles for the Government of the Navy, and the disciplinary laws of the Coast Guard, and to enact and establish a Uniform Code of Military Justice, U.S. Statutes at Large* 64 (1950): 107–149, http://www.loc.gov/law/help/statutes-at-large/81st-congress/session-2/c81s2ch169.pdf.

68 *Kinsella* v. *Kreuger*, 351 U.S. 470 (1956), https://casetext.com/case/kinsella-v-krueger.
69 *Reid* v. *Covert*, 354 U.S. 1 (1957), https://casetext.com/case/reid-v-covert-kinsella-v-krueger.
70 *Relford* v. *U.S. Disciplinary Commandant*, 410 U.S. 355 (1971), https://casetext.com/case/relford-v-us-disciplinary-commandant.
71 *Solorio* v. *United States*, 483 U.S. 435 (1987), https://casetext.com/case/solorio-v-united-states.
72 Counter Extremism Project, "Al-Qaeda," https://www.counterextremism.com/threat/al-qaeda#violent_history.
73 *Joint Resolution To authorize the use of United States Armed Forces against those responsible for the recent attacks launched against the United States, U.S. Statutes at Large* 115 (2001): 224–225, https://www.govinfo.gov/content/pkg/STATUTE-115/pdf/STATUTE-115-Pg224.pdf.
74 *An Act to deter and punish terrorist acts in the United States and around the world, to enhance law enforcement investigatory tools, and for other purposes, U.S. Statutes at Large* 115 (2001): 272–402, https://www.govinfo.gov/content/pkg/STATUTE-115/pdf/STATUTE-115-Pg272.pdf.
75 *An Act to establish the Department of Homeland Security, and for other purposes, U.S. Statutes at Large* 116 (2002): 2135–2321, https://www.govinfo.gov/content/pkg/STATUTE-116/pdf/STATUTE-116-Pg2135.pdf; *An Act To reform the intelligence community and the intelligence and intelligence-related activities of the United States Government, and for other purposes, U.S. Statutes at Large* 118 (2004): 3638–3872, https://www.govinfo.gov/content/pkg/STATUTE-118/pdf/STATUTE-118-Pg3638.pdf.
76 Military Order of November 13, 2001, "Detention, Treatment, and Trial of Certain Non-Citizens in the War Against Terrorism," https://www.govinfo.gov/content/pkg/FR-2001-11-16/pdf/01-28904.pdf.
77 Geneva Convention relative to the Treatment of Prisoners of War, August 12, 1949, 75 UNTS. 972, https://treaties.un.org/doc/Publication/UNTS/Volume%2075/volume-75-I-972-English.pdf.
78 Convention against Torture and Other Cruel, Inhuman or Degrading Treatment or Punishment, December 10, 1984, 1465 UNTS 85, https://treaties.un.org/doc/Treaties/1987/06/19870626%2002-38%20AM/Ch_IV_9p.pdf; *Torture, U.S. Code* 18 (2019) §§ 2340–2240A, https://uscode.house.gov/browse/prelim@title18/part1/chapter113C&edition=prelim.
79 Beyond Guantanamo Bay, the United States also came under heavy criticism for abuses committed in Abu Ghraib, a prison in Iraq in which the military held detainees during and after its invasion of the country in 2003 (Danner 2004).
80 *Rasul* v. *Bush*, 542 U.S. 466 (2004), https://casetext.com/case/rasul-v-bush; *Hamdi* v. *Rumsfeld*, 542 U.S. 507 (2004), https://casetext.com/case/hamdi-v-rumsfeld.
81 *Detainee Treatment Act of 2005, U. S. Statutes at Large* 119 (2005): 2739–2744, https://www.govinfo.gov/content/pkg/STATUTE-119/pdf/STATUTE-119-Pg2680.pdf.
82 *Hamdan* v. *Rumsfeld*, 548 U.S. 557 (2006), https://casetext.com/case/hamdan-v-rumsfeld.
83 *An Act to authorize trial by military commission for violations of the law of war, and for other purposes, U.S. Statutes at Large* 120 (2006): 2600–2637, https://www.govinfo.gov/content/pkg/STATUTE-120/pdf/STATUTE-120-Pg2600.pdf.
84 *Boumediene* v. *Bush*, 553 U.S. 723 (2008), https://casetext.com/case/boumediene-v-bush-5.
85 *Military Commissions Act of 2009, U.S. Statutes at Large* 123 (2009): 2574–2614, https://www.govinfo.gov/content/pkg/STATUTE-123/pdf/STATUTE-123-Pg2190.pdf.

86 The Guantanamo Docket, *The New York Times*, https://www.nytimes.com/interactive/projects/guantanamo.

87 Drone strikes have occurred most prominently in Afghanistan and Pakistan, as well as in Somalia, Yemen, Libya, and Iraq. One estimate is that the United States has conducted over 14,000 drone strikes since 2004, see The Bureau of Investigative Journalism, "Drone Warfare," https://www.thebureauinvestigates.com/projects/drone-war.

88 Department of Justice White Paper, "Lawfulness of a Lethal Operation Directed Against a U.S. Citizen Who Is a Senior Operational Leader of Al-Qa'ida or An Associated Force," November 8, 2011, https://fas.org/irp/eprint/doj-lethal.pdf.

89 The Islamic State (IS) is also known as the Islamic State of Iraq and the Levant (ISIL), the Islamic State of Iraq and Syria (ISIS), and Daesh.

90 "Sayfullo Saipov Charged With Terrorism and Murder in Aid of Racketeering in Connection With Lower Manhattan Truck Attack," United States Department of Justice, Office of Public Affairs, November 21, 2017, https://www.justice.gov/opa/pr/sayfullo-saipov-charged-terrorism-and-murder-aid-racketeering-connection-lower-manhattan.

91 *United States* v. *Tsarnaev*, 157 F. Supp. 3d 57 (D. Mass. 2016), https://casetext.com/case/united-states-v-tsarnaev-15.

References

Bravin, Jess. 2013. *The Terror Courts: Rough Justice at Guantanamo Bay.* New Haven: Yale University Press.

Britton, Rick. 2005. *General George Washington: A Military Life.* New York: Random House.

Buttaro, Andrew. 2016. "*Ex Parte Quirin*: The Nazi Saboteur Case and the Tribunal Precedent." *National Security Law Brief* 6 (1): 37–65.

Chertoff, Michael. 2009. *Homeland Security: Assessing the First Five Years.* Philadelphia: University of Pennsylvania Press.

Chomsky, Carol. 1990. "The United States-Dakota War Trials: A Study in Military Injustice." *Stanford Law Review* 43 (1): 13–98. DOI: 10.2307/1228993.

Coakley, Robert W. 2011. *The Role of Federal Military Forces in Domestic Disorders 1789–1878.* Washington, DC: United States Army Center of Military History.

Cole, David, ed. 2009. *The Torture Memos: Rationalizing the Unthinkable.* New York: New Press.

Congressional Research Service. 2018. "The Posse Comitatus Act and Related Matters: The Use of the Military to Execute Civilian Law." R42659. https://fas.org/sgp/crs/natsec/R42659.pdf.

Cushing, Harry Alonzo, ed. 1907. *The Writings of Samuel Adams.* Vol. III. 1773–1777. New York: GP Putnam's Sons.

D'Errico, Jonathan G. 2018. "Executive Power, Drone Executions, and the Due Process Rights of American Citizens." *Fordham Law Review* 87 (3): 1185–216.

Danner, Mark. 2004. *Torture and Truth: America, Abu Ghraib, and the War on Terror.* New York: New York Review of Books.

Effron, Andrew S. 2002. "The Fiftieth Anniversary of the UCMJ: The Legacy of the 1948 Amendments." In *Evolving Military Justice*, eds. Eugene R. Fidell and Dwight H. Sullivan. Annapolis: Naval Institute, 169–72.

Feller, Daniel, ed. 2015. *The Papers of Andrew Jackson Digital Edition.* Charlottesville: University of Virginia Press, Rotunda. https://rotunda.upress.virginia.edu/founders/JKSN.html.

Force, Peter, ed. 1833. *American Archives: Fourth Series, Containing a Documentary History of the English Colonies in North America, From the King's Message to Parliament of March 7, 1774, to the Declaration of Independence by the United States.* Vol. I. Washington, DC: M. St. Clair Clarke and Peter Force. https://babel.hathitrust.org/cgi/pt?id=umn.31951002076378c&view=1up&seq=1.

Ford, Worthington Chauncey. 1905a. *Journals of the Continental Congress 1774–1779.* Vol. II. Washington, DC: Government Printing Office. https://memory.loc.gov/cgi-bin/query/r?ammem/hlaw:@field(DOCID+@lit(jc0021)).

Ford, Worthington Chauncey. 1905b. *Journals of the Continental Congress 1774–1779.* Vol. III. Washington, DC: Government Printing Office. http://memory.loc.gov/cgi-bin/query/r?ammem/hlaw:@field(DOCID+@lit(jc0031)).

Ford, Worthington Chauncey. 1906. *Journals of the Continental Congress 1774–1779.* Vol. V. Washington, DC: Government Printing Office. http://memory.loc.gov/cgi-bin/query/r?ammem/hlaw:@field(DOCID+@lit(jc0051)).

Gerges, Fawaz A. 2011. *The Rise and Fall of Al-Qaeda.* New York: Oxford University Press.

Gerges, Fawaz A. 2016. *ISIS: A History.* Princeton: Princeton University Press. DOI: 10.2307/j.ctvc77bfb.

Hafetz, Jonathan. 2016. *Obama's Guantánamo: Stories from an Enduring Prison.* New York: New York University Press.

Halperin, Terri Diane. 2016. *The Alien and Sedition Acts of 1798: Testing the Constitution.* Baltimore: Johns Hopkins University Press.

Hayashi, Brian Masaru. 2004. *Democratizing the Enemy: The Japanese American Internment.* Princeton: Princeton University Press.

Haymond, John A. 2016. *The Infamous Dakota War Trials of 1862: Revenge, Military Law and the Judgement of History.* Jefferson, NC: McFarland.

Howell, Beryl A. 2004. "Seven Weeks: The Making of the USA PATRIOT Act." *George Washington Law Review* 72 (6): 1145–1207.

Human Rights Watch. 2011. "Getting Away with Torture: The Bush Administration and Mistreatment of Detainees." New York: Human Rights Watch. https://www.hrw.org/report/2011/07/12/getting-away-torture/bush-administration-and-mistreatment-detainees.

Huntington, Samuel. 1957. *The Soldier and the State: The Theory and Politics of Civil-Military Relations.* Cambridge: Belknap. DOI: 10.2307/j.ctvjf9wx3.

Kraft, Michael, and Edward Marks. 2012. *U.S. Government Counterterrorism: A Guide to Who Does What.* Boca Raton, FL: CRC Press.

Laurie, Clayton D., and Ronald H. Cole. 1997. *The Role of Federal Military Forces in Domestic Disorders 1877–1945.* Washington, DC: United States Army Center of Military History.

Lokken, Roy N. 1952. "The Martial Law Controversy in Washington Territory, 1856." *The Pacific Northwest Quarterly* 43 (2): 91–119.

Madison, James. 1788. "Federalist Papers No. 41: General View of the Powers Conferred by The Constitution." https://avalon.law.yale.edu/18th_century/fed41.asp.

McPherson, Edward, ed. 1871. *The Political History of the United States of America During the Period of Reconstruction, (From April 15, 1865, to July 15, 1870).* Washington, DC: Solomons & Chapman. https://ia800702.us.archive.org/32/items/politicalhistory00lcmcph/politicalhistory00lcmcph.pdf.

Mitchell, Ian. 2012. "The Trial of Jefferson Davis and the Treason Controversy." *Northern Kentucky Law Review* 39 (4): 757–84. DOI: 10.2139/ssrn.2102911.

Mohamedou, Mohammad-Mahmoud Ould. 2018. *A Theory of ISIS: Political Violence and the Transformation of the Global Order*. London: Pluto. DOI: 10.2307/j.cttlx07z89.

Moore, Frank, ed. 1862. *The Rebellion Record: A Diary of American Events with Documents, Narratives, Illustrative Incidents, Poetry, etc.* Vol. III. New York: GP Putnam. https://www.google.com/books/edition/The_Rebellion_Record_Sept_61_Jany_62/VWMPAAAAYAAJ?hl=en&gbpv=1.

Mudd, Philip. 2019. *Black Site: The CIA in the Post-9/11 World*. New York: Liveright.

Myers, Erika. 2008. "Conquering Peace: Military Commissions as a Lawfare Strategy in the Mexican War." *American Journal of Criminal Law* 35 (2): 201–40.

Neely, Mark E. 1991. *The Fate of Liberty: Abraham Lincoln and Civil Liberties*. New York: Oxford University Press.

Open Society Foundation. 2013. *Globalizing Torture CIA Secret Detention and Extraordinary Rendition*. New York: Open Society Foundation. https://www.justiceinitiative.org/uploads/655bbd41-082b-4df3-940c-18a3bd9ed956/globalizing-torture-20120205.pdf.

Pargellis, Stanley, ed. 1936. *Military Affairs in North America, 1748–65: Selected Documents from the Cumberland Papers in Windsor Castle*. New York: D. Appleton. https://archive.org/details/militaryaffairsi00cumb/mode/2up.

Peskin, Allan. 2003. *Winfield Scott and the Profession of Arms*. Kent, OH: Kent State University Press.

Reed, John S. 1995. "External Discipline during Counterinsurgency: A Philippine War Case Study, 1900–1901." *The Journal of American-East Asian Relations* 4 (1): 29–48. DOI: 10.1163/187656195X00039.

Reed, Thomas J. 2017. *America's Two Constitutions: A Study of the Treatment of Dissenters in Time of War*. Madison, NJ: Fairleigh Dickinson University Press.

Rehnquist, William. 1997. "Civil Liberty and the Civil War: The Indianapolis Treason Trials." *Indiana Law Journal* 72 (4): 927–38.

Richardson, James D., ed. 1897. *Messages and Papers of the Presidents 1789–1897*. Vol. VI. Washington, DC: Government Printing Office. https://books.google.com/books?id=0SVKAAAAMAAJ.

Rosen, Deborah A. 2008. "Wartime Prisoners and the Rule of Law: Andrew Jackson's Military Tribunals during the First Seminole War." *Journal of the Early Republic* 28 (4): 559–95. DOI: 10.1353/jer.0.0037.

Rossiter, Clinton L. 1948. *Constitutional Dictatorship: Crisis Government in Modern Democracies*. Princeton: Princeton University Press.

Rutman, Darrett B. 1960. "The War Crimes and Trial of Henry Wirz." *Civil War History* 6 (2): 117–33. DOI: 10.1353/cwh.1960.0007.

Scheiber, Harry N., and Jane L. Scheiber. 1990. "Constitutional Liberty in World War II: Army Rule and Martial Law in Hawaii, 1941–1946." *Western Legal History: The Journal of the Ninth Judicial Circuit Historical Society* 3 (2): 341–78.

Scheips, Paul J. 2012. *The Role of Federal Military Forces in Domestic Disorders 1945–1992*. Washington, DC: United States Army Center of Military History.

Steers, Edward, Jr., ed. 2003. *The Trial: The Assassination of President Lincoln and the Trial of the Conspirators*. Lexington: University Press of Kentucky.

United Nations Human Rights Council. 2010. "Report of the Special Rapporteur on extrajudicial, summary or arbitrary executions, Philip Alston: Addendum: Study on targeted killings." A/HRC/14/24/Add.6. https://undocs.org/A/HRC/14/24/Add.6.

Vagts, Detlev F. 2008. “Military Commissions: The Forgotten Reconstruction Chapter.” *American University International Law Review* 23 (2): 231–74.

Vestal, Allan W. 2017. “The First Wartime Water Torture by Americans.” *Maine Law Review* 69 (1): 1–66.

Vladeck, Stephen I. 2004. “Emergency Power and the Militia Acts.” *Yale Law Journal* 114 (1): 149–94. DOI: 10.2307/4135718.

Ward, Harry M. 2006. *George Washington’s Enforcers: Policing the Continental Army.* Carbondale: Southern Illinois University Press.

Warren, Charles. 1926. *The Supreme Court in United States History, Volume Two, 1836–1918.* Boston: Little, Brown, and Company.

Warshauer, Matthew. 2006. *Andrew Jackson and the Politics of Martial Law: Nationalism: Civil Liberties, and Partisanship.* Knoxville: University of Tennessee Press.

Weiser, Benjamin. 2013. “Terrorist Has Cooperated with U. S. Since Secret Guilty Plea in 2011, Papers Show.” *The New York Times*, March 25. https://www.nytimes.com/2013/03/26/nyregion/since-2011-guilty-plea-somali-terrorist-has-cooperated-with-authorities.html.

Wilson Center. 2019. “Timeline: The Rise, Spread, and Fall of the Islamic State.” October 28. https://www.wilsoncenter.org/article/timeline-the-rise-spread-and-fall-the-islamic-state.

Winthrop, William. 1920. *Military Law and Precedents.* 2nd ed. Washington, DC: Government Printing Office. https://www.loc.gov/rr/frd/Military_Law/pdf/ML_precedents.pdf.

8 Conclusion

Introduction

Democracy demands that the military answers to civilian leaders who ultimately answer to the voting public. The rule of law requires that everyone is treated equally under the law, regardless of status. Respect for human rights only thrives where perpetrators are held accountable when violations occur. Military justice systems have the potential to serve all of these goals or to gravely threaten them. Militaries have an inherent need to maintain systems of justice to enforce unique rules of service necessary to maintain good order and discipline in the forces, which are essential to command and military effectiveness. Militaries, however, should not be able to use their justice systems to insulate themselves from accountability or to deploy them as a tool of repression against civilians.

Our study examines the politics of military justice globally and historically. By analyzing a new dataset and conducting detailed case studies, we are able to provide a comprehensive assessment of how military justice systems were established, how and why they evolved over time, and the nature of their relationship to democracy, human rights, civil-military relations, and the rule of law.

Key findings

Our most important finding is that military legal subordination has increased over time, remaining steady for much of the twentieth century until experiencing dramatic improvements coinciding with the Third Wave of democratization and again after the end of the Cold War. Despite the global improvements, we identify ongoing problematic practices in military justice in many places. Moreover, we caution that change is not uniformly positive. Much like democratization, gains can be reversed. The aggregate pattern of overall improvement should be celebrated as progress and viewed as evidence that change is possible in the places where it has not yet been achieved, but we should not be lulled into a false sense of security. Subordinating the legal powers of the military to civilian rule requires hard work and vigilance.

Our findings provide further confirmation that the objective is worth it. Higher levels of military legal subordination are associated with better democratic practices and respect for human rights. Indeed, gaining control over legal jurisdiction is a crucial first step in the successful pursuit of human rights trials to hold former authoritarian actors accountable and to prevent continued impunity in a new democracy.

Implications for theory and practice

If the goal is to fully subordinate the military's legal power to civilian leaders, how do we get there? The answer to this question is complicated. We find that military justice systems are, in many ways, persistent and resistant to change. Militaries fight to hold on to the power to judge their own behavior. Military justice also tends to fly under the radar of human rights activists and those advocating for judicial reform, though in recent years this has started to change. Because of this, the nature of the creation of military justice systems in each country has an outsized impact on present day practices.

Military justice as we know it in the world today grew out of European state building and military development from the late modern period to the nineteenth century. Military legal privileges existed alongside those of other groups, all of which were permitted to enforce professional, vocational, or community standards separately from the general laws of nascent states. The centralizing pressure of the threat of external war (Porter 2002) simultaneously consolidated state control over lands and people while also prompting formalization of the first military justice systems, moving the practice of disciplining troops from the sole domain of individual commanders to a form of law. States sought to rationalize punishment "to make military service tolerable to the masses" as they mobilized populations in ever larger numbers, especially in conscript armies, to face off against their neighbors in total war (Dolman 2004, 132). Thus, the initial establishment of first systems in European states evolved over time, frequently influenced by developments across the continent. Military justice systems were also established in the context of state (re)formation in three settings—independence from a colonial power primarily in the latter half of the twentieth century, at the breakup of the Soviet Union and Yugoslavia at the end of the Cold War, and installation by an external power following defeat in foreign war. Those advocating for reform of military justice systems must understand the nature of these critical junctures in national politics and the role that the military played in them. Where militaries see themselves as the ones responsible for liberating the country from a colonial power, for example, they are more likely to resist civilian efforts to infringe on their core prerogatives. Where most aspects of the political and judicial system persist from a former state to a successor state, a type of institutional inertia exists that makes it difficult to initiate serious debates over reform.

Changes—positive and negative—in military systems after their initial establishment are the result of a dynamic interaction between three principal domestic actors—the government, the military, and high courts—in a decision-making nexus, and a variety of international and domestic influences that shape the political environment. Our model shows that international human rights courts, non-governmental organizations, international organizations, and external states have the ability to pressure the principal actors in a variety of ways, from giving domestic courts international rulings to use in their judgments to publishing reports that expose the abuses of military justice systems. Likewise, public sentiment and domestic civil society organizations can pressure government officials to take a stand on military justice. We find, however, that these efforts only matter at the margins and to be successful need to be sustained, sometimes for decades. We see the greatest successes when actors take a combined approach, pressuring government through multiple avenues to shape public sentiment in favor of reform and shift politicians' incentives to establish clear control over military legal prerogatives.

The creation of new institutions, or changes in their composition, provides a major opportunity for reform. Thus, democratization is associated with positive change, as is the establishment of new high courts or the presence of justices ready to challenge military legal prerogatives. These critical junctures are the driving force behind much of the positive change we observe in the world.

At the same time, episodes of backsliding occur through civilian governments utilizing military courts to persecute political opponents or empowering the armed forces to combat internal security threats such as terrorism. Alarmingly, we find too many examples of countries with few problems related to military justice quickly abandoning established practices and empowering the military to handle crises. We caution that politicians must resist the temptation to turn to the military in pursuit of a quick fix. The military is the one tool of the state with the specific purpose to fight and win wars; it must not be seen as the one to solve all of the problems a country faces. Politicians and the public alike must not unduly "pull" the military into politics, weakening civilian government and the rule of law and threatening human rights in the process (Bove, Rivera, and Ruffa 2020). Societies must approach the public order issues they face by taking seriously the need for civilian institutions that provide for effective policing and courts rather than expecting military legal instruments and force to substitute for them. Civil society actors must be prepared to stand up for legal, civilian approaches to dealing with security threats.

Finally, backsliding also occurs through outright military coups and imposition of military rule, which brings government under military control. Under these circumstances, high courts have little ability to resist military action against them either. Moreover, militaries often fight to retain legal prerogatives after leaving power for fear of being held accountable for abuses committed during their rule. In such scenarios, advocates of reform must strike a delicate balance, working to chip away at the military's legal power while avoiding aggravating it and instigating another coup. As we have shown, activists should not underestimate the level of importance militaries place on their legal prerogatives and the degree to which they will fight to maintain them.

Directions for future research

Our study establishes a comprehensive understanding of military justice systems in countries around the world that have been democratic at some point from the Third Wave of democratization to today—whether those countries began the period as democracies or transitioned during it. We focus on democracy because as a regime type it is the one in which there is a clear expectation of equality before the law, respect for human rights, and leaders who answer to their constituencies through free, fair, and frequent elections thereby allowing the people to exercise civilian control over the armed forces. Given the historical depth with which we study these countries, however, we examine them in many non-democratic periods allowing us to assess the impact of regime change and other major political developments on military justice systems. A potentially fruitful area of future research would be to study the world's non-democracies through this same lens. Expectations of the rule of law (Ginsburg and Moustafa 2008), civil-military relations (Escribà-Folch, Böhmelt, and Pilster 2020), and government responsiveness are different for non-democracies (Williamson and Magaloni 2020), but as we have shown, military justice reform is possible even within non-democratic regimes and the persistence of undesirable military justice systems (or backsliding into them) is possible within democracies.

Investigating non-democracies in full would shed more light on the relationship between regime type and military justice as well as the role this specific military prerogative plays in civil-military relations in authoritarian settings. We find some preliminary evidence that military justice systems may be more likely to be subordinated to civilian control in one-party states than other authoritarian systems, but this remains unanswered. We also identified a number of examples of authoritarian leaders, for a variety of political reasons, striving to subvert the military's legal power, but the mechanisms by which they do so, and the level of their success, are unclear. Finally, the military's use of military courts when it controls government remains understudied. The insular nature of military justice is exacerbated in such settings and military regimes go to great lengths to hide their human rights abuses—the military knows that its hold on power will be temporary and that the institution must continue to exist afterwards. Are military-led regimes more likely to use their court systems to prosecute opponents and the general population or do they more frequently rely solely on extrajudicial, physical violence? Does the military-as-institution resist the military-as-government in the use of military courts in order not to compromise their internal effectiveness? Our conceptualization of the interaction between high courts, the military, and the government allows flexibility in identifying who occupies those roles and what preferences they maintain, which would permit our model of change to serve as a point of departure for future study of military courts in non-democracies.

Second, our research raises a question about military court jurisdiction over police. In this study, we focused specifically on active-duty regular militaries and their use or abuse of their court systems. A potentially valuable future area of research would be to understand the extent to which police or quasi-military bodies (e.g. national guards, gendarmes) are subject to military court jurisdiction and what the operations of those courts look like in handling cases of potential abuse by police and others who are not personnel of the regular army. As we discuss in the case of Brazil, Military Police (*Polícia Militar*)—civilian police responsible for day-to-day policing—fall under military court jurisdiction in some circumstances, and this is a clear source of impunity for abuses against the general public. Moreover, in states as varied as Cote d'Ivoire (Human Rights Watch 2015), Niger (Narey 2009), and Hungary (United States Department of State 2008) police can be subject to military trial. Military courts exercised jurisdiction over police in Mongolia (Tseveen, Battsetseg, and Shagdarsuren 2009) and Romania (Macovei 2000) in their communist eras. The military and the police are different institutions with distinct roles and missions, but if military courts or other special tribunals serve as a source of impunity for police accused of wrongdoing, including human rights abuses against the general public, the same dynamic we study here could be taking place. A systematic study of police in military courts would be a valuable contribution to our understanding of sources of impunity and how to combat them.

Third, criminal legal proceedings have many stages—investigation, arrest, charging, pre-trial detention, trial, sentencing, and imprisonment, among others. The venue for a trial is not the only point of potential friction between military and civilian authorities or the only way in which military legal powers can become a problem for the rule of law and human rights. We address this issue in part through our consideration of military compliance or lack thereof with civilian authorities. Militaries often carry out parallel investigations of crimes and refuse to turn over any evidence collected. A comprehensive study into military investigatory powers and practices relative to their civilian counterparts would shed light on the potential for impunity born of different standards of investigation and charging decisions. Similarly, studying the steps after trial, especially military corrections, would provide valuable insight into the role of military prisons in military justice. This is another element of the parallel system that demands civilian oversight in order to safeguard the basic rights of military prisoners and to prevent military prisons from being used against civilians without trial. In our study, we focus on military trial of civilians as military overreach, but in notable instances, militaries use their parallel prison systems to hold civilians without charge or trial. This practice has been documented in Nigeria, for example, with military detention of children in the fight against Boko Haram (Human Rights Watch 2019). As we discuss at length with the cases of Fiji and the United States, military prisons can become sources of human rights abuses in the context of domestic repression and international conflict. Investigating how military corrections are carried out and overseen is an important part of understanding military justice.

Conclusion

We began this study by asserting that the politics of military justice is poorly understood. We hope that it is less so now. At the same time, our study has limitations. The massive scope of the project necessitated a concise typology of military justice systems: full subordination, jurisdictional contestation, and military overreach. There are significant variations within those categories, however, and now that we have mapped the world for the first time, we hope that others will follow our work and undertake more fine-grained qualitative case studies of the subject. Finally, given that we were breaking new ground in many areas, we see a large contribution of this work as theory building. Future research should further test and refine our theory. Building new knowledge of what we have shown is a crucial step in improving human rights, civil-military relations, the rule of law, and democracy.

References

Bove, Vincenzo, Mauricio Rivera, and Chiara Ruffa. 2020. "Beyond Coups: Terrorism and Military Involvement in Politics." *European Journal of International Relations* 26 (1): 263–88. DOI: 10.1177/1354066119866499.

Dolman, Everett Carl. 2004. *The Warrior State: How Military Organization Structures Politics*. New York: Palgrave. DOI: 10.1057/9781403978264.

Escribà-Folch, Abel, Tobias Böhmelt, and Ulrich Pilster. 2020. "Authoritarian Regimes and Civil-Military Relations: Explaining Counterbalancing in Autocracies." *Conflict Management and Peace Science* 37 (5): 559-79. DOI: 10.1177/0738894219836285.

Ginsburg, Tom, and Tamir Moustafa, eds. 2008. *Rule by Law: The Politics of Courts in Authoritarian Regimes*. Cambridge: Cambridge University Press. DOI: 10.1017/CBO9780511814822.

Human Rights Watch. 2015. "Côte d'Ivoire: Extortion by Security Forces," July 29. https://www.hrw.org/news/2015/07/29/cote-divoire-extortion-security-forces.

Human Rights Watch. 2019. "'They Didn't Know if I Was Alive or Dead': Military Detention of Children for Suspected Boko Haram Involvement in Northeast Nigeria." https://www.hrw.org/sites/default/files/report_pdf/nigeria0919_web.pdf.

Macovei, Monica. 2000. "Police Impunity in Romania: Military Jurisdiction over Misconduct Cases." *Policing and Society* 10 (1): 107–20.

Narey, Oumarou. 2009. "Brèves Réflexions Sur La Loi Portant Code De Justice Militaire De La République Du Niger." *Revue Juridique de L'Océan Indien* 9: 34–68.

Porter, Bruce D. 2002. *War and the Rise of the State: The Military Foundations of Modern Politics*. New York: The Free Press.

Tseveen, Odgerel, Ganbold Battsetseg, and Badmaarag Shagdarsuren. 2009. "The Mongolian Legal System and Laws: A Brief Overview." Hauser Global Law School Program. http://www.nyulawglobal.org/globalex/Mongolia1.html.

United States Department of State. 2008. "Hungary: Country Reports on Human Rights Practices 2007." https://2009-2017.state.gov/j/drl/rls/hrrpt/2007/100563.htm.

Williamson, Scott, and Beatriz Magaloni. 2020. "Legislatures and Policy Making in Authoritarian Regimes." *Comparative Political Studies* 53 (9): 1525–43. DOI: 10.1177/0010414020912288.

Appendix
Military legal subordination in the modern world

Country	*Military legal subordination*
Albania	1948–2017: Full subordination
Algeria	1963–2017: Military overreach
Argentina	1810–1973: Jurisdictional contestation
	1974–1982: Military overreach
	1983–2008: Jurisdictional contestation
	2009–2017: Full subordination
Armenia	1991–1994: Military overreach
	1995–2017: Full subordination
Australia	1901–2017: Full subordination
Austria	1920–1937: Full subordination
	1945–2017: Full subordination
Azerbaijan	1991–2012: Military overreach
	2013–2017: Full subordination
Bangladesh	1971–1974: Jurisdictional contestation
	1975–1976: Military overreach
	1977–1981: Jurisdictional contestation
	1982–1985: Military overreach
	1986–2017: Jurisdictional contestation
Belarus	1991–2012: Military overreach
	2013–2017: Full subordination
Belgium	1831–2003: Jurisdictional contestation
	2004–2017: Full subordination
Benin	1960–1989: Jurisdictional contestation
	1990–2017: Full subordination
Bolivia	1825–2017: Jurisdictional contestation
Botswana	1966–1976: Full subordination
	1977–2017: Jurisdictional contestation
Brazil	1822–1888: Jurisdictional contestation
	1889–1893: Military overreach
	1894–1930: Jurisdictional contestation
	1931–2017: Military overreach
Bulgaria	1949–2017: Jurisdictional contestation
Burkina Faso	1960–2017: Jurisdictional contestation
Burundi	1965–1979: Military overreach
	1980–1992: Jurisdictional contestation
	2005–2017: Jurisdictional contestation
Cambodia	1954–1974: Military overreach
	1981–2017: Military overreach

Country	*Military legal subordination*
Canada	1950–2017: Jurisdictional contestation
Chile	1818–1924: Jurisdictional contestation
	1925–2009: Military overreach
	2010–2017: Jurisdictional contestation
Colombia	1832–1885: Full subordination
	1886–1986: Military overreach
	1987–2009: Jurisdictional contestation
	2010–2017: Full subordination
Costa Rica	1838–1868: Military overreach
	1869–2017: Full subordination
Croatia	1996–2017: Full subordination
Cyprus	1960–2017: Full subordination
Czech Republic	1993–2017: Full subordination
Czechoslovakia	1948–1992: Full subordination
Denmark	1919–2017: Full subordination
Dominican Republic	1844–1873: Military overreach
	1874–1952: Jurisdictional contestation
	1953–2009: Military overreach
	2010–2017: Full subordination
Ecuador	1831–1868: Jurisdictional contestation
	1869–1877: Military overreach
	1878–2007: Jurisdictional contestation
	2008–2017: Full subordination
El Salvador	1841: Military overreach
	1842–1863: Jurisdictional contestation
	1864–1991: Military overreach
	1992–2017: Full subordination
Estonia	1991–2017: Full subordination
Ethiopia	1944–1973: Full subordination
	1974–1980: Military overreach
	1981–1987: Full subordination
	1988–1990: Military overreach
	1996–2017: Full subordination
Fiji	1970–1986: Full subordination
	1987–2017: Jurisdictional contestation
Finland	1920–2017: Full subordination
France	1791–1917: Military overreach
	1918–1927: Jurisdictional contestation
	1928–1938: Full subordination
	1939–1981: Jurisdictional contestation
	1982–2017: Full subordination
Gambia	1965–2017: Full subordination
Georgia	1995–2017: Full subordination
Germany/West Germany	1919–1932: Full subordination
	1933–1944: Military overreach
	1949–1989: Full subordination
	1990–2017: Full subordination
Ghana	1957–2017: Full subordination
Greece	1954–1966: Jurisdictional contestation
	1967–1972: Military overreach
	1973–2017: Jurisdictional contestation

(Continued)

Country	*Military legal subordination*
Guatemala	1878–1981: Jurisdictional contestation
	1982: Military overreach
	1983–2017: Jurisdictional contestation
Guinea	1958–2017: Jurisdictional contestation
Guinea-Bissau	1974–1993: Military overreach
	1994–2017: Full subordination
Guyana	1966–2017: Jurisdictional contestation
Honduras	1881–1905: Full subordination
	1906–1981: Military overreach
	1982–2010: Jurisdictional contestation
	2011–2017: Military overreach
Hungary	1946–1956: Military overreach
	1957–2017: Full subordination
India	1947–1949: Full subordination
	1950–2017: Jurisdictional contestation
Indonesia	1946–1996: Military overreach
	1997–2017: Jurisdictional contestation
Iran	1940–1978: Military overreach
	1979–2017: Jurisdictional contestation
Ireland	1922–2017: Full subordination
Israel	1948–1966: Jurisdictional contestation
	1967–2017: Military overreach
Italy	1861–1945: Military overreach
	1946–2017: Full subordination
Jamaica	1962–2017: Full subordination
Japan	1946–2017: Full subordination
Kenya	1968–2017: Full subordination
Kyrgyzstan	1993–2015: Jurisdictional contestation
	2016–2017: Full subordination
Latvia	1991–2017: Full subordination
Lebanon	1968–2017: Military overreach
Lithuania	1992–2017: Full subordination
Luxembourg	1881–2017: Full subordination
Madagascar	1960–2017: Military overreach
Malawi	1966–2017: Jurisdictional contestation
Malaysia	1972–2017: Full subordination
Mali	1960–1990: Jurisdictional contestation
	1991–2017: Full subordination
Mauritius	1968–2017: Full subordination
Mexico	1824–1909: Jurisdictional contestation
	1910–1916: Military overreach
	1917–2017: Jurisdictional contestation
Moldova	1992–2017: Full subordination
Mongolia	1924–1992: Jurisdictional contestation
	1993–2017: Full subordination
Montenegro	2006–2017: Full subordination
Mozambique	1979–1988: Military overreach
	1989–2017: Full subordination
Myanmar	1947–1958: Full subordination
	1959–1961: Jurisdictional contestation
	1962–2017: Military overreach
Namibia	1990–2017: Full subordination

Country	*Military legal subordination*
Nepal	1959–2017: Jurisdictional contestation
Netherlands	1814–1990: Jurisdictional contestation
	1991–2017: Full subordination
New Zealand	1971–2017: Full subordination
Nicaragua	1841–1947: Jurisdictional contestation
	1948–1978: Military overreach
	1979–1993: Jurisdictional contestation
	1994–2017: Full subordination
Niger	1960–2002: Full subordination
	2003–2017: Jurisdictional contestation
Nigeria	1960–1975: Jurisdictional contestation
	1976–1977: Military overreach
	1978–1982: Jurisdictional contestation
	1983–1990: Military overreach
	1991–2017: Jurisdictional contestation
North Macedonia	1991–2017: Full subordination
Norway	1814–2017: Full subordination
Pakistan	1947–1952: Jurisdictional contestation
	1953: Military overreach
	1954–1957: Jurisdictional contestation
	1958–1961: Military overreach
	1962–1968: Jurisdictional contestation
	1969–1971: Military overreach
	1972–1976: Jurisdictional contestation
	1977–1984: Military overreach
	1985–1997: Jurisdictional contestation
	1998: Military overreach
	1999–2006: Jurisdictional contestation
	2007: Military overreach
	2008–2014: Jurisdictional contestation
	2015–2017: Military overreach
Panama	1953–1977: Military overreach
	1978–1986: Jurisdictional contestation
	1987: Military overreach
	1988–1989: Jurisdictional contestation
	1990–2017: Full subordination
Papua New Guinea	1975–2017: Full subordination
Paraguay	1811–1886: Jurisdictional contestation
	1887–1938: Full subordination
	1939–1991: Military overreach
	1992–2017: Full subordination
Peru	1821–1898: Jurisdictional contestation
	1899–1916: Military overreach
	1917–1929: Full subordination
	1930–1938: Military overreach
	1939–1948: Full subordination
	1949–1955: Military overreach
	1956–1962: Full subordination
	1963–1967: Jurisdictional contestation
	1968–2002: Military overreach
	2003–2014: Jurisdictional contestation
	2015–2017: Full subordination

(Continued)

Country	*Military legal subordination*
Philippines	1946–1971: Jurisdictional contestation
	1972–1981: Military overreach
	1982–1990: Jurisdictional contestation
	1991–2017: Full subordination
Poland	1945–2017: Full subordination
Portugal	1763–1894: Jurisdictional contestation
	1895–1944: Military overreach
	1945–1973: Jurisdictional contestation
	1974–1975: Military overreach
	1976–2017: Full subordination
Romania	1948–1992: Military overreach
	1993–2003: Jurisdictional contestation
	2004–2017: Full subordination
Russia	1992–2017: Military overreach
Senegal	1960–2017: Full subordination
Serbia	2008–2017: Full subordination
Sierra Leone	1961–1966: Full subordination
	1967: Military overreach
	1968–1990: Full subordination
	2002–2017: Jurisdictional contestation
Slovakia	1993–2017: Full subordination
Slovenia	1991–2017: Full subordination
Solomon Islands	1978–2017: Full subordination
South Africa	1957–2017: Jurisdictional contestation
South Korea	1962–1971: Jurisdictional contestation
	1972–1980: Military overreach
	1981–2017: Jurisdictional contestation
Spain	1701–1767: Jurisdictional contestation
	1768–1930: Military overreach
	1931–1939: Full subordination
	1940–1990: Military overreach
	1991–2017: Full subordination
Sri Lanka	1949–2017: Jurisdictional contestation
Sudan	1957–2002: Military overreach
	2003–2012: Jurisdictional contestation
	2013–2017: Military overreach
Suriname	1975–2017: Jurisdictional contestation
Sweden	1809–2017: Full subordination
Switzerland	1889–2017: Jurisdictional contestation
Taiwan	1949–1986: Military overreach
	1987–2013: Jurisdictional contestation
	2014–2017: Full subordination
Tanzania	1964–2017: Full subordination
Thailand	1955–1956: Jurisdictional contestation
	1957–1967: Military overreach
	1968–1970: Jurisdictional contestation
	1971–1972: Military overreach
	1973–1975: Jurisdictional contestation
	1976–1978: Military overreach
	1979–1990: Jurisdictional contestation
	1991: Military overreach
	1992–2003: Jurisdictional contestation
	2004–2017: Military overreach

Country	*Military legal subordination*
Timor-Leste	2002–2017: Full subordination
Trinidad and Tobago	1962–2017: Jurisdictional contestation
Tunisia	1957–2017: Military overreach
Turkey	1961–2002: Military overreach
	2003–2009: Jurisdictional contestation
	2010–2017: Full subordination
Uganda	1962–1972: Jurisdictional contestation
	1973–2017: Military overreach
Ukraine	1993–2017: Full subordination
United Kingdom	1689–2017: Full subordination
United States	1789–1813: Full subordination
	1814: Military overreach
	1815–1860: Full subordination
	1861–1869: Military overreach
	1870–1940: Full subordination
	1941–1943: Military overreach
	1944–2017: Full subordination
Uruguay	1825–1830: Jurisdictional contestation
	1831–1883: Full subordination
	1884–1942: Military overreach
	1943–1971: Jurisdictional contestation
	1972–1984: Military overreach
	1985–2017: Jurisdictional contestation
Venezuela	1938–2017: Military overreach
Zambia	1964–2017: Full subordination
Zimbabwe	1980–2017: Jurisdictional contestation

Index

Note: Page numbers in italics refer to figures and those in bold refer to tables.